Language, Borders and Identity

LANGUAGE, BORDERS AND IDENTITY

Edited by Dominic Watt and Carmen Llamas

EDINBURGH
University Press

Edinburgh University Press Ltd
The Tun – Holyrood Road, 12(2f) Jackson's Entry, Edinburgh EH8 8PJ

www.euppublishing.com

Typeset in 10/12 Ehrhardt by
Servis Filmsetting Ltd, Stockport, Cheshire,
and printed and bound in Great Britain by
CPI Group (UK) Ltd, Croydon CR0 4YY

A CIP record for this book is available from the British Library

ISBN 978 0 7486 6976 9 (hardback)
ISBN 978 0 7486 6978 3 (webready PDF)
ISBN 978 0 7486 6977 6 (paperback)
ISBN 978 0 7486 6980 6 (epub)

Contents

Acknowledgements

We would like to thank the following people for the help and advice they gave us when planning and editing this book. Special thanks are due to Nikolas Coupland and Adam Jaworski, who gave us detailed feedback on the proposed structure and content. We are also grateful to the staff of Edinburgh University Press, in particular James Dale, Anna Glazier, Michelle Houston, Gillian Leslie, Rebecca Mackenzie, Jenny Peebles and Richard Strachan. For seeking and granting permissions to reproduce some of the illustrations we thank Dominique Bürki, Jo Dean, Diane Grosse, René Kontic, Rob Lawson, Olivia Middleton and Bettina Müller. We must also acknowledge our gratitude towards Daniel Ezra Johnson for his input to the early phase of the AISEB project, to Victoria Watt for assisting with matters bibliographical, and to Paul Watt for the image on the cover. Lastly, many thanks are due to the colleagues who devoted their time, enthusiasm and expertise to anonymously reviewing chapter drafts.

List of Tables, Figures and Extracts

Tables

Figures

Extracts

Notes on Contributors

Wendy Baker-Smemoe is an Associate Professor in the Department of Linguistics and English Language at Brigham Young University, Salt Lake City, Utah, USA. She teaches varieties of English and phonetics, as well as classes in psycholinguistics and speech perception. Her main research interest in sociophonetics is the study of language and religion, especially in Utah English.

Michel Bert is a lecturer in linguistics at the Université Lumière-Lyon 2 in Lyon, France, where he teaches general linguistics and sociolinguistics in the departments of linguistics and anthropology. A member of the Dynamique du Langage (DDL) laboratory at the Institut des Sciences de l'Homme (ISH) in Lyon, he is a leading expert on Francoprovençal and has contributed significantly to the sociolinguistics and the dialectology of this domain. He was the coordinator of the Francoprovençal and Occitan in Rhône-Alpes (FORA) project (2007–9) that led to the recognition of both languages by the regional government, and he is now a member of the regional steering committee for language policy in Rhône-Alpes.

Jaine Beswick is Senior Lecturer in Linguistics at the University of Southampton. She teaches general sociolinguistics, articulatory and instrumental phonetics, Iberian dialectology and language variation and change in multilingual societies. She has research interests in Portuguese and Galician sociophonetics and phonology, and the relationships between language, ideology and identity in migratory contexts. Her publications include *Regional Nationalism in Spain: Language Use and Ethnic Identity in Galicia* (Multilingual Matters, 2007), *Linguistic Ideologies in Institutional Settings: the Pronunciation of Galician in Radio Broadcasts* (Spanish at Work: Discourse and Institutional Settings in the Spanish-Speaking World, 2010), *Portuguese-Speaking Diaspora in Great Britain and Ireland* (special issue of *Portuguese Studies*, 2010, co-edited with Mark Dinneen) and *Ideology and language: assumed and authentic linguistic practices of Portuguese migrants in British workspaces* (Ideological Conceptualisations of Language: Discourses of Linguistic Diversity, Peter Lang, 2013). She is currently writing a book on the sociolinguistics of migration on Jersey.

Garland D. Bills is Professor Emeritus of Linguistics and of Spanish & Portuguese at the University of New Mexico. His scholarly interests lie principally in the fields of syntax, sociolinguistics, US Spanish and the Quechua languages. The breadth of his research career is illustrated by two books: *An Introduction to Spoken Bolivian Quechua* (with Bernardo Vallejo and Rudolph Troike, University of Texas Press, 1969) and *The Spanish Language of New Mexico and Southern Colorado* (with Neddy Vigil, University of New Mexico Press, 2008). In retirement he lives in rural southwestern New Mexico and continues to work on the data from the *Spanish Language of New Mexico and Southern Colorado* project and to establish an archive of those data at the University of New Mexico.

Charles Boberg is Associate Professor of Linguistics at McGill University in Montreal, Canada, where he teaches courses in language variation and change. His research focuses on variation and change in North American English, particularly phonetic and lexical variation in Canadian English. He is co-author, with William Labov and Sharon Ash, of the *Atlas of North American English: Phonetics, Phonology and Sound Change* (Berlin: Mouton de Gruyter, 2006); author of *The English Language in Canada: Status, History and Comparative Analysis* (Cambridge: Cambridge University Press, 2010); and co-editor, with John Nerbonne and Dominic Watt, of the forthcoming *Blackwell Handbook of Dialectology*.

David Britain is Professor of Modern English Linguistics at the University of Bern in Switzerland. His research interests embrace language variation and change, varieties of English (especially in Southern England, the Southern Hemisphere and Micronesia), dialect contact and attrition and the dialectology-human geography interface, with particular interest in applying insights from social geography's Mobilities paradigm to social dialectology. He is editor of *Language in the British Isles* (Cambridge University Press, 2007), co-editor (with Jenny Cheshire) of *Social Dialectology* (Benjamin, 2003), and co-author of *Linguistics: an Introduction* (with Andrew Radford, Martin Atkinson, Harald Clahsen and Andrew Spencer) (Cambridge University Press, 2nd edn 2009). He is also currently an Associate Editor of the *Journal of Sociolinguistics* and is on the editorial board of *Journal of Linguistic Geography* and *English World-Wide*.

James Costa is a postdoctoral research fellow at the Center for Multilingualism in Society across the Lifespan (MultiLing) at the University of Oslo, Norway, where he is part of a research programme on language standardisation in European minority languages (STANDARDS). He looks more specifically at social issues involving users and non-users of language standards in Scots and Gaelic. Previously he was a researcher at the Ecole Normale Supérieure (ENS) in Lyon where he sought to understand the ideological underpinnings of language revitalisation movements in Provence and Scotland. He has recently edited an issue of *Langage & Société* (number 145, 2013) on language revitalisation and co-edited (with Médéric Gasquet-Cyrus) an issue of *Lengas – Revue de Sociolinguistique* (number 72, 2012) on language ideological debates in language revitalisation movements.

Nikolas Coupland is Distinguished Professor of Sociolinguistics at the University of Technology, Sydney, and Research Professor at the University of Copenhagen. He is an elected Fellow of both the UK Academy of Social Sciences and the Australian Academy of the Humanities. He was founding editor, with Allan Bell, of the *Journal of Sociolinguistics* (Wiley-Blackwell). With Adam Jaworski he edits the book series, *Oxford Studies in Sociolinguistics* (Oxford University Press). His main research interests are speech style and social identity, sociolinguistic theory, language and ageing, and the sociolinguistics of Wales. He is currently editing *Sociolinguistics: Theoretical Debates* (Cambridge University Press, forthcoming).

Gerard Docherty is Professor and Dean (Research) at Griffith University, Brisbane, Australia, where he is also affiliated to the School of Languages and Linguistics. His research focusses on phonetic variability and its implications for phonetic theory. Much of his work has been focussed on sociophonetic variation in adult speakers, but he has also investigated the acquisition of speech-sound patterning in children and the nature of speech in populations of speakers with impaired speech production. He is currently Chief Investigator (with Paul Foulkes) on an Australian Research Council-funded Discovery Project entitled *The Social Dynamics of Language: A Study of Phonological Variation and Change in West Australian English* (2013-2015).

Paul Foulkes is a Professor in the Department of Language and Linguistic Science, University of York. His teaching and research interests include forensic phonetics, laboratory phonology, phonological development, and sociolinguistics. He has published papers in *Language, Journal of Phonetics, Journal of Sociolinguistics, Laboratory Phonology, Journal of Linguistics, Phonology, International Journal of Speech, Language and the Law, Language Variation and Change, Linguistics* and *Lingua*, as well as state-of-the-art review chapters in *The Blackwell Handbook of English Linguistics, Blackwell Handbook of Phonetic Sciences* (2nd edn), *Oxford Handbook of Language and Law, Blackwell Handbook of Language Emergence* and *Oxford Handbook of Historical Phonology*. With Gerry Docherty he is co-editor of *Urban Voices* (Arnold 1999). His current collaborators include Cathi Best, Jean-Pierre Chevrot, Gerry Docherty, Bronwen Evans, Peter French, Bill Haddican, Jen Hay, Vince Hughes, Jason Shaw, Marilyn Vihman and Kim Wilson. He has worked on over 200 forensic cases in the UK, Ghana and New Zealand.

Damien Hall is Lecturer in French Linguistics at Newcastle University. After a PhD in Linguistics at the University of Pennsylvania, working with Gillian Sankoff and William Labov, he worked with Carmen Llamas and Dominic Watt as a Research Assistant on the *Accent and Identity on the Scottish/English Border* project (University of York). Since then he has worked at the University of Kent and Newcastle University, beginning a major project on the contemporary dialectology of France, *Towards A New Linguistic Atlas of France*.

Breana Jones recently graduated from Brigham Young University, Salt Lake City, Utah, USA, with an undergraduate degree in linguistics. She is currently working in industry.

Jeffrey L. Kallen is an Associate Professor of Linguistics and Phonetics at Trinity College Dublin, Ireland, where he is head of the Centre for Language and Communication Studies. His work on Irish English (or Hiberno-English) includes *Irish English – volume 2: The Republic of Ireland* (De Gruyter Mouton, 2013), co-directorship of the International Corpus of English project for Ireland (ICE-Ireland), and papers on linguistic politeness, lexicon, syntax and phonology. He has also published on the Linguistic Landscape in Ireland, Japan and elsewhere, and on other topics in semiotics, discourse analysis and dialectology. His teaching and research supervision includes the study of world Englishes, language variation and change, language acquisition, language policy and bilingualism.

Carmen Llamas is Senior Lecturer in Sociolinguistics at the University of York, UK. Her research interests lie in phonological variation and processes of change. She is particularly interested in the identity-making and -marking functions of language, and in sociolinguistic fieldwork methods. She was a principal investigator, with Dominic Watt and Gerry Docherty, on the *Accent and Identity on the Scottish/English Border* (AISEB) project (2008–11), and has co-authored or edited several books on topics relating to sociolinguistics and language and identity, including *Urban North-Eastern English: Tyneside to Teesside* (with Joan Beal and Lourdes Burbano-Elizondo, Edinburgh University Press, 2012), *Language and Identities* (with Dominic Watt, Edinburgh University Press, 2010) and *The Routledge Companion to Sociolinguistics* (with Louise Mullany and Peter Stockwell, Routledge, 2007).

Chris Montgomery is Lecturer in Dialectology at the University of Sheffield, UK. His research interests are primarily in the field of perceptual dialectology, and specifically the methodological approaches to the study of non-linguists' perceptions. His research has focussed on locations in the north of England and southern Scotland, and has discussed the role of (real and imagined) borders in perception. He is also interested in the wider field of folk linguistics and language attitudes. He has investigated ways of integrating techniques used in the field of Geographical Science with those used in the study of language variation and perception, with a particular focus on the possibilities offered by GIS technologies. Alongside these topics, he is interested in sociolinguistic and dialectological methodologies, lexical erosion, and language variation and change.

Jennifer Nycz is an Assistant Professor of Linguistics at Georgetown University in Washington, DC. Her research interests include the quantitative analysis of variation in its social context and modelling such variation in phonological theory, and she has worked on a variety of projects spanning sociolinguistics, phonology and phonetics. She has previously held positions at Haskins Laboratories (New Haven, USA), University of York (UK) and Reed College (Portland, USA). She is currently pursuing studies involving dialect change over the lifespan, individual variation in phonetic accommodation and style-shifting, and statistical methods in sociophonetic research.

Elizabeth S. Parks is a doctoral student in the Department of Communication at the University of Washington. Parks holds an MA in Communication from the University of Washington, an MA in Deaf Studies: Cultural Studies from Gallaudet University, a BA in Communication Studies from Creighton University and an AAS in Sign Language Interpreting from Iowa Western Community College. From 2006 to 2012, Parks worked with an international development organization to better understand the linguistic landscape of deaf communities and signed languages in the Americas. She has published this research in 21 electronic reports available through SIL Electronic Survey Reports online and presented at international professional and academic conferences in the United States, Barbados, the United Kingdom, Colombia, Thailand and the Netherlands.

Daniel Redinger has research interests in the study of language and identity and its connection with language planning and policy initiatives in multilingual contexts. As a Luxembourgish national, he has extensive first-hand experience of the ways in which spatial and linguistic borders are closely linked to the concept of identity. He undertook his PhD research at the University of York, UK, completing a large-scale sociolinguistic study of language attitudes and multilingual language behaviour in Luxembourg. An investigation of the various factors determining language in education policies lies at the heart of his research. He is currently Head of Upper School at an international school in Germany where he also teaches English to a linguistically diverse group of students.

Neddy A. Vigil is a Research Professor in the Department of Spanish and Portuguese at the University of New Mexico. His major research interests have been Portuguese and New Mexican Spanish, and he has published in both areas. With Garland Bills he is co-author of *The Spanish Language of New Mexico and Southern Colorado: A Linguistic Atlas* (University of New Mexico Press, 2008).

Mark Waltermire is an Assistant Professor of Linguistics at New Mexico State University. His main research areas are sociolinguistic variation and language contact, particularly regarding the linguistic results of Spanish in contact with Portuguese along the Uruguayan-Brazilian border and Spanish in contact with English in the United States. He has published original research findings in these areas in the *International Journal of Bilingual Education and Bilingualism, Journal of Language Contact, Sociolinguistic Studies, Southwest Journal of Linguistics*, and *Spanish in Context* as well as the edited collection *Laboratory Approaches to Spanish Phonology* (2004, Mouton). He recently edited a special issue of *Sociolinguistic Studies* titled *The Influence of English on U.S. Spanish* and serves as an associate editor for the *International Journal of the Linguistic Association of the Southwest* (IJLASSO).

Dominic Watt is Senior Lecturer in Forensic Speech Science at the University of York, UK. He teaches forensic phonetics and sociolinguistics, and also has research interests in speech perception and the study of language and identity. With Carmen Llamas and Gerry Docherty, he co-directed the *Accent and Identity on the Scottish/English Border* (AISEB) project (2008–11), and is currently developing novel sociophonetic data analysis and presentation methods with Anne Fabricius (Roskilde) and Tyler Kendall (Oregon). His publications include *Language and Identities* (Edinburgh University Press 2010, with Carmen Llamas) and the 5th edition of *English Accents and Dialects* (Hodder Education 2012, with Arthur Hughes and Peter Trudgill). He is co-editor, with Charles Boberg and John Nerbonne, of the forthcoming *Blackwell Handbook of Dialectology*.

Kim Wilson is a PhD student in the Department of Language and Linguistic Science, University of York. She holds an MSc in Forensic Speech Science from York, where she has also taught forensic phonetics. Her research is on the topic of language for the determination of origin (LADO).

Introduction

Dominic Watt and Carmen Llamas

Recent years have seen a flourishing of social scientific research on the construction and negotiation of identity in border regions (e.g. Newman 2006a, b; Diener and Hagen 2009, 2010, 2012; Donnan and Wilson 2010; Wastl-Walter 2011; Wilson and Donnan 2012). The study of these issues has attracted scholars from a broad spectrum of disciplines, including the political sciences, human geography, sociology, law, social psychology, anthropology, history and environmental studies, contributing to what has been described as a 'major growth industry' and 'a major renaissance' of inquiry into borderland zones (Newman 2006a: 144). There is a clear consensus in the literature emerging from this drive to describe and theorise such regions: scholars of borderlands agree that as sites of social scientific inquiry they possess unusual potential to reveal the processes that motivate the establishment and ongoing negotiation of human relations, with perceptions of sameness and difference among social groups at the core of these processes. At least in part, this expansion of interest is undoubtedly a function of the global proliferation of borders during the twentieth and twenty-first centuries. The number of international land borders runs into the hundreds in the contemporary world, with each to a greater or lesser degree being the locus of contestation of some kind. The contestation may be one concerning a claim to geographical territory, perhaps linked to a desire for greater or less costly access to natural resources, or inequities in material affluence that may accrue from such resources or from economic development of other types. Alternatively, or indeed simultaneously, the border may reify less tangible differences such as ethnic identity and the antagonisms it can engender, asserting in concrete terms the boundary dividing one national homeland from its neighbour. Borders are difficult things to generalise about; each stands as the product of a unique set of historical contingencies, and its existence can symbolise very different things to different groups.

For sociolinguists with interests in the topic, this wealth of new literature is naturally very welcome. At the same time, though, a lack of engagement with linguistic factors among researchers in the agglomeration of disciplines known collectively as 'borderland studies' can be a little puzzling, and at times even frustrating. In study after study, it is observed that language is central to how borderlanders portray themselves and perceive their neighbours, and that linguistic traits may override practically every other marker of belonging; claims to such-and-such an identity are hard to sustain if the language, dialect or accent 'does not fit' (see for example Kiely et al. 2000). An individual's language patterns are in these circumstances taken to signal his/her 'authentic' identity, trumping other types of evidence (birthplace, parentage, citizenship, etc.) that might underwrite the identity claim (e.g. Joseph 2010). Attitudes of this kind are probably linked to the difficulty of convincingly 'faking' linguistic competence that one does not possess, even for a short time, let alone for more extended periods (Eriksson 2010; Neuhauser 2011; Wilson and Foulkes, this volume), and to the idea that people sometimes claim identities that others feel they (the claimants) are not really entitled to. Thus, the speaker's language behaviour might be taken by the listener to be a more foolproof indicator of the speaker's background than are other behavioural cues.

However, in spite of the acknowledged primacy of language factors in the claiming and projection of identities in borderlands, relatively few social scientific studies pursue this theme. It is as though once the point has been made that accent and dialect are crucial, nothing much more needs to be said about the matter; readers are left to fill in the gaps for themselves. Although names of individual languages are listed, it is perhaps telling that language as a theme in its own right – 'language with a capital L', so to speak – fails to make it into the indexes of some significant recent volumes on the theme of borderlands (e.g. Donnan and Wilson 1999; Diener and Hagen 2010, 2012). Neither 'dialect' nor 'accent' appear in the indexes of these books, moreover, and they are also absent from other recent milestone texts (Wilson and Donnan 1998; Donnan and Wilson 2010).

It is perfectly understandable that social scientists lacking a background in linguistic or phonetic description might feel that discussion of the specifics of the role played by language in the formation and maintenance of borderland identities transcends their expertise. It is also possible, on the other hand, that some see talking about dialect words or the pronunciations of speech sounds as an interesting but not very serious aspect of borders scholarship, or a distraction from weightier matters concerning, say, informants' political leanings, the fates of trans-border economic migrants, or borderlanders' socio-psychological orientations towards 'self' and 'other'. However, as sociolinguists who have for more than a decade preoccupied ourselves with how language variation relates to claimed and attributed identity in borderland regions (e.g. Watt and Ingham 1999; Llamas 2001; Llamas et al. 2009; Watt et al. 2010; Docherty et al. 2011), we believe it is vital that linguists be more closely integrated into future programmes of research in this burgeoning interdisciplinary area of inquiry.

This is because borderlands, linguistically speaking, tend to be remarkable places. There can be few geographical areas better suited to the investigation of how language relates to identity. The linkage between how one talks, writes or signs and how one is labelled – or chooses to be labelled – is nowhere more obvious than in these liminal zones. The linguistic afterimage of arbitrary political boundaries may persist long after the divide has vanished, and sometimes bundles of dialect heteroglosses are practically all that remains to show that the political boundary ever existed (Hall 2005; cf. Haag 1898, cited in Roeder 1926: 292). After the unification of hitherto independent nations, the former border may continue for many centuries to be marked using, as it were, 'linguistic fenceposts'. Similarly, while in some parts of the world the relaxation of border controls has meant that trans-border movement is free or even encouraged, pressures to perpetuate linguistic differences at the border may still be exerted. The eminent theorist of borderlands David Newman observes that 'Even if we have become more mobile and find it easier to cross the boundaries that previously hindered our movement, most of us retain strong ethnic or national affiliations and loyalties, be they territorial-focused or group affiliations' (Newman 2006a: 147). An immediate, accessible means of encoding these affiliations and loyalties is the use of linguistic markers associated with populations on one or other side of the border. The words, sounds and signs with which border dwellers signal their group affiliations are therefore not just epiphenomena. Their part in how identity construction and perception are achieved through the verbal, semiotic and symbolic interactions that characterise daily social life is absolutely pivotal. Be they the outcome of invididual speakers' choices or the diktats of policymakers, the linguistic behaviours we study are a crucial element of how identity in borderlands is made and marked, and if we fail to recognise them as such we can hope to form only a partial picture of the nature of the societies that inhabit such regions.

The fourteen chapters in this volume were brought together as an exploration and an illustration of the themes discussed in the preceding paragraphs. While the balance of topics is perhaps inevitably tipped towards the Anglophone and Hispanophone worlds, with an especial focus on the internal and external borders of the United Kingdom, there are contributions on a range of continental European countries, and the Americas and the Caribbean are also represented. While we cannot claim comprehensive geographical coverage, the list of languages dealt with in the book is not a short one: other than English and Spanish, there is discussion of Welsh, Portuguese, French, Luxembourgish, German, Irish, American Sign Language, other signed languages of the Western Hemisphere and varieties for which full-blown language status is moot (Galician, Scots, Occitan, Francoprovençal, and others). Indeed, it is often the very presence of borders that has led to the debate about the 'languagehood' of varieties in the last of these sets. Determining where the territory in which a variety is spoken stops is made much easier if there is a pre-existing line on a map (a national border, for instance) that can be used to demarcate such a limit, even if the political borderline coincides with the linguistic one only loosely, or not at all. Governments have imposed such boundaries on language communities on countless occasions, thereby creating situations in which dialect continua over generations become ever more discontinuous.

The extent to which speakers subscribe to such imposed divisions of geographical and linguistic space is of course one of the key research questions that are investigated by the authors of the chapters in this book. We begin by considering boundaries that have served both to foster and to hinder contact between communities that are geographically close together, but which do not necessarily share sets of common values with respect to the cultural or linguistic spheres. The first chapter deals with results from a large-scale study of phonological variation along the Scottish/English border (*Accents and Identities on the Scottish/English Border*, AISEB) that was carried out between 2008 and 2011. To make sense of the often large differences between the speech patterns of people living in Scottish and English towns sometimes just a few miles apart, we had to refer to attitudinal data elicited from the towns' residents. In particular, we found it beneficial to consider our informants' opinions of the border and the two nations that it separates. These recapitulate themes that have developed over hundreds of years in this part of the United Kingdom, and that show how long-lived attitudes towards ingroups and outgroups can be. Factors of a comparable antiquity are argued by David Britain in

Chapter 2 to account for linguistic discontinuities in the Fens of eastern England. Here, instead of social divides rooted in centuries of political conflict, it was a physical barrier imposed by seasonally impassable low-lying marshland that resulted in low levels of contact between settlements separated by only short distances. The tensions between geographical and psychological space, and their effects on how sound changes take hold or are resisted by communities of speakers, are amply illustrated by the case of English in the Fenland.

Divisions between varieties of English on a much larger geographical scale are explored by Charles Boberg in Chapter 3. Alongside a discussion of major dialect boundaries within the United States and Canada and a critique of some of the dialectological approaches to mapping them, Boberg draws a focus on the border between the two countries, which is well known for being the longest shared international border in the world. Given that the majority of Canadians live close to the US border, high levels of regular contact between speakers of Canadian and American English is to be expected, and thus, on the face of it, the conditions for the two varieties to influence one another are very favourable. The relationship between Canadian and American English is a highly asymmetrical one, however: the influence is practically all in one direction. Boberg examines the sociohistorical underpinnings of this skewing, placing a heavy emphasis on the questions surrounding what makes social identity operate differently in Canada from how it works in the United States.

Chapter 4 gives another perspective on language and identity in the United States, this time in the south-west of the country, where it borders on Mexico. The US state of New Mexico, and its northerly neighbour Colorado, have been part of Spanish-speaking North America for several centuries. However, in the face of rigidly prescriptive attitudes towards the promotion of English on the part of the US federal government and mainstream American society more generally, the fortunes of Spanish in the south-west have been very mixed. Neddy Vigil and Garland Bills consider the forces that have shaped New Mexico Spanish, with a focus on the effects of contact with English on the one hand and Mexican Spanish on the other, and the identity issues that are implicated in the ways in which New Mexico Spanish speakers exhibit loyalty to their language.

Contact between the Hispanophone and the Lusophone zones of the Americas, in this case between bilingual residents of a town on the border between Uruguay and Brazil, is the topic discussed by Mark Waltermire in Chapter 5. Waltermire provides a clear demonstration of how attitudes towards Spanish and Portuguese in the region correlate with speakers' participation in ongoing sound changes affecting the fricative /s/ in their spoken Spanish. Orientation towards or away from the Portuguese language, speakers' occupations and a number of other attitudinal and identity factors are shown to have a hand in the complex distribution of /s/ variants. Fine-grained patterns of variation in the speech of bilinguals in Latin America are also examined by Wendy Smemoe-Baker and Breana Jones, in their account (Chapter 6) of English and Spanish as they are used by inhabitants by a number of Anglophone Mormon 'colonies' in northern Mexico. The authors address questions relating to whether speakers' ethnicity and religious preferences can be found to have an influence on their pronunciation of English and Spanish. Their results show that, of the non-linguistic variables tested, ethnicity and religion have the strongest effect in terms of whether speakers show evidence of their participation in a key set of vowel mergers and consonant substitutions. These data contribute significantly to the relatively scant literature on the role played by religious affiliation in the enmeshing of language and identity practices in daily life.

Interactions between neighbouring populations on the border of Galicia (north-west Spain) and Portugal are investigated in Chapter 7. The results of Jaine Beswick's recent ethnographic fieldwork in towns on either side of the river that divides Galicia from Portugal are illustrative of the formation through face-to-face accommodation of speech codes as markers of locally-focused identities, instead of – or as well as – identities at broader (e.g. national) levels that speakers might seek to project to others. A principal motive in the present case is a commercial one: Beswick's informants are service-sector workers responsible for sustaining the local 'knowledge economy' that ensures the survival of mutually dependent trans-border communities. Their shared accent serves both as a token of this solidarity and as a means of excluding those who do not have a stake in these crucial commercial interactions.

There is then a shift of focus in the chapters occupying the second half of the book. In Chapters 8 (by Chris Montgomery) and 9 (by Nikolas Coupland) the emphasis is on perceptions of separateness and distinctiveness as these relate to linguistic behaviour. Montgomery's perceptual dialectological research on the Scottish/English border complements that discussed in Chapter 1, by probing how readily high-school students can recognise and label major varieties of British English, and locate on blank maps the areas in which they are spoken. The asymmetry of Montgomery's results, whereby Scottish respondents are able to discriminate English accents about as well as English respondents can, but English respondents cannot distinguish Scottish accents as consistently as Scottish respondents can, brings to mind the patterns seen in Chapter 3, whereby a large disparity between neighbouring countries in terms of population size and economic power correlates with an 'unequal balance' with respect to speech production. Related themes are explored by Coupland, who devotes his attention to the use of the Welsh language in Wales, another constituent country of the United Kingdom that has for centuries been overshadowed culturally and economically by its larger neighbour. In this case, Welsh is an entrenched emblem of Welshness in multiple senses: it is a positive badge of identity via the language's semiotic functions as a fundamental element of what makes Wales unique, while its use also serves to distance Wales from England by drawing attention both to the obvious and numerous differences between Welsh and English, and the implied 'exclusivity' of entitlement to use Welsh. We encounter here the mobilisation of Welsh in the public sphere for a broad variety of purposes, including signage in urban spaces. On the other side of the Irish Sea, Jeffrey Kallen's study of the 'linguistic landscape' of the border zone between the Republic of Ireland and Northern Ireland (Chapter 10) shows how a discourse of anti-English linguistic resistance similar to that observed by Coupland in Wales is visibly enacted through the use of Irish language and iconography on street signs, decorative masonry, monuments, shop fronts and the like. Everyday objects such as street furniture could scarcely be more mundane, and yet careful thought on the part of local, regional and national planning committees has gone into the degree to which English and Irish are integrated into the visual scene at sites close to a divide which has over its 400-year history been a flashpoint of contestation and conflict. Investigations of the linguistic ecology of border zones are shown to be of indubitable value when attempting to understand the symbolic significance of languages and dialects in identity formation.

Language planning and policy in a more conventional sense are explored in a continental European context in Chapter 11. Here, Daniel Redinger and Carmen Llamas describe in detail the results of a study of language use and attitudes towards languages in the education system of Luxembourg, the tiny independent state that sits at the meeting point of the Germanic and Francophone domains. Multilingualism is the norm among Luxembourgers, in part because of Luxembourg's position between two major European powers – France and Germany – and because of its population's unusually high proportion of immigrants, in particular from Portugal. But multilingualism is also enforced by an education system which requires students to master French and German, because each is used as the medium of instruction in Luxembourgish schools. A high level of attainment in English is also particularly valued. Luxembourgish, though it stands as a marker of national belonging, is perhaps inevitably rather sidelined. Redinger and Llamas consider how young Luxembourgers negotiate the complexities of their linguistic environment while retaining a sense of distinctness from their close neighbours across the French, Belgian and German borders.

France is, of course, itself far from being a uniformly French-speaking country, as Michel Bert and James Costa remind us in Chapter 12. Their account of the changes in the ways that language scholars have chosen to subdivide the Romance language continuum in southern France (as well as adjacent parts of its neighbours Italy and Spain) reveals how the delimitation and labelling of language varieties is subject to strategic but sometimes arbitrary-looking political considerations, and often simply to the whims of individual 'stakeholder' linguists. The rationales used by linguists when demarcating the Occitan- and Francoprovençal-speaking regions – both from each other, and from 'French' – are contrasted with those offered by non-linguist interest groups, which often seek to distort the linguistic facts to fit their regional identity-driven agendas. The example of the Rhône-Alpes region invites the reader to reflect upon the assumptions that underlie the classification and nomenclature of dialects elsewhere in Europe and indeed in other parts of the world.

In the penultimate chapter (Chapter 13), by Elizabeth Parks, we are introduced to a number of sign languages that are used in the Caribbean and Latin America. Each is in competition with American Sign Language (ASL), which has a disproportionately strong influence on other sign languages across the world. Indeed, it has been cast as a 'killer language' by some commentators, in the same way that the global spread of English is often said to endanger (spoken) minority languages. Among members of the deaf communities in the countries that Parks has investigated through her applied linguistics research for the Summer Institute of Linguistics, ASL is seen in both positive and negative lights, with some learners and users seeing it as a valued international standard and others resenting its domination over local varieties. The focusing of national sign languages in the regions that Parks's chapter deals with, with sometimes heavy borrowing from ASL and other sign languages, is interpreted as the outcome of processes that implicate users' identities as members of national groupings as well as representatives of national and supranational deaf communities.

A detailed understanding of the links between a speaker's national origin – or 'community of socialisation' – and his or her language behaviour is clearly of importance when we are seeking to develop models of how language and identity interact with one another in borderland contexts. However, as described in Chapter 14 by Kim Wilson and Paul

Foulkes, there are circumstances in which the speaker's welfare, or even his/her life, may depend upon others identifying these links correctly, raising the stakes enormously. In the field of language analysis for the determination of origin (LADO), linguists attempt on the basis of linguistic evidence to evaluate the claims to national or ethnic identities that are made by asylum seekers hoping to obtain leave to remain in the destination country. The linguist's task may be to try to discredit the claimant's story by pinpointing linguistic features that would indicate that the story is false, or it may (in addition) be to give an opinion on the likely origin of the claimant. Fulfilling either task requires the analyst to have a solid grounding in how language and identity are mutually dependent upon one another. As yet, very little empirical research has been done on this topic from a LADO perspective specifically, but the work of Wilson and Foulkes represents a significant series of early steps in this direction. It is to be hoped that the practices of the LADO agencies will be modified as new results emerge from this critically important application of research being conducted on language and identity in the context of international migration.

The compilation of the present volume was inspired by the first *Borders and Identities Conference* (BIC2010), which took in Newcastle upon Tyne, England, in January 2010 as part of the programme of dissemination activities we had planned during the course of the AISEB project. Several of the chapters in the book are elaborations of presentations that were delivered at BIC2010. Enthusiasm for turning what had been intended as a one-off conference into an ongoing series was shared by many of the conference delegates, and so it was that the second BIC meeting was held in early 2013 in Rijeka, Croatia, a city bisected by a historic national border and lying close to several modern ones. The third conference in the series will take place in the self-evidently appropriate city of Berlin in 2015. We are confident that events such as the BIC conference series, and publications like the present volume, will serve to raise already high levels of interest in an area of linguistics so deserving of detailed scrutiny.

I

Language and Identity on the Scottish/English Border

Dominic Watt, Carmen Llamas, Gerard Docherty, Damien Hall
and Jennifer Nycz

1. Introduction

For many people, discussion of language and identity at national borders will first bring to mind contexts in which different languages – perhaps mutually unintelligible or unrelated ones – are spoken on either side of an international frontier, across which the movement of people, goods and services, and even ideas, is controlled. Examples of such boundaries are plentiful, and some of them are described in other chapters in this book. However, there are also cases in which borders between nations are uncontrolled, and where the linguistic varieties spoken on either side of the border are dialects of one language. Several such contexts are also examined in this volume (see the chapters by Boberg, Coupland, Kallen, Redinger and Llamas, and Montgomery). In contexts of this second type, the role played by language behaviour in how social groups self-identify and how they are identified by others, and the significance of the border in these identity-construction processes, are factors that deserve every bit as much attention from researchers as do situations of the first kind. Indeed, in regions where trans-border movement is uncontrolled and where a language is shared by populations living on either side of the border, the dependencies between subtle accent/dialect differences and speakers' identities may become particularly meaningful and finely balanced. The border between Scotland and England is one such region.

In this chapter we first consider the Scottish/English border in the context of the British dialect continuum, before looking more closely at the results of an analysis of consonant variation in varieties of English spoken in four border localities: Carlisle, Gretna, Eyemouth and Berwick-upon-Tweed (see Figure 1.1). The results derive from the *Accent and Identity on the Scottish/English Border* (AISEB)[1] project, a large-scale study of phonological variation in an area that is geographically compact yet surprisingly rich in terms of accent diversity.

Figure 1.1 Map of the AISEB fieldwork locations (reproduced, with permission, from Watt et al. 2014).

2. Context

Readers of this volume are likely to be familiar with the observation that the variety of dialects found in Great Britain is prodigious, despite the island's comparatively small surface area. There has been plenty of time available for dialect divergence in British English, it is true, and (as has happened in many other areas of the globe) Britain's sociopolitical history has been characterised by radical shifts and mixtures of population through trade and conquest, and by rapid spurts in societal and technological change. The conditions have in this sense been right for dialect diversification for well over a millennium. However, it is easy to exaggerate the geographical factors that may have played a role in the diversification of British English over this period. To talk of communities in mainland Great Britain as 'remote' or 'isolated' – even those on the far-flung Atlantic coasts of Cornwall or the north-west Scottish Highlands – seems an overstatement when considered against the huge distances between localities in the large Anglophone countries (Canada, the United States, Australia) and the true isolation of New Zealand and the islands of the south Atlantic.

Yet significant dialect differences continue to exist in Britain, and make their presence felt over sometimes very short distances. The accurate demarcation of British dialect zones has, of course, long been a central preoccupation of dialectologists, and while the focus of attention in research on language variation has moved from traditional rural vernaculars onto urban varieties of English, major dialect divides still figure prominently in discourse about language among both the general public and academic linguists (e.g. Wales 2000; Britain 2010b, this volume; Flynn 2013). The break in the dialect continuum that occurs at the Scottish/English border is sufficiently abrupt and deeply entrenched that lay people and linguists alike (e.g. Aitken 1992; Johnston 1997; Jones 2002; Kay 2006;

McColl Millar 2010) have argued that two continua should in fact be posited: an English continuum that stops at the border, and a Scots one that begins north of it. Many proponents of this view contend that Scots is in fact a language distinct from English but with a close relation to it (see further Montgomery, this volume).

Appeal to historical, political and legal factors is often made in support of this stance. Scotland and England were separate kingdoms until the seventeenth century, and still retain distinct legal systems. The Edinburgh parliament was restored in 1999, and other hallmarks normally associated with fully autonomous polities – distinct school and university education systems, Scottish banknotes that differ from English ones (in part by not featuring the Queen's likeness), a separate Church of Scotland, and so forth – lend further weight to arguments that Scotland is 'different' (see further Rosie and Bond 2003; Bechhofer and McCrone 2008, 2010; Kiely et al. 2001, 2005). A test of just how different Scottish people feel Scotland to be is the 2014 referendum, which asked the question 'Should Scotland be an independent country?' The pro- and anti-independence campaigns have encouraged people in Scotland to think harder about what it means to be Scottish on the one hand and British on the other, and since people living close to the border on the English side are likely to have been exposed to the same nationalist and unionist rhetoric via television broadcasts, advertising hoardings, etc., they may have had cause to reappraise how they feel about their Scottish neighbours and the meanings of national identity labels.

When attempting to account for the fact that the border marks a cultural and linguistic boundary as well as a political one, we ought also to factor in its status as a discontinuity in the population map of Great Britain. Figure 1.2 is a 'gridded' map of the United Kingdom showing where population is concentrated. In this distorted depiction of the country the border area, marked with an arrow, forms a conspicuous population bottleneck, exaggerating the way it spans a relatively narrow isthmus in physical space. Northumberland and Cumbria are England's most sparsely populated unitary authorities (Office for National Statistics 2012), and the population density of the Scottish Borders is approximately as low as that of Sweden, placing it among Europe's least populated regions (Scottish Borders Council 2010). Away from the coasts, the border bisects agriculturally poor country that is given over largely to rough grazing, grouse moorland and forestry, and the transport infrastructure is basic. In 2014 there were no motorways nor even a single railway station in the whole of the Scottish Borders region (see Figure 1.1), and the east–west road network is poorly developed. However, some distance to the north and south there are significant conurbations: the Scottish Central Belt (Edinburgh, Glasgow and the towns in between) is home to around 70 per cent of Scotland's population of 5.3 million, while the Tyneside conurbation (population approximately 800,000) is the largest urban centre in the far north of England (Office for National Statistics 2012), as well as the principal centre of economic and cultural gravity not just for north-eastern England but for large parts of the north-west of the country too. Newcastle's reach also extends into southern Scotland, which is unsurprising given that travel times by road to Newcastle from Scottish border towns such as Hawick or Jedburgh are about the same as they are to the Scottish capital, Edinburgh.

The border is highly porous: there are no border controls whatever, many people live on one side but work on the other, and the trans-border exchange of goods and services is vigorous. As we point out elsewhere (Watt et al. 2014) the separate Scottish and English education systems mean that the catchment areas for schools in the border towns do not

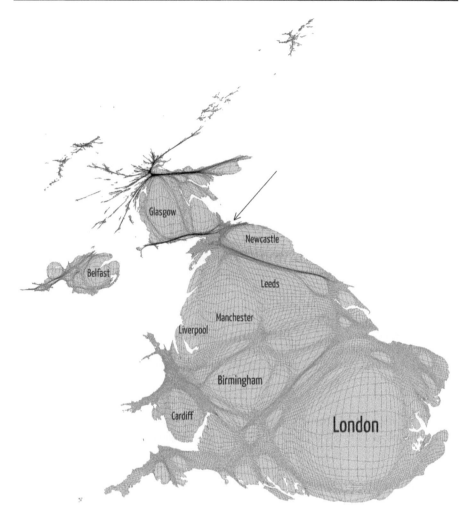

Figure 1.2 Gridded population map of the United Kingdom © Benjamin D. Hennig, *Worldmapper Project* (www.worldmapper.org). The arrow denotes the location of the Scottish/English border.

straddle the border. There are thus few opportunities for Scottish and English children to interact during school hours, and we might speculate about the longer-term effects this could have on their language behaviour. At other times, however, they are free to mix, and since retail and leisure amenities and general infrastructure are superior on the English side of the border owing to the greater sizes of the communities there, there are many more reasons for people living on the Scottish side of the border to cross into England than the reverse.

Given how readily people cross the border for all these reasons, promoting plentiful face-to-face contact and opportunities for exposure to linguistic innovations spreading into the border region, the following findings are perhaps unexpected. A study of UK-internal

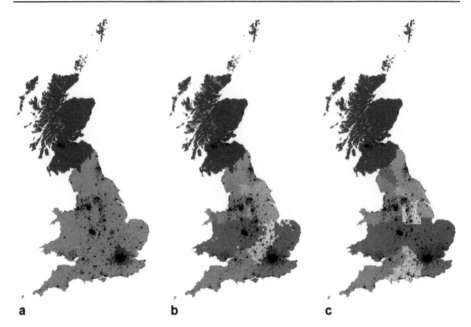

Figure 1.3 Regions of Britain defined using a spectral modularity optimisation algorithm run on a database of 12 billion landline telephone calls placed over a one-month period. Map (a) after two iterations; (b) final partitioning; (c) after further fine-tuning following M. Newman (2006). From Ratti et al. (2010: e14248, p. 3).

telephone traffic by Ratti et al. (2010) plainly shows that, at least over the landline network, Scottish people tend to talk far more to other people in Scotland than to people elsewhere in Britain. Using a database of 12 billion calls made over a one-month period, Ratti et al. sought to identify geographical areas where telephone traffic was most internally intensive, using a partitioning technique based on that of M. Newman (2006). This algorithm isolates areas of high 'modularity', i.e. areas which are well demarcated from each other, such that regions begin to emerge as iterations of the algorithm are run. Map (a) in Figure 1.3 shows that after just two iterations, two main geographical zones are resolved: Greater London and Scotland. It seems intuitively obvious that, as the capital city of the UK and one of the world's primary economic centres, London should figure disproportionately with respect to locally-focused telephone traffic. Why Scotland, on the other hand, should be comparably inward-looking is perhaps harder to explain, and is a question we cannot adequately grapple with in the current chapter. It is worth noting nevertheless that in map (a) the boundary between Scotland and everywhere else aligns with the political border with England, save for a small southward dip at the western end which presumably indicates that Carlisle is a city to which landline calls are regularly placed by Scottish callers. Berwick, on the east coast, also seems to be part of this Scottish region, though the geographical granularity used (9.5 km × 9.5 km pixels) makes the pattern harder to see. By the final iteration and some subsequent minor adjustments, Scotland has continued to cohere as a single region, while northernmost England is divided into north-eastern and north-western zones, partitioned along the Pennine watershed much as the counties of Northumberland

and Cumbria are. In map (c) the contrast between Scotland and Wales is striking; the latter does not appear to operate as a unit separate from England. As Ratti et al. observe, 'Scotland is the region least connected to Great Britain . . . [and] appears to be loosely coupled with the rest of Great Britain in a way that Wales emphatically is not' (2010: e14248).

While we must be careful not to assume that landline traffic over this brief period necessarily correlates with how borderers conduct their face-to-face interactions the rest of the time – and we should remember also that landline telephony tends to be used more heavily by older people than younger ones (e.g. Hardill and Olphert 2012) – Ratti et al.'s data lend objective support to the notion that Scottish English is markedly different from the English of northern England in part because Scottish people tend to interact with one another more than they do with their near-neighbours. More intensive contact with one's compatriots than with other groups would on balance tend to perpetuate or even amplify conservative linguistic behaviour (e.g. Barlow and Kemmer 2000), such that northward-spreading sound changes might meet strong resistance at the border. David Newman again anticipates this sort of emphatic insistence on distinctiveness among inhabitants of borderlands where one might reasonably expect to see signs of cultural homogenisation: 'We tend to view transition zones as being akin to a sort of borderland space, straddling the line on both sides and constituting a place of contact where difference is diluted and reconstructed as a sort of borderland hybridity. But . . . transition zones can equally be places in which the contact between different groups . . . strengthens the notion of border as barrier despite . . . the contact that takes place in these new spaces' (Newman 2006a: 151). We have elsewhere related this possibility to the phenomenon of group polarisation (Watt et al. 2014; see Sunstein 2011), whereby discussion of shared values among groups of like-minded people tends not just to reinforce the consensual view but to push it towards a more extreme version of itself.

Though the Scottish/English border can scarcely be described as a 'new space', Newman's generalisation seems to ring true. In spite of what Ratti et al.'s data suggest, the region is certainly a place of contact, and there are plentiful signs of cultural and linguistic hybridity. It is hard to see how things could be otherwise. Nevertheless, the assertion by Aitken (1992: 895) that the border between Scotland and England coincides with 'the most tightly-packed bundle of isoglosses in the English-speaking world, effectively turning Scotland into a "dialect island"' invites one to wonder why, if Aitken's depiction is accurate, such a situation might persist. Identity is without doubt implicated, but explanations based on identity factors can sound trite unless the notion of identity is unpacked, as the contributors to Llamas and Watt (2010a) attempt to do. A key AISEB objective was to put Aitken's claim to the test, and to examine the roles played by local and national identity in the sociolinguistic life of the border region.

We turn in the following sections to focus on one of the phonological variables examined for the AISEB project, following a brief account of the overall project design.

3. AISEB: project design

In designing AISEB we were motivated by a hypothesis that we could arrive at a better understanding of how (and perhaps why) speakers use language to indicate group affiliation if we scrutinised not just patterns in their speech production, but also their overtly-expressed opinions and attitudes towards language variation, national identity, locally relevant ingroups and outgroups, and towards the border itself. Evidence of hypothesised correlations between phonological production and attitudinal data would bolster our view – and that of earlier researchers whose work provided a springboard for our own (Kiely et al. 2000; Glauser 2000) – that linguistic factors are paramount when inhabitants of the Scottish/English border region seek to define themselves and to categorise one another. By examining these correlations we could thereby learn a great deal about how speaker groups choose to adopt or resist incoming sound changes. Furthermore, we felt that our generalisations would be strengthened if we could assess the level of discrimination, consistency and automaticity with which listeners could bring into play their socioindexical knowledge about phonetic variation in the region. We did this by running a variety of perception tests on a subset of the AISEB interviewees, some of which used a reaction time latency paradigm to probe the strength and directness of participants' associations between certain pronunciations and speaker traits of different kinds (Docherty et al. 2012).

AISEB's tripartite structure (production, perception, attitudes) is an attempt to mini-mise the second-guessing of speakers' motivations that has led to criticism of variationist sociolinguistics in the past. By having interviewees answer a standard set of questions about their evaluations of issues of day-to-day significance to them, we could come closer to knowing what social imperatives might be driving their (non-)participation in linguis-tic changes. Triangulation of informants' production patterns and their questionnaire responses with data relating to more involuntary perceptual evaluations of spoken utter-ances gave us additional confidence in the validity of our models of the identity-making and -marking functions of phonological variation.

We recorded a minimum of forty speakers in each of four border localities, two at either end of the border, and no more than a few miles from it. The fieldwork sites were in pairs: Gretna (Scotland) and Carlisle (England) near the west coast, and Eyemouth (Scotland) and Berwick (England) on the east (see Figure 1.1). Speakers of both sexes in two age groups (Young = 16–25; Older = 57+), categorised as working class or middle class using educational criteria, were recorded either singly or in friend/spouse pairs, mainly in their own homes. Other than the interview questionnaire, which was divided into sections relating to identity and language, informants were asked to read aloud a wordlist and a text passage. The data we discuss below are drawn from the read material only.

4. Voice Onset Time in the border region

In earlier outputs from the project (Llamas et al. 2009; Llamas 2010; Watt et al. 2010) we focused fairly heavily on (r), looking simultaneously at patterns of rhoticity ('r-fulness') and at the distribution of (r)'s phonetic variants. In both respects, variation in (r) is some-thing which speakers appear to be highly aware of. However, we opted also to examine variables which are less likely to be subject to overt commentary or stereotyping, but which might vary – albeit quite subtly – in line with factors such as the speaker's country of residence, the coast on which he or she lives, his/her age, gender, etc. The variable we discuss below is Voice Onset Time (VOT), the duration of the period between the release of the stop closure for the consonants /p t k b d g/ and the onset of voicing for the following vowel (Lisker and Abramson 1964; Docherty 1992). The VOT data presented below have previously been described in Docherty et al. (2011), but here we consider them alongside the attitudinal findings presented in Section 7.

The literature on the phonetic properties of stop consonants in British English accents suggests that voiceless stops are occasionally unaspirated in varieties spoken in Scotland and the north of England (Lodge 1966; Wells 1982; Catford 1988; Scobbie 2006). This would be reflected in small positive ('short-lag') VOT values for /p t k/. Where short-lag VOTs are used in Scottish and northern English varieties, in order for contrast between the voiceless and voiced stops to be maintained, the VOT values of voiced stops must be close to zero, or even negative (i.e. the voicing may coincide with the stop release for /b d g/, or precede it, thus producing pre-voiced stops). Johnston (1997: 505) contends that traditional Scottish vernaculars – those most heavily influenced by the Scots language (Jones 2002) – feature unaspirated /p t k/. That set of varieties would include the traditional rural dialects of the border region, which were indeed the focus of study of Johnston's doctoral research (Johnston 1980).

In the light of this previous work, we might then ask whether the border coincides with VOT differences between groups of speakers on either side of it, and, if so, whether these differences are in line with what previous researchers have found for Scottish and English varieties of English.[2] The possibility that we might encounter age-related differences in VOT values within the same community was also considered (Benjamin 1982; Torre and Barlow 2009; Docherty et al. 2011), and we were careful to take this factor into account when interpreting our results. Note that the VOT results we report in following sections are summarised by speaker groups, rather than being presented for individual speakers.

5. Method

We isolated a total of 4,662 tokens of pre-vocalic voiceless (N = 3,319) and voiced (N = 1,343) stops in stressed syllables. These mainly, but not exclusively, occurred in word-initial position; the exception was the first /t/ in the word *potato*. VOT was measured using the *Praat* spectrographic analysis package (Boersma and Weenink 2013; see also Foulkes et al. 2010; Thomas 2011). Figure 1.4 shows an example. Multiple regression analyses were then run on the data to test for the effects of the independent variables *Nation* (England/Scotland), *Coast* (West/East) and *Speaker* (*Age* [Older/Young], *Sex* [Male/Female] and *Class* [Working/Middle]).

6. Results

The results for each of the four fieldwork sites, broken down further by speaker age, can be seen in Figure 1.5. The patterns in Figure 1.5 are, overall, rather similar across the four sites. Looking first at the results for the voiced stops (the upper panel in each of the four pairs), we can see that for older speakers, whose pooled figures are denoted by the solid lines, the VOT values follow a bimodal (two-peaked) distribution. This is because VOT values for /b d g/ tend to cluster around zero for non-prevoiced tokens, while for the bimodally distributed pre-voiced tokens there is a peak between around –50 and –100ms. The older Eyemouth speakers differ somewhat from the other older speaker groups in that pre-voiced tokens of /b d g/ seem marginally to predominate: the left-hand peak in the pair is somewhat taller than the right-hand one.

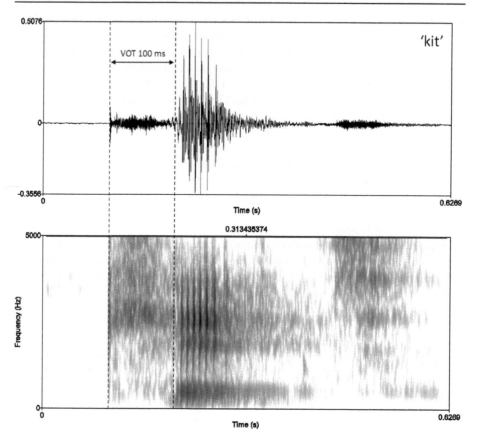

Figure 1.4 Pressure waveform (upper pane) and wide-band spectrogram (lower pane) of the word *kit* spoken by a 22-year-old male from Berwick. The period of aspiration following the /k/ release, which occupies the gap between the release burst and the onset of voicing for the vowel, is demarcated using dashed vertical lines. Its duration is 100 milliseconds.

Differences between the older and the young groups in each locality are also clear: the bimodal curves are replaced by steep unimodal ones, with practically all of the VOT values for /b d g/ in the positive short-lag range (10–15ms). Owing to the apparent avoidance of pre-voiced realisations of these consonants among young speakers, it appears that in this sample of read speech the average VOT for the voiced stops /b d g/ has risen substantially over one or two generations in each of the four localities, and there is considerably more consistency in VOT durations for /b d g/ among young speakers than older ones. The regression test results for an overall comparison of data for the two age groups strongly bear out the generalisation that average VOT for /b d g/ has increased in recent decades ($t_{1,1337}$ = 20.02, p < .001).

A duration increase pattern from old to young can also be identified in the data for /p t k/. In spite of a considerable level of overlap in the distributions for young and older speakers in each community, VOT values for the voiceless stops are significantly longer among young speakers than among older ones ($t_{1,3313}$ = 16.15, p < .001). The differences between the four sites can be more clearly appreciated in Figure 1.6, in which it can also

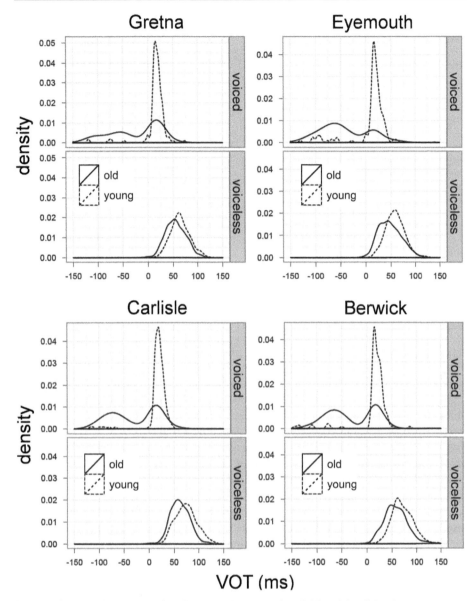

Figure 1.5 Probability density functions for VOT in the four fieldwork localities, by age group (solid lines = older speakers; dashed lines = young speakers). The upper pane in each pair shows results for the voiced stops /b d g/, while the lower pane is for their voiceless counterparts /p t k/, pooled across place of articulation (figure reproduced from Docherty et al. 2011).

be seen that for both older and young speakers the grey curves (for the Scottish sites) sit somewhat to the left of the black (English) ones. That is, VOT for /p t k/ is lower by an average of about 10ms in the Scottish varieties than in the English ones, and there is a higher frequency of tokens with VOT values below 50ms. Again, the curves overlap a

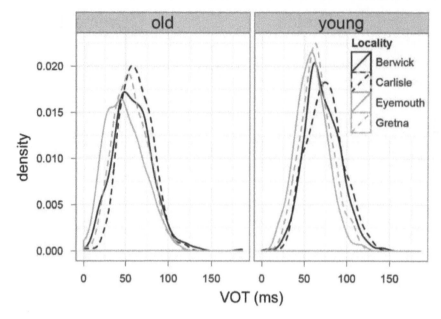

Figure 1.6 Probability density functions for VOT of the voiceless stops /p t k/ in the four fieldwork localities, by age group (black lines = England, grey lines = Scotland; solid lines = east coast, dashed lines = west coast; figure reproduced from Docherty et al. 2011).

good deal, but there is enough of a separation between them to yield a small but significant effect for *Nation* ($t_{1,3313} = 14.19, p < .001$). *Coast* is also revealed to influence VOT duration, with the two eastern localities each having slightly shorter VOT values for /p t k/ than their western counterparts ($t_{1,3313} = 7.40, p < .001$).

Overall, then, we see a picture which suggests that change may be underway with respect to this variable. Pre-voiced tokens of /b d g/ are very much rarer in the speech of young borderers than they are in that of older ones, and VOT duration for the voiceless stops /p t k/ is apparently increasing. Note that from a perceptual point of view, a change in which tokens of /b d g/ with zero or short-lag VOT come to predominate over pre-voiced variants of these consonants is not simply one of degree; such a change also represents a shift of category (Flemming 2005; see further below). An equivalent increase in VOT for /p t k/, whereby speakers make adjustments to the level of aspiration on stops that are already aspirated, would, by contrast, be a purely quantitative matter. Maintaining phonetic distinctions between the voiced and voiceless sets is important, given the high functional load of the /p ~ b/, /t ~ d/ and /k ~ g/ contrasts. We therefore might predict that an increase in VOT in the voiced set would lead to an increase in VOT in the voiceless set, or perhaps *vice versa*. The latter scenario seems less likely because the phonemic distinction would be augmented, not reduced, by a wider durational gap. The differences in question are relatively small ones, it is true, but they are all in line with the direction which is predicted, and as we shall see below they relate to findings from the attitudinal data in ways that accord with the trends we have discussed in other AISEB outputs (Llamas 2010; Watt et al. 2014). Before turning to examine attitudinal factors we should, however, take into account the cross-linguistic studies showing that older speakers tend to exhibit shorter VOT values for voiceless stops than do younger ones (Benjamin 1982; Liss et al. 1990; Ryalls et al. 1997; Torre and Barlow 2009). We see plain evidence of this in the AISEB data and could put the differences down to the physiological effects of ageing. But the effects of the *Coast* and *Nation* variables cannot be accounted for in this manner, even if they interact with the effect of speaker age in complex ways. Local and national identity may have a part to play, a hypothesis we set out to test by examining attitudinal data elicited from the AISEB speakers.

7. Attitudinal factors

Having looked at the VOT results we will next turn briefly to examine some of the relevant attitudinal data that we collected from the AISEB informants, with the aim of seeing whether their responses to questions about national identity can cast any light on the patterns observed in their speech production.

The section of the questionnaire devoted to identity matters is comprised of twenty-one questions designed to elicit our speakers' opinions on a) the local area (e.g. 'What do you consider the best and worst things are about growing up and living in this town?'; 'If you wanted a day out shopping, where would you go?'), b) the border (e.g. 'How often do you cross the border?'; 'Do you see the border as a divide of some sort?') and c) the informant's language (e.g. 'Do you think older and younger people talk the same here (pronounce things the same and use the same words)?'; 'Where, geographically, would you say people stop talking the same as you and start sounding different?'). There were also tasks that required informants to respond to key questions using 'visual analogue scales' (Llamas and Watt 2014; see also Redinger and Llamas, this volume). One of these, the Relational Analogue Scale (RAS), asked informants to rank identity labels by how important they felt the labels were in relation to their identities. They did this by arranging the labels along the RAS, a horizontal line running between 'most important' at one end and 'least important' at the other. The generic labels provided were *British*, *English*, *Scottish*, *Borderer* and *European*, together with a label specific to the town the informant came from (e.g. *Berwicker*, *from Gretna*, etc.). Participants were also free to come up with their own preferred labels instead of or in addition to those provided.

Because informants were asked to mark the precise positions of each label using a vertical stroke through the RAS line, it was possible to log the labels' relative locations by expressing them as values on a 0–100 scale, where 0 is 'least important' and 100 is 'most important'. In addition, we used the *British* label as an anchor point, since it represents a shared identity and so is – at least in principle – the label that all the AISEB informants, as UK citizens, could apply to themselves (though note that in Kiely et al.'s 2000 study in Berwick not a single interviewee chose to self-identify as British, and the label also tends to be unpopular in Scotland, so it could not automatically be assumed that it would always be chosen). The distances between *British* and other labels ranked above or below it on the importance scale were also measured.

The results yielded by this task were complex, and we have space to briefly summarise just three main findings here. First, we are particularly interested in informants' location of the national identity labels *Scottish* and *English* (which we collectively refer to as *Nation*) in both absolute terms and relative to the location of *British*, if *British* was indeed chosen. The second finding relates to the size of the preference, if any, for one label over the other,

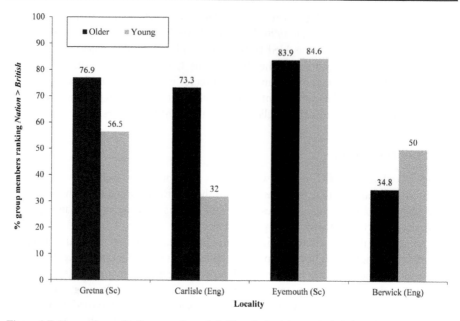

Figure 1.7 Proportions of informants in each fieldwork site who ranked their respective national identity labels (*Scottish* or *English*) higher in importance than *British*, by age group.

quantified as the distance between *British* and *Nation* on the RAS continuum in percentage points. Third, we think it is informative to examine the frequency with which informants opted *not* to choose the labels *British* and *Nation* when carrying out the RAS task.

For each locality, we can as a first approximation see how highly informants rated the *Nation* labels relative to *British*. Figure 1.7 shows this for the 132 informants who included both *Nation* and *British* in their RAS responses. In the two western communities, Gretna and Carlisle, *Nation* outranks *British* except among the young Carlisle group. In both Gretna and Carlisle, the majority of older respondents favour *Nation* over *British*, but this preference is much less clear among the young speakers from Gretna, and those young speakers who rank *English* higher than *British* in Carlisle are in a minority. The situation is quite different in the eastern localities Eyemouth and Berwick, by contrast. Practically all of the respondents in Eyemouth who chose both *British* and *Scottish* for inclusion among the labels on their RAS ranked *Scottish* higher than *British*, and the proportion of young speakers who favoured *Scottish* over *British* was only marginally higher, at 84.6 per cent, than the proportion of older speakers who did likewise (83.9 per cent). It appears, in other words, that this preference is fairly stable across the generations. The proportion of respondents who rank *Nation* higher than *British* in Berwick is also higher among the young interviewees (50 per cent) than it is among the older ones (34.8 per cent). Overall, then, it seems that while 'Britishness' is gaining favour among young people in the western localities, it is losing favour in this age cohort in the eastern towns.

This picture is sharpened somewhat when we look at the size of the gaps between *Nation* and *British* for the 132 participants who used both labels on their completed RAS. The individual and group mean distances (in percentage points on the 0–100 scale) between *British* and *Nation* for the two age groups in each of the four localities are shown in Figure 1.8. These data reveal several things. Probably the most obvious is that the slopes of the lines linking the means for the two age groups per locality are negative in three cases (Gretna, Eyemouth and Carlisle), and that the corresponding line for Berwick is more or less horizontal. These slopes indicate that in three of the four localities young interviewees chose the relevant *Nation* label over *British* less consistently than their older counterparts did, while in Berwick both age groups exhibit more of a mix of preferences. However, in Berwick there is a slightly greater concentration of positive and negative values close to zero among young speakers than among older ones, who exhibit a broad spread of values between the $+/-$ 100 extremes. The slopes of the lines for Eyemouth and particularly Carlisle are steep, showing that the age difference is more pronounced in those localities than in Gretna. In Carlisle, the preference among young interviewees for ranking *British* higher than *English* is reflected by the comparative sparsity and tighter spread of (low) positive values relative to the results for the older Carlisle group, as well as the large number of individual points lying in the range between zero and 100 for the younger speakers. Overall, there is a conspicuous difference between the two Scottish localities and the two English ones, in that (with the notable exception of the older Carlisle speakers) the tendency south of the border is for respondents to treat *English* and *British* as more equal in importance than is the case for the *Scottish* and *British* labels among the Scottish participants.

A second immediately visible trend in the data concerns the strong preference for positive values (i.e. *Scottish* was ranked higher than *British*) among the Eyemouth respondents. This recalls what we saw in Figure 1.8, though here we can see that although there is a reduction in the overall size of the gap between *Scottish* and *British* on the RAS scales completed by young Eyemouth speakers relative to older ones, the responses still indicate that *Scottish* is by far the preferred self-identity label in the town. For older Eyemouth respondents, the mean distance represents practically half of the RAS continuum, and it is around a third of its length for the young Eyemouth speakers. It is worth comparing this finding with the equivalent figures for Gretna, where the trend is similar but less prominent, and with those for Berwick, just nine miles across the border to the south, in which much more ambivalence about the relative appropriateness of *English* and *British* is in evidence (cf. Kiely et al. 2000, who report that the local and national identities professed by Berwick interviewees frequently confounded the researchers' expectations).

Finally, the proportions of interviewees who did not choose *British* or *Nation* when completing the RAS task (i.e. they opted not to select the label at all, rather than just assigning it zero by placing it at the 'least important' pole of the RAS), again split by locality and age group, can be seen in Figure 1.9. Note that there were no individual respondents for whom both labels were missing, i.e. no-one felt neither *British* nor *Scottish/English*. In no case is the proportion very large, but four columns in particular stand out from the rest. These are the three columns for *British* in Gretna, Eyemouth and Berwick, and that for *English* in Berwick. In all four cases it is older speakers who are avoiding the use of these labels. Fully a quarter of the older Eyemouth speakers reject *British* as an appropriate self-identifying label, and the older Gretna and Berwick speakers are not far behind (15.4 per cent and 17.4 per cent, respectively). It is perhaps telling that the Berwick older speakers omit *English* from their RAS responses at about the same rate (13 per cent). Far fewer young speakers overall reject *British* and *Nation*; the proportions are

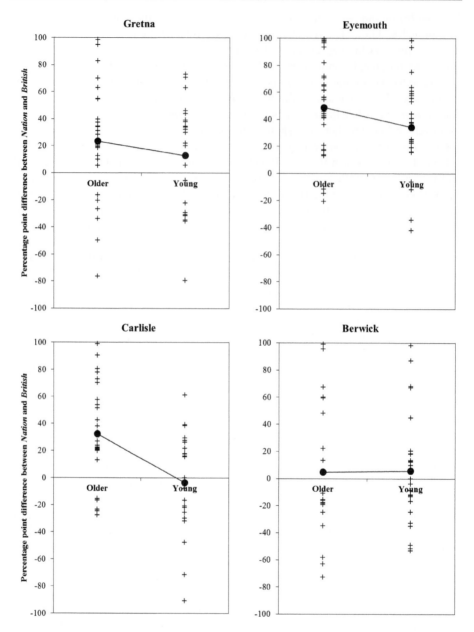

Figure 1.8 Individual and mean group distances, in percentage points, between the *Nation* and *British* labels on the Relational Analogue Scale (RAS) in the four fieldwork sites, by speaker age. Positive values indicate that *Nation* was ranked higher for importance than *British*. The means for each pair of age groups per locality are denoted by filled circles linked by a solid line.

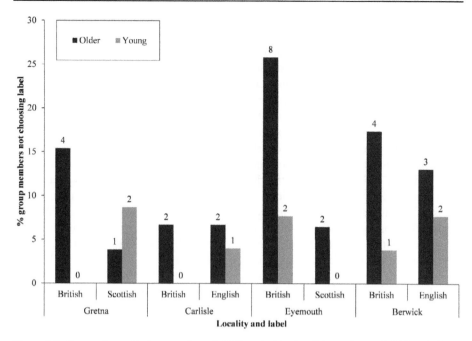

Figure 1.9 Proportions of informants in each fieldwork site who did not choose *British* or their respective national identity labels (*Scottish* or *English*) during the RAS task, by age group. The numbers of speakers that the percentages are based on are indicated above each column (N = 34).

highest among the young Gretna speakers with respect to *Scottish*, and a small number of individuals avoid *British* in Eyemouth and *English* in Berwick. It must be remembered, of course, that even if labels which are absent in the responses given by older people are chosen by their young counterparts, it does not mean that the labels are necessarily popular among young speakers; *English* might be included on a respondent's RAS but ranked low for importance (it could be assigned a score of zero, for instance). The zero scores in Figure 1.9 are also worth considering: significantly, no young people in Gretna or Carlisle omitted *British* from their RAS responses, and *Scottish* was never excluded by young Eyemouth interviewees.

In the final sections of this chapter we consider the potential link between the RAS scores and the VOT data, as a way of testing our hypotheses about connections between linguistic behaviour and national identity.

8. Relating phonetic production to identity factors

We saw in the discussion of VOT in the read speech of people from the four fieldwork sites that VOT values were conditioned by the non-linguistic factors *Nation, Coast* and *Speaker Age*. While in all four localities VOT was longer for both voiced and voiceless stops among young speakers than among older ones, in /p t k/ it was significantly shorter in the two Scottish towns than it was in the English communities. It was also significantly shorter on the east coast than the west coast. VOT was therefore shortest overall in Eyemouth, in keeping with the predictions of Johnston (1980, 1997), and longest in Carlisle. We have found in our research on other phonological variables investigated for the AISEB project – especially (r) and the NURSE vowel (Watt et al. 2012) – that Eyemouth and Carlisle represent the extremes of 'Scottishness' and 'Englishness' with respect to the characteristics of the accents spoken there (see also Maguire 2014). It is notable that the VOT patterns appear to be lining up in way that is consistent with what we found for /r/.

If we are correct in our assumption that there is a link between the way people living on the Scottish/English border choose to label themselves *vis-à-vis* the categories *Scottish* and *English* and how they pronounce certain vowels and consonants, we would expect to find correlations between those who sound the most 'Scottish' or 'English', and those who claim to be the most 'Scottish' or 'English' when they are asked to classify themselves using these adjectives. The group-level evidence discussed in this chapter suggests that this is indeed the case. Eyemouth speakers, irrespective of their age group, rank *Scottish* much higher than *British* if they choose *British* as a self-identifying label at all (around 1 in 6 of Eyemouth speakers did not). They also use the shortest VOT, on average. Gretna speakers exemplify a similar, if less polarised, pattern, and have slightly longer VOT values overall. Carlisle speakers, who exhibit the longest (i.e. least 'Scottish') VOT patterns in both the older and the young age cohorts, show among the older group a preference for *English* over *British* as a self-descriptive label. The choice of ranking *British* over *English* among young Carlisle interviewees does not seem incongruous with the fact that VOT values for this group would be typical of speakers of other varieties of (English) British English. A pattern for Berwick is rather more difficult to discern, but since the speech of that part of Northumberland is classified by some analysts as a variety of Scots (Speitel and Mather 2010) and identity in the town is often described as a Scottish/English hybrid (Watt and Ingham 1999; Kiely et al. 2000), it is not altogether surprising that we fail to resolve a clearer picture. The real test of the generalisations we have made on the basis of looking at group behaviour will come when we correlate VOT production patterns with attitudinal responses at the level of the individual speaker, as is planned in future research.

9. Conclusions

The patterns in the production and attitudinal data described in previous sections support our initial hypotheses about the correlation between phonological variation and identity factors in this region, even if the variable we chose to focus on in this chapter varies more subtly than others we have previously discussed, in particular (r). The extent of the differences between the distributions of VOT values is quite small, though VOT variations of as little as 10ms are known to be large enough to be noticeable by listeners (Cole et al. 1978; Blumstein et al. 2005), and there appears to be no bar on perceptually marginal durational and spectral differences acquiring socioindexical functions (e.g. Labov and Baranowski 2006; Langstrof 2009; Clopper and Pisoni 2005; Scobbie 2006; Kendall and Fridland 2012). There are limiting factors, of course: VOT is anchored in perceptual space by fairly sharply-defined durational thresholds (Flemming 2005), and because an adequate phonetic distance between the homorganic pairs of voiced and voiceless stops must be maintained if they are to fulfil useful phonemic contrasts, speakers do not have free rein to modify VOT durations as markers of (for example) local and national affiliation. It may be, in view of the large degree of overlap between the VOT distributions for the four localities and age groups, that the socioindexical functions of VOT variation in the region are performed more by tokens lying at the extremes of the distributions than they are by tokens with more typical VOT durations. However, word- and syllable-initial stop consonants are very frequent sounds, so listeners are given ample opportunity to hear exemplars of each of the six phonemes in interlocutors' speech within a relatively short time. Alongside the other phonological features that characterise the different varieties spoken in the four AISEB fieldwork sites (see further Watt and Ingham 1999; Llamas et al. 2009; Watt et al. 2010), it seems reasonable to argue that VOT has the potential to denote a variety of social characteristics, some of which we have encoded here by age group, *Coast* and *Nation*.

We cannot discount altogether the possibility that the physical consequences of speaker age have a bearing on the VOT durations observed in these data, as mentioned earlier. In spite of what we have argued above, the VOT patterns may depend to an appreciable degree upon the age of the speakers who produced them. However, if this were the case we might expect to see more homogeneity among the young speakers, and fewer indications that the VOT distributions we have abstracted from the speech of the young speakers parallel those of their older contemporaries, though the former are slightly positively skewed with respect to duration.

We have barely scratched the surface with the attitudinal data: the RAS is just one of a host of fieldwork instruments with which we have gauged the AISEB interviewees' opinions and orientations towards local and national identities. The relative positions of the other identity labels that respondents chose to attribute to themselves (*Borderer*, *European*, *local of town X*, etc.) on the RAS are of great interest to us, as are the ways in which the identity data quantified using this simple technique relate to findings gathered using other instruments. Future publications will shed further light on the complex interconnections between the speech patterns used by inhabitants of this dialectologically dynamic region and relevant non-linguistic aspects of how they go about making and marking social identities.

The United Kingdom is a country in which, to quote Dorling (2013), 'divides . . . have over time become clearer and clearer'. Dorling is talking about social divides rather than linguistic ones, but widening social divides are, on balance, likely to foster conditions in which linguistic divergence will take place (see also Dorling 2010). In the case of the Scottish/English border, an already strongly entrenched political divide buttressed by long-standing institutional differences (legal, educational, monetary, ecclesiastical) may sharpen still further following the 2014 independence referendum. As David Newman puts it, 'The notion that good fences make good neighbours often accurately reflects the disposition of peoples who wish to maintain and perpetuate their difference, even where this is not necessarily accompanied by animosity or outright political exclusion. Not every trans-border region results in the meeting of minds, nor do they necessarily bring about a form of transitional hybridity consisting of a mix of characteristics from each side of the border. Not all peripheral regions can, or want to be, transformed into transition zones' (Newman 2006b: 181). While Newman's generalisations might apply quite well at the eastern end of the Scottish/English border, however, the signs of linguistic convergence and the greater acceptance of Britishness as a self-identifying label seen in Gretna might argue against their aptness in the present context. We must, in other words, be careful not to view the Scottish/English border all of a piece, and guard against glib predictions of the likely linguistic consequences of the shifting social and political currents along this particular border and other borderland zones to which it might be compared.

Notes

1. We gratefully acknowledge the support of the UK Economic and Social Research Council (RES-062-23-0525). See <http://www.york.ac.uk/res/aiseb/>.
2. For reference, Docherty (1992: 116) cites mean VOT values in milliseconds for initial pre-vocalic stops in Southern British English (Received Pronunciation) as follows: /p/ = 42; /t/ = 63; /k/ = 63; /b/ = 18; /d/ = 26; /g/ = 31. Docherty's VOT values for pre-voiced tokens of /b d g/ were not included in the averaging.

2

Where North Meets South? Contact, Divergence and the Routinisation of the Fenland Dialect Boundary[1]

David Britain

1. Introduction

Before the seventeenth century, the Fenland of eastern England – low-lying marshland, subject to frequent flooding and with few suitable locations for settlement – represented a considerable barrier to communication between East Anglia, especially Norfolk and Suffolk, to the east, and northern England and the East Midlands to the west. Perhaps not surprisingly, then, it also marked the location of an important dialect boundary. From the mid-seventeenth century onwards the Fens began to be drained, and today the area is home to some of the richest agricultural land in the UK. Despite the drainage, however, the dialect boundary has persisted. This chapter explores some of the reasons for this persistence. I argue that the physical, but also subsequent and consequent perceptual, attitudinal, military, political and institutional barrier of the Fenland has shaped people's spatialities in the area, and that the routinisation of these spatial practices has significantly contributed to the preservation of the dialect boundary to this day. Fundamentally, the chapter argues that dialect boundaries such as this one are actively created and maintained by the geographies of our practice and mobility, but in circumstances not entirely of our own choosing. I begin with a brief social history of the Fens, to highlight how many boundary effects resulted from the original barrier caused by the marshland. I then provide both traditional dialectological and sociolinguistic evidence from the area of the robust and multiplex (and stable) dialect isoglosses and transitions that run through the area. It is here that the persistence of the dialect boundary at all levels – phonological, grammatical and lexical – despite the drainage of the Fens, becomes clear. I then turn to attempt an explanation of this persistence, adopting Giddens' (e.g. 1984) ideas on routinisation as a system-maintenance mechanism and applying them to the Fenland situation. The discussion ends with a specific case study on the role of political borders in shaping spatialities and thereby, in this area at least, shaping dialects.

2. A brief sociohistory of the Fens

The Fens were once an area of low-lying marshland. They are located at the north-western edge of East Anglia, in eastern England, and cover parts of the counties of Lincolnshire, Cambridgeshire, Norfolk and Suffolk. Figure 2.1 shows the Fenland in Anglo-Saxon times. The Fens sat at the border between East Anglia to the east and Mercia to the west. Settlement was limited to a very few patches of higher land on fenland islands (such as Ely), as well as locations on what was then the northern coastline (e.g. Wisbech, Spalding, Boston). A map of Domesday settlement in the area – Figure 2.2 – highlights particularly well the sparse settlement density and the string of coastline settlements. Most parts of the Fens were simply uninhabitable, with Darby describing how 'even those portions that escaped winter flooding were subject to an annual heaving motion, the mud absorbing water and swelling' (Darby 1931: 18). It was variously described as a 'wide wilderness . . . a waste untilled, devoid of settled habitation' (Darby 1934: 188), 'accessible neither for man nor beast, affording only deep mud' (Paris 1256, in Darby 1934: 190) and as 'swamps and bogs, an occasional black pool, exuding dark mists, sprinkled with islands of marshy heaths and crisscrossed by winding waterways' (St Guthlac of Crowland, an eighth-century monk, cited in Stafford 1985: 16). Samuel Pepys was none too impressed either. In a diary report from 18 and 19 September 1663, he describes his travels 'over most sad fenns, all the way observing the sad life which the people of the place do live, sometimes rowing from one spot to another and then wading'; later he 'begun a journy . . . with much ado through the Fens, along Dikes, where sometimes we were ready to have our horses sink to the belly, we got by night, with great deal of stir and hard riding, to Parsons drove, a heathen place' (Latham and Matthews 1971: 310–11; spellings as per the original).

Serious and systematic attempts to drain the Fens began in the mid-seventeenth century, but this was an ongoing project that lasted right into the twentieth century. It was not until the nineteenth century that the Fens became relatively secure from regular flooding. Locals in the late seventeenth century claimed that 'most of the draines, sewers, dykes . . . are grown upp obstructed and very defective for want of ditching and scouring soe as the waters cannot pass . . . Where wee should now be plowing the fowles of the ayre are swimming' (jury comment from a 1688 'Session of Sewers', cited in Summers [1976: 94]; spellings as per the original). Elizabeth Harris, in 1763, remarked in a letter to her son that

> 1400 cows are kept in the parish of Cottenham, which feed on the fens in summer. The water is, in this dry season, up to their bellies . . . Mr Harris took a ride to survey these fens, and he says nothing can be so detestable. He talked with the natives, who told him, that during the winter the water was constantly above their ancles [sic] in their houses. (Malmesbury 1870: 91)

Not surprisingly, then, the Fens created a significant physical barrier to east–west communication at the time.

The physical barrier, however, created the context for other 'barrier effects' to emerge. One such effect was military. Anglo-Saxon settlers, Darby suggested, 'coagulated into political entities . . . until the Fenland remained as the great obstacle between the big states . . . Barrier boundaries have their military aspect . . . by holding neighbouring

Figure 2.1 Map of the Fenland in Anglo-Saxon times (from Stafford 1985: 7). Note not just the marshland, but also the then coastline (bold), south of the present-day coastline.

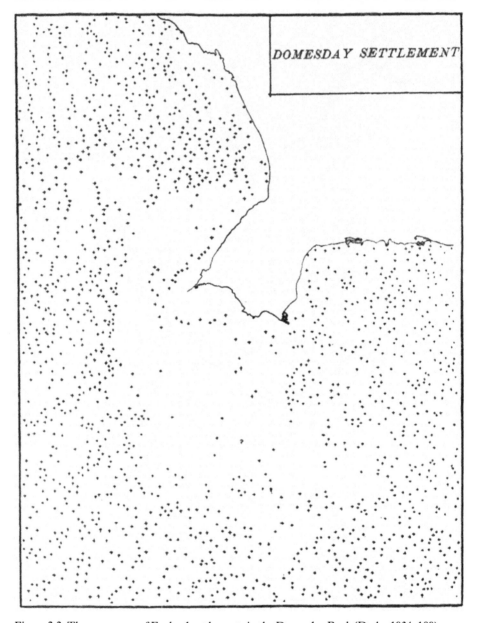

Figure 2.2 The sparseness of Fenland settlements in the Domesday Book (Darby 1934: 189).

peoples apart it reduces that contact and friction which so often provoke hostilities. The Fenland . . . constituted such a frontier' (1934: 186–90).

Very importantly, in addition, the Fens became a psychological barrier. Darby (1931: 61) cites St Felix of Burgundy, who argued that there arose

> a mythical fear of a land inhabited by demons and dragons, ogres and were-
> wolves . . . especially obscure, which ofttimes many men had attempted to
> inhabit, but no man could endure it on account of manifold horrors and fears
> and the loneliness of the wide wilderness – so that no man could endure it, but
> everyone on this account had fled from it.

Not just the area, but also its inhabitants, became demonised. Macaulay (1855, in Darby
1932: 432) claimed that 'In that dreary region, covered by vast flights of wild-fowl, a
half-savage population, known by the name of Breedlings, then led an amphibious life,
sometimes wading and sometimes rowing from one islet of the firm ground to another.'
It was 'an abode of monsters and demons . . . a landscape inhabited by evil against
which saints and heroes might battle' (Stafford 1985: 16). St Botolph found the Fens
'infested with devils of various kinds' (in Darby 1934: 191). The barrier effect, then,
was psychological as well as physical. Eventually the Fens were drained, and a complex
network of drainage channels and overflow plains now keeps the water out of most of
the fenland. But the Fens today remain at the boundary of different counties and different regions, and infrastructure has done little to break down the east–west divide. It
remains peripheral in every sense. It sits at the fringes of all four counties it occupies,
located, especially in Norfolk, Suffolk and Lincolnshire, well away from the major urban
centres in each where political and economic power resides. It sits at the edges of both
East Anglia to the east and the East Midlands to the west. It even sits at the edge of three
regional TV reception areas.[2] Major train lines run either side of the Fens, with just one
line passing east–west, and only some of the trains using it actually stop at Fenland sta-
tions. Road connections are also poor, with no motorways and only a few miles of dual
carriageway. The area is predominantly rural, with few urban centres of any kind. The
main urban centres for service provision are located either side of the Fens, for example
in Peterborough to the west and King's Lynn to the east. Region-internally, the extensive drainage channel network makes road and rail infrastructure relatively expensive,
and some of the major channels have only a very few crossing points. Post-reclamation
political, infrastructural and economic developments have not helped the Fens shed
their peripheral border status.

3. Historical linguistic evidence of a dialect boundary

It is not, then, at all surprising that the physical impenetrability of the Fens, the almost
demonic way in which the area was perceived, and the positioning of the major sociopolitical spheres of influence to the east and west have led to the Fens becoming a major
linguistic boundary too. Within the dialectological tradition, the pioneering researchers
of the nineteenth century provided evidence of major dialect boundaries in the Fens.
Prince Louis Lucien Bonaparte (1875–76) showed East Anglia and the East Midlands as
clearly distinct (see Viereck 1992: 25–6). Alexander Ellis (1889) placed the Norfolk and
Suffolk Fens in his 'East Eastern subsection of the Eastern Division', Cambridgeshire in
the 'North Eastern' subsection, what was then Huntingdonshire in Variant 3 of the Mid-
Eastern subsection, and most of Lincolnshire in the Border Midland subsection of the
Midland Division, though he has no evidence from South-East Lincolnshire (see Britain
2012: 27).

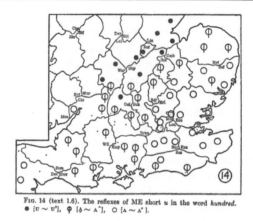

FIG. 14 (text 1.6). The reflexes of ME short *u* in the word *hundred*.
● [ʊ ~ ʊˑ], ⊕ [ɤ ~ ʌˑ], ○ [ʌ ~ ʌˑ].

Figure 2.3 Map from Kurath and Lowman (1970: 17) showing variable realisations of /ʌ/ on either side of the Fens.

In the twentieth century, Kurath and Lowman's (1970) research from southern England in the 1930s similarly shows a number of clear isoglosses running north-east to south-west through the Fens. Figure 2.3, for example, shows the distribution of the STRUT vowel in the word 'butter'. Similar patterns were found, for example, for raised and fronted [æ] realisations of the TRAP vowel (present to the east, absent to the west) (1970: 19), for [ɐ] variants of NURSE (present to the east, absent to the west) (1970: 29), and for the realisation of /h/ (absent to the west, present to the east) (1970: 33).

Most evidence of the Fenland's boundary status in traditional dialectological work comes from the *Survey of English Dialects* (SED; Orton et al. 1962–71), both in the *Atlas* derived from the *Basic Materials* (Orton, Sanderson and Widdowson 1978) and in the extensive processing and re-analysis (computerised or otherwise) that the *Basic Materials* have undergone since (e.g. Anderson 1987; Viereck 1986a, 1986b, 1990; Shackleton 2010). Anderson (1987: 4) specifically points to the Fenland:

> Linguistic boundaries which seem to bear little relation to current geographical features often follow the edges of earlier marshes or forests. Perhaps the most important boundary of this type is the Fens which, until the seventeenth century, was an impassable morass with a few scattered island communities. The dialects of these areas contrast sharply with Lincolnshire to the north and Norfolk to the east.

Viereck's aggregate maps of phonological, morphological and lexical features from the *SED* all show the boundary distinctly, but highlight the fact that while the east is clearly distinct from the west, there is, in fact, an intermediate transition 'buffer' zone between the two (Figures 2.4–2.6; see also Shackleton 2010: 163).

Kontic (1990), focusing predominantly on lexical variation in the south-east of England from the *SED*, also finds a number of isoglosses running through the Fens. These include the words used for 'donkey' (*dickey* to the east, *pronkus* to the west; 1990: 88), 'farm cart'

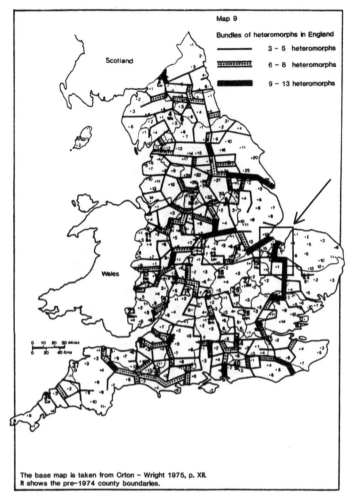

Figure 2.4 Viereck's multivariable map of morphological isoglosses, based on the *Survey* of *English Dialects* (Viereck 1986b: 250), with Fenland highlighted.

(*tumble* or *tumbril* to the east, *cart* to the west; 1990: 100), 'gutter' (*trough(ing)* to the west, *spout(ing)* to the east; 1990: 112) and the possessive pronouns (-*s* forms such as *hers, yours, ours* to the east, and -*n* forms *hern, yourn* and *ourn* to the west; 1990: 207–12).

4. Sociolinguistic evidence

Variationist evidence of the situation at this boundary comes from my own work over twenty years on the accents and dialects of the Fenland (see, especially, Britain 1997, 2001, 2005, 2010c). This work has been able to shed light on the geographical positioning of this dialect transition in somewhat more detail (given that much of the more traditional work had relied on only a few speakers across the area), and to examine whether the

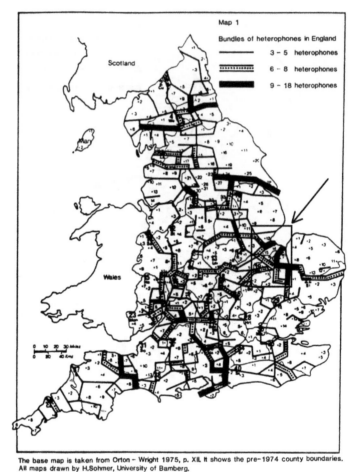

The base map is taken from Orton – Wright 1975, p. XII. It shows the pre-1974 county boundaries.
All maps drawn by H.Sohmer, University of Bamberg.

Figure 2.5 Viereck's multivariable map of phonological isoglosses, based on the *Survey of English Dialects* (Viereck 1986b: 245), with Fenland highlighted.

boundary is shifting to any degree, as well as considering the outcomes of dialect contact in the boundary transition zone itself. Importantly, it was able to revisit specific linguistic variables that had both already been subjected to special focus in the traditional literature and become iconic in introductory texts, especially the realisation of words in the STRUT and BATH classes. Both, but especially the latter, have gained a highly salient status in distinguishing 'Northerners' from 'Southerners' in England, although as the traditional studies show, the 'northern' forms [ʊ] (in STRUT-class words) and [a] (in the BATH set) respectively reach quite far south. These [ʊ] and [a] realisations have become enregistered as quintessential characteristics of 'northernness', such that Wales (2006: 150) was able to claim that 'these two vowels [have become] significant symbols of a "North–South divide" . . . Wells' comment (1982: 354) that many educated Northerners "would feel it a denial of their identity . . . to say BATH words with anything other than short [a]" rings

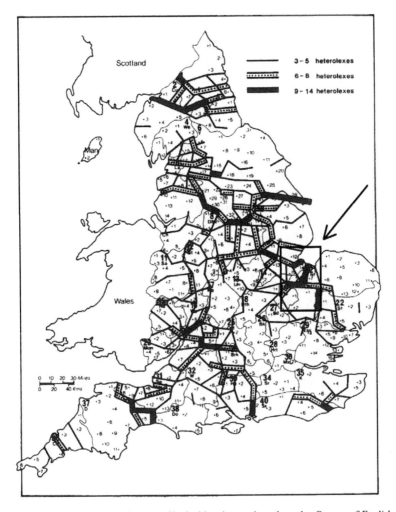

Figure 2.6 Viereck's multivariable map of lexical isoglosses, based on the *Survey of English Dialects* (Viereck 1986a: 734), with Fenland highlighted.

true even twenty years later.' This 'North–South divide' for BATH and STRUT runs, at its eastern end, right through the Fens.

My variationist analyses of BATH and STRUT suggest that the dialect boundary has barely moved, in this area at least, since the early traditional dialectological studies. As Ellis (1889) and the *SED Basic Materials* had logged, Chambers and Trudgill (1998 [1980]) had analysed, but the *Linguistic Atlas of England* maps had oversimplified (see, for example, Orton et al.'s 1978 Ph50 map of the isogloss for the word 'butter'), the [ʊ/ʌ] boundary for STRUT was, in fact, a rather broad and very heterogeneous transition zone (see Britain 2013). Inside this transition zone were the sort of interdialect forms that research on dialect contact (e.g. Trudgill 1986) would lead us to expect – the central Fenland area housed phonetically intermediate [ɤ] forms, with closer forms to the north(-west) and more open forms to the south(-east). What is more, these interdialectal forms seemed to be stabilising and becoming the dominant form among the young. In the north of the Fenland, the Lincolnshire–Norfolk border – a sparsely populated area, separated by a wide drainage channel crossed at only one point – there was little evidence of a transition zone but a much clearer boundary, with [ʊ] to one side and [ʌ] to the other. An apparent-time comparison, however, showed little evidence, firstly, of a northward movement of the transition, as some had expected (e.g. Wolfram and Schilling-Estes 2003: 722). Secondly, however, the results showed that the transition area was geographically narrower for the younger speakers than for the older ones. This dialect boundary continues, then, to straddle the Fens.

The picture for BATH is even more indicative of the stability of the dialect boundary. Chambers and Trudgill (1998) had found interdialect forms present in the *Basic Materials* of the *SED*. A rather different picture was drawn from my variationist analysis of conversational data from the Fens. Firstly, variability was relatively uncommon. Most speakers, old and young, categorically or near-categorically chose one variant, [a] or [aː]. Tokens of intermediate length were not found in my data, and the long forms were often very long indeed. For the vast majority of speakers their majority variant accounted for well over 85 per cent of their tokens. Secondly, the apparent-time comparison showed a rather narrow transition zone, where variability was more robust, among the older speakers, and an even narrower transition zone, located in a very sparsely populated strip between Wisbech and March in the central Fens and Peterborough to the west, among the young. Furthermore, the younger speakers were even more categorical users of one or the other variant than the old had been. There were very few robustly variable young speakers at all (see Britain 2013). Again, the boundary appears to be stable, and even sharpening.

Analyses of other variables not only highlighted further evidence of the boundary status of this area, but was also able to distinguish two boundaries, rather than one: one between the eastern edge of the Fens and a central 'belt' of towns from Wisbech in the north through March to Chatteris in the south, and the other between these towns and Peterborough and Spalding to the west. Both lie within very sparsely populated farmland. The BATH boundary, for example, is located between these central towns on the one side, and Peterborough on the other. An example of a boundary at the east is the realisation of the MOUTH diphthong. In the east, this is realised as [ɛʊ], whereas in the central towns, and further west, it is a monophthongal [ɛː] (see Britain 2003). Also to the east, third-person present tense -*s* is (variably) absent, while in the central towns and the west it is not. These 'twin boundaries' can be seen in the traditional dialectological data too (see Figures 2.4–2.6).

These maps provide clear visual evidence, not of the transitional nature of this dialect boundary (as we have seen, in some places and for some variables the border is not especially gradient), but of the clearly distinct linguistic nature of this intermediate zone, distinct from the dialects to both east and west. I have argued elsewhere (Britain 1997, 2010c) that in this central area a distinct koine has developed as a result of the mixture of dialects from the east and west once the Fens were finally drained. My data provide ample evidence of the effects of koineisation in this area. The central belt, for example, has an allophonic patterning of PRICE phonologically similar to that found in Canada. So while the east has [əɪ] and the west has [ɑɪ ~ ɑː], the central towns have [əɪ] before voiceless consonants and [ɑɪ ~ ɑː] elsewhere (Britain 1997). And levelling is also prevalent. If either

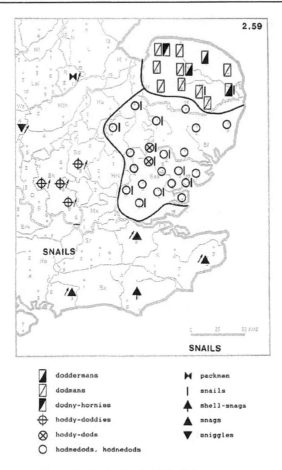

Figure 2.7 'Snail' in Eastern England (Kontic 1990: 181).

the east or the west use forms which are rather locally restricted, the central towns have tended to avoid them, and adopt the more supralocal and widely distributed form. So, for example, western Fenland [ɛ] forms of /ei/ in the words *take* and *make* are avoided in the central Fenland towns, as is the east's retention of a ROSE [ʊu] ~ ROWS [ʌʊ] split.

Kontic (1990) also provides lexical evidence of levelling, showing the absence of locally restricted lexis when areas to the west, or the east, or both present localisms. The Fens avoid the western forms *hissen* for 'himself' (1990: 218) and *mysen* for 'myself' (1990: 219) and the eastern forms *hodmedod* and *dodman/dodderman* for 'snail' (1990: 181) (Figure 2.7). The fact that a distinctive koine has developed here is further evidence, I would argue, of the stability of this boundary zone.

5. Boundaries and routinised spatialities

The question, then, to be addressed here is: given that the marshland has been drained and this physical barrier to east–west communication is no longer present, why is this area still the site of such a dense clustering of dialect boundaries and transitions? In order to attempt to address this question, I draw on work on the power of routines and routinisa-tion (see, for example, Giddens 1984 and Britain 1997 for a different linguistic example) to shape and reinforce social behaviour, while highlighting the importance of understand-ing the social and attitudinal dimensions of space, as well as the physical. I introduce the ideas here first, before demonstrating how, together, they can inform explanations of the persistence of the Fenland dialect boundary.

Routines provide an important frame for examining dialect maintenance and change. Giddens (1984) argues strongly for the important role of routinisation in the consoli-dation and perpetuation of social structures. He defines routines as 'whatever is done habitually' (p. xxiii), 'the habitual, taken for granted character of the vast bulk of activities of day-to-day social life, the prevalence of familiar styles and forms of conduct' (p. 376). Most important for our discussions here is Giddens' claim that routines are the 'material grounding of . . . the recursive nature of social life' (1984: xxiii). In other words, many activities in our daily lives are routinised and the structure of these activities is repro-duced by their very performance. Cohen explains:

> Structure is reconstituted in each instance where a pervasive and enduring procedure is reproduced. This reconstitution of structures 'regrooves' agents' familiarity with established cognitive outlooks, it reinforces the mutual knowl-edge of rules . . . both for those who actually participate in them as well as for those who recognise that these practices are being performed. This point equally applies to the reproduction of context. In every instance where agents reflex-ively monitor physical, social and temporal elements of their circumstances in a routine manner, they reflexively regenerate the contextual relevance of these elements. (Cohen 1989: 46)

Regular re-enactment of routines helps, according to this account, to preserve, reiterate and reinforce the behaviours performed in those routines. In a sense, they act in ways similar to those proposed for strong social network ties (e.g. Milroy 1980; Milroy and Milroy 1985), reinforcing and enforcing established behaviours. Giddens (1984: xxiii) argues, further, that we gain 'ontological security' from routines. Pica and Kakihara (2003: 1559) explain this as 'the security derived from familiarizing ourselves with an environment and acting in and/or interacting with it', while Gregory (1989: 197) describes it as 'a mode of self-reassurance brought about by the agent's involvement in the conduct of everyday life'. Craib (1992: 157) summarises the role of routines in Giddens' theoretical model neatly when he claims that it is a 'major source of patterning, producing the most deeply embedded institutions of social life and social systems . . . we have a need for routine, we develop routine practices and pass them on from generation to generation.' I argue below that the role of routines in system preservation can help us understand the stability of the Fenland dialect boundary.

In other work, I have argued that our understanding of space in dialectology needs to be informed by the fact that space is at once physical, social and perceptual (see Britain 2010a, 2013), and I here introduce the importance of routines into this understanding of spatiality. Human settlement and our manipulation of physical space, our movement and interaction within that space, our attitudes towards that space and the way we interact with the social, economic and political institutions that regulate or mould our behaviour 'colonise' this physical space, and our actions subsequent to that colonisation are guided (often strongly) as a result. If I want to go from A to B, my journey – if I can afford it and if I am allowed to make it (children in England, for example, may need explicit permission to do so at 10 o'clock in the morning on a Tuesday in early October; the law says they should be in school!) – will be guided by the transportation infrastructure that is or is not present. It may be an onerous, unpleasant, uncomfortable journey on a crowded train or on congested roads, or it may be swift, comfortable, efficient and affordable. If I am able (financially, physically, legally) to travel, I am free to do so, but my journey is strongly shaped by forces and structures outside my control. Past events and manipulations of space (the construction of roads and bridges and tunnels, the building of shopping malls, the location of industrial developments) and our past spatial practices can shape future ones. And as I have argued elsewhere (Britain 2010b), our actions, and those of industry and the state, have the potential either to trigger change or to cement past practices even further.

The performance of face-to-face interaction entails mobility: 'Mobility can be understood as the ordinary and everyday achievement of planning and organising co-presence with other people and with material objects such as tables, chairs and occasionally also cake' (Peters et al. 2010: 349), and to the extent that interactions become regular and routinised, spatialised patterns of interaction – life-paths – are built up for both individuals and communities. Some of these 'paths' become very well-worn: at home, our journey to work, our trips to pick up bread and milk, popping in for a beer after the football match on a Saturday. These paths aren't just physical, they are also social, taking into account not just our personal choices but also the ways institutions have shaped the options available to us to make these choices (Britain 2010a). And they are psychological in that our paths through space are also shaped by the way we perceive the social and physical space around us. Over time and on a community scale, through the practice of everyday routines, 'places' and 'regions' emerge. Viewing places and regions in this way – as processes rather than as objects – emphasises that they are shaped by practice, practice that is of course nevertheless constrained by institutional factors. So through our practices we produce places and regions, but they in turn provide the context – enabling as well as constraining – for that production. We are therefore guided to a great extent by what our predecessors have done in creating place and region (see Britain 2010a).

I would argue that the dialect boundary has survived and been reinforced in the Fens because the boundary effect of the original marshland, and the consequent boundary effects that this engendered – attitudinal, infrastructural, socio-economic – has shaped people's routine socio-spatial behaviours. People can, fairly readily, travel from east to west in the Fens, but, on the whole, routinely, they do not do so. These routines have been reinforced by three main factors:

1. **Political and local government borders**. These, at a particularly crucial time in people's dialect socialisation – adolescence – strongly routinise social mobilities (for linguistic examples of the effects of political borders specifically on adolescents, see further below).
2. **Infrastructure**. Good road and rail and public transportation connections that might have facilitated and encouraged east–west travel are lacking. The largely rural nature of the area, and the poor service provision in the central Fenland towns, mean that residents orient either to the east – to King's Lynn and beyond

to Norwich – or to the west (to Peterborough) for non-everyday shopping,
cinema and other forms of consumption.
3. **Negative stereotyping**. The central Fenland is perceived relatively negatively
by people living to either side. As an area of countryside that does not conform
to stereotypical images of England's rural idyll, it is viewed as a rather poor and
somewhat lawless rural backwater full of 'carrot crunchers'.

So people to the west of the Fens had neither encouragement nor desire to venture east,
and local infrastructure did not facilitate such travel anyway. Their daily spatial routines
kept them in the west, talking and socialising (and developing strong social network ties)
mostly with people from the west. And local schools kept western children in the west.
The same can be said for those in the east. People's routines led them to remain 'on
their own side of the fence', and political institutions and infrastructure did nothing to
encourage them to do otherwise. The deep grooving (to use Cohen's term) of routines has
perpetuated socio-spatial behaviours and in doing so reinforced and reiterated the specific
local dialect into which people are socialised.

Of course it is impossible to say which of these 'border effects' is more responsible than
others (though, as we will see, the political effects are, in this area at least, quite significant), and I would want to argue that they are all mutually reinforcing. Ratti et al. (2010)
showed that there was a good match between regional government boundaries and breaks
in the density of landline telephone calls, and their maps of areas of call density even provided a fairly good match with Trudgill's (1999) proposed map of regional dialect areas,
with particularly strong correlations between the East Anglian dialect region (i.e. the
eastern Fenland and further east) and intra-regional call density (see also Watt et al. and
Montgomery, this volume). I have shown in earlier work that there was a close correlation
between the existence of bus routes between the eastern and central Fens (Britain 2002:
615) and some salient dialect isoglosses. But are bus-riding people's spatialities determined by where the buses go, or are the bus routes responding to pre-existing tendencies
and desires of people to go to particular places? Probably both. Together these factors are
both context-creating and context-renewing. The factors that serve to create, maintain
and reiterate the border combine factors driven by agency of the human subject, as well
as factors driven by structural, economic and political power. We create spaces but not
under circumstances totally of our own choosing; we are free to explore, but are 'chan-
nelled' by the explorations of those who went before us, and those who seek to control us
(Britain 2010a).

In order to emphasise and exemplify the institutional constraints that shape our
mobilities and thereby our dialects, I conclude by examining the potential role of political boundaries in the creation and perpetuation of dialect boundaries. Trudgill's (2000)
now famous tour, firstly through East Anglia, and then through west Germanic-speaking
continental Europe, emphasised that geographical dialects, for the most part, lie on a
dialect continuum:

> If you travel from Norfolk into Suffolk . . . investigating conservative rural
> dialects as you go, you will find, at least at some points, that the dialects change
> *gradually* from place to place. There is no clear *linguistic* break between Norfolk
> and Suffolk dialects. It is not possible to state in *linguistic* terms where people

stop speaking Norfolk dialect and start speaking Suffolk dialect . . . If we choose to place the dividing line between the two at the county boundary, then we are basing our decision on *social* (in this case local-governmental-political) rather than on linguistic facts . . . [a]t some places along the Netherlands–Germany frontier the dialects spoken on either side of the border are extremely similar. If we choose to say people on one side of the border speak German and those on the other Dutch, our choice is again based on social and political rather than linguistic factors. (Trudgill 2000: 3–4)

Trudgill's discussion is primarily to argue for the essentially sociopolitical nature of dialect and language labels, and he is careful to recognise that this continuum occurs only 'at least at some points' and 'at some places' and not everywhere. Recent research at certain places along the Dutch–German border has found that linguistic differences between the two sides appear to be increasing over time, suggesting that political borders are (increasingly) important loci of linguistic isoglosses. De Vriend et al. (2008) investigated the Kleveland area of the border between Germany and the Netherlands. A historical dialect continuum had once passed through this area, and it was only in 1830 that the location of today's national border became fixed. Since then, though, people's everyday lives have been moulded, shaped and guided by the implications of this boundary. Giesbers (2008: 66–7) points to the importance of compulsory schooling, an issue that I will return to below. In this case it led to children who happened to have ended up living in the Netherlands being taught Standard Dutch in Dutch schools and those who ended up in Germany being taught Standard German in German schools. Consequently, as Trudgill (2000) also makes clear, each set of children was presented with distinct autonomous standard varieties to acquire, despite the original similarities in their vernacular dialects. The border also, ultimately, determined the languages used in the local and national media. But Giesbers also demonstrated, importantly, that local spatialities were affected by and adapted to the increasing importance of the border. She pointed (2008: 66–7) to the fact that political disputes between the two countries occasionally led to the border being closed. She also highlighted (2008: 63) the fact that there were ever fewer cross-border marriages, fewer friendships that straddled the border, fewer trans-border shopping trips. And infrastructure both reflected and reinforced this decline in cross-border contact – few local bus routes cross the political border to facilitate such contact. Ultimately, the consequences of this emergent divergence of spatialities were that 'cross-the-border dialects are nowadays separated by a plain gap' (De Vriend et al. 2008: 10), that the dialect boundary corresponded to people's assumed geographical spatialities (actual movement was not examined), and that people perceived the political boundary to be a linguistic one too. These researchers concluded that 'the dialect variation in our research turns out to be more closely related to socio-geographic structures than to the geographic spatial configuration. This can be seen as the consequence of dialect variation paralleling or reflecting contact data, dialect variation being the product of social entities (people, groups of people) interacting with each other. When there is no or scarce social interaction and no cohesive social system . . . dialect variation maximizes' (De Vriend et al. 2008: 14; see Kremer 1979 and Gerritsen 1999 for other Dutch–German boundary studies, and Smits 2012 for an examination of different levels of dialect supralocalisation either side of the border). The political boundary, then, is a linguistic boundary because of its socio-spatial implications for people's everyday lives.

The case above involves the boundary between nation-states, where institutional and infrastructural differences either side of a border are likely to be relatively great. But the implications for spatial mobilities of political boundaries at the more local, intra-national level can be critical for dialect boundary formation too. In England, county boundaries strongly determine which school a child will attend, because schools' catchment areas tend not to straddle county boundaries. In rural areas, these catchment areas can be quite large, meaning children have to travel quite some distance to attend school. Compulsory schooling, of course, represents a significant institutionally and legally imposed constraint on the mobilities of almost all children. For roughly six or seven hours per day, for much of the year, almost all children from wherever they live within their politically determined catchment area are brought together. So a great deal of adolescent dialect socialisation – so important for the transmission and reorganisation of local dialect – takes place in and around the confines of the school.

As the foregoing discussion and associated maps show, the boundary, in the far north of the Fens, between Norfolk in the east and Lincolnshire in the west is a particularly major and sharp isogloss. The border runs for about 15 km (9 miles), partly following the course of the River Nene, with just one river-crossing point between the two counties, and then heading north-eastwards to the Wash (an inlet of the North Sea), rather anomalously trapping a small, relatively recently reclaimed and extremely sparsely inhabited strip of farmland, Wingland Marsh, between the Nene and the Norfolk border. The (very few) children living close to the border on the Norfolk side travel east or south-east for primary school, with a somewhat longer trip for secondary school, into areas where the predominant dialect is an eastern Fenland, East Anglian one (so, [ʌ] in STRUT, [aː] in BATH, [ɛʊ] in MOUTH; [əɪ] in PRICE, some retention of a ROSE~ROWS distinction, low levels of third-person present-tense zero, /h/ present, etc.). Children close to the border on the Lincolnshire side travel west for primary school, and further west still for secondary school, into areas where the predominant dialect is a western Fenland one ([ʊ] in STRUT, [a] in BATH, [ɛː] in MOUTH; [ɑɪ ~ ɑː] in PRICE,[3] ROSE~ROWS fully merged, no third-person present-tense zero, /h/ variably absent, variable [ɛ] in *make* and *take*, etc.). Children who may live a hundred metres apart, but on either side of the county boundary, end up (at least) 15 km (9 miles) apart from each other at secondary school. As in the Netherlands–Germany study discussed above, the political boundary has become a sharp linguistic boundary because of the implications of the border for, in this case, young people's routinised spatialities. Political boundaries determine school catchment areas, which, generation after generation, bring together all young people into one place and reinforce the dialect norms on either side of the boundary. It is important to note that this is subject to change. If county boundaries are moved, or educational policies change (for example, by a decision to send children to their nearest school, even if this is in a different county), then significant dialectological consequences might result.

6. Conclusion

In this chapter, I have attempted to present a practice-based explanation for the persistence of dialect boundaries in the Fens. Having demonstrated the long-standing location of dialect boundaries in the area, despite the drainage of the Fenland, I argued that the marshland-as-barrier created a whole set of other barrier effects that lasted long after the Fens were drained, effects that have strongly shaped people's everyday spatialities. The routine nature of these spatialities has, following Giddens, enabled the social practices performed through them to be stabilised, reinforced and enforced. People have, through their everyday mundane and routine practice, maintained these borders. They have done so, though, I have argued, not entirely in circumstances of their own choosing. A number of political factors and infrastructural developments have also served to reiterate these boundaries between east and west, and shape and even control people's movement. The mutual engagement of people's practice and political and economic structure has perpetuated social spatialities on either side of the Fens, and thereby perpetuated the long-standing dialect boundary in the area.

Notes

1. This article was due to be presented for the first time at the inaugural *Borders and Identities* conference in Newcastle upon Tyne in January 2010, but heavy snow prevented me from attending. I am grateful to Dom Watt and Carmen Llamas for giving me the opportunity to brush the snowflakes off this paper and present it in writing. Somewhat different versions were also later aired to audiences in Sheffield, Neuchâtel and Gent. I am very grateful to the people present for their very useful comments and suggestions.
2. Consequently, some people living in north-west Norfolk, who would like to see programming from their county town of Norwich, receive instead news about Leeds and Sheffield, in West and South Yorkshire respectively.
3. So there is very little evidence, at this part of the border, of the 'Canadian Raising'-type allophonic reallocation of variants of PRICE.

3

Borders in North American English

Charles Boberg

1. Different types of border

Research on North American English has been primarily concerned with two kinds of borders: dialect borders, such as those dividing the North, Midland and South dialect regions of the eastern United States, as conceived by Kurath (1949) and Kurath and McDavid (1961); and political borders, particularly the United States/Canada border, the linguistic status of which was first studied by Avis (1954–1956) and Allen (1959). There has also been some research on a third kind of border: the points of contact between English and other languages of North America. Poplack (1978, 1980, 1989, 2008) has been a key figure in examining the mixed varieties of speech that arise among bilinguals along these partly figurative borders between the domains of English, Spanish and French. Less work has been done on the borders between English and the many indigenous languages still spoken in North America. An even more figurative type of border, which has also received copious attention in previous research, is that between ethnic or social groups, such as are normally studied by quantitative sociolinguists. Though some of these social borders are well defined and have accordingly substantial linguistic effects, such as when neighbourhoods are divided along racial, ethnic or socio-economic lines, or when cultural minority groups send their children to segregated schools, social borders will not concern us here. This chapter will focus instead on the more literal types of border: those that separate regional and national varieties of North American English.

2. Different views of regional borders in American English

Serious study of regional variation in North American English, and of the borders implied by that regional variation, was initiated by Hans Kurath and his collaborators in the 1930s, with a never-completed project that was intended to generate a *Linguistic Atlas of the United States and Canada*. Complete data were published only for the New England region, where the project began, but summary data for a wide variety of lexical and phonological variables were eventually published for the whole Atlantic seaboard, from Maine down to Georgia (Kurath 1949; Kurath and McDavid 1961), and later for the Midwest

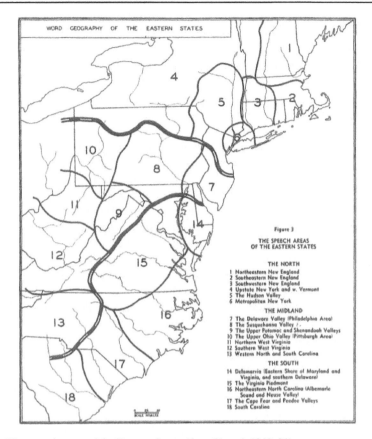

Figure 3.1 The speech areas of the Eastern States (from Kurath 1949: 91).

(Allen 1976; Marckwardt 1957; Shuy 1962) and the South (Pederson et al. 1986–93). Kurath's analysis of the data produced by the Atlas project along the Atlantic coast found evidence for three main dialect regions: North, Midland and South (1949, his Figure 3, reproduced here as Figure 3.1). These seemed to result from distinct settlement histories in each region. The northern region reflected the westward expansion of the Massachusetts Bay settlements established by Pilgrims and Puritans in the early seventeenth century. The southern region reflected the inland expansion of several English coastal settlements established between the early seventeenth and early eighteenth centuries (especially Jamestown, Virginia; Charleston, South Carolina; and Savannah, Georgia). Between these, the Midland had been formed by the inland migration of groups originating in the region around Philadelphia, which was established by William Penn in 1680. In Kurath's analysis, these three regions are separated by clear borders, shown as thick black lines on his map; thinner lines divide the main regions into smaller sub-regions.

Kurath demonstrates how his borders are built up from the geographic coincidence of a set of individual isoglosses, each of which represents the outer margin of the spatial distribution of a single dialect feature. Some of these isogloss bundles are tighter than others, depending on the degree of isolation between the communities on either side. Isolation is primarily a factor of settlement patterns and topography, each of which can impose communication barriers of varying strength, thereby preventing innovations arising in one dialect from diffusing across borders to adjacent dialects. The border between the North and Midland, for example, appears as a transition zone of loosely bundled isoglosses in northern New Jersey, just to the south of New York City, but then extends inland along the Allegheny Plateau of northern Pennsylvania as a tighter bundle of isoglosses separating western New York State, in the North, from southern Pennsylvania, in the Midland. This focusing of the border reflects the transition from the easily traversed fertile plains of New Jersey to the barren, rocky terrain of north-western Pennsylvania, which remains sparsely settled to this day. The border between the Midland and South crosses the upper ends of the Delaware and Chesapeake bays and continues inland, north of Washington DC, along the spine of the Appalachian Mountains, thereby separating the coastal regions of Virginia and the Carolinas, in the South, from their inland regions in the Midland.

Later investigations were able to extend Kurath's borders farther west, into the Midwest and Gulf Coast regions: as far as Illinois in the North (Shuy 1962; see Thomas 2010 for a recent analysis of the North–Midland–South split in Ohio), and as far as Texas in the South (Pederson et al. 1986–93). However, it became increasingly difficult to identify clear dialect borders as the comparatively old and densely settled European-origin population of the east gave way to a sparser, more recently settled population in the west, displaying a much larger degree of mixture in its regional origins. It has never been possible to establish clearly demarcated dialect regions west of the Mississippi River.

Even in the east, however, the isoglosses forming the bundles that marked off Kurath's regions were evidently selected by him for that purpose from a larger set that might have obscured his divisions if displayed in its entirety. His analysis appears to proceed from an implicit and rather idealised view of dialects as internally homogeneous regions that can be demarcated by relatively clear boundaries (consistent with a 'family tree' model of linguistic evolution), rather than as broad transition zones of overlapping feature distributions (consistent with a 'wave' model; see Trask 1996: 181–7; Labov 2007). In conducting his investigation, Kurath expected dialect divisions to reflect what he knew about the historical patterns of English-speaking settlement, then looked for isoglosses that would confirm that expectation. These aspects of Kurath's work are criticised, quite justifiably, by Kretzschmar (1996), but Kurath's view of American dialect geography nevertheless remains the dominant one among people only superficially acquainted with the subject.

A different approach to establishing dialect regions and the borders among them was developed by Carver (1987), using data collected in the 1960s for the *Dictionary of American Regional English* (Cassidy and Hall 1985–2012). Carver grouped regionally specific terms into 'layers': sets of lexical variants associated with each historical or cultural region of the United States. The number of variants from each set occurring at each location was then plotted on a map, and an isogloss drawn to enclose the locations with the highest numbers. Divisions along the continuum of index values were made according to Carver's own judgement, at points where they appeared to fall off sharply; these thresholds were taken to indicate the edges of each layer. This method produced an alternate view of American dialect geography, one that extended for the first time to the Pacific coast, reflecting the nationwide coverage of the *Dictionary of American Regional English*, but that was limited to lexical data. It was summarised in a national map of American regional dialects that has also been widely disseminated (Carver's Map 8.1, reproduced as Figure 3.2).

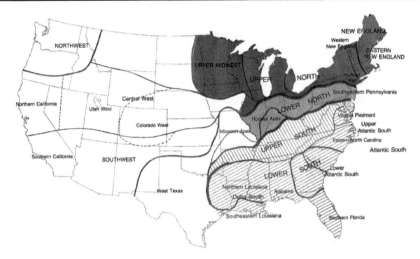

Figure 3.2 The major dialect regions of the continental United States (from Carver 1987: 248).

Apart from its wider geographical range, Carver's view contradicts that of Kurath insofar as Carver finds evidence for two main dialect regions in the eastern United States – North and South – rather than three. In Carver's map, Kurath's Midland region is split by the Ohio River, its northern half becoming the Lower North sub-region of the North, its southern half the Upper South sub-region of the South. While these sub-regions retain a transitional character, compared to the more highly differentiated dialects found in the Upper North and Lower South, the primary division is clearly a binary one between the North and South as a whole, following the Ohio River (Pennsylvania to Illinois in the North; Virginia and Kentucky in the South). This binary classification, it might be said, agrees better than Kurath's three-way split with the common view of the general public that American dialect geography essentially involves an opposition between southern and non-southern speech, in addition to the more regionally focused coastal dialects spoken around New York City and Boston (Preston 2010).

Carver's method, too, was criticised by Kretzschmar (1996) on several grounds, which further illuminate some of the conceptual problems associated with notions of dialect borders in North America. Not only was Carver's placement of layer boundaries rather arbitrary, involving subjective judgement rather than an automated or more objective procedure, but the representation of the layers themselves as relatively homogeneous regions of uniform vocabulary was misleading. There was no requirement that a location display even the majority of the terms associated with a layer, let alone all of them, in order to qualify for inclusion within the layer boundary, or that the particular terms recorded in each location within the layer be the same. The sets of words found at two locations within a layer might therefore be completely different (one subset of regional terms recorded in location A, another in location B), a possibility that alters considerably our sense of how well Carver's abstract view of dialect regions and the borders among them actually describes the speech to be found in any given location. Similar issues of objective versus subjective analysis and quantitative approaches to border identification have recently been explored in a European context by Heeringa and Nerbonne (2001) and Nerbonne (2009).

Kretzschmar's own analysis applies computerised quantitative analysis to data from the Middle and South Atlantic states portion of Kurath's Linguistic Atlas project to show that the borders between North, Midland and South along the Atlantic seaboard are not the sudden, clearly delineated breaks implied by Kurath's isogloss bundles or Carver's layer boundaries, but gradual shifts in the frequency or probability of occurrence of regional variants, with the transition from one region to another occurring at different points for different variables. Kretzschmar demonstrates this with probability maps, which divide the eastern seaboard into small sampling cells and shade each cell according to the probability with which a given feature will occur in that location. While this analysis finds evidence for 'core' areas in which most of the forms identified with a given region are found, intermediate areas such as New Jersey, straddling Kurath's North–Midland border, are recast as broad transition zones. In some of the maps he presents, frequencies are so gradient that it is not at all clear whether any sort of isogloss could be drawn with confidence. These transitional regions reflect not only a mixed settlement history but more recent influence from competing urban centres. New Jersey, for example, is split between a northern sphere of influence dominated by New York City and a southern sphere dominated by Philadelphia, with a zone of mixed influence in the centre (see Coye 2009 for a recent study of this area).

While Carver presents a national view of dialect boundaries in American English, his data are confined to lexical variables. When his book appeared, there was still no national or continental map of the borders among regional varieties of North American English at the phonetic and phonological levels. Yet pronunciation has more influence on people's impressions of regional variation than lexicon, because phonetic variables occur with much greater frequency, at a rate largely independent of the topic of conversation. This gap was addressed by Labov et al. (2006), who analysed acoustic phonetic data on vowel pronunciation and phonemic contrasts to produce the *Atlas of North American English* (*ANAE*). In this approach, approximately 700 individuals in cities and large towns across North America were interviewed by telephone, and the resulting recordings, which included direct questions about contrasts between minimal pairs like *cot* and *caught*, were analysed impressionistically to determine the set of phonemic distinctions maintained by each person. A subset of over 300 recordings was then subjected to acoustic analysis, involving the extraction of first and second formant values from approximately 300 vowel productions per person, in order to measure the phonetic quality of each vowel phoneme. Using these data, the *ANAE* sought to study the sound changes currently in progress in North American English, both at the phonological level, involving phonemic mergers and splits, and at the phonetic level, involving coordinated sets of shifts in the phonetic quality of vowel phonemes known as chain shifts and parallel shifts. A new dialect geography of American English was then put forward on the basis of these changes in progress, involving alternative ways of thinking about dialect differences that are rooted in the structural dialectology of Weinreich (1954) and Moulton (1960, 1962). Low-level output phenomena, involving purely phonetic differences in the production of vowels, were seen to result from higher-level, more abstract phenomena, such as the number and type of phonemic oppositions maintained by each dialect.

Like its predecessors, the *ANAE* did not resist the temptation to suggest relatively sharp transitions between dialect regions by employing isoglosses, despite the small number of speakers in many of the towns at the edges of those regions (most locations were represented by only two people, some smaller centres by a single participant).

Nevertheless, the starkly different phonetic character of the regions corresponding loosely to Carver's Upper North and South, as well as to several of Kurath's smaller regions along the Atlantic seaboard, is amply demonstrated, and maps in which individual speakers are colour-coded according to the number or degree of variable features they exhibited reveal a striking degree of uniformity across these regions, particularly in the eastern half of the continent. Thus, while the number of individuals in each community is small, the number of communities in each region is fairly large, and the true regional sample could be taken to include the several dozen people in the set of towns within its borders. These larger regional samples made possible a quantitative and statistical analysis of social factors such as age and sex, which would not have been possible on an individual community level over the entire continent, thereby providing a secondary sociolinguistic component to what was primarily a regional or dialectological project.

In the *ANAE*, borders were identified as those regions where structurally associated sets of phonetic or phonological changes – like the low-back vowel merger, the monophthongisation of /ay/ (the PRICE vowel), the Northern Cities chain shift, or the Southern chain shift – were found to recede sharply. That is, the *ANAE*'s dialect borders are essentially compound isoglosses marking the outer edges of regions where a particular set of phonetic or phonological features is found among most people in the sample of participants. In the case of phonetic variables such as vowel shifts, the isoglosses marking borders naturally represent points on a continuum of values, rather than the presence or absence of a variant. In preparing the maps, several thresholds along each continuum were examined in order to find the one that presented the most coherent distributions of values on either side of an isogloss. Unlike in traditional dialect geography, where we might say that the territory of a given dialect is where we find a certain word or grammatical construction used by most people, in the *ANAE* a dialect region is more often identified as the territory where the first or second formant of a given vowel is above or below a certain threshold. Like any other means of drawing isoglosses, this system had to contend with variation on either side of the line: the robustness of each isogloss was quantified by reporting the proportion of the total instances of the feature in question it enclosed, the proportion it excluded, and the proportion of speakers within its territory who displayed the feature. In this way, some isoglosses could be objectively characterised as being more robust or informative than others. The result of this analysis, presented in Figure 3.3 (*ANAE* Map 11.15, Labov et al. 2006: 148), comprises eight major dialect regions: Eastern New England; Western New England; the Northern Mid-Atlantic region (including the distinctive New York City sub-region); the Southern Mid-Atlantic region; the South (corresponding in its extent largely to Carver's South); the Inland North (corresponding to Kurath's North or Carver's Upper North); the Midland (Carver's Lower North); the West; and Canada.

An important contrast can be observed between different degrees of sharpness in the borders identified by the *ANAE*. The North–Midland border, for example, is an impressively sharp line delimiting the southern extent of the Inland North. It separates the band of large, Midwestern industrial cities along the southern shores of the Great Lakes (Buffalo, Cleveland, Detroit and Chicago) from the central and southern parts of Ohio, Indiana and Illinois, despite the absence of any physical boundary that might explain the retention of such robust differences. The crispness of this division would appear to be an inheritance from the settlement patterns assumed by Kurath to be the basis of today's dialect borders. On the other hand, the Midland–South border is a broader transition

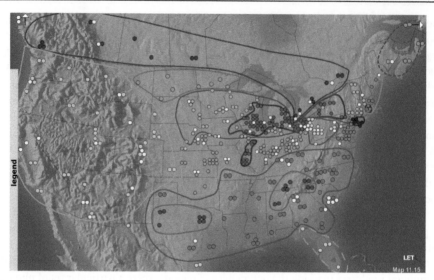

Figure 3.3 North American English dialects (Map 11.15 from Labov, Ash and Boberg (2006), reproduced with permission).

zone over which southern pronunciation features gradually intensify as one moves southward. There have been several studies of the incursion of southern features into Midland territory in southern Illinois, Indiana and Ohio, such as Frazer (1978); while the Ohio River does constitute an important linguistic divide, it should be thought of as the focal point of a transition zone rather than as a well-defined border between North and South. The border between the eastern regions and the west, approximately along the Mississippi River, is even less well defined, while that between the American West and western Canada proved particularly difficult to establish with any clarity. In several places, moreover, certain towns and territories have an indeterminate status, lying in an unidentified space between the borders circumscribing adjacent regions, since they did not qualify for inclusion in either region. These are, in general, areas of relatively sparse population and recent settlement, such as parts of the Great Plains, or of intensive dialect mixture, such as southern Florida. The existence these transitional areas, which do not lend themselves to an analysis that assumes clearly defined dialect borders, is explicitly acknowledged in the *ANAE* (Labov et al. 2006: 141–2).

Even with this reservation, however, it might be pointed out that where the *ANAE* does assert the existence of clear dialect boundaries, as between the Inland North and the Midland, or around the major metropolitan areas of the east coast, these divisions are based not on the sort of quantification across an entire set of data advocated by Nerbonne (2009), but on a selection of data determined by a theoretical analysis of the most important structural and phonetic variables in each region. The selectivity may have been more principled than that of Kurath, which involved more or less arbitrary choices among structurally unconnected lexical variables, but it nevertheless entails some degree of analytical bias. For instance, while the *ANAE* regions are based mostly on the analysis of vocalic variables, another important variable, the vocalisation of /r/, reveals regional divides that cross-cut many of those made by vocalic variables, joining Boston and New York City within an isogloss, and severing Boston from other regions that share its low-back merger. If to this we add isoglosses established by lexical variables, such as the different generic terms for carbonated beverages (*soda, pop, coke, soft drink*, etc.) – one of the first things that comes to mind when ordinary Americans are asked about dialect differences – we find a much greater degree of non-conformity. If all of these isoglosses were plotted on a map, it would look more like a plate of spaghetti than an orderly set of internally homogeneous dialect regions. Some degree of selectivity therefore seems necessary, if useful facts about regional differences in language, or about the mechanism of language change and diversification, are to emerge from the complex mass of data produced by most dialect surveys. It is important to recall, however, that any coherent view is by necessity an abstraction that chooses to focus on some facts and ignore others, according to the interests of the analyst.

3. The United States/Canada international boundary as a linguistic border

If different regional settlement histories have contributed to the rise of linguistic borders within the United States, we might equally expect the separate histories of the United States and Canada to have produced different varieties of English on either side of the international boundary between them. This is in spite of the fact that much of the initial English-speaking settlement of Canada came from what would become the United States, when 30,000–40,000 pro-British Loyalists fled the threat of retribution from their victorious countrymen during and after the American Revolution, settling down in Nova Scotia, New Brunswick and Ontario. Subsequent immigration directly from Britain to Canada during the early nineteenth century seems to have modified the basic speech patterns laid down by the Loyalists in only superficial ways, which accounts for the generally North American sound of Canadian English today (Chapter 2 of Boberg 2010 gives this question more careful consideration). This ex-American, Loyalist speech was then spread across the country as eastern Canadians, particularly Ontarians, took the leading role in settling the western half of Canada in the late nineteenth and early twentieth centuries.

Nevertheless, the international boundary has long had an important influence on the development of English-Canadian culture and identity, moderating and in some cases even blocking the ever-present and massively powerful force of American influence on Canadian life. The eastern section of the boundary was established by the Treaty of Paris, which ended the American Revolution in 1783, and its western section, along the 49th parallel, by subsequent Anglo-American treaties in 1818 and 1846, well before the founding of Canada as an independent dominion in 1867. While non-North Americans may be puzzled by the proposition that there are any substantial cultural or linguistic differences between English-Canadians and Americans, they are quite apparent to Canadians, who sometimes make more of them than they merit, in an effort to stake out for themselves a cultural identity independent from that of their southern neighbours. The United States has generally had about ten times the population of Canada, with a corresponding difference in cultural, commercial, industrial, military and political power, so if Canadians spent their first decades seeking an identity separate from Britain, their more recent history has been focused on trying to find their own voice amid a constant deluge of American influence. On a linguistic level, the original similarities established by the Loyalist immigration have been augmented by this trans-border influence, yet Canadian English has never disappeared as a distinctive variety, or set of varieties, within the North American context. Despite American domination of Canada's entertainment industry, frequent Canadian visits to the United States and a relatively high degree of economic integration between the two countries, the international boundary prevents the daily, face-to-face interaction between the majority of the respective populations that would produce full linguistic assimilation. Most Canadians continue to interact mostly with other Canadians, so that Canadian speech patterns are reinforced among adults and passed on to children, while recent American influence has been restricted to relatively superficial domains such as the lexicon (*elevator* vs. *lift*; *flashlight* vs. *torch*), discourse particles (such as the use of quotative *be like*, as reported by Tagliamonte and D'Arcy 2004) or phonemic incidence (the choice of phonemes in variable words like *either, lieutenant, schedule* or *vase*).

The first attempts to characterise the linguistic status of the United States/Canada border operated from either side of it: Avis (1954, 1956) collected data on Ontario speech, which he contrasted with an American standard for which he provided no documentation; Allen (1959) extended his research on the American Upper Midwest into western Canada, on the basis of only a few isolated subjects. While these efforts made many accurate and useful observations of national differences in speech, concentrated efforts to study the border as a linguistic division by collecting binational sets of data began later. Miller (1989), Zeller (1993), Chambers (1994) and Burnett (2006) present small sets of such data at specific locations, which in some cases show a clear discontinuity in variant frequency at the international border, suggesting its effectiveness as a barrier to interpersonal communication. On the other hand, other studies have revealed the failure of the border to prevent the northward diffusion of American English into Canada (Nylvek 1992; Chambers 1995). Boberg (2000), a study of trans-border diffusion, finds evidence for both views: the border acts as a barrier to diffusion of phonetic patterns related to underlying differences in phonemic contrast (such as those studied by Labov et al. 2006), but is relatively permeable for less structurally embedded features such as variation in phonemic incidence. In particular, this study found that one of the most important transborder differences in phonemic incidence, involving the vowels used in nativisations of foreign words spelled with <a> such as *avocado, llama, pasta* and *taco*, was gradually receding. Traditionally, Canadians used the /æ/ vowel of TRAP in these words, while Americans preferred the /ah/ vowel of PALM, but younger Canadians in the study seemed to be using more American pronunciations than their older counterparts, thereby reducing the national difference (Boberg 2010: 137–40). Of course, pronunciation of individual words such as *pasta* or *taco* is just the sort of variation that can be transmitted through mass media channels such as television or movies, so it is not surprising that this is a domain where American influence is to be found.

Most recently, Boberg (2010) finds that the linguistic significance of the United States/Canada boundary varies along its length, depending on which variables are taken into account. In the middle of the continent, its lexical significance is comparatively lessened, while its phonological and phonetic significance is paramount. Here, it separates two major vowel shifts: the Canadian Shift in Ontario, which involves a backing of TRAP into low-central position in response to the merger of LOT and THOUGHT in low-back position; and the Northern Cities Shift in the American Inland North, which involves a raising of TRAP and a fronting of LOT as a strategy for avoiding merger with THOUGHT. As a result, the phonetic qualities of the vowels in American LOT and Canadian TRAP are very close if not identical, producing confusion when Canadians hear *salad* for American *solid*, *black* for American *block*, etc. Boberg (2000) showed that the transition between these patterns is remarkably sharp, being as narrow as the width of the river separating Detroit from Windsor, Ontario (see Willis 1972 for a study of sound differences on either side of the Ontario/New York border).

Further west, by contrast, structural phonological differences resolve themselves in a vast region of relative phonological and phonetic homogeneity, in which the LOT–THOUGHT merger straddles the border, producing similar vowel sounds on either side. In particular, the effects of the Northern Cities Shift fade out across Minnesota and North Dakota, being lost entirely along the Pacific Coast, so that Calgary and Denver, or Vancouver and Seattle, share more or less identical phonological systems. Nevertheless, one important phonetic variable, the Canadian Raising of MOUTH and PRICE (the occurrence of non-low nuclei in the low diphthongs before voiceless obstruents), remains as a national shibboleth, with a virtual absence of raising on the American side. This is not true further east, especially not with respect to PRICE, which is significantly raised in several eastern US dialects (Labov et al. 2006: 114). In the West, however, it is lexical differences that seem to play the greatest role in giving a linguistic character to the international boundary. For instance, Boberg (2010) reports high frequencies of unique local terms such as *parkade*, *runners* and *scribbler* in western Canada. These have no currency in the United States, where *parking garage*, *sneakers* or *tennis shoes* and *notebook* would be the American equivalents.

Because of the settlement patterns and strong American influence referred to above, the international boundary often separates relatively invariant usage of Americanisms on its southern side from an alternation among American, British and sometimes Canadian terms to its north. Not only is the vocabulary of Canadian English generally North American rather than British, but where American and Canadian usage do differ, relatively few variables show a categorical division across the border. Many of those that do have some sort of institutional support, such as the use of *first grade*, etc., to designate the successive years of elementary school in the United States, against *grade one*, etc., in Canada. Though some Americanisms, such as *candy bar*, *restroom* and *silverware*, enjoy very little usage in Canada (where *chocolate bar*, *washroom* or *bathroom* and *cutlery* or *utensils* are generally used instead), most British and Canadian terms, such as *tap*, *bachelor apartment* and *bank machine*, compete with their American equivalents (in this case, *faucet*, *studio* and *ATM*) in varying proportions across the country.

4. Dialect borders within Canada

Boberg (2010) also examines borders within Canada, beginning with a large set of relatively small regions from west to east across the country, and testing which of these is associated with a substantial number of linguistic divisions. The analysis of phonetic and phonological borders, first presented in Boberg (2008), finds that Canadian English is comprised of five main regional types: the West, including north-western Ontario; southern and eastern Ontario; Quebec (mostly greater Montreal); the Maritimes; and Newfoundland. The western region can be subdivided into British Columbia and the Prairies, to make six regions (Boberg 2010: 209). Apart from the well-known features distinguishing Newfoundland and Maritime English, statistical analyses demonstrate that

Ontario and the West differ on several phonetic measures, such as the phonetic output of Canadian Raising and the allophonic distribution of /æ/ (TRAP).

Data on lexical differences within Canada come from the *North American Regional Vocabulary Survey*, first reported in Boberg (2005). Frequencies of variants of forty-four lexical variables from the survey were tabulated for sixteen Canadian regions. For each regional division, the mean difference in variant frequencies was averaged over the forty-four variables; the number of frequency differences of greater than 50 per cent was also calculated. By both measures, the strongest lexical borders in Canada were found to separate Quebec from its neighbours to the east (New Brunswick) and west (eastern Ontario), a result that might be expected, given the unique status of Quebec English as a minority language in intimate contact with French (Boberg 2010: 184; 2012). In addition, Quebec's English-speaking community is cut off from adjacent regions by a considerable physical distance, particularly to the east. Strong lexical borders were also found to divide Newfoundland and Prince Edward Island from other parts of Atlantic Canada and to split southern Ontario from north-western Ontario and the Prairies. By contrast, lexical borders within Ontario and the Prairies, areas that are both culturally homogeneous and continuously settled, are comparatively difficult to identify. A summary of these data supports a six-region division of Canada, corresponding closely to the view that emerges from the phonetic and phonological analysis (2010: 178).

5. Conclusion

This brief consideration of borders in North American English leads us to observe that their nature and strength are highly variable. On one extreme, we find a sharply defined perimeter surrounding the American Inland North and its Northern Cities Shift, so clearly marked off from the Canadian and Midland phonetic patterns to its north and south. Inland Northern speech immediately strikes the ear as strongly distinctive and can be heard only in a tightly circumscribed set of urban communities along the southern shores of the Great Lakes. Another example is the Canadian province of Newfoundland, with its long history as a separate British colony, which still preserves most of its distinct linguistic identity intact, despite convergence at higher social levels with mainland Canadian English, and retains perhaps the clearest linguistic borders of any English dialect region in North America (Clarke 2010). On the other extreme, we find the subtle and gradual shifts in small sets of variables that characterise the vast expanses of western North America, where one can drive for hundreds, even thousands, of miles without encountering anything that would qualify as a dialect border in Britain or even in the eastern United States. Between these extremes we find the American South. Here, the core regions, identified by Labov et al. (2006) as northern Texas and eastern Tennessee, have traditionally been highly distinct, but are now undergoing gradual erosion through assimilation to global, 'General' American norms (Dodsworth and Kohn 2012). More to the point, they are surrounded by a broad transition zone of less strongly southern speech, which gradually blends into the Western, Midland, Mid-Atlantic and South Florida dialect regions that surround the South. The extent to which any of these borders remains in place over the course of the twenty-first century will be determined by larger forces of continental linguistic diffusion, and by the interplay of cultural forces that pit local identity against global prestige.

4

Spanish Language Variation and Ethnic Identity in New Mexico: Internal and External Borders

Neddy A. Vigil and Garland D. Bills

1. Introduction

In the United States, as in other countries, speakers of any minority language confront major challenges to the retention of their ethnic identity and the maintenance of their ethnic language. When that minority language variety happens also to be a minority dialect within the same country, the pressures to abandon the heritage language and identity become even more pronounced. Such intriguing identity issues surface in the case of the Spanish language in New Mexico.

New Mexico is a US state on the Mexican border. Spanish speakers first settled in the area in 1598, and for 250 years the region belonged to Spain and then Mexico, until it became a US territory in 1848. Today, New Mexico displays considerable ethnic diversity; it is a 'majority-minority' state in which the varied minorities represent the majority of the population. The largest of these minorities is composed of persons of Spanish-language heritage, estimated at 46.3 per cent in 2010 by the US Bureau of the Census (another 9.4 per cent are Native Americans). These persons of Spanish-language heritage are commonly referred to as 'Hispanics' in this region, as elsewhere in the US. Most of this Hispanic population is reported to be Spanish-speaking, as measured by the Census (see U.S. Bureau of the Census 2013).

This chapter draws on data from a survey of the Spanish of New Mexico and southern Colorado that we have been working on since 1988. The project, supported by the US National Endowment for the Humanities from 1991 to 1995, attempts to document the Spanish language as it is currently spoken across the region. This documentation effort is most fully described in Bills and Vigil (2008). The survey collected data from 357 native-born Spanish speakers in face-to-face tape-recorded interviews averaging about two hours in length. We use the data from this survey to explore the dynamics of language and dialect contact, ethnic identity and Spanish-language loss in this sociolinguistic situation.

Our survey covers the entire state of New Mexico and sixteen counties of southern Colorado, the state immediately to the north.[1] Because of the history of settlement, the Spanish spoken in this region is generally referred to as 'New Mexican Spanish'.

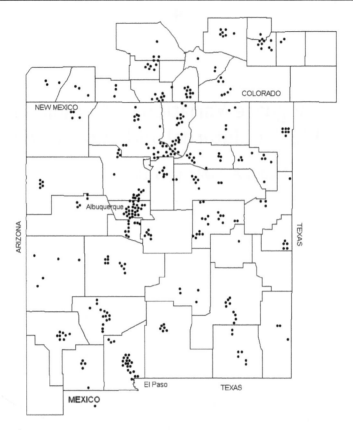

Figure 4.1 Geographical distribution of consultants (N = 357) across New Mexico and southern Colorado.

Figure 4.1 shows the distribution of our 357 consultants according to the places where they were born and raised. Reflecting the settlement patterns in this arid land, these persons are distributed principally along the major waterways, such as the Rio Grande, which rises in central Colorado and curves down through the middle of New Mexico to finally form the border between Texas and Mexico. Note that approximately half of the southern border of New Mexico is directly adjacent to Mexico, while the eastern half lies on the narrow western tip of Texas. Note also the location of El Paso, Texas, and its twin city across the Mexican border, Ciudad Juárez, just a few miles from the New Mexico border.

The Spanish speakers in our survey represent two major dialects. One dialect is concentrated in the northern two-thirds of New Mexico and much of southern Colorado. This variety derives from early Hispanic settlement beginning in 1598, and is labelled 'Traditional Spanish'. The other dialect, which we call 'Border Spanish', is represented primarily in the southern third of New Mexico, but also along the Arkansas River of south-eastern Colorado, in cities such as Albuquerque and less prominently elsewhere on the eastern and western fringes. This variety is more closely aligned historically and linguistically with the Spanish speakers of northern Mexico. Most of these Border Spanish speakers derive from immigration from Mexico during the twentieth century.

Ethnic identity is closely associated with three features of the survey region: this linguistic division in Spanish, the status of Spanish as a minority language in the larger English context and the proximity to Mexico, where Spanish is of course the national language. This sociolinguistic situation results in identity issues that are varied and complex, revealing the significance of both external and internal borders. A quick linguistic overview of the history of the situation will begin to shed a little light on these issues.

2. Development of Traditional Spanish

Let us first sketch the development of Traditional Spanish through the colonial period, first under Spain and later under independent Mexico. The colonists who entered New Mexico in 1598 accepted a life of relative isolation far from their birthplaces. In 1598 the limit of the Spanish crown's influence in western New Spain (that is, modern Mexico) was the city of Durango. The straight-line distance from Durango to the first settlement in northern New Mexico is over 1,200 km (750 miles). Not only was the distance great but the trip was harsh, requiring months of travel through semi-desert sparsely populated with antagonistic Native Americans. Contact between the New Mexico colonists and the larger Hispanic world was through a yearly wagon train, which could on occasion be delayed up to three years (Simmons 2001).

Thus, extreme physical and psychological isolation from the rest of the Spanish-speaking world characterised the New Mexico Hispanics for two centuries. Then in 1821 the area passed to Mexican authority. But New Mexico still remained far from the central life of Mexico, even though trade and contact increased as other Spanish speakers continued expansions in northern Mexico and the greater south-west of the United States. The centuries of isolation contributed to the development of the special dialect that is today's Traditional Spanish. Though this variety derives from the Mexican Spanish of the sixteenth and seventeenth centuries, it differs from modern Mexican Spanish in its retention of older forms and in unique innovations. We illustrate this development briefly here with a few lexical items.

Like all Spanish varieties in the New World, most of the lexicon derives directly from pre-Conquest Spain, though not uniformly so. For example, *albaricoque* ('apricot') was borrowed into Spanish from Arabic prior to the conquest of the Americas and was brought to the New World by the earliest explorers. However, the use of *albaricoque* and its several variants in New Mexico today is characteristic only of the Traditional Spanish area. By contrast, the neologism *chabacán* or *chabacano*, which has become the dominant form across Mexico, is characteristic of the Border Spanish areas of our survey.

Other features of Traditional Spanish derive from New World contacts. Figure 4.2, for example, shows the distribution of terms used for 'slip' (the female undergarment). As indicated on the map, the word preferred in Traditional Spanish is *naguas*, or variants of that form, displaying a distribution almost identical to that of *albaricoque*. The word *naguas* results from very early contact with the Taino Indians of the Caribbean. Although the word occurs regularly in early Mexican documents, the form that is usual in Mexico today is the Standard Spanish word *fondo* (Lope Blanch 1990–2000, map 906). Again, as expected, *fondo* is typical of the Border Spanish region of our survey.

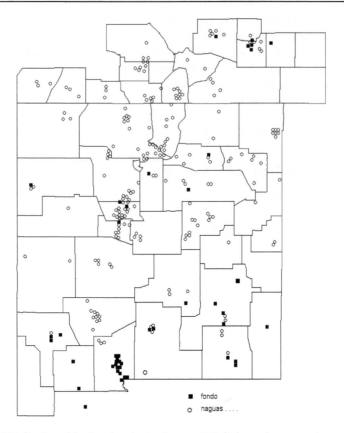

Figure 4.2 Distribution of *fondo* and variants of *naguas* ('slip', the undergarment) across New Mexico and southern Colorado.

'Tub' is another variable that shows the sharp differentiation between Traditional Spanish and Border Spanish, and the distribution of the two principal variants patterns very similarly to those of 'apricot' and 'slip'. In this case, *cajete* is an early borrowing from Nahuatl, spoken by the Aztecs of central Mexico. In New Mexico it now refers to a metal container used for washing clothes or bathing, a semantic broadening from the Nahuatl meaning of 'cup, bowl, vessel'. The term employed in Mexico is *tina*, and not surprisingly that is the Border Spanish term. In Mexico the term *cajete* is still used, but it is restricted to refer to an earthenware bowl or basin.

Many features of Traditional New Mexican Spanish came about as a result of independent developments. An example of such innovations can be seen in the terms used for 'bat' (the flying mammal). The label now characteristic of Traditional Spanish is *ratón volador*, literally 'flying mouse', a compound rarely attested elsewhere in the Spanish-speaking world. In Mexico as well as in the Border Spanish areas, the preferred label is the general Spanish *murciélago*, a Latin-derived compound with the same literal, but less transparent, meaning. Once more, these two variants of 'bat' exhibit the same dialect distributions.

To summarise this section, then: the language brought into New Mexico was the Spanish of sixteenth- and seventeenth-century Mexico, supplemented with contributions from later colonists in the eighteenth and nineteenth centuries. This Traditional Spanish contains early loanwords from native Caribbean and Mexican languages. It retains forms that are no longer used in Standard Mexican Spanish, and it lacks innovations that have occurred in Mexico, but has adopted its own linguistic innovations. It became a unique Spanish dialect that was spoken throughout the New Mexico province up until the twentieth century, when the Border Spanish variety began to develop via greatly increased immigration from Mexico.

3. US impact on language and identity

Prior to the linguistic impact of modern Mexico, however, the English language and its speakers profoundly altered the sociolinguistic landscape. The political connection to Mexico came to an abrupt end after the Mexican–American war of 1845–48, when the Treaty of Guadalupe Hidalgo ceded to the United States the vast territory that stretches from Texas to California. In addition to physical isolation there was now political isolation, and contact with mainstream Spanish was further reduced. Demographically there was a rapid and steady increase in the percentage of 'Anglos', i.e. the non-Hispanic, non-Indian minority. The Anglo newcomers quickly became economically dominant. And much like the attitudes of the earlier invading Hispanics towards the local Native Americans, the invading Anglos tended to hold the local Hispanic culture and language in low esteem.

In fact, New Mexico remained a United States territory for sixty-four years primarily because of a low regard for Hispanics and concerns about the predominance of Spanish speakers. But as the Anglo population and therefore the use of English increased, New Mexico was finally admitted to the Union as a state in 1912. Along with statehood, the institutions of government increased, and English became the language of instruction in schools.

Quite naturally, the Hispanic–Anglo contact led to ethnic differentiation and conflict. The residue of this century and a half of inter-ethnic contact is reflected in comments offered by our survey consultants. Example 1 illustrates the simple recognition that the two ethnic groups manifest distinct linguistic behaviours. (The coding following each example represents interview number, gender, age and place represented, so this first example comes from interview 77, a 63-year-old female from Carriso, New Mexico.)

> 1. *Entre los hispanos hablamos español y inglés y entre el anglo puro inglés.* 'Among ourselves we Mexicanos speak Spanish and English, and among themselves Anglos speak only English.' (77: F, 63, Carriso, NM)

More insidious is the overt linguistic discrimination shown towards the Spanish language. Many older consultants commented on being punished for speaking Spanish in school, a practice that once was common. The description in 2 is typical:

> 2. *En la escuela, fíjese, yo me acuerdo cuando—, si hablábanos español cuando salíanos a recess, nos daban una cubeta pa' que levantáranos piedras, pa' quitar las piedras del playground.* 'At school, listen, I remember when—, if we would

speak Spanish when we went out for recess, they would give us a bucket to pick up rocks, to clear the rocks off the playground.' (336: F, 70, Truth or Consequences, NM)

In situations of less overt power control, the contact between ethnic groups produced open conflicts, as reported in example 3:

3. *Los mexicanos con los gringos tenían unas peleas de moquetes bárbaras en los bailes.* 'The Mexicanos had some terrible fistfights with the Anglos at the dances.' (109: M, 77, Clayton, NM)

Notice in examples 1 and 3 that Mexicano is the ethnic self-identity label for these Traditional Spanish speakers. For reasons that will become clear below, we do not translate this label as 'Mexican'.

Examples 4 and 5 show two kinds of social discrimination enforced by the dominant Anglos: restricted seating in the cinema and residential segregation:

4. *A los negritos y a los mexicanos nos echaban allá arriba; no nos dejaban sentarnos abajo.* 'They would put the Blacks and the Mexicanos up above [in the balcony of the cinema]; they wouldn't let us sit below.' (99: M, 62, Fort Sumner, NM)

5. *Ahi en Hurley, de este lado de los traques las escuelas para los mexicanos y para el otro lado para los anglos.* 'There in Hurley, on this side of the railroad tracks, [were] the schools for the Mexicanos and on the other side for the Anglos.' (336: F, 70, Truth or Consequences, NM)

As noted above, the invading Anglos quickly became economically dominant, and this situation continues today, though perhaps less markedly so. The next two examples show the effects of this economic differentiation in some communities.

6. *Todos los mexicanos o Spanish o como quieres decirlos trabajan por hueros, gringos.* 'All the Mexicanos or Spanish, or whatever you want to call them, work for Anglos.' (267: F, 34, Clayton, NM)

7. *Fíjese, los trabajos más duros en las plantas eran de mexicanos, y los anglos lo mejor.* 'Look, the Mexicanos had the hardest jobs in the plants, and the Anglos the best.' (336: F, 70, Truth or Consequences, NM)

Nevertheless, Hispanics have often maintained considerable economic and political power in their communities, as illustrated in example 8:

8. *[En] la casa de corte todos son mexicanos, el asesor, el tesorero.* '[In] the courthouse they are all Mexicanos, the tax assessor, the treasurer.' (109: M, 77, Clayton, NM)

Such community influence and solidarity is more common in rural areas, especially in less accessible villages such as the tiny hamlet of Chise, described by the man quoted in example 9.

9. *Todo el pueblito éranos puros mexicanos; puro mexicano hablábanos aquí.* 'The whole town was solely Mexicanos; we spoke only "Mexican" here.' (356: M, 60, Chise, NM)

The words of the speaker in example 9 also illustrate clearly how the term 'Mexicano' is used not only as the ethnic label, but also to name the Spanish language.

Nevertheless, it is in the nature of human beings to hang on to dignity in the face of discrimination by a dominant group. Many of our consultants reported a maintenance of pride in their language, as shown by the next two examples:

> 10. *Se me hace que la idioma mexicana es más romántica también que el inglés.* 'I think the "Mexican" language is also more romantic than English.' (264: F, 47, Lake Arthur, NM)
>
> 11. *Yo les digo a estos gabachos que yo estoy más rico con mi inglés que le sé porque ellos no saben nada de mexicano.* 'I tell these Anglos that I am richer with the English that I know because they don't know anything about "Mexican".' (356: M, 60, Chise, NM)

Still, few are willing to unflinchingly embrace the heritage language as it is manifest in the survey region. Because of criticisms from other speakers of Spanish and the societal pressure of English, they are quite aware of regrettable changes regarding their language behaviour:

> 12. *Tengo una maña de hablar mitá inglés y mitá mexicano.* 'I have a habit of speaking half English and half "Mexican".' (192: F, 58, Socorro, NM)

And of course, change affects not only the language but also people's identities, as poignantly illustrated by this life-long resident of the major city in the region:

> 13. *Sí, seigo mexicano, pero seigo más gabacho.* 'Yes, I'm Mexicano, but I'm more Anglo.' (88: M, 45, Albuquerque, NM)

With the steady expansion of economic, governmental and educational control by Anglos, there was a steady increase in the influence of English on New Mexican Spanish lexicon and language behaviour. For example, Figure 4.3 shows the distribution of terms for 'quarter' (the 25-cent US coin). The map shows the usual distribution for the Border Spanish term *peseta*, an old (unofficial) Mexican label for the fourth part of a monetary unit. In contrast, two variants characterise the Traditional Spanish dialect area. For hundreds of years in the New Mexico province the label was *dos reales*, the official fourth part of the early Spanish *peso*. However, the borrowing from English, *cuara* (reflecting the American English flapped pronunciation of the medial /t/), is now firmly established in the Traditional Spanish region.

A particularly intriguing case of the lexical influence of English concerns the preferred term for 'baking soda', as displayed in Figure 4.4. The Traditional Spanish term is *salarata*, a borrowing from English in the nineteenth century, when the label *salaratus* was used in the United States. The Border Spanish term is *soda de(l) martillo*, literally 'hammer soda' or 'soda of the hammer', an innovative Spanish compound describing the logo image carried on the Arm and Hammer product made in the United States.

The more devastating linguistic impact of the English presence in our survey region concerns the displacement of Spanish, through the gradual abandonment by Hispanics of their heritage language in favour of English. We treat this issue more fully below.

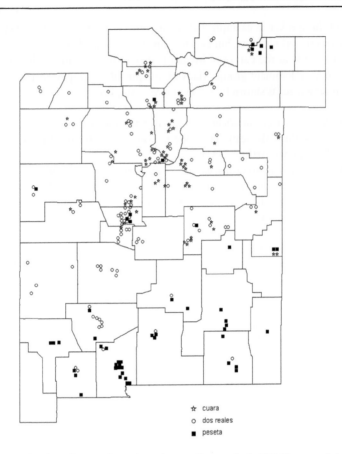

Figure 4.3 Distribution of *cuara*, *dos reales* and *peseta* ('quarter', the US 25-cent coin) across New Mexico and southern Colorado.

4. Border Spanish impact on language and identity

As the distinct Spanish dialect and culture of New Mexico began to wither under the Anglo and English language assault from one side, the rise of the United States as an economic powerhouse also brought an assault from a different direction, from Mexico. The period from the end of the nineteenth century up to the present has seen steadily increasing immigration from Mexico, introducing into our region a modern Mexican Spanish which diverges significantly from Traditional Spanish. The result is the two New Mexican Spanishes that we have seen delineated so markedly in the previous maps.

The burgeoning Mexican immigration that began in earnest with the Mexican revolution of 1910 also created a new situation of ethnic differentiation in the midst of the Anglo–Hispanic contact and conflict. The newcomers differed both culturally and linguistically from the established Hispanics, and the development of the classic ethnicity paradigm 'us' vs. 'them' was not long in surfacing. Again, a prominent manifestation of this ethnic consciousness revolved around language. The differences between Traditional Spanish and Border/Mexican Spanish are readily perceived. The terse comment in

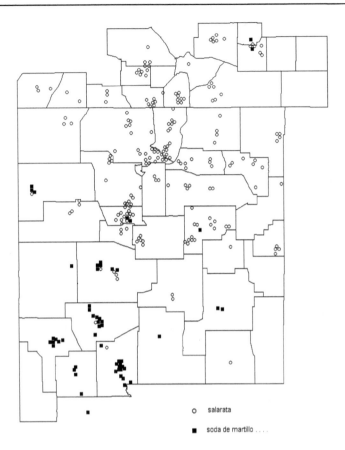

Figure 4.4 Distribution of *salarata* and *soda de(l) martillo* ('baking soda') across New Mexico and southern Colorado.

example 14 comes from a Traditional Spanish speaker from an area that has seen significant immigration from Mexico.

> 14. *La gente de México habla mucho diferente de nojotroj.* 'People from Mexico speak a lot different than us.' (318: F, 72, Cortez, CO)

Example 15, on the other hand, describes an agricultural community that was settled in the twentieth century by migrants moving up from New Mexico, as well as by Mexican immigrants:

> 15. *Para mí hay como dos modos de hablar aquí en Rocky Ford mexicano. Uno es el de la comunidad, de la gente de Nuevo México más, y luego ahi son los mexicanos que vienen de, parece principalmente de Chihuahua . . . Pero la diferencia no es MUY distinta.* 'It seems to me there are two ways to speak Spanish here in Rocky Ford. One is that of the community, mostly of people of New

Mexico, and then there are the Mexicans that come from, it seems, principally from Chihuahua [the state of northern Mexico]. But the difference
isn't VERY distinctive.' (304: M, 51, Pueblo, CO)

Moreover, the newcomers considered their variety of Spanish to be less rustic and more
representative of modern international Spanish. These newcomers were not reluctant
to express their disdain for the local variety. The lament in example 16, expressed by a
woman who married a Mexican immigrant, illustrates the sense of linguistic inferiority
shared by many New Mexicans:

16. *Hasta me da a mí pena hablar mi español que hablo, porque sometimes él me dice
que si hablo chino o japonés.* 'It even makes me sad to speak the Spanish I
speak, because sometimes he asks me if I'm speaking Chinese or Japanese.'
(320: F, 82, Hobbs, NM)

This inferiority complex derives also from the negative assessments of teachers and educated foreigners. Speakers of Standard Spanish are prone to disparage and even ridicule
the Spanish spoken in New Mexico and elsewhere in the United States. Hidalgo (1983),
for example, examined the attitudes of Mexicans in Juárez concerning the Hispanics
living just across the border in El Paso. Several comments from those Mexicans, for
whom Spanish was the medium of instruction, are presented here in examples 17–19.

17. *La gente de allá batalla mucho para hablar el español, o no puede terminar lo que
quiere decir, o lo dice todo revuelto.* 'People over there [in El Paso] struggle a
lot to speak Spanish, or they can't finish what they want to say, or they say
it all mixed up.' (Hidalgo 1983: 175)
18. *Si los de El Paso quieren llamarse mexicanos deberían de hablar como los de
Juárez.* 'If those in El Paso want to call themselves Mexican they ought to
talk like those in Juárez.' (Hidalgo 1983: 161; also cited in Hidalgo 1986:
209)
19. *A nadie se le olvida el idioma de sus padres. La gente no habla porque no quiere
o porque le da vergüenza.* 'Nobody forgets the language of their parents.
They don't speak [Spanish] because they don't want to or because they're
ashamed.' (Hidalgo 1983: 182)

Speakers of Traditional Spanish have developed a pervasive sense of insecurity about
their Spanish with the rise of awareness of the broader Spanish language represented by
Border Spanish. Yet at the same time, they have generally considered themselves culturally superior to the more recent immigrants, adopting a condescending attitude as negative as that of the Anglos towards Hispanics. Those of Traditional Spanish heritage tend
to own land and have a tradition of political power and economic stability, whereas the
Border Spanish speakers are seen as menial, often migrant, labourers with less wealth and
little power. Consequently, the speakers of Traditional Spanish tend to reject identification with the more recently arriving speakers of Border Spanish.

Self-identification in English diverges strongly across the two groups. Traditional
Spanish speakers prefer to call themselves 'Hispanic', 'Spanish' or 'Spanish American'

(as per the labels used in numerous studies of this ethnic group, e.g. Brisk 1972; González 1967; Nieto-Phillips 2004). This use of Spanish as an ethnic label harkens back to a desired European source, leapfrogging the historically closer Mexican origins, and is therefore distinct from the more inclusive use of 'Spanish' in New York as 'roughly equivalent to Hispanic or Latino' (Callahan 2007: 30). In contrast, speakers of Border Spanish are likely to prefer 'Mexican' or 'Mexican American'. This difference in self-identification in English shows up clearly in the findings of the 2000 Census. For example, 71 per cent of the Hispanics in Doña Ana county, on the Mexican border, placed themselves in the 'Mexican/Mexican American/Chicano' category, while in Río Arriba county in northern New Mexico only 13 per cent so identified themselves, with 87 per cent choosing the 'Other Hispanic' category.

As we would expect, terms exist to differentiate the two ethnic groups. Traditional Spanish speakers are called *Manitos*. In accordance with the general principle that more labels exist for the more disdained, there are several terms for Border Spanish speakers (and Mexican nationals): *Surumato, Mateo, Chúntaro, Mojado, Wetback*. Examples 20–23 illustrate the variety of ethnic labels used.

> 20. *Mateo les dicen porque vienen del otro lado y ellos a nosotros nos dicen los manitos.* 'They're called Mateo because they come from the other side [of the border] and they call us Manitos.' (211: M, 78, Chama, CO)
> 21. *Todos nos dicen manito y nosotros chúntaro.* 'They all call us Manito and we [call them] Chúntaro.' (43: M, 34, Pastura, NM)
> 22. *Mi amá le decía a mi papá surumato.* 'My mother [native-born] used to call my father [Mexico-born] Surumato.' (235: F, 57, Gallup, NM)
> 23. *Era el surumato que venía, inmigrante, que venía buscando la vida.* 'It was the Surumatos who came [here], immigrants, who were looking for a better life.' (233: M, 71, La Junta, CO)

These terms have negative associations that are rarely absent in the speech of the other ethnicity. In example 24 a Traditional Spanish woman quotes the reactions of her Mexican in-laws to the way she speaks:

> 24. *Tonta manita, no sabe nada.* 'Stupid Manita, she doesn't know anything.' (307: F, 83, Ratón, NM)

In contrast, example 25 shows a Border Spanish speaker's reaction to being called *manita* after having lived and worked many years in a Traditional Spanish community:

> 25. *La primera vez que me noté yo que alguien me había llamado manita, ¡Ay manita! ¡Yo no soy manita! ¡Jai, grama, me llamaron manita!* 'The first time I noticed that someone had called me Manita, Oh Manita! I'm not a Manita! Hey, Grandma, they called me a Manita!' (237: F, 45, La Junta, CO)

In a marvellously ironic twist, however, both populations typically label themselves as *mexicano* in Spanish, as we saw in many of the previous examples, such as 3–7. Speakers of Traditional Spanish had called themselves *mexicanos* for centuries, but these clearly different newcomers also called themselves *mexicanos*. Example 26 illustrates the growing insecurity of identity among New Mexico Hispanics:

> 26. *La comida mex-, de nojotros. No quiero decir que mexicano, porque no semos mexicanos nojotros. Dicemos mexicanos, pero no semos. México está al otro lado.* 'The food of us Mex-, of us. I don't mean Mexicano, because we're not Mexicano. We say Mexicanos, but we're not. Mexico's over there on the other side [of the border].' (219, F, 96, Medanales, NM)

How does one resolve the labelling conflict? How does one clearly label the other group, the 'them'? The speaker in example 27 reveals the need for redundancy to unambiguously identify a girl from Mexico:

> 27. *Mi ayuda era una muchacha mexicana de México.* 'My help [in taking care of my husband] was a Mexicano girl from Mexico.' (108: F, 83, Santa Fe)

But equally problematic is the label for 'us'. Like the woman speaking in example 26, many Traditional Spanish speakers find themselves in a quandary about what term to use to describe their own ethnicity, as seen in example 28:

> 28. *En esos tiempo era puro español, puro mexicano.* 'In those days [the town of Chama] was totally Spanish, totally Mexicano.' (211: M, 78, Chama, CO)

The use of *español* as an identity label appears to be a translation from the 'Spanish' label that Traditional Spanish speakers adopted for use with English speakers to maintain their separateness from the 'Mexican' group. Such is the usage of the speaker in 29, and see also example 6 above.

> 29. *La mayor de la gente era ahi españoles.* 'Most of the people there [in McPhee, CO] were Spanish.' (194: M, 64, Cortez, CO)

Consequently, the quandary finishes up by not being simply about labels, but about what one's identity actually is. A sad expression of cultural anomie is example 30. We find many poignant comments of this sort in our interviews.

> 30. *Sabía que no era español, pero también no quería ser mexicano.* 'I knew I wasn't really Spanish, but I also didn't want to be Mexicano.' (304: M, 51, Pueblo, CO)

5. Consequences of multiple borders

What happens when one has language contact, dialect contact and ethnic contact producing identity issues such as these in New Mexico? A typical result when two languages come into contact is the gradual loss of the language perceived to have lesser status, a consequence suffered by virtually all minority languages in the United States. New Mexican Spanish is certainly no exception to the trend. Over the hundred years since statehood, many New Mexican Hispanics have become English monolinguals. But different situations, different concerns about identity and different experiences of discrimination may lead to different degrees of abandonment of the use of Spanish.

The contact between speakers of Traditional Spanish and speakers of Border Spanish produces different reactions in the two ethnic groups. The generalisation captured by consultant 304 holds true wherever that contact takes place:

> 31. *[L]a cosa es que, es muy extraño, es que los mexicanos no quieren aprender inglés porque los chicanos se burlan de ellos. Y los chicanos no quieren aprender mexicano porque los mexicanos se burlan de ellos. Tienen vergüenza los chicanos de hablar mexicano porque los mexicanos se burlan de ellos. Y los mexicanos tienen miedo de hablar inglés adelante de los chicanos.* 'The thing is, it's very strange, it's that the [immigrant] Mexicans don't want to learn English because the [native-born] Chicanos make fun of them. And the Chicanos don't want to learn Spanish because the Mexicans make fun of them. The Chicanos are ashamed to speak Spanish because the Mexicans make fun of them. And the Mexicans are afraid to speak English in front of the Chicanos.' (304: M, 51, Pueblo, CO)

There is a strong tendency, then, for greater abandonment of Spanish among those of Traditional Spanish heritage. In addition, greater distance from the Mexican border is associated with greater loss of Spanish (see, for example, Bills et al. 1995). Jenkins (2009) plots a measurement of Spanish retention by county on a map for six states of the US south-west (see his Map 5). This map shows the region of our survey to be the area of least retention. In addition, it shows that the Border Spanish areas have somewhat greater retention than the Traditional Spanish areas.

But both areas suffer considerable shift from the heritage language under the influence of the language of still higher prestige, English. The English language has an overwhelming presence in New Mexico, dominating in education, government, the media and all aspects of public participation outside the home or village or sometimes specific neighbourhood. These societal forces severely limit access to Spanish. Example 32 affirms one typical limitation:

> 32. *Oyemos las nuevas en inglés porque no la podemos agarrar en mexicano.* 'We listen to the news in English because we can't get it in "Mexican".' (356: M, 60, Chise, NM)

But those same societal forces have a psychological impact that restrains the use of Spanish and facilitates the shift to English. Example 33 comes from a young woman, a speaker of Border Spanish, explaining what she used to say to high-school friends about to introduce her to some new people:

> 33. *Yo decía, "No les digan que sé español"* . . . *Si ya sabías el español es que tus padres eran mojados.* 'I would say, "Don't tell them I know Spanish" . . . If you knew Spanish it meant your parents were Wetbacks [immigrants from Mexico].' (149: F, 21, Las Cruces, NM)

Reflecting those same societal pressures, the man cited in example 34 reports the reasons for his deliberate abandonment of Spanish in the home:

> 34. *Los gabachos o gringos se rían de tí y a tí te daba muncha vergüenza, so yo dije a mis muchachas, 'No les vamos a hablar en mexicano'.* 'The Anglos or Gringos would laugh at you and that would cause you a lot of shame, so I told my girls, "We're not going to talk to you in Spanish".' (218: M, 53, Grants, NM)

Laments about the loss of Spanish among younger Hispanics are common in our interviews. The woman in example 35 describes her grandson's limited ability in Spanish:

> 35. *Sabe qué está dijiéndole en mexicano pero en inglés le responde pa' atrás.* 'He knows what you're telling him in "Mexican" but he responds in English.' (47: F, 54, Albuquerque, NM)

Another explains in example 36 the unlikely way her grandson finally learned Spanish:

> 36. *Mi nieto jue hasta Spain a aprender mexicano allá.* 'My grandson went to Spain to learn "Mexican" there.' (324: F, 81, Watrous, NM)

Example 37 is another woman's response when asked if young people were maintaining Spanish:

> 37. *No. Ya – aquí no. Ya, los jóvenes que aprenden español ahora, ah, son gente que se casan con obreros que vienen de California o de Texas, o de Arizona o de México. Y ya es otro dialéctico de, de lo que era aquí. So, está cambiando. Porque está entrando eso. Pus, ya los jóvenes de aquí ya no tienen la idioma de nuestros viejitos. Ya, ya, se está acabando.* 'No. Now – not here. Now, the young people who learn Spanish now, uh, are people who get married to workers who come from California or Texas, or Arizona or Mexico. And it's already a different dialect from, from what was here. So, it's changing. Because that's coming in. Well, now the young people here no longer have the language of our old folks. Now, now, it's disappearing.' (212: F, 37, Antoñito, CO)

This example shows another aspect to the loss. The special Traditional Spanish dialect is rapidly being undermined by the new wave of Spanish, losing many of the features that make the dialect unique. In Table 4.1 we give a few examples of the decline in use of several Traditional Spanish lexical items across three generations.

6. Conclusions

The implications of this research are far-reaching, but just two major points may be highlighted. First, dialect geography reveals that internal borders may be as significant as international political borders in the development of ethnic differentiation and identity conflicts. Second, insecurities about ethnic identity are apt to be strengthened across these internal dialect borders where a distinct language (English in the present case) happens to hold higher prestige.

Table 4.1 Decline of Traditional Spanish forms across generations (%)

Lexical variable	Younger (ages 15–40)	Middle (ages 41–64)	Older (ages 65–96)
ánsara 'goose'	2.4	9.6	22.6
pariagüe, paragüe 'umbrella'	6.3	50.0	57.4
camalta 'bed'	6.5	10.1	20.4
horno 'skillet'	7.6	15.6	16.1
cuerpo 'blouse'	15.4	23.1	34.5
chupilote 'buzzard, vulture'	15.9	21.6	36.6
mora 'strawberry'	16.0	32.8	33.6
almendras 'nuts' (in general)	16.0	31.9	38.5
ratón volador 'bat'	18.1	51.9	68.5
tresquilar 'shear'	19.0	37.3	55.3
paisano 'roadrunner'	19.3	45.5	58.9
chile/chilito de perro 'sty'	26.3	50.4	59.8
cuerpoespín/corpoespín 'porcupine'	27.8	53.7	63.6
bolita 'marble'	41.3	65.9	63.0
metate 'grinding stone'	43.2	53.5	77.2
petaquilla 'trunk'	45.0	82.1	79.5
tútano 'marrow'	45.2	81.1	83.4
pescuezo 'neck'	46.8	59.4	67.8
chuparrosa 'hummingbird'	47.6	66.7	72.8

The latter point is highly relevant to the study of language maintenance and shift. It is clear that some degree of ethnic solidarity (or 'the maintenance of intracultural bounda-ries' in Joshua Fishman's terms) 'is crucial for intergenerational minority group mother tongue maintenance' (Fishman 1989: 226). Likewise, any constraints on ethnic solidarity can be expected to facilitate language shift. For the Spanish speakers of New Mexico and southern Colorado (and indeed throughout the United States; see Bills 2005), it is the internal borders that form barriers to the establishment of ethnic solidarity. This type of situation may inhibit dialect levelling between two dialects, e.g. Traditional and Border Spanish. But more significantly, the internal barrier to ethnic solidarity is likely to promote a more abrupt abandonment of the heritage language in favour of the higher-status language. In addition, heritage language loss is likely to be particularly manifest in the group (Traditional Spanish speakers here) that holds a more negative attitude towards speakers of the other dialect.

Note

1. The survey area is quite large: at around 390,000 km^2 (c. 150,500 sq. miles), it is some 1.6 times the size of the United Kingdom.

5

Language Use and Attitudes as Stimuli for Phonological Change in Border Uruguayan Spanish

Mark Waltermire

1. Introduction

Thanks to hundreds of years of territorial dispute between the Spanish and Portuguese in what is now north-eastern Uruguay, a situation of language contact exists along the national border that this country shares with Brazil. Previous research on the bilingualism of this region has focused primarily on Portuguese (Carvalho 1998, 2003; Elizaincín 1979, 1992; Elizaincín et al. 1987; Hensey 1972; Rona 1965). While the Spanish spoken along this border has only received significant attention in recent years (e.g. Carvalho 2006a, b; Elizaincín 2008; Thun and Elizaincín 2000; Waltermire 2006, 2008, 2011), the investigation of language use and attitudes towards local language varieties, especially as these relate to the construction of social and national identities, has only received significant attention in Waltermire (2010). Results from this research show that there is a statistical correlation between these factors and the use of language-specific articulations in the Spanish of Rivera, the largest metropolitan area on the Uruguayan side of the border. Using inter-vocalic /d/ as a conflict site for the analysis of the use of language-specific articulations (a stop in Portuguese versus a fricative or phonetic zero in Spanish), Waltermire (2010) shows that Portuguese-dominant speakers who display positive attitudes towards Border Portuguese tend to incorporate loan articulations from this language into their Spanish, whereas speakers who prefer Spanish and have positive attitudes towards language mixing tend to delete intervocalic /d/ in an attempt to distance themselves from Brazil. As Spanish and Portuguese differ primarily in their phonological inventories, there are mul-tiple variables that demand analysis of the kind pursued in Waltermire (2010), including syllable- and word-final /s/, one of the most studied variables in Spanish linguistics.

2. Variants of syllable- and word-final /s/ in the Spanish of Rivera

The realisation of syllable- and word-final /s/ as a sibilant is standard in both Uruguayan Spanish and Brazilian Portuguese. The use of a full sibilant is also common in the

Table 5.1 Phonological contexts for the aspiration of syllable- and word-final /s/ in Spanish

Phonological context	Example and gloss	Phonetic form and source
Pre-consonantal, word-internal	*respeto* 'respect'	[ɾeh.ˈpe.to] (18/A:059/27)
Pre-consonantal, word-final	*muchas veces* 'many times'	[ˈmu.tʃah.ˈβe.ses] (32/A:220/50)
Pre-vocalic (atonic), word-final	*años atrás* 'years ago'	[ˈa.ɲo.ha.ˈtras] (10/A:188/10)
Pre-vocalic (tonic), word-final	*tenemos una* 'we have one'	[te.ˈne.mo.ˈhu.na] (04/A:165/03)
Phrase-final	*portugués* 'Portuguese'	[por.tu.ˈɣeh] (13/A:191/15)

Spanish of Rivera, and has traditionally been thought to be more frequently used along the border than in other areas of Uruguay due to contact with Portuguese, a language that demonstrates strong tendencies towards the maintenance of sibilant articulations. With respect to the full production of /s/, both languages exhibit patterns of voicing assimilation when this consonant is followed by a voiced consonant (as in *mismo*, 'same' (Sp.), pronounced as [ˈmiz.mo] or *mesmo*, 'same' (Port.), as [ˈmɛz.mu]). Unlike in Southern Brazilian Portuguese, however, syllable- and word-final /s/ is commonly reduced to an 'aspirant' ([h]) in border Uruguayan Spanish (e.g. *mismo*, 'same', as [ˈmih.mo]). The aspiration of syllable- and word-final /s/, which has never traditionally been associated with the Spanish of Rivera, has become relatively frequent in this bilingual dialect in the past decade. As shown in Table 5.1, /s/ aspiration occurs in multiple phonological contexts. The aspiration of /s/ in initial positions does not occur with any notable frequency within the community. For this reason, only syllable- and word-final occurrences of /s/ will be analysed in this chapter.

In addition to maintenance and reduction, /s/ is also deleted in the Spanish of Rivera, with *mismo*, 'same', therefore, potentially receiving the pronunciation [ˈmi.mo]. As with aspiration, the deletion of this consonant occurs in all possible final phonological environments, but not in initial environments. In Portuguese, the deletion of /s/ is limited exclusively to word-final environments (*mesmo*, 'same', *[ˈmɛ.mu]). Although the deletion of word-final /s/ is characteristic of practically all varieties of colloquial Brazilian Portuguese, regardless of social factors related to class or educational level (Azevedo 1989), we shall see that the processes of conditioning differ in Brazilian Portuguese and border Uruguayan Spanish. This being the case, there are competing patterns of deletion along the border. It is likely that factors related to the individual, such as language use, preference and attitudes, affect these patterns of deletion within the community.

3. Linguistic and social associations of /s/ variants in Rivera

Patterns of phonological conditioning, like the production of certain sound variants, are closely associated with distinct language varieties in contact situations. That is, specific phonological variants and the conditioning of their use are tied inextricably to the languages in which their use is most common. In this sense, the production of some consonants is perceived as typically Portuguese in nature or typically Spanish in nature. Each of these perceptions is continually reinforced through continued use in each language. The realisation of syllable- and word-final /s/ as the aspirant [h] is much more characteristic of Spanish, since this articulation is common among multiple geographically distinct dialects of this language (Lipski 1994), whereas it occurs in only a handful of dialects of Brazilian Portuguese (most notably in the north-east of Brazil; see Ferreira 2001; Palácio 1989). Of even greater importance to the current study is the fact that /s/-aspiration has never been reported for dialects of Southern Brazilian Portuguese (Koch et al. 2002). As such, there is virtually no association whatever between this articulation and Border Portuguese.

Although the aspiration of syllable- and word-final /s/ cannot be seen as typically Portuguese for these reasons, the deletion of this phoneme in word-final positions in the Spanish of Rivera is conditioned by Portuguese plural-marking patterns, in which plural /s/ is retained for determiners and first-position noun phrase (NP) constituents in general, but deleted for other constituents of the NP (as in *as casa*[Ø] *antigua*[Ø], 'the old houses') (Carvalho 2006a; Waltermire 2011). The deletion of /s/ for head constituents of nominal phrases, therefore, constitutes a typically Portuguese process along the border, and is associated more highly with this language than with border Uruguayan Spanish. Since the deletion of /s/ in the Spanish of Rivera is possible in all syllable-final contexts regardless of other factors, whereas /s/-deletion in Portuguese is restricted to plural nouns and adjectives of nominal phrases (Azevedo 1989; Guy 1981; Scherre 2001), it can safely be claimed that this pattern of conditioning is more highly associated with Portuguese than with Spanish, at least for the dialect in question.

Naturally, there are also social values ascribed to the use of these variants. Aspiration, once assumed to be non-existent in border varieties of Uruguayan Spanish, has recently emerged as a marker of social prestige owing to its associations with the Spanish of Montevideo (Carvalho 2006b). The use of aspirated variants of /s/ in Rivera is most frequent among young members of the middle class (Carvalho 2006b) and female students (Waltermire 2006). This contrasts greatly with the deletion of syllable- and word-final /s/, which is socially stigmatised not only in border Uruguayan Spanish, but in practically every dialect of the language (Lipski 1994). The deletion of this phoneme is highly frequent among community members of Rivera who have had little exposure to formal education (Waltermire 2006). The current research seeks to answer questions related to the use of /s/ variants in border Spanish as markers of social and national identity. Since linguistic attitudes are a manifestation of a speaker's sociolinguistic identity (Ben-Rafael et al. 1998; Hoare 2001; Joseph 2004: 71; Lawson and Sachdev 2004), these factors will be analysed, along with factors related to language use, to determine the potential effects they might have on the use of articulations associated with either Spanish or Portuguese within the community of Rivera. Perceptions of identity will be based on four independent factor groups: 1) frequency of language use, 2) language preference, 3) attitudes towards Border Portuguese and 4) attitudes towards language mixing. As was found in Waltermire (2010) with respect to the use of language-specific variants of intervocalic /d/, it would be expected that these factors would play a conditioning role in the aspiration and deletion of syllable- and word-final /s/ in the Spanish of Rivera.

4. Data collection and methodology

An analysis of the conditioning role of usage and attitudinal factors on the variable realisation of syllable- and word-final /s/ was conducted using a total of 3,091 tokens, which were extracted from an extensive database of Spanish recorded by the author in Rivera, Uruguay, from mid-March to mid-May 2003.[1] This database consists of over fifty hours of colloquial speech from a representative sample of sixty-three Spanish/Portuguese bilinguals, who were interviewed both individually and in groups, often in the presence of in-community contacts. Conversations were completely unguided, with topics of great personal interest being pursued in order to attain the most informal samples of colloquial speech possible. Using 2003 Uruguayan census data, consultants were chosen based on age, sex and occupation relative to their general representation among the city's population.[2] Of the sixty-three total consultants, eighteen speakers represented the youngest generation (16–25 years of age), twenty-seven represented speakers of the second generation (26–50 years of age) and eighteen speakers were selected to represent the oldest generation. With respect to sex, there is a greater representation of female speakers (N = 35), which is consistent with actual figures for Rivera, according to census data. Unfortunately, 2003 census data did not include information related to the occupations of community residents. This being the case, relatively equal distributions of speakers by general occupational classes (professional, non-professional and students) were chosen for each generational grouping. Professionals (N = 28) included educators, lawyers, doctors, health inspectors and engineers. Non-professionals (N = 23) worked in professions that do not require advanced education. They were hotel owners and their employees, shopkeepers and their employees, secretaries, police officers, currency exchangers, waiters, street vendors and taxi drivers. The youngest generation, however, includes members of all three occupational classes owing to the fact that they occupy a professionally transitional life stage during which speakers eventually enter the community's workforce. Of the eighteen consultants of the youngest generation, twelve were students, while four speakers had non-professional occupations and two had professional occupations. For each speaker, frequency of language use, preference and attitudes towards Border Portuguese and language mixing were determined.

5. Language use

The analysis of language use by each consultant is crucial to the sociolinguistic analysis of bilingual communities, in view of the evidence that suggests that bilinguals access language-specific phonological forms based on exemplars in stored memory (Brown and Harper 2009; Bybee 2001; Pierrehumbert 2001). Bybee (2001: 28) explains that 'since tokens of use map onto existing representations, high-frequency items grow strong and therefore are easier to access'. For bilingual speakers, of course, there are competing levels of access to phonological forms relative to the frequencies with which such speakers use both languages. Whichever language a bilingual speaker chooses to use more often will, then, be likely to have an effect on the type of articulations that he or she produces. Given this evidence, it is expected that Spanish-dominant speakers will use phonological variants that are characteristic of this language more frequently than variants associated with Portuguese. It should be noted, however, that this is only a tendency, and that other factors influence the use of language-specific articulations. As a result of the different frequencies of use of both languages, the use of these articulations is variable even for the same speaker in the same stretch of discourse, as shown in the following example from the Rivera corpus.

1. *Ahora saben lo*[s], *eh, ya saben inglé*[s], *eh, ba*[s]*tante. La profesora también de inglé*[s], *entra al salón hablando solo inglé*[s]. *Lo*[s] *hace entender por seña*[s] *o lo que sea, no necesariamente e*[h]*pañol para nada. Tienen todo*[h] *lo*[h] *día*[h], *creo que cuarenta y cinco minuto*[h], *pero todo*[h] *lo*[z] *día*[Ø].
'Now they know, uh, they already know English, uh, well. The English teacher enters the classroom speaking only English. She makes them understand through signs or what have you, not necessarily Spanish at all. Every day, they have, I believe, forty-five minutes, but every day.' (15/A:172-176/19)

This example demonstrates that bilinguals have access to all possible variants from both Spanish and Portuguese, but will use variants from one language more often than those from the other language due to more frequent access of the forms that typify the dominant language. As both languages demonstrate maintenance of full sibilants, only aspiration and deletion will be analysed for the sixty-three consultants who represent the community of Rivera for this study. Since aspiration of syllable- and word-final /s/ is characteristic of Spanish, we would expect speakers who use this language frequently and who have negative attitudes towards Border Portuguese to use [h] more often than speakers who use this language less frequently. We would expect the inverse pattern with respect to the deletion of this phoneme.

Despite differences exhibited by individual consultants in terms of use, preference and attitudes, each consultant in the current study must be considered bilingual, since they use Spanish and Portuguese in their daily lives. Although some speakers almost never use Portuguese in their daily interactions, they are nevertheless capable of communicating in the language and have been influenced by it to some extent, as a natural result of having been raised on the border with Brazil. These speakers fall on the more monolingual Spanish end of what Silva-Corvalán refers to as the bilingual continuum, which 'goes from a standard or non-reduced variety to an emblematic one and vice versa in the other language, depending on the greater or lesser knowledge that the bilingual has of both languages' (2001: 270, translation mine). There are also consultants who speak Portuguese much more frequently than Spanish on a daily basis, and naturally fall on the Portuguese end of the bilingual continuum. The remaining speakers represent the majority of this continuum.

Speakers' varying frequencies of language use were categorised according to percentages of use that they provided through a written questionnaire, which appears in its entirety in the appendix to this chapter. Although soliciting frequencies of language use via a questionnaire is limiting since speakers do not always accurately report their actual use of both languages, their reported frequencies of use do match their actual use as observed during fieldwork. In an attempt to maintain the greatest possible levels of informality during the interviews by directing attention away from the linguistic purposes of the data collection, questionnaires were given to consultants only after the interviews had taken place, sometimes after an appreciable period of time had elapsed. As a result, some speakers were never relocated, and so a total of only fifty-seven consultants filled in the questionnaire, thereby reducing the number of tokens for this factor group. Frequencies of language use in churches, banks, post offices, restaurants and bars were not included in final tabulations, due to the fact that many speakers indicated that their choice of language in these environments depended on whether they were actually in Uruguay or Brazil. Furthermore, it seems fairly clear that speakers spent the majority of their time in work and home environments. In these domains, with their respective interlocutors, a majority of speakers (N = 33) indicated that they used Spanish 80 per cent of the time or more overall. These speakers were categorised as the group representing the more monolingual Spanish end of the bilingual continuum in Rivera. Consultants who indicated that they used Spanish between 40 and 80 per cent of the time (N = 16) represent speakers with a high level of competing phonological influence from both languages. Those who spoke Spanish 40 per cent or less of the time (N = 8) represent the more Portuguese end of the bilingual continuum.

6. Language preference

Although bilinguals are capable of using both languages at any given moment, the choice of using one language over another depends largely on pragmatic factors related to inter-locutors' level of familiarity with one another, their knowledge of each other's language preferences, and the linguistic domains in which speech occurs. For example, in Rivera, the use of Portuguese – though possible – has been shunned historically in schools and other publicly sanctioned domains owing to its unofficial status and the historical 'threat' it has posed to monolingual ideologies.[3] To use Portuguese in these domains would be tantamount to 'calling attention to oneself'. Similarly, if all speakers participating in a conversation are speaking Spanish, it would be unusual for another speaker to use only Portuguese if he or she can communicate in the language already chosen by the rest of the group. In both situations just described, the speaker may actually prefer to use Portuguese. The external situation, however, prohibits (or at least greatly limits) the pos-sibility of using this language, which would almost certainly guarantee that outlier status would be assigned to this individual. Since language preference and language use are not identical, the former factor will also be analysed in the current investigation.

Language preference was determined for each consultant through the strict analysis of metalinguistic commentaries provided by the consultants during interviews, along with the author's knowledge of these preferences. The qualitative analysis of metalinguistic commentary has been effective in the determination of attitudes and perceptions of iden-tity in other studies (e.g. Coupland and Jaworski 2004; Giles and Coupland 1991: 53; Hoare 2001; Hyrkstedt and Kalaja 1998: 346–8) and has been extended here to include language preferences. Soliciting information related to speakers' language preferences by way of a questionnaire may be somewhat unreliable due to the fact that most consultants associate preference with actual use. As we shall see, these two factors do not neatly coincide for all speakers. For these atypical speakers, Portuguese is the language with which they feel the most comfortable, even though they speak Spanish more frequently overall. They use Portuguese (referred to by many as *portuñol* to distinguish it from a more standard variety) at home and with close personal friends, but primarily use Spanish outside the home. This is the case for consultants 63 and 34, as shown by the following comments:

2. C: *El portugués es como el idioma dentro de casa [Exacto]. Este, y después, si sales, hablas español.*
   'Portuguese is like a home language [Exactly]. Umm, and later, if you leave, you speak Spanish.'
   I: *Exacto. Así que en casa el portugués y en las calles [Claro] el, el, el español.*
   'Exactly. So, at home Portuguese and on the streets [Of course] Spanish.'
   C: *O con alguien que no, no conoces o que no sabe español, ¿no?, [Ah, sí] pero en familia, digamos, se habla el portuñol.*
   'Or with someone that you don't, don't know or that doesn't know Spanish, right?, [Oh, yes] but with family, let's say, we speak Portuñol.' (34/B:120-124/63)
3. *Se habla el portuñol prácticamente sólo entre familiares y personas conocidas. Yo, por lo menos, con mis amigos hablo portuñol, (¿?) pero no voy a hablar en portuñol en la escuela donde estoy yendo porque te empiezan a reír.*
   'Portuñol is spoken practically only among family members and close acquaintances. I, for one, speak Portuñol with my friends, (??) but I'm not going to speak in Portuñol at the school I'm going to because they'll start laughing at you.' (24/A:289-293/34)

Language use and preference do not coincide for nine speakers, all of whom speak Spanish more frequently overall than Portuguese, but nevertheless prefer Portuguese. Despite the fact that the representation of these speakers in the sample is not overwhelming (at a mere 15.8 per cent), language preference may be an important factor in the determination of consultants' use of typically Spanish or typically Portuguese phonological variants. At the very least, the inclusion of this factor group will enable us to draw finer distinctions with respect to speakers' linguistic choices.

7. Language attitudes

Although language use and preference are important factors from a cognitive standpoint, in that frequency of use may affect bilinguals' production of divergent articulations, they do not directly indicate the values that these speakers ascribe to each language and their phonological variants. That is, simply because a bilingual chooses to speak one language more often than another does not mean that he or she values that language more than the other. This seems to be the case with the majority of speakers in Rivera. As mentioned in Section 5, the majority of speakers in this community (57.9 per cent, N = 33/57) speak Spanish 80 per cent of the time or more in their daily lives. This, however, does not mean that they value Portuguese any less than Spanish. It is for this reason that the examination of language attitudes is so crucial to the study of bilingual communities. The value that bilinguals place on both languages and mixed varieties is revealing of speakers' social and cultural identification.

As with language preference, sociolinguistic attitudes were also determined through the analysis of metalinguistic commentary provided by the consultants during interviews.

The use of questionnaire responses to assess speakers' attitudes is less reliable than the analysis of unsolicited responses given in casual interviews, in that the former do not always match speakers' actual linguistic perceptions (Auer et al. 2005: 251; Chin and Wigglesworth 2007; Coulmas 2005: 152). According to Chin and Wigglesworth (2007: 252), 'self-report data can be unreliable, especially when bilinguals view language mixing negatively'. This is the case for bilingual varieties, in that they form part of a local identity but may not reflect prestige norms inside the community and will almost certainly not reflect prestige norms outside the community (i.e. in monolingual communities). In other words, since there is a variable acceptance of local and/or mixed varieties within the community, there is at least a certain degree of reluctance on the part of many speakers to criticise local varieties frankly. If a questionnaire were used to assess attitudes in Rivera, the proportion of positive responses towards language mixing and local varieties of Portuguese would probably be unrealistically high.

Since the decision to assess language attitudes was determined from the outset of the data collection process, discussions about language mixing and the use of Border Portuguese occurred in almost every interview. It is important to note, however, that these attitudes were never solicited directly from consultants, who were encouraged to speak freely on a broad variety of topics, the majority of which were related, naturally, to the community. Many discussions centred on the use of Portuguese in Rivera – its characteristics, whether it is acceptable to speak the language in certain environments, its prestige, etc. As it was apparent that few consultants displayed negative feelings towards unmixed, more standard varieties of Portuguese, it was decided that only their attitudes towards local varieties of Portuguese would be assessed. Of course, in most bilingual communities the discussion of language mixing is also common. The general impression given by most consultants is that language mixing, though somewhat acceptable, is certainly not prestigious, though this may not be the case when one examines factors relating to in-group membership and social networks, issues that are beyond the scope of the current investigation. Discussions related to local language varieties and speakers' perceptions of them are crucial for the determination of speakers' linguistic attitudes, which may condition the use of language-specific articulations in the Spanish of Rivera. For each of these attitudes, consultants were assigned a positive or negative value. Despite the general nature of these designations, they seem appropriate for use in the current study, given that the objective of the study is not to determine speakers' attitudes towards linguistic phenomena in Rivera per se, but rather to examine the effect they may have on the use of language-specific articulations within the community.

Although relatively few community members displayed negative attitudes towards local varieties of Portuguese, some consultants for the current study (N = 8/63) indicated that these varieties are badly spoken and represent a departure from Standard Portuguese. The Portuguese spoken along the border is seen by these speakers as an aberration from acceptable, unmixed Portuguese, which most community members claim not to speak. Many of these speakers associate the use of local varieties of Portuguese with a lack of education and, consequently, with members of the lowest socio-economic class. To these consultants, the use of a local variety is a negative influence that separates Rivera from other parts of the country, where the permeation of Portuguese and Brazilian heritage has not been felt to the same degree. Consider, for example, the following comments:

4. I: *¿Hablás el portugués mucho?*
'Do you speak Portuguese much?'
C: *Mirá, digamos que sí, pero claro, hablamos más un portuñol, ¿no es? Es más una mezcla del español con portugués. Portugués- portugués mismo, no. Eso no. Es más un portuñol, así la mezcla.*
'Look, let's say yes, but of course, we speak more of a Portuñol, you know? It's a mix of Spanish with Portuguese. Portuguese- Portuguese, no. Not that. It's more of a Portuñol, like a mix.'
I: *¿Pero lo, lo ves como mal hablado el portugués (de Rivera)?*
'But, do you see it as badly spoken, the Portuguese (of Rivera)?'
C: *Sí.*
'Yes.'
I: *¿Verdad?*
'Really?'
C: *Sí.*
'Yes.'
I: *¿Por qué?*
'Why?'
C: *Acá, generalmente es muy mal hablado.*
'Here, generally it's badly spoken.'
I: *¿Por qué?*
'Why?'
C: *Porque, como que, como es frontera y se mezclan los idiomas, como que no se habla bien ni el de allá ni el de acá.*
'Because, since it's, since it's the border and the languages are mixed, neither the language there nor the language here is spoken well.' (36/B:056–062/57)

5. *Se me parece que hay un problema porque el español está perdiendo, como, sus características con muchos, tantas cosas de los brasileños, ¿no es?*
'It seems to me that there's a problem because Spanish is losing, like, its characteristics with many, so many things from Brazilians, isn't it?' (24/A:282–283/35)

6. C50: *El más educado trata de hablar mejor, sin, sin el tal portuñol, que a mí no me gusta.*
'More educated people try to speak better, without, without (speaking) Portuñol, which I don't like.'
I: *¿No te gusta?*
'You don't like it?'
C50: *No, no. A mí no me gusta.*
'No, no. I don't like it.'
C51: *A mí tampoco.*
'Me neither.'
I: *¿Tampoco?*
'You neither?'
C50: *En los barrios pobres por allí, sí.*
'In the poor neighbourhoods over there, yes.'

C51: *Pero, pero, mi amor, tú decís en los, en los barrios pobres, pero por aquí se habla el portuñol tranquilamente, ¿no ves? Hasta el portuñol hay una diferenciación – entre el portuñol del barrio de allí, como tú decías de los barrios modestos, [Sí] y este otro que se usa aquí que se va a echar una palabra. Es un portuñol también.*
'But, but, my love, you say in the, in the poor neighbourhoods, but Portuñol is spoken casually around here (also), don't you see? Even with Portuñol, there's a difference – between the Portuñol of the neighbourhood over there, like you were saying about the modest neighbourhoods, [Yes] and this other one that is used here where a word will be thrown in. It's also Portuñol.'
(32/A:069-074/50,51)

With respect to speakers' attitudes towards language mixing, there is a much wider range of variation. Although many members of the community feel that language mixing is natural, over half of the consultants interviewed for the current study (N = 32/59) revealed negative attitudes towards this characteristic of language use in Rivera.[4] Any consultant who referred to language mixing as ungrammatical, incorrect, improper, uneducated or inferior, whether linguistically or socially, was assigned a negative value for this factor group. As shown in examples 7–9, language mixing does not hold any linguistic prestige for the community in general.

7. *Las maestras actualmente tienen eso, la mezcla, con el dialecto. Una vez, estaba en la peluquería y estaba a los altos escuchando a una maestra y pensaba, 'Pobres de los niños que caigan en las manos de esta maestra.' No van a saber hablar. No saben. No saben en ese dialecto.*
'Nowadays, teachers have that, mixing, with the dialect. Once I was in a hair salon and I was upstairs listening to a teacher and I was thinking, "Poor children that wind up with this teacher." They aren't going to know how to speak. They don't know. They don't know in that dialect.'
(14/A:334-339/16)

8. *La segunda hijita que tengo, que te, esa que te decía, que tiene, eh, tiene once años, eh, está por el mismo camino. Cuando habla portugués, habla portugués, o sea, brasileño, portugués, ¿no? Este, es aquel idioma. Y cuando habla el castellano, habla un castellano limpio, claro, bien definido, lo que a mí me satisface mucho porque me gusta así.*
'The second daughter that I have, that, the one I was telling you about, that is, uh, that's eleven years old, uh, is on the same path. When she speaks Portuguese, she speaks Portuguese, or rather, Brazilian, Portuguese, you know? So, it's that language. And when she speaks Spanish, she speaks a clean, clear, well-defined Spanish, which really satisfies me because I like it that way.' (03/A:176-181/02)

9. *La gente que tiene menos, menos, menos, menos orgullo así del español es el que entrevera eso. Yo siento que es así.*
'People who have less, less, less, less pride in Spanish are the ones who jumble it all up. I feel that it's that way.' (32/A:075/50)

These metalinguistic commentaries illustrate the lack of prestige associated with border language varieties and their characteristics. Bilingualism on the border, though common for everyone, is seen as imperfect, in that few speakers feel that they speak a 'proper' (i.e. unmixed, idealised) Portuguese.

8. The contribution of usage and attitudinal factors to the realisation of syllable- and word-final /s/ in the Spanish of Rivera

We will examine next the contribution of usage and attitudinal factors to the realisation of syllable- and word-final /s/ as an aspirant [h] or a phonetic zero in the Spanish of Rivera. Since /s/-aspiration is characteristic of Spanish, it is to be expected that the use of this variant would be more frequent among speakers who use this language often, prefer to use it in discourse and hold negative attitudes towards Border Portuguese. It is also to be expected that consultants who aspirate /s/ would express negative attitudes towards language mixing, which lacks linguistic prestige, whereas aspiration is seen as a prestige marker of monolingual Uruguayan Spanish. We will first examine the rates of use of all three variants of syllable- and word-final /s/ according to each of the four usage and attitudinal factors just described. These rates appear in Table 5.2.

Although the maintenance of /s/ as a full sibilant will not be pursued in the current study, it is important to note that, of all possible variants, it is the most commonly used. This is a feature of a Portuguese substrate that has existed in border Uruguayan Spanish since these two languages came into contact (Rona 1965). It is compounded by the fact that the aspiration of /s/ is a recent phenomenon in border Uruguayan Spanish which, as such, represents a change in progress. Furthermore, the deletion of word-final /s/ in pre-vocalic contexts in Spanish is extremely infrequent, since it often becomes the onset of the following syllable during the process of resyllabification.[5] The data in Table 5.2 show that the aspiration of syllable- and word-final /s/ corresponds to our predictions. Consultants who use Spanish frequently in their daily lives (80 per cent of the time or more) aspirate /s/ much more frequently than those who do not use Spanish as often. At 31.1 per cent, their [h]-usage rate greatly exceeds the rates for speakers who use Spanish less than 80 per cent of the time ([h] accounts for just 13.3 per cent of tokens for consultants who use Spanish between 40 and 80 per cent of the time, and 12 per cent for those who use the language 40 per cent of the time or less). Likewise, and at rates similar to those for frequency of Spanish use, consultants who prefer to speak Spanish aspirate syllable- and word-final /s/ much more frequently than those who prefer Portuguese (at rates of 30.7 per cent and 9.8 per cent, respectively). For each of these factors, consultants who align themselves with Spanish use the one phonological variant that is truly characteristic of Spanish, and they do so three times as often as do speakers who align themselves more closely with Portuguese.

The rates of aspirant use are not so disparate between speakers with positive and negative attitudes towards Border Portuguese or language mixing. It is worth noting, however, that the tendencies just mentioned for language use and preference also exist for language attitudes. That is, consultants who view Border Portuguese negatively aspirate /s/ more frequently than do those who view it positively (at a rate of 37.3 per cent compared to 22.6 per cent). Similarly, those with negative attitudes towards language mixing aspirate more than those who view the phenomenon positively (29.9 per cent, as

Table 5.2 Distribution of variant use of syllable- and word-final /s/ according to usage and attitudinal factors in the Spanish of Rivera

Factor group	Factor	[s]	[h]	[Ø]	Total
		\multicolumn{3}{c}{Phonetic variant}	
Spanish use	≥ 80%	968 / 1,650 (58.7%)	513 / 1,650 (31.1%)	169 / 1,650 (10.2%)	650 / 2,816 (58.6%)
	40%–80%	561 / 791 (70.9%)	105 / 791 (13.3%)	125 / 791 (15.8%)	791 / 2,816 (28.1%)
	≤ 40%	267 / 375 (71.2%)	45 / 375 (12.0%)	63 / 375 (16.8%)	375 / 2,816 (13.3%)
Preference	Spanish	1,297 / 2,175 (59.6%)	668 / 2,175 (30.7%)	210 / 2,175 (9.7%)	175 / 3,091 (70.4%)
	Portuguese	665 / 916 (72.6%)	90 / 916 (9.8%)	161 / 916 (17.6%)	916 / 3,091 (29.6%)
Attitudes towards Border Portuguese	Positive	1,757 / 2,691 (65.3%)	609 / 2,691 (22.6%)	325 / 2,691 (12.1%)	691 / 3,091 (87.1%)
	Negative	205 / 400 (51.2%)	149 / 400 (37.3%)	46 / 400 (11.5%)	400 / 3,091 (12.9%)
Attitudes towards language mixing	Positive	895 / 1,316 (68.0%)	232 / 1,316 (17.6%)	189 / 1,316 (14.4%)	316 / 2,916 (45.1%)
	Negative	953 / 1,600 (59.6%)	479 / 1,600 (29.9%)	168 / 1,600 (10.5%)	600 / 2,916 (54.9%)

Spanish use: $\chi^2 = 131.74$; $df = 4$; $p \leq .001$; Preference: $\chi^2 = 165.44$; $df = 2$; $p \leq .001$; Attitudes towards Border Portuguese: $\chi^2 = 41.26$; $df = 2$; $p \leq .001$; Attitudes towards language mixing: $\chi^2 = 61.79$; $df = 2$; $p \leq .001$.

opposed to 17.6 per cent). These data suggest that speakers who are critical of language mixing choose prestige variants more often than do consultants who are more accepting of it. The phonological choices that these speakers make seem to be a direct reflection of their linguistic attitudes.

When compared to rates of aspiration, rates of deletion among consultants are not remarkably divergent. This is especially true for attitudes towards Border Portuguese, which are approximately the same for consultants who view this language variety positively (325/2,691, or 12.1 per cent) as for those who view it negatively (46/400, or 11.5 per cent). Attitudes towards language mixing do not show a strong correlation with deletion either, though this linguistic process is slightly more common for those who view language mixing positively. It seems that speakers who are less conservative in their variant use are also less conservative in their views concerning the 'correctness' of language use (i.e. that it should not incorporate elements of another language). This was revealed with respect to the deletion of intervocalic /d/ in the Spanish of Rivera in Waltermire (2010).

Rates of deletion are more marked according to language use and preference. Consultants who use Spanish frequently and prefer to speak the language over Portuguese demonstrate lower rates of deletion than those who speak Portuguese frequently and prefer that language. While rates of deletion reach only 9.7 per cent among consultants who prefer Spanish, /s/-deletion occurs at nearly twice the rate (17.6 per cent) among those who prefer Portuguese. Also, those who speak Spanish 80 per cent of the time or more do not delete the consonant as often as do consultants who speak Spanish less than 80 per cent of the time (10.2 per cent, compared to rates of 15.8 per cent for those who use Spanish between 40 and 80 per cent of the time, and 16.8 per cent for those who speak Spanish 40 per cent of the time or less).

8.1 The conditioning of /s/-aspiration in Rivera

Although these rates do indicate important differences in the realisation of /s/ by speakers who demonstrate notable differences in language use, preference and attitudes, they are simply too similar to allow for any definitive conclusions with regard to their relative contributions to the realisation of this phoneme. In order to determine the relative contributions of each of the independent factor groups, a multivariate analysis using *GoldVarb X* (Sankoff et al. 2005) was conducted. *GoldVarb X* generates probability weights corresponding to observed frequencies in a corpus by determining the relative contribution that each factor makes to the occurrence of a linguistic variant when all factors are considered together. The applied variant for the first statistical analysis of the contribution of usage and attitudinal factors to the realisation of syllable- and word-final /s/ was the aspirant [h] (versus the use of the sibilant [s] or the deletion of the phoneme). After conducting this analysis, a crossover between percentages of variant use and probability weights was encountered for Spanish use.[6] In order to remedy this methodological problem, the three original speaker divisions according to this factor were reduced to two general groups: 1) those that use Spanish 80 per cent of the time or more, and 2) those that use this language less than 80 per cent of the time. The probability weights generated during this analysis appear in Table 5.3.

When two or more factors are determined to be significant in speakers' choice of the dependent variable, it is necessary to determine the range of each factor group in order to establish the relative strengths of each group on their co-occurrence with the dependent variable. Language preference is the most significant factor in the aspiration of syllable- and word-final /s/ in the Spanish of Rivera, with a range of 26. Probability weights confirm that consultants who prefer to use Spanish in their daily lives are likely to aspirate /s/, as shown by the probability weight of .58. It is statistically improbable, however, that those who prefer to speak Portuguese will use the aspirant [h] for /s/, which is clear from a mere .32 probability weight for aspiration among these speakers. Similarly, consultants who use Spanish 80 per cent of the time or more in their daily activities will most likely use an aspirant (with a weight of .53), while those who use this language less than 80 per cent of the time will most likely avoid the use of this articulation. These results show that the aspiration of syllable- and word-final /s/ is a direct consequence of using Spanish frequently. Such speakers prefer to align themselves more closely with the monolingual varieties that typify the rest of Uruguay. As already discussed, these dialects are socially prestigious, whereas the local dialect of Spanish spoken in Rivera lacks prestige

Table 5.3 Multivariate analysis of the probabilities of co–occurrence of the aspiration of /s/ and usage and attitudinal factors in the Spanish of Rivera ($p < .05$, N = 3,091 (except where indicated), Input = 0.222, Log likelihood = -1627.964)

Factor group	Factor	N	% [h]	Factor weight
Preference	*Spanish*	2,175	30.7	.58
	Portuguese	916	9.8	.32
				Range 26
Attitudes towards Border	*Negative*	400	37.3	.57
Portuguese	*Positive*	2,691	22.6	.49
				Range 8
Spanish use	⩾ *80%*	1,650	31.1	.53
(N = 2,816)	< *80%*	1,166	12.9	.46
				Range 7

Other factor group included in analysis: (1) Attitudes towards language mixing

due to the notable influence of Portuguese on its phonological patterns. It is also likely that consultants with negative attitudes towards Border Portuguese will use an aspirant for /s/, with a probability weight of .57, providing further support for examining the role of sociolinguistic identity in the variable realisation of language-specific articulations in this community. When these factors are taken into account, it appears that aspiration is a salient marker of linguistic identity for speakers who do not want to be associated with border varieties of Spanish, which have historically demonstrated characteristics derived from a Portuguese substrate.

The frequent use of Spanish or a preference for this language, of course, does not lead categorically to high rates of /s/-aspiration for all speakers of the community. There are myriad other factors that potentially condition the use of [h], such as word stress, following phoneme, the speaker's sex, gender, occupation or age, acts of accommodation, discourse topic, style shifting, etc. These factors certainly merit further investigation, but are simply outside the scope of the current study and cannot be pursued here in detail. With respect to language use, however, which should be seen as an integral part of one's sociolinguistic identity, we see a general pattern of higher rates of /s/-aspiration among Spanish-dominant speakers. On average, speakers who use Spanish frequently in their daily lives produce a greater number of aspirants than do speakers who use the language infrequently, though this is by no means categorical. By plotting tokens of aspiration relative to the use of Spanish for all consultants who participated in the current investigation, we will arrive at a better understanding of the variability with which consultants realise /s/ as [h] according to this factor. These data are displayed in Figure 5.1.

Although Figure 5.1 shows that the frequent use of Spanish does not guarantee that a speaker will aspirate /s/ at any given moment, it also shows that frequencies of use of Spanish do serve as indicators of rates of aspiration. All speakers who use Spanish more than 70 per cent of the time in their daily lives produce at least six tokens of [h], with only

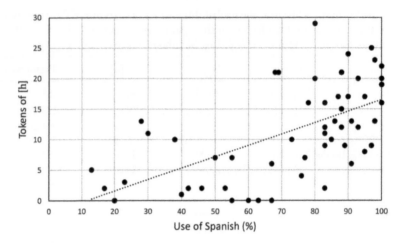

Figure 5.1 Tokens of aspirated syllable- and word-final /s/ according to individual consultants' use of Spanish.

two exceptions. It is important to note that these two speakers are both males with non-professional occupations, which are the two factors that most disfavour /s/-aspiration in the Spanish of Rivera (Waltermire 2006). All speakers who use Spanish less than 70 per cent of the time in their daily lives produce a maximum of seven tokens of [h], with only five exceptions. These five speakers all hold professional occupations. Their use of this socially prestigious variant may well be related to their social standing. Three of these speakers, however, use Portuguese more often than Spanish in their daily lives. This would seem to override the use of [h]; however, it does not, because of their frequent use of Spanish in work domains. Each of these speakers uses Spanish 80 per cent of the time or more at work, where they spend the majority of their time during the week. Their use of Portuguese dominates in the home with family and friends (at a rate of not less than 80 per cent), but their frequent use of Spanish for professional reasons reinforces the use of [h], the typically Spanish phonological variant. This is important because it shows that the use of language-specific phonological variants can be the result of not just overall frequency of use of a particular language, but rather the frequency of use of that language in certain domains. Part of these speakers' identities is related to their professions and the social prestige associated with them, which may override other factors such as family background.

8.2 The conditioning of /s/-deletion in Rivera

The deletion of syllable- and word-final /s/ is characteristic of both Spanish and Portuguese. However, as discussed in Section 3, the deletion of /s/ in the Spanish of Rivera is conditioned by morphological constraints, as it is in Brazilian Portuguese. As we have already seen, the aspiration of /s/ in final positions is much more characteristic of speakers who wish to identify with the prestige norms of monolingual Spanish that characterise non-border varieties. The deletion of /s/, on the other hand, lacks sociolinguistic prestige in almost all varieties of Spanish, including those of Uruguay (Lipski 1994). This

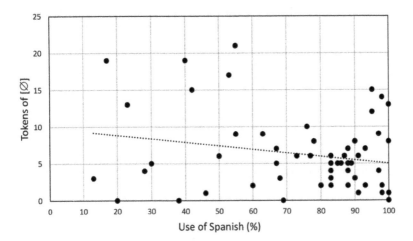

Figure 5.2 Tokens of deletion of syllable- and word-final /s/ according to individual consultants' use of Spanish.

being the case, it seems that there will be a greater likelihood that speakers who identify with Brazil will delete syllable- and word-final /s/.

Portuguese-aligned speakers who identify more closely with Brazilian social and cultural norms are likely to delete /s/ as the result of using Portuguese more frequently than Spanish. To confirm whether this is the case or not, we now look at the distribution of tokens of /s/-deletion for the fifty-seven individuals for whom language use was ascertained. The overall frequency of /s/-deletion for each consultant relative to his or her use of Spanish is shown in Figure 5.2. Although the effect of the use of Spanish on the deletion of /s/ is not as great as that for aspiration (as shown in Figure 5.1), there is a trend among speakers who use Spanish 80 per cent of the time or more to delete /s/ infrequently. Four speakers deviate from this trend. As displayed in Figure 5.2, these four individuals use Spanish 95 per cent of the time or more, but deleted 12–15 tokens of /s/ (i.e. at rates of 24 per cent to 30 per cent). These rates far exceed the overall rate of deletion of /s/ among Spanish-dominant speakers (10.2 per cent) and even that for Portuguese-dominant speakers (16.8 per cent; see Table 5.2). The fact that these four consultants all have non-professional occupations may account for how frequently they delete /s/. Two are hotel receptionists, while the other two operate a food trailer on the border. Since they use Spanish so frequently, it would be expected that they would not delete /s/ in accordance with the morphological patterns of Portuguese discussed in Section 3. This is true for three of the four: consultants 42, 43 and 62 deleted /s/ in strictly phonological contexts 60 per cent of the time or more. The remaining consultant, however, deleted /s/ nine out of twelve times in accordance with the patterns of Portuguese. One possible explanation for this is that he works at a hotel on the main thoroughfare of Rivera (Avenida Sarandí) that accommodates primarily Brazilian guests. Most Brazilians, even those living right across the border in Santana do Livramento, do not speak Spanish. As such, this consultant indicated on the questionnaire that he speaks Portuguese 80 per cent of the time while at work. This explanation seems plausible and parallels that given for the high rates of

Table 5.4 Multivariate analysis of the probabilities of co-occurrence of the deletion of /s/ and usage and attitudinal factors in the Spanish of Rivera ($p < .05$, N = 3,091, Input = 0.119, Log likelihood = -1113.297)

Factor group	Factor	N	% [Ø]	Factor weight
Preference	*Portuguese*	916	17.6	.62
	Spanish	2,175	9.7	.45
				Range 17

Other factor groups included in analysis: (1) Spanish use, (2) Attitudes towards Border Portuguese and (3) Attitudes towards language mixing

aspiration among the three Portuguese-dominant exceptions to the general trend of aspiration correlated with Spanish use that was discussed in the previous section. In each of these exceptional cases, both language use in the workplace as well as occupational type in general seem to override the effects of overall language use.

As shown in Figure 5.2, the effect of Spanish use on the deletion of /s/ does not seem to be overly powerful, especially considering that there are ten speakers using Spanish less than 80 per cent of the time who deleted /s/ five times or fewer (i.e. at rates of 10 per cent or less). The case for the role of Spanish use on the deletion of this phoneme is not a very convincing one. This being so, a separate multivariate analysis using *GoldVarb X* was conducted in which the applied variant was the zero variant, in order to determine the conditioning role of each factor group on the deletion of /s/. The same usage and attitudinal factors used in the analysis of aspiration were included in this analysis, the results of which appear in Table 5.4. Although neither attitudes nor language use condition the deletion of /s/ in the Spanish of Rivera, language preference is significant in its deletion. As shown in Table 5.4, there is a statistically relevant probability that consultants who prefer speaking Portuguese will delete syllable- and word-final /s/. The probability weight generated for this factor (.62) differs greatly from that for Spanish preference (.45), yielding a range of 17. The patterns of /s/-deletion according to language preference are the exact inverse of those for /s/-aspiration. That is, when choosing a variant of /s/, speakers who prefer Portuguese will most likely delete /s/, while those who prefer Spanish will aspirate it.

One major question still remains, however. Do speakers who prefer Portuguese follow the patterns of /s/-deletion that characterise this language? As shown in Table 5.4, these speakers delete /s/ more frequently than do speakers who prefer Spanish, but is this deletion restricted to non-initial NP constituents, as it is in colloquial Brazilian Portuguese? In order to further explore this possibility, a cross-tabulation using morphological status and language preference was conducted. For morphological status, tokens were coded as nouns or adjectives, determiners or non-plurals. The results of this cross-tabulation appear in Table 5.5. These results provide strong evidence that speakers who prefer Portuguese delete plural /s/ according to the morphological constraints that characterise this language. For these speakers, the rate of /s/-deletion is 25.5 per cent for plural nouns and adjectives, which is almost twice the rate of deletion in these contexts for speakers who prefer Spanish. That said, it is true that community members who

Table 5.5 Cross-tabulation of rates of /s/-deletion, as opposed to retention ([s]) or aspiration ([h]), according to morphological status and language preference

Preference	Variant	Morphological status			
		Noun/Adjective	Determiner	Non-plural	Total
Portuguese	[Ø]	64 / 251 **(25.5%)**	2 / 74 (2.7%)	95 / 591 (16.1%)	161 / 916 (17.6%)
	[s / h]	187 / 251 (74.5%)	72 / 74 (97.3%)	496 / 591 (83.9%)	755 / 916 (82.4%)
Spanish	[Ø]	85 / 590 **(14.4%)**	7 / 163 (4.3%)	118 / 1,422 (8.3%)	210 / 2,175 (9.7%)
	[s / h]	505/590 (85.6%)	156/163 (95.7%)	1304/1422 (91.7%)	1965/2175 (90.3%)
Total	[Ø]	149 / 841 (17.7%)	9 / 237 (3.8%)	213 / 2,013 (10.6%)	371 / 3,091 (12.0%)
	[s / h]	692 / 841 (82.3%)	228 / 237 (96.2%)	1,800 / 2,013 (89.4%)	2,720 / 3,091 (88.0%)

prefer Portuguese delete /s/ more overall, even for non-plurals (at 16.1 per cent). Since the deletion of /s/ is not restricted to plurals in Uruguayan Spanish, this implies that these speakers have mutual influences from both Spanish and Portuguese and, as a result, have expanded morphological and phonological repertoires. It is important to note that consultants who prefer Spanish also delete /s/ for plural nouns and adjectives, at a rate of 14.4 per cent. Given that this rate of deletion is higher than the rate of /s/-deletion overall for these speakers, it is fair to say that they too have been influenced by the use of Portuguese within the community. Since this pattern of deletion forms an integral part of the morphological structure of Portuguese, speakers who frequently access this pattern of deletion through the use of the language and a close personal identification with it tend to delete plural /s/ accordingly.

9. Conclusion

Results from this study show that Spanish-dominant speakers tend to aspirate sylla-ble- and word-final /s/ to a much greater extent than Portuguese-dominant speakers. Conversely, the deletion of the consonant, a process lacking sociolinguistic prestige within the community, is statistically favoured among speakers who prefer Portuguese. More importantly, since the conditioning of /s/-deletion patterns in exactly the same way in the Spanish of Rivera as it does in local varieties of Brazilian Portuguese (Carvalho 2006a; Waltermire 2011), deletion is perceived as typically Portuguese, not Spanish. The current research has shown that speakers who prefer Portuguese exhibit plural-marking patterns from this language in their Spanish. It has also been shown that community members, to greater and lesser degrees, exhibit some characteristics borrowed from Portuguese. Those who infrequently utilise Portuguese show very little influence from this language in the use of /s/ articulations, while those who more frequently use Portuguese exhibit a greater degree of influence from Portuguese plural-marking patterns. When choosing a variant of /s/, we may hypothesise that Spanish-dominant speakers tend to aspirate the phoneme in line with the frequency with which they access aspirated articulations of /s/ from stored memory. Similarly, the frequent access of Portuguese morphological patterns results in higher rates of deletion for speakers who prefer to use that language. This is only a general trend, however, as was shown via the analyses of variant usage according to individual consultants' use of Spanish. Several consultants do not conform neatly to the trend. Portuguese-aligned speakers who often aspirate /s/ and Spanish-aligned speakers who often delete it do so as a result of their professional identities and use of the other language in the workplace. With respect to sociolinguistic attitudes, multivariate analysis shows that the aspiration of syllable- and word-final /s/ is favoured by speakers who display negative attitudes towards local varieties of Portuguese. This indicates that these members of the community are trying to distance themselves from local linguistic varieties, while simultaneously aligning themselves more closely with the prestige varieties of monolingual Uruguayan Spanish. In this way, the use of language-specific articulations and patterns of morphological conditioning in the Spanish of Rivera seem to be means by which speakers assert their social and national identities.

Appendix

| Nombre: _____ | Edad: ___ |

Profesión: _____

Nacionalidad: _____

Nacionalidad de padre: _____

Nacionalidad de madre: _____

Frecuencia con que usa el español: %

En casa	20	40	60	80	100
En el trabajo / la escuela	20	40	60	80	100
En la iglesia	20	40	60	80	100
En el banco	20	40	60	80	100
En el correo	20	40	60	80	100
En restaurantes / bares	20	40	60	80	100
Con el marido / la mujer	20	40	60	80	100
Con los hijos	20	40	60	80	100
Con los padres	20	40	60	80	100
Con los parientes	20	40	60	80	100
Con los amigos	20	40	60	80	100
Con el jefe / los maestros	20	40	60	80	100

MUCHÍSIMAS GRACIAS.

Notes

1. Fifty tokens were analysed for each consultant, with three exceptions. Two speakers did not produce enough language during their interviews to reach this number, only producing twenty-five tokens each. A third speaker produced only forty-one tokens. The total number of tokens for all consultants (3,091) was not reached for two factor groups (Spanish use [N = 2,816] and attitudes towards language mixing [N = 2,916]), for reasons described in Sections 5 and 7.

2. Since economic status is not highly divergent for different residents of the community described in this chapter, and as such cannot be seen as the primary determinant of social class, I decided to choose speakers based on occupation, which is perhaps the best overall indicator of social class. Following Labov (2001: 60), 'it is generally agreed that among objective indicators, occupation is the most highly correlated with other conceptions of social class, and much effort has gone into determining the prestige assigned to various occupations.'

3. Although recent policies which have expanded bilingual programmes in the country may reverse this situation gradually over time, the inferior status of Portuguese is unequivocal. As recently as 2003, I observed a sign on a local bus that read *Hablar español es ser uruguayo*, 'To speak Spanish is to be Uruguayan'.

4. Four of the sixty-three consultants did not make comments related to language mixing and, therefore, were excluded from calculations for this factor group.

5. Most notably, Lipski (1988: 315) reports not even a single case of word-final /s/-deletion in pre-vocalic contexts for monolingual Uruguayan Spanish.

6. A crossover, or non-equivalence, in hierarchy rankings between percentages and probability weights for individual factors of a factor group was discovered for speakers claiming ≥ 80 per cent Spanish use and those claiming ≤ 40 per cent use of this language. As shown in Table 5.2, the former group aspirates /s/ at a rate of 31.1 per cent, while the latter aspirates this phoneme only 12 per cent of the time. The ranking of probability weights of the likelihood of aspiration of /s/ by groups according to Spanish use, however, was incongruous with these rates. The probability weight for aspiration of /s/ for the group using Spanish ≥ 80 per cent of the time was only .51 (i.e. very weak), whereas that for the group claiming ≤ 40 per cent use of Spanish was .55.

6

Religion on the Border: The Effect of Utah English on English and Spanish Use in the Mexican Mormon Colonies

Wendy Baker-Smemoe and Breana Jones

1. Introduction

This chapter examines whether religion affects language use in a group of bilingual English–Spanish speakers on the US/Mexico border. This community of small towns and farmlands is called by the local community the 'Mexican Mormon colonies'. The community is composed of descendants of English speakers who purchased lands in Mexico in 1885 to escape what they perceived as religious persecution as members of the Church of Jesus Christ of Latter-day Saints (LDS), the adherents of which are commonly known as Mormons (Romney 1938). This study examines the phonological features of their descendants as well as those of local residents already settled in the area, some of whom also became LDS. The region provides a unique opportunity to study the influence of religion, ethnicity and bilingualism on regional dialects, since the inhabitants use both English and Spanish and are divided socially into ethnic and religious groups, living 'on the border' with respect to culture, language and religion. In particular, this research was conducted to determine whether the participants' English is influenced by Utah English, if these features are carried into their Spanish (by both native English and native Spanish speakers) and if these features mainly occur in speakers who self-identify as LDS.

2. Religion, identity and language use

Numerous studies of language and identity have shown that different groups index their identities by using different lexical, phonological and grammatical features to distinguish themselves from other groups (Silverstein 2003). These linguistic features may index a speaker's gender, age, socio-economic class and ethnicity (Labov 2001), as well as less overarching demographics such as musical tastes (Morgan 2001) and even membership of a club or organisation (Moore 2010). Use of such features, like one's identity, is fluid, and their use can differ depending on the person with whom the speaker is conversing (through accommodation; Llamas et al. 2009), what aspects of one's identity or self are important at the time (stance; Eckert 2000) and what stage in life the person is at (Bowie 2010; Sankoff and Blondeau 2007).

More and more researchers are examining the specific effects that one's religious affiliation can have on language use and change (Di Paolo 1993; Baker and Bowie 2009; Fox 2010; Samant 2010). Such research has found that a speaker's religious affiliation can impact the language someone speaks (Hamburger 2005), the people someone identifies and interacts with (Watson-Gageo and Gageo 1991) and even where someone lives (Kingsmore 1995). These differences can be as large as differences in languages (Johnson-Weiner 1998) or as small as the production of a single sound (Benor 2001).

One difficulty with previous studies is teasing apart religion from variables such as ethnicity and region. For example, Kingsmore (1995) found that language differences between Belfast Catholics and Protestants were more geographical than religious. In fact, in areas such as Belfast, neighbourhoods are often designated as being inhabited by people of one religion (and/or ethnic group) or another. However, recent studies have also determined that religion can impact language use even in non-segregated communities, at least in areas where religion is an especially salient social characteristic. One area of this kind is Utah in the western United States, especially northern Utah. A large percentage (61–72 per cent) of the population of this region self-identify as members of the LDS Church (US Religious Landscape Survey 2008). Di Paolo (1993) and Baker and Bowie (2009) have compared the linguistic behaviour of Mormons and non-Mormons in Utah, finding that the two groups exhibit significant differences from one another. For example, Baker and Bowie (2009) demonstrated that listeners trained in phonetics were able to hear a difference between vowels spoken by Mormons and non-Mormons, all of whom had been raised in Utah.

In addition, several recent studies have determined that religion may play an especially significant role in immigrant populations whose ethnicity differs from that of the majority, as is the case for the LDS community studied in this chapter. Samant (2010) examined whether Lebanese Muslims living in Michigan exhibited features of the Northern Cities Shift (NCS) by interviewing high-school students who differed in terms of gender, religious activity and ethnicity. Samant demonstrated that whether or not features of the NCS were found in an informant's speech was related in part to how actively involved that speaker was in the Muslim community. Importantly, she also showed that even those speakers who used features of the NCS did so differently from the non-Muslim speakers in the area. Similarly, Fox (2010) found that young Bangladeshi Muslims living in Tower Hamlets, London, used fewer of the typical vowel features found in traditional working-class London English ('Cockney') than did the other inhabitants. Instead, their vowels were more strongly influenced by their native language, Sylheti. In addition to demonstrating the influence of religion on language use, Fox's findings also suggest that bilingualism may be one way in which different religious groups assert their religious and ethnic identity.

What if groups have the same religion but different ethnicities? What occurs when religion and ethnicity intersect in a bilingual community, as is the case in the Mexican Mormon colonies? Non-Hispanic native English speakers immigrated to this area and interacted with Hispanic native Spanish speakers, some of whom converted to the LDS Church. Others in the area did not. This has created three groups: non-Hispanic

LDS native English speakers, Hispanic LDS native Spanish speakers and Hispanic non-LDS native Spanish speakers, all of whom are raised in a bilingual community. These groups provide us with the opportunity to determine how religion, language and ethnicity interact in border towns along the boundary between two nations.

3. LDS religion and features of Utah English

Although no known studies have previously examined the phonological features of English (or Spanish) in the LDS settlements in Mexico, previous research has examined the effect of being LDS on language use in other LDS settlements. LDS members settled areas across the borders of the United States and both Canada and Mexico. Research focusing on LDS settlements in Alberta, Canada, suggests that the LDS Canadians in this area use fewer features of Canadian English than do other residents of the same area (Meechan 1998). More recent research has demonstrated that the LDS Canadians also use a feature of Utah English – the *card~cord* merger – and have this merger more than do other Canadians (Chatterton 2008). In other words, religion is related not only to whether or not the speakers use features of Utah English, but also to how much they use features typical of the area in which they live. In the current study, we examine whether features of Utah English are in evidence in the speech of the LDS native English speakers of the community, and whether they have also been acquired by the native Spanish speakers. We also consider whether the speakers have acquired features of Northern Mexican Spanish, and how religion and ethnicity affect their use of the forms of interest. In particular, the following research questions guide this study:

1. Do religion and ethnicity influence whether features of Utah English are used in the English spoken in the Mexican Mormon colonies?
2. Do religion and ethnicity influence whether features of Utah English are used in the Spanish spoken in the Mexican Mormon colonies?
3. Does religion influence how features of Northern Mexican Spanish are used?
4. Are differences between LDS and non-LDS speakers the result of different religions or different demographic variables (such as ethnicity, age and gender)?

4. Historical/social context

The geographical context of this study is the area comprising the towns of Nuevo Casas Grandes, Casas Grandes, Colonia Dublán and Colonia Juárez in Casas Grandes Valley, Chihuahua, Mexico. These colonies were settled in 1885 by Utah Mormons escaping what they perceived to be religious persecution in the United States. The current residents still have ties to, and in many ways still identify with, Utah. Most of the non-Hispanic inhabitants are descendants of these early settlers, they often have dual citizenship with the USA and Mexico, and they often own land in Texas or Arizona (although at the time of the study they typically spent most of their time in Mexico). The largest city has approximately 50,000 residents, and the entire area has a population of approximately 100,000, about 5 per cent of whom are LDS. The majority of people own and live or work on farms. Most new native English-speaking residents and teachers are from Utah, which helps to strengthen ties to this English variety. Although the non-Hispanic inhabitants of the area are in the minority, they tend to be the ones who own the land and are perceived to be the district's most prestigious residents.

The other participants in the study are Hispanics whose families have lived for genera- tions in the area. When the US LDS settlers bought the land in Mexico, the Mexican government required that native Mexicans also move into the area at the same time. During the hundred years since the Casas Grandes valley was settled, some of the native Mexicans who settled there have joined the LDS Church, and church services began to be conducted in both English and Spanish.

In 1889 a bilingual school was established in Casas Grandes, which today is where most LDS residents attend school. The school is also the place where many learn either Spanish or English, depending on which is dominant in their homes. The demographic profile of the school shows that students are approximately 70 per cent LDS and 30 per cent non-LDS; 90 per cent are native Spanish speakers and 10 per cent are native English speakers. All participants in this study graduated from this bilingual school.

5. Methodology

5.1 Participants

As explained above, participants were divided into three groups: native English speak- ers who grew up in the Mexican colonies (hereafter 'English LDS') (N = 19), native Spanish speakers who grew up in the same area and who are members of the LDS Church (hereafter 'Spanish LDS') (N = 19) and native Spanish speakers who grew up in the same area but are not members of the LDS Church (hereafter 'Spanish non-LDS') (N = 10). None of the speakers we examined was raised bilingually in the home, because it is very rare for people from different racial groups to intermarry. Most families speak only one language in the home (either English or Spanish) and speak both languages in the community. In addition, if native English speakers decide to leave the LDS Church, they also tend to leave the area, so that there are very few non-LDS native English speakers.

The participants' ages, their proficiency in English and Spanish, and their amount of English and Spanish daily use, as well as other demographic data, are given in Table 6.1. Spanish and English use was determined by asking the participants how often they used English and Spanish in different situations (at home, school, church, etc.) and their overall use of English in a typical week. Statistical analyses determined that the three groups did not differ according to speaker age ($F(2,49) = 2.56$, $p < .05$), although they did differ in terms of self-rated Spanish and English ability and the degree to which they reported using Spanish and English (all F's > 3.56, all p's $< .05$). As shown in Table 6.1, the Spanish LDS sample contained more males than females. This is not a result of properties of the population, but of the sampling methods.

5.2 Procedure

Data were taken from semi-structured interviews in which the participants were asked to answer questions designed to elicit the phonetic features of interest. Participants completed the interview in both English and Spanish, since our intention was to examine

Table 6.1 Demographic characteristics of the three participant groups

	Mean age	Gender	Spanish ability	English ability	Total Spanish use	Total English use
LDS English (N = 19)	30.47	55% M, 45% F	8.3	9.7	35%	65%
LDS Spanish (N = 19)	30.7	78% M, 22% F	9.8	7.2	79%	21%
Non-LDS Spanish (N = 10)	28.5	50% M, 50% F	10	8.6	83%	17%

phonetic features in both languages. They also read a short story that contained these features. Participants were interviewed by a resident of the area who spoke in both Spanish and English to the participants.

5.3 Features examined

5.3.1 English

We examined whether features of Utah English were used by the participants in this study. Many researchers have examined the features of Utah English that distinguish it from other western varieties of American English (e.g. Baker and Bowie 2009). Most of this variation concerns tense-lax vowel mergers (or near-mergers; see Di Paolo and Faber 1990) before /l/ (*fail~fell*, *fill~feel*, *pool~pull~pole*) and mergers before /r/ (*card~cord*). Other salient features include releasing glottal stops orally rather than nasally before nasals (as in the word 'mountain') (Eddington and Savage 2012) and epenthetic [t] between laterals and other sonorants (*Nelson* pronounced as *Nel*[t] *son*). Previous research on Utah English suggests that these differences between Utah English and other western varieties may be the result of a higher percentage of the first settlers coming from England and other foreign countries (Bowie 2003; Di Paolo 1993) and a consequence of the influences of the dialect of Missouri (Bowie 2003; Morkel 2003).

Importantly, the *card~cord* merger may have been part of the Utah dialect since at least the late 1800s, that is, before the Mexican colonies were settled (Bowie 2003). This makes it likely that at least some of the first inhabitants may have had the merger when they settled in the colonies. We also examined pre-lateral laxing because of its prevalence in Utah English today, and because these mergers distinguish LDS from non-LDS Utah English speakers in Utah (Baker and Bowie 2009). In particular, we chose to examine three pre-lateral tense-lax vowel mergers (*feel~fill* merged to *fill*; *pool~pull~pole* merged to *pole*; *fail~fell* merged to *fell*) and one pre-rhotic vowel merger (*card~cord* merged to *card*). For ease of description, we will refer to these mergers by these names, even when discussing parallel forms in Spanish or when talking about only the tense vowels in the vowel pair. In nearly every case, we examined the mergers in monosyllabic words, since mergers typically occur when the lateral is in the same syllable (for example, *feel* vs. *feeling*). The only word where this rule was not followed was the word *really*. However, we confirmed that the merger takes place in this environment as well. The Appendix contains a list of all the words analysed in this study.

5.3.2 Spanish

We asked our participants to complete the semi-structured interviews in both English and Spanish. In Spanish, we also examined pre-lateral laxing and the equivalent of the *card~cord* merger in their Spanish vowel system. In addition, we examined the use of the voiced bilabial stop when the sound is orthographically depicted by the letter <v>. Most modern dialects of Spanish, including Northern Mexican Spanish, produce words traditionally spelled with a <v> as [b] in initial position and [β] intervocalically (Alba 1998). Probably because of orthography, there is a tendency to produce words spelled with <v> with [v], especially by non-native Spanish speakers.

It is difficult to determine whether or not vowel mergers, if found in the speech of our participants, are a result of Utah English influence on this region. There are several reasons that mergers may occur. Pre-lateral laxing occurs independently in several English varieties, including those of areas directly across the border from the Mexican colonies (see Labov et al. 2006). In addition, it is possible that laxing may occur in Mexican Spanish and may influence dialect variation. However, the most comprehensive examination of Mexican Spanish carried out to date suggests that laxing does not in fact occur in Northern Mexican Spanish (Alvar 2010). In fact, Spanish vowel laxing in the Americas does not seem to occur in any phonetic environment (Lipski 2008), even among bilingual speakers (see Willis 2005 and his analysis of vowels of varieties spoken in New Mexico).

Our main goal in this study is to examine whether the three groups examined – English LDS, Spanish LDS and Spanish non-LDS – differ in how the mergers are manifested in their speech, regardless of the origin of these phenomena. Where the mergers come from historically is not the focus of this study.

6. Data analysis

The data were analysed using two methods. First, both authors listened to every participant's interview and determined the number of phonologically tense vowels that were produced as lax vowels before /l/, and productions of /ɔr/ (as in *cord*) produced as /ɑr/ (as in *card*). Any disagreements between the two authors were resolved via re-evaluation of the material in question. Second, acoustic analyses were made of a subset of the vowels of interest, /i e o u ɑ/. These vowels were measured in both pre-lateral and pre-rhotic positions as well as in other phonetic environments, in order to compare vowel differences across pre-liquid versus other environments. Fundamental frequency and the two lowest-frequency formants were measured to determine variations in vowel height (estimated from F1) and frontness (F2) at the temporal midpoint of each of the vowels. F3, as a correlate of lip rounding, was also measured, but for ease of discussion the F3 results are not given here. Formant frequencies were converted to the Bark scale using the formula given by Syrdal and Gopal (1986).

7. Results

7.1 Research question 1: vowel mergers in English

We first examined whether the three groups (English LDS, Spanish LDS, Spanish non-LDS) differed in the number of English vowel mergers they exhibited by listening to the interviews and categorising vowels produced before /l/ (the *feel~fill, fail~fell* and *pool~pull~pole* mergers) and /r/ (the *card~cord* merger). The average percentage of the time that each group produced pre-lateral (phonologically) tense vowels as lax, and (historical) /ɔr/ vowels as /ɑr/, is given in Figure 6.1.

A series of one-way ANOVAs was run on the data from this analysis for each of the mergers, with the percentage of phonologically tense vowels produced as their lax counterparts as the dependent variable, and speaker group (English LDS, Spanish-LDS, Spanish-non-LDS) as the independent variable. We found a significant difference between the three groups for the *feel~fill* and the *fail~fell* mergers (both F's (2,49) = 3.95, $p < .02$, $\eta_p^2 < .144$), but not for the other two mergers (F(2,49)'s < .279, p's < .780, η_p^2's < .012). Post-hoc Tukey tests found that for both mergers where a significant effect was reported there was a significant difference between the English LDS and Spanish-non-LDS groups, but no such difference between those two groups and the Spanish LDS group. This analysis suggests that religion and ethnicity may, as hypothesised, influence the production of vowels in English.

To double-check the validity of our perceptual observations, we ran another analysis on the same vowels, this time using the acoustic measurements described above. Specifically, we ran a series of repeated-measures ANOVAs on both the height (F1) and frontness (F2) of the vowels in question. We ran two analyses for the pre-lateral vowels: one where we compared tense and lax vowels before /l/, and a second one in which we compared tense vowels pre-laterally (*really, feel*) versus other phonetic contexts (*free, me, feed*). Since the results of these two analyses came to the same conclusions, we report

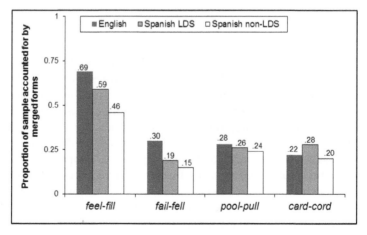

Figure 6.1 Average proportion of sample accounted for by merged forms, by speaker group and vowel pairing (English).

here only the analysis of tense vowels before laterals versus other phonetic contexts. We report this analysis because it allows us to make comparisons with a similar analysis on Spanish vowels. We hypothesised that if the vowels in pre-lateral position were lower and more centralised, it would suggest that the tense vowels were produced more like their lax counterparts. For the vowels before /r/, a merger would occur if there were no significant difference between the vowels /ɔ/ and /ɑ/ where they precede /r/. Another series of repeated-measures ANOVAs were run for each group's productions of each of the vowel pairs. The results of these analyses of each of the mergers for each of the three groups are given in Table 6.2.

As Table 6.2 indicates, there are differences between the three participant groups. First, the English LDS speakers seem to lax all three tense vowels (/i/, /e/ and /u/) in pre-lateral position, with vowels before /l/ being more centralised than vowels in other phonetic environments. Only the height of the vowel /i/ did not differ in cases where it occurred before /l/ versus its realisation in other phonetic environments. The English LDS speakers also merge *card* and *cord* in both vowel height and frontness. Second, the Spanish LDS group also seem to lax all three pre-lateral vowels, but they did not exhibit the *card~cord* merger, nor did they lower /i/ and /u/ pre-laterally. Finally, the Spanish non-LDS speakers tended towards laxing on the vowel frontness (F2) dimension only for English /u/, but they did have the *card~cord* merger. The results of this analysis concur in part with the perceptual analyses: there is a difference between each of the three speaker groups, with the English LDS group producing the most features of Utah English, followed by the Spanish LDS and then Spanish non-LDS group.

7.2 Vowel mergers in Spanish

The next research question was to determine whether tense vowels are laxed before /l/ in Spanish. We hypothesised that the mergers found in Utah English might have 'transferred' into their Spanish, as sometimes occurs with second-language learners or bilinguals (O'Brien and Smith 2010). It is also possible, of course, that laxing might occur in Spanish as an independent language change, although no such change has been documented in the area (Alvar 2010).

As with the English analysis, we first transcribed the vowels in pre-/l/ and pre-/r/ positions, and in other phonological contexts. Unlike in English, however, there are few contexts in which laterals and rhotics occur in the same syllable as the target vowels, although they do occur in some words (such as *ulcero*, *aquel*). Nevertheless, we still found that some of the vowels even in these environments were produced more like lax vowels. The results are given in Figure 6.2. As with the English vowels, a series of one-way ANOVAs were run on the data with the number of lax vowels as the dependent variable, and speaker group as the independent variable. The results of these analyses revealed that there was a significant difference between the groups with respect to the merger of /i/ before /l/ (F(2,49) = 4.88, p = .012, η_p^2 = .172) and the *card~cord* (F(2,49) = 6.27, p = .003, η_p^2 = .224) merger. Post-hoc Tukey tests revealed that for /i/ the English LDS group had the highest proportion of laxed vowels, followed by the Spanish LDS group and finally the Spanish non-LDS group. This was not the case with *card~cord*: while the English LDS group had the most *card~cord* mergers, the Spanish non-LDS group had more mergers than did the LDS Spanish group.

Table 6.2 Comparisons of vowel height (F1) and vowel frontness (F2) in pre-liquid versus other phonetic contexts in English for each of the tense vowels examined (shaded boxes indicate vowels pronounced with their typical Utah English qualities)

	/i/-/il/		/e/-/el/		/u/-/ul/		/ɔr/-/ɑr/	
	F1	F2	F1	F2	F1	F2	F1	F2
English LDS	F(1,18) = .001 p = .975 η_p^2 = .000	F(1,18) = 44.92 p = .0001 η_p^2 = .714	F(1,18) = 6.51 p = .02 η_p^2 = .266	F(1,18) = 22.15 p = .0001 η_p^2 = .552	F(1,18) = 51.73 p = .0001 η_p^2 = .742	F(1,18) = 151.94 p = .0001 η_p^2 = .894	F(1,18) = .303 p = .589, η_p^2 = -.017	F(1,18) = .852 p = .368 η_p^2 = .045
Spanish LDS	F(1,18) = .038 p = .847 η_p^2 = .001	F(1,18) = 57.51 p = .0001 η_p^2 = .650	F(1,18) = 9.823 p = .005 η_p^2 = .223	F(1,18) = .306 p = .587 η_p^2 = .018	F(1,18) = 11.00 p = .004 η_p^2 = .379	F(1,18) = 78.29 p = .0001 η_p^2 = .813	F(1,18) = 40.7 p = .0001 η_p^2 = .693	F(1,18) = 17.578 p = .001 η_p^2 = .494
Spanish non-LDS	F(1,9) = 1.02 p = .324 η_p^2 = .054	F(1,9) = 4.32 p = .06 η_p^2 = .194	F(1,9) = 3.15 p = .110 η_p^2 = .259	F(1,9) = .132 p = .725 η_p^2 = .014	F(1,9) = .214 p = .655 η_p^2 = .023	F(1,9) = 40.27 p = .0001 η_p^2 = .817	F(1,9) = 9.38 p = .015 η_p^2 = .508	F(1,9) = 1.53 p = .251 η_p^2 = .161

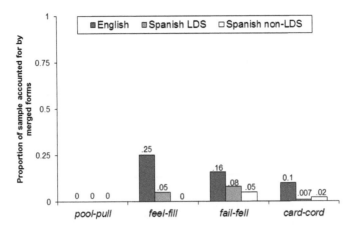

Figure 6.2 Average proportion of sample accounted for by merged forms, by speaker group and vowel pairing (Spanish).

The acoustic analyses of the Spanish vowels before laterals and rhotics revealed similar results. Spanish has only tense vowels, but we examined whether there were differences in the vowels produced before laterals and rhotics versus those in other phonetic contexts. These results are given in Table 6.3, with the highlighted cells suggesting laxing for pre-lateral tense vowels and merging of pre-rhotic vowels. As with the English vowels, the English LDS group demonstrated vowel laxing in all three vowels, either in terms of vowel height or vowel frontness and merged /ɔr/~/ɑr/ vowels. The same was true for the Spanish LDS group. By contrast, the Spanish non-LDS group showed differences between pre-lateral and pre-rhotic positions and other phonetic contexts for only vowel frontness in two of the vowels.

7.3 Merger of /b/-/v/ in Spanish

Our third research question was to determine if the three groups also differed in their productions of Spanish features not related to vowel mergers. To do this, we determined whether the three groups differed in their use of [b] for [β] or [v]. Unlike what was done for the above analyses, we performed a perceptual and acoustic analysis at the same time, in which we examined whether sounds orthographically depicted as <v> were produced as stops or fricatives. In order to do this, we listened to speakers' productions at the beginnings of words, where it was easier to determine whether the initial sound was produced as a stop or a fricative, while simultaneously examining the waveform. If we detected a burst and Voice Onset Time (as is found in stops), the production was marked as a [b]. If we observed frication and aperiodicity, we marked the initial sound as [v]. No attempt was made to determine the difference between bilabial [β] and labiodental [v], since determining the difference between these is difficult without using equipment that can measure lip movement (Maddieson 2005).

After determining the number of times each participant produced as a bilabial stop the initial sound of words with written forms that start with the letter <v>, we ran a

Table 6.3 Comparisons of vowel height (F1) and vowel frontness (F2) in pre-liquid versus other phonetic contexts in Spanish for each of the vowels examined (shaded boxes indicate vowels pronounced with their typical Utah English qualities)

	/i/-/il/		/e/-/el/		/u/-/ul/		/ɔr/-/ɑr/	
	F1	F2	F1	F2	F1	F2	F1	F2
English LDS	$F_{(1,18)} = 1.19$ $p = .29$ $\eta^2_p = -.066$	$F_{(1,18)} = 6.99$ $p = .01$ $\eta^2_p = .29$	$F_{(1,18)} = 9.91$ $p = .006$ $\eta^2_p = .355$	$F_{(1,18)} = 9.17$ $p = .007$ $\eta^2_p = .338$	$F_{(1,18)} = .001$ $p = .001$ $\eta^2_p = .000$	$F_{(1,18)} = 27.68$ $p = .0001$ $\eta^2_p = .634$	$F_{(1,18)} = 6.89$ $p = .001$ $\eta^2_p = .277$	$F_{(1,18)} = 1.77$ $p = .2$ $\eta^2_p = .09$
Spanish LDS	$F_{(1,18)} = .409$ $p = .530$ $\eta^2_p = .022$	$F_{(1,18)} = 13.76$ $p = .002$ $\eta^2_p = .433$	$F_{(1,18)} = 6.2$ $p = .02$ $\eta^2_p = .279$	$F_{(1,18)} = 3.99$ $p = .06$ $\eta^2_p = .20$	$F_{(1,18)} = 7.80$ $p = .01$ $\eta^2_p = .31$	$F_{(1,18)} = 13.01$ $p = .002$ $\eta^2_p = .434$	$F_{(1,18)} = 41.38$ $p = .000$ $\eta^2_p = .709$	$F_{(1,18)} = .269$ $p = .611$ $\eta^2_p = .016$
Spanish non-LDS	$F_{(1,9)} = .027$ $p = .874$ $\eta^2_p = .003$	$F_{(1,9)} = .252$ $p = .629$ $\eta^2_p = .031$	$F_{(1,9)} = 1.22$ $p = .317$ $\eta^2_p = -.111$	$F_{(1,9)} = 17.05$ $p = .003$ $\eta^2_p = .655$	$F_{(1,9)} = .301$ $p = .596$ $\eta^2_p = .03$	$F_{(1,9)} = 4.42$ $p = .06$ $\eta^2_p = .33$	$F_{(1,9)} = 20.74$ $p = .001$ $\eta^2_p = .697$	$F_{(1,9)} = .990$ $p = .346$ $\eta^2_p = -.09$

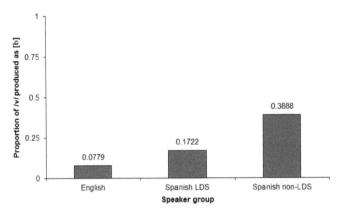

Figure 6.3 Average proportion of sample accounted for by production of /v/ as [b] in spoken Spanish, by speaker group.

one-way ANOVA with the number of tokens of [b] versus [v] for each of the three groups as the dependent variable, and speaker group as the independent variable. This analysis revealed a significant effect of group (F(2,44) = 18.13, p = .0001, η_p^2 = .463). Post-hoc Tukey tests determined that the English LDS and Spanish LDS groups did not differ from each other statistically, but did differ in this way from the Spanish non-LDS group. The Spanish non-LDS group produced significantly more bilabial stop productions in this phonetic context than did the other two groups; see Figure 6.3.

8. The effect of other demographic variables

The final research question asked whether it is religion or other demographic variables (gender, age, ethnicity) that is more related to the use of Utah English forms in the participants' English and Spanish. We ran three linear stepwise multiple regression analyses and three sets of correlations on the frequency counts of tense vowels which had been produced as lax pre-laterally and pre-rhotically as against the number of productions of bilabial stops when the written form of a word began with the letter <v>. The demographic variables included in these analyses were age, religion, gender and ethnicity (Hispanic or non-Hispanic). The results revealed the following:

1. Tense vowels in English. Religion, gender and ethnicity were all correlated with the percentage of laxed tense vowels in English (correlations: religion, .336, gender, .334, ethnicity, .302, all significant at the .05 level); religion (r^2 = .11) and gender (r^2 = .14) were the only significant predictors of the proportion of laxed tense vowels in English when a multiple regression analysis (MRA) was run.
2. Tense vowels in Spanish. Only ethnicity correlated with, and was found to be a significant predictor of, laxed tense vowels in Spanish (correlations: ethnicity, .497, significant at the .01 level; MRA r^2 = .247).
3. [b] for [v] in Spanish. Religion was highly correlated with the production of labiodental fricatives in place of bilabial stops or fricatives, as was ethnicity

(correlations: religion, .65, ethnicity, .44, both significant at the .01 level); MRA demonstrated that only religion was shown to be a significant predictor: $r^2 =. 385$.

Thus, religion, gender and ethnicity were all found to influence the variables we studied, though determining whether or not these non-linguistic variables *caused* the differences in pronunciation is difficult. Moreover, without data from a group of non-LDS non-Hispanic participants, it is difficult to tease apart the influence of religion and ethnicity. What these findings do suggest, however, is that religion and ethnicity are related to the nature of speakers' productions more than age and gender are.

9. Discussion and conclusions

The results of this study demonstrate that features of Utah English may be found in the English and Spanish of the residents of the Mexican Mormon colonies. Moreover, although earlier studies have found effects for age, location, ethnicity and gender on language use, this is perhaps the first study in which language use is related most closely to the speaker's religion and ethnicity. Also, although previous studies have demonstrated a linguistic difference in sectarian and non-sectarian groups in other areas (Huffines 1986), this is the first study to demonstrate such differences in terms of ethnicity and religion. The results of the present study have specific implications for the study of language and identity, especially in border situations where speakers of two languages across two political or social borders interact.

First, residents of this area seem to express separate identities through the number of Utah English features they use, as well as the number of Spanish features they *don't* use. These divisions also appear to enhance or reflect participants' membership of religious and/or ethnic groupings. For example, the Spanish LDS group, which is similar to the English LDS group in terms of religion and similar to the Spanish non-LDS group in terms of ethnicity, seem to distinguish themselves from both the LDS English speakers (by using fewer and different features of Utah English) and from the non-LDS Spanish speakers (by distinguishing between word initial [b] and [v]). They seem to straddle two identities and use features of Utah English and Northern Mexican Spanish in ways that make them both similar to and separate from the other two groups. These results can be seen to demonstrate that the identities of speakers in the Spanish LDS group are created in the 'negotiation of participation in multiple communities of practice' (Eckert and Wenger 1993), these communities being defined by both religion and ethnicity. Such results also reflect the fact that the two features in their community where identity is maintained most are those of religion and ethnicity.

Second, unlike the colonies in Canada, the colonists from Utah in Mexico seem to have held on to forms of Utah English. Similar LDS colonies in Canada have lost most of the features of Utah English, except for the *card~cord* merger (Chatterton 2008). In addition, the LDS Mexico settlers seem to have maintained features now possibly dying out in Utah, such as the *card~cord* merger (Lillie 1998). In fact, these features are prevalent among both older and younger speakers, suggesting their pervasiveness and fortitude across time.

Why the LDS Mexico settlers have kept these features may be because most colonies tend to retain older forms for longer than is the case in the mother country (or mother region; Trudgill 1999); or it may be that doing so helps in retaining these speakers' identity as members of the LDS Church. Future studies that compare historical examinations of the features of interest (especially the *card~cord* merger) would be helpful. The settlers may also have kept these features because native English speakers interact mainly with native Spanish speakers in Spanish, and only with each other in English. Therefore, the social networks and communities of practice in which English is used only involve the members of these colonies, and typically relatives from Utah. This was especially true during the development of the variety, when travel was difficult. Moreover, even today these English speakers are insular, separated from other speakers by farmlands, religion and ethnicity.

Finally, the non-LDS Spanish speakers have adopted features of Utah English (although fewer of them) in both English and Spanish. Their only interaction with native English speakers is with the English LDS group, and it was from them that they would have learned their English. What is surprising is that, despite this, members of the Spanish non-LDS group have opted not to adopt many of the Utah English features in their speech, at least not to the degree of the other groups. These findings also demonstrate that dominant groups may accommodate to features of a non-dominant group, while still keeping their identity through not adopting them to the same degree.

Perhaps the differences among the groups' use of Utah English features is not as simple as merely differences in religion and ethnicity. Along with ethnicity, there is most likely a difference in participants' attitudes towards living in the area, differences in languages and differences in the level of active involvement and identification with one's religious and ethnic groups. For example, it is difficult to determine whether the English LDS group has maintained features of Utah English in their Spanish across several generations so as to keep a distinction between them and other religions or other ethnicities, as Bakos (2008) found for Lebanese Muslims in Michigan. It also may be that converts to Mormonism may exhibit fewer (or indeed more) features of the dialect than those who are not converts, or those with a long versus a short family history in the Church. Moreover, it is unknown whether speakers of these varieties are participating in sound changes otherwise taking place in the region. Future studies will hopefully tease apart these questions, and will therefore better illuminate how languages interact with identity along the US/Mexico border.

Appendix: English and Spanish words subjected to acoustic analysis

English

	/i/	/ɪ/	/e/	/ɛ/	/u/	/ʊ/	/ɔr/	/ar/
Before /l/ or /r/	kneel feel sealed really	fill filling milk pill	bail fail available	fell	school rules cool pool fool	bullet pulled full pull	divorced horrible oral born	Laura warm ward barn
Other contexts	she's week cheat free	did hit	hey break	memorize tests stress bed	you true	would could	know both	mom got

Spanish

	/i/	/e/	/u/	/or/	/ar/
Before /l/ or /r/	ilegal, 'illegal'	aquel, 'that' sellados, 'sealed' religión, 'religion'	fulano, 'somebody'	jornada, 'day' divorciada, 'divorced' horrible, 'horrible'	barba, 'beard'
Other contexts	vivir, 'to live' dieras, 'give'	desafortunado, 'unfortunate' sentirías, 'feel'	tuberculosis, 'tuberculosis' fugarias, 'escape'		

7

Borders within Borders: Contexts of Language Use and Local Identity Configuration in Southern Galicia

Jaine Beswick

I. Introduction

Although the River Minho constitutes both a geographical and political state border between Galicia and Portugal (see Figure 7.1), local communities maintain regular cross-border commercial contact and communication with each other. Initial research in the area carried out in the late 1990s[1] raised the question of whether, from a linguistic perspective, the degree of mutual intelligibility and structural similarity between the respective language varieties and the presence of certain phonological features might be facilitating such inter-group contact. However, this research did not take into consideration the multilingual configuration of the area or the sociolinguistic relationship of Galician with Castilian Spanish within a society in which bilingualism may be widespread but does not imply allegiance to the state-sponsored language. Nor did it consider Galician's sociohistorical relationship with Portuguese, which was ostensibly the same language until the Middle Ages. In order to address these issues, the role of the localised language variety in cross-border identification practices necessitated further investigation, and to this end, in the present chapter we draw on data collected in 2010 and 2011 from speakers living and working in the towns of Tui (Galicia) and Valença (Portugal) in the borderlands of the River Minho.

In line with socio-psychological approaches to identity such as Social Identity Theory (Tajfel 1978), we consider individual linguistic repertoires and the role of symbolic borders that determine group inclusion and exclusion in the configuration of local identities. The objectives of the present research are threefold:

1. to document the continued presence of certain phonological phenomena in a language contact scenario: specifically, in inter-group commercial interactions between individuals of the Minho borderland communities;
2. to observe the use of such phenomena as part of a localised linguistic variety;
3. to examine and analyse speakers' perceptions regarding their use of such

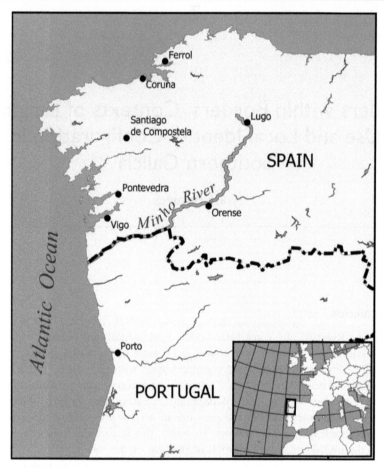

Figure 7.1 Map of the Minho River in Portugal and Spain (Norman Einstein, 25.8.2005.
Permission is granted to copy, distribute and/or modify this document under the terms of the
GNU Free Documentation License.)

phenomena and their value in the utilisation of localised identification
strategies.

The main hypothesis is that individuals may identify with their interlocutors whom they
consider to be part of a particular in-group through the use of particular phonological
habits in specific contexts, irrespective of any other identification practices, allegiances
to the nation, etc. We investigate how speakers' attitudes towards accent variation, code-
switching phenomena and phonological production strategies in socio-economic interactions across the geo-linguistic border interact with their socio-psychological perceptions
regarding in-group and out-group membership. However, we also examine pervading
ideological precepts concerning language status and contexts of use in Galicia, since
current issues regarding the levelling of Galician accent and dialect variation and the
functional distribution of Castilian in the region may in a sense be engendering other

socio-psychological borders. These borders would be made visible through behaviours relating to identity inclusion and exclusion exhibited by the local Galician group in ways that are distinct from those of their Portuguese neighbours.

2. The Galician–Portuguese borderlands

The research discussed in this chapter was carried out between 2010 and 2011 in Valença do Minho and Tui. Valença is a small fortified walled town of some 15,000 inhabitants located in the most northerly Portuguese province of Viano do Castelo (Guia Turístico de Valença 2014: 3). Tui is located in the southern Galician province of Pontevedra and has about 17,000 inhabitants. Both towns sit on the River Minho, Valença on its left bank and Tui on its right. The river thus constitutes a geographical, national border between Spain and Portugal. Indeed, and exacerbated no doubt by centuries of military and political disagreement, traditional narratives concerning the nature of Spanish and Portuguese identity have generally highlighted differences rather than similarities between the two nations, and, in a similar vein, historical accounts of Galicia and Portugal have until recently also focused on perceived differences rather than on their shared ethnic and linguistic origins. As far back as the sixth century, competing urban and religious centres were established on either side of the current border; by the thirteenth century Galicia was subsumed into the Kingdom of Castile, and the newly created Kingdom of Portugal had transferred its power base southward to Lisbon. Yet despite the differing political, social and historical trajectories that Portugal and Galicia were to take over the centuries, the communities living in and around the fertile river valley of the Baixo Minho (in Portuguese; Baixo Miño, in Galician) long maintained cross-border alliances and commerce involving illegal trade by boat in coffee, linen and alcohol (Beswick 2005: 45), facilitated by the lack of a clearly demarcated political border until the early twentieth century and by the linguistic similarities between the varieties spoken along the river.[2] Even the imposition of strict border controls after the Second World War did not stop these transactions, and the incipient economic growth of the region in the 1960s and 1970s, as well as the attendant development of new railway and public transport systems,[3] membership of the EU and the opening up of European borders under the terms of the Schengen Agreement have now legitimised such cross-border movement and trade.[4]

Agriculture and fishing still play significant roles in the area, and in Valença there are thriving textile and artisanal industries, the majority of which are located in the historic district of the town, which acts as a pilgrimage centre and is the site of a huge outdoor market of goods such as gold jewellery, pottery, lingerie and towelling.[5] This not only provides a focus for contact between the communities under discussion, but also serves the burgeoning tourism industry catering to visitors principally from Spain who support the cafés, restaurants, shops, hotels, museums and historical sites.

In recent times, Tui has developed a noteworthy construction industry and several commercial and trading estates on the outskirts of the town. However, agriculture, fishing and – in particular – tourism are also important to its economic success; its historic quarter is regularly visited by tourists from other parts of Spain as well as from Portugal, but it is also part of the town's commercial focus. Again, the service sector is the most important employer, and people who work in it are the focus of the research discussed here.

3. Conceptual issues

Central to our discussion of the Galician–Portuguese border is the conceptualisation of identity. We adopt Tajfel's Social Identity Theory, an essentially socio-psychological approach that moves away from the focus on external social categories such as age, gender, etc., that assign to individuals membership of social groups. Here, an individual's self-image, self-identity and sense of belonging are based on how (internally) they relate to, value and understand this membership, and how they articulate it through external relationships and behaviour (Tajfel 1978; Isajiw 1992; Joseph 2010). In sociolinguistic terms, 'identity is the social positioning of self and other' (Bucholtz and Hall 2010: 18). Individuals perceive, enact and reinforce symbolic boundaries of identification by reference to characteristics which define membership (inclusion) and non-membership (exclusion; Padilla 1999: 116). Inclusion leads to a sense of positive distinctiveness and self-esteem (Reizábel et al. 2004: 4, 13). Both in-group and out-group members may categorise individuals in terms of belonging, even if they no longer actively share all the relevant identity traits and features, as long as some form of historical link can be made.

Ethnicity is one socio-psychological process that affords such a feeling of individual belonging and identity, but it also embodies an implicit reference to the collective: we may choose to demonstrate membership in a given context by identifying with communal ancestral heritage, such as through ethnic origin, or with some other primordial artefact, such as language (Beswick 2007: 43–5), as in the present research. In other contexts we may choose to enhance our sense of nationhood – here, that of 'being Spanish' or 'being Portuguese'. A discussion of in-groups, out-groups and identity can apply equally across political boundaries if members of a specific group recognise and choose to reinforce traits that are indicative of implicitly conceptualised boundaries, rather than of existing national ones.[6]

In this chapter we explore the existence of a cross-border localised identity in the borderlands between Galicia and Portugal, enacted and reinforced through communication strategies, in particular commercial activities. Roudometof (2005) highlights the relevance of transnational social spaces to movement across state borders, through which such borders become less significant than those between the localised in-group and the externalised out-group. Thus, even places on the border may become distinct alternative centres of their own borderland regions, spanning the political divide (Llamas 2010: 228). They may retain their own discrete inter-group categorisations, but in relevant contexts individuals may also identify and ally themselves with their interlocutors, and often language is a key element of such processes.

Language is the medium through which self-conceptions of identity are transmitted (Bucholtz and Hall 2010: 19), and is also employed to assign identities indirectly when value judgements regarding the characterisation of individuals are based on the way they speak (Llamas and Watt 2010b: 1). Linguistic varieties and linguistic forms may thus acquire and retain extra-linguistic characteristics and social meaning above and beyond interpersonal communication needs (Padilla 1999: 115–16). Shared linguistic behaviour may lead to local or regional varieties being labelled 'prestigious' in certain contexts, but not in others. In other words, all sociolinguistically competent language users have at their disposal a range of linguistic resources for highlighting different facets of their identities according to context (Llamas and Watt 2010b: 1; Joseph 2010: 20).

In contact situations between two communities employing differing language varieties for intragroup communications, intersystemic variation may be reduced as individuals start to adjust their linguistic behaviour to that of their interlocutors. This process is termed *convergence* (Giles 1973: 90).[7] Although there is a pragmatic communicative function to this behaviour, there may also be an intention to accommodate to the interlocutor on socio-psychological grounds (Hinskens et al. 2000: 3) in order that the speaker be seen as 'inclusive', or to identify with the interlocutor through the specific linguistic choices made by the speaker. Over time, the general community may come to replicate this behaviour. At national borders, a transitional language variety may thus develop, so as to facilitate cross-border communications and transmissions as well as to demonstrate in-group identity allegiance (Llamas 2010: 228).

4. Research aims and methodology

The main aims of this research were:

1. to document the continued presence of certain phonological phenomena in a language contact scenario: specifically, in inter-group commercial interactions between individuals of the Minho borderland communities;
2. to observe the use of such phenomena as part of a localised linguistic variety;
3. to examine and analyse speakers' perceptions regarding their use of such phenomena, and their value in localised identification strategies.

A multi-method empirical and qualitative approach was employed, with the focus throughout being on individual language use, attitudes and identification strategies.

The research was carried out in September 2010 and April 2011. Respondents who had participated in a previous study in the area (see Beswick 2005) were asked to participate a second time, since it was felt that a re-examination of their linguistic behaviour and attitudes some twelve years after the initial study had taken place would clarify whether the earlier results were valid from a longitudinal perspective. Furthermore, all the speakers satisfied various sociolinguistic and extra-linguistic criteria: all were born and raised in their particular community, and at the time of the second study all still resided within the confines of the town. This ensured parity regarding the use of an urban setting. At the time of the 2010–11 fieldwork all respondents were aged between 30 and 60 and were thus of working age; all worked either in the service or commercial sectors, satisfying our requirements regarding their accessibility to cross-community interactions. There was an equal split between men and women. In total, nineteen L1 Galician-speaking respondents and seventeen Portuguese respondents (i.e. the majority of those from the original study of twenty in each town) agreed to participate. All gave informed consent to the use of the data, and they were assured of anonymity at all times.

Three complementary data-generation techniques were employed: researcher observations were used in order to evaluate respondents' linguistic competencies and behaviour in cross-border discourse, semi-structured ethnographic interviews were carried out in order to understand participants' attitudes and opinions regarding language use and group membership, and a Matched Guise technique was utilised in order to elicit participants' opinions regarding the character of a speaker based on accent cues.

Observations of respondents' conversations during commercial transactions took place in their place of work or in commercial exchanges across the river, and each respondent was observed on at least five different occasions in different contexts. As a control, respondents were also observed in intra-group contexts to ensure that any phonological variation not generally found in their variety only occurred in interactions with interlocutors residing on the other side of the border.

Interviews took place in the informal setting of a quiet bar or café after the final observed transaction. Respondents were not made aware of the detailed research objectives, but were asked to recount anecdotal stories and opinions about what it was like to live and work so close to a state border. They were also given the opportunity to talk about the context beforehand. The researcher employed an informal, open-ended interview technique to guide the conversation when the participant failed to engage with the issues specific to this research, as it was sometimes difficult to elicit information on individuals' own perceptions of how they used the localised language variety.

Finally, the Matched Guise tests were composed of four short pieces of spoken discourse recorded by a southern Galician speaker and a northern Portuguese speaker. Two included the phonological traits we found to be indicative of cross-border commercial exchanges, and two did not. These were played once to each respondent, and a brief set of questions was posed regarding the perceived character of the speaker.

5. Discussion: the linguistics of Galician-Portuguese

From a political perspective, Galician, Portuguese and Castilian are separate language varieties with their own standard forms. However, from a linguistic perspective, even the standard forms of Portuguese and Galician share a degree of structural similarity and mutual intelligibility, owing to their historical provenance. Spain became a parliamentary democracy in the 1970s, and the decentralising policy embedded within the 1978 Spanish Constitution paved the way for the creation of seventeen self-governing communities and two self-governing cities within the *Estado de las autonomías* ('State of Autonomies'). Devolution has thus afforded Galicia, Catalonia and the Basque Region in particular the legitimate opportunity to seek political self-determination, and to have their languages officially recognised as representative of their respective ethnicities and given formal co-official status with Castilian.[8] In Galicia, this has also encouraged the two prominent regionalist movements to highlight the role of the autochthonous language as a symbol of identity, albeit from different perspectives. The so-called *independentistas* (advocates of independence) have long advocated language policy and planning initiatives based on the premise that the Galician standard should be as linguistically independent as possible from both Castilian and Portuguese,[9] whereas the *reintegracionistas* (reintegrationists) believe that Galician's only chance of survival in the long term is to free itself of Castilian's long-held dominance, and to ally itself linguistically once again with Portuguese. What is clear is that Galician-Portuguese was ostensibly the popular vernacular of the area until the end of the *Reconquista* (the 'reconquest' of Iberia by Christian kingdoms), that the political cleavage of what became Galicia and Portugal also engendered the start of diversification of their linguistic varieties, and that this period also marked the beginning of Castilian influence on the linguistic systems of Galician, particularly in urban areas. Historically, as far as Portuguese is concerned, central and southern varieties of the language were strongly influenced by Mozarabic, yet the north of the country was largely isolated from such influence, retaining certain characteristics (Pharies 2007). These are discussed further below.

Until recently, Castilian influence had polarised dialectal variation in Galicia and linguistic fragmentation was rife, but the most prominent surveys of the last thirty years have shown that while the general stratification of such variation into western, central and eastern dialectal zones simplifies the situation somewhat, many phonological traits are now being lost as a consequence of standardisation (see, for example, Instituto de Língua Galega 1999) and the fact that spoken Galician is increasingly influenced by Castilian, particularly since virtually the entire population of Galicia is now considered to be functionally bilingual (Beswick 2007: 196–9). In contrast, Portuguese dialectal and accentual variation remains somewhat limited; Portugal is a nation with one overriding language variety used by the indigenous population which displays a high level of geo-linguistic uniformity and homogeneity. However, the northern Portuguese varieties of Tras-os-Montes, the areas surrounding the Rivers Minho and Douro and parts of Beira-Baixa do exhibit limited dialectal variation, and as well as certain idiosyncratic lexical phenomena, this generally takes the form of marked phonological and other linguistic similarities to southern Galician varieties.[10] We may hypothesise, therefore, that structural similarity between Galician and Portuguese, together with the degree of mutual intelligibility this affords, has facilitated and sustained cross-border commercial activities. Indeed, our earlier research (Beswick 2005, 2007) established that some form of localised language variety was often used around the Minho, based on a set of shared phonological traits in cross-border communications that were present in one or other of the varieties under consideration. The present control data demonstrate dialect features common to northern Portuguese and southern Galicia:

1. Paragogic /e/ after infinitives in -ar or nouns in -al: pescar[e], 'to fish', Portugal[e], 'Portugal'. This is not found in either standard variety.
2. The diphthong /ei/ > [ej] (madeira, 'wood') is also generally retained. However, both diphthongs are consistently monophthongised by a few respondents, possibly in line with the Castilian form.
3. The homogeneous Galician and Castilian realisation of /b/ and /v/ by positional allophones [ß] intervocalically and [b] elsewhere (e.g. boca, 'mouth', vaga, 'wave', cabo, 'cape, headland') is prevalent on both sides of the Minho. Standard Portuguese retains /b/ and /v/ for orthographic <b> and <v>.
4. The word-initial palatal affricate articulation /tʃ/ of orthographic <ch> (e.g. chama, 'flame') is found in both varieties, in contrast to the Standard Portuguese palatal fricative /ʃ/.
5. Neither variety employs the gheada, the Galician 'aspirate' pronunciation of word-initial and intervocalic orthographic <g>, which is realised as [h], [x] or [xʰ].

Moreover, our re-examination of cross-border interactions confirms the presence of a further shared set of features that has not altered significantly over the last decade, although some new traits appear to have embedded themselves in what seems to be a fairly well-established localised linguistic variety:

1. Non-tonic <a> is realised as the Portuguese [ɐ]; the Standard Galician realisation, as in Castilian, is [a] (e.g. *falar*, 'to speak').
2. Post-tonic /e/ is raised to /i/ (e.g. *xente*, 'people'), mirroring the northern Portuguese cognate. The Standard Portuguese pronunciation is [ə]; the Standard and dialectal Galician realisation is said to be [e], as in Castilian. This raising also applies in pre-tonic position (e.g. in *Espanha/España*, 'Spain'), even though it is reported not to occur around the Minho (Teyssier 1984: 59–63).[11]
3. Word-final /o/ (e.g. in *burro*, 'donkey') is consistently raised to [u], as in standard Portuguese along the Minho. In Standard Galician it is /o/, as in Castilian.
4. The pronunciation of the diphthong /ou/ as [ow] (as in e.g. *ouro*, 'gold') is a northern Portuguese marker and is also the Standard Galician cognate. In our research it is retained in the borderland varieties, although in urban Galician areas it is progressively monophthongised in line with the Castilian form.
5. [Vŋ] (the Standard Galician pronunciation also found in southern varieties) or [Ṽ] (the Standard Portuguese version) are used in free variation for orthographic Gal. *can* and Port. *cão*, 'dog'. However, even in Valença the nasalisation of the vowel was not markedly present.
6. The Portuguese voiced palatal fricative [ʒ] is found in Galician cognates (Gal. *xente*, Port. *gente*, 'people'). The Standard Galician counterpart is voiceless [ʃ].
7. Contrary to previous research, the Standard Galician voiceless interdental fricative /θ/ for intervocalic <z> and <c> before <e, i> was not consistently attested here, often being replaced by the voiceless sibilant /s/ found in Portuguese cognates and sporadically in western Galician varieties such as those used in Tui (Gal. *nación*, Port. *nação*, 'nation').
8. Similarly, our data often attest the palatalisation /ʃ/ of <s> in Galician tokens, particularly in plurals (e.g. *camas*, 'beds'), in line with Portuguese realisations.
9. Pre-dental and apico-alveolar sibilants are maintained in northern Portuguese, but our data demonstrate simplification in Valença to the apico-alveolar realisations [s̺] and [z̺] prevalent further south, and also generally through Galicia.

It would appear that, at any rate for these speakers, some form of accommodation of phonological forms in cross-border exchanges has been occurring for the last decade at least, although it is too soon to predict whether this is indicative of a convergence process that will be replicated in future generations' linguistic behaviour, or whether it is simply a feature of this particular set of respondents. Nonetheless, it would seem to represent a generally reciprocal and mutual adjustment of forms, irrespective of the (variable) direction the convergence moves in. Furthermore, the interviews reveal that most of our respondents (80 per cent) recognize these particular linguistic behaviours both in general and in cross-border exchanges, and are aware that they use such traits. Statements made during the interviews regarding the notion of a shared accent (Gal. *o noso acento axuda nas transacións comerciais*, 'our accent aids commercial transactions'; Port. *partilhamos uma pronunciação cá no Minho*, 'we share a pronunciation here on the Minho'; *somos todos minhotes*, 'we are all people from the Minho') signal an intention on the part of these individuals to accommodate on socio-psychological grounds (Hinskens et al. 2000: 3), based upon their desire to be seen as inclusive towards their interlocutors as part of an alternative cross-border community.

However, a few respondents (20 per cent) maintain that they do not modify their phonological output in the direction of that of their interlocutor in such interactions, stating that a code-switched conversation ensues, in spite of the fact that in our observations, shared phonological data was used by all respondents. For these respondents, then, convergence on these forms occurs below the level of awareness, yet even they give positive responses towards the intersystemic variation employed in the Matched Guise recordings, when tested. Irrespective of the respondents' L1, the recorded speakers are characterised as having empathy or sincerity (Gal./Port. *empatia*, *sinceridade*) or of being 'kind', 'one of us', 'one of our group' (*amizade*, *gente como nós*, *um do noso grupo*) when they are using the shared traits. The overriding comments were more negative when the speakers did not use such traits, however. Independent of any pragmatic function, then, these forms have thus acquired social meaning in such communications (Padilla 1999: 115–16), whereby an in-group identity is assigned to the speakers based on the linguistic forms they use in line with language-mediated attribution of identity (Llamas and Watt 2010b: 1). Where respondents feel they have much in common with neighbours across the border, irrespective of their national affiliation, language may thus become a unifying tool, the vehicle for localised identification practices, even if speakers do not realise that they accommodate phonologically to their interlocutors.

Palmeiro Pinheiro believes that a decrease in cross-border interaction in the area is occurring despite the relaxation of border controls, with the result that shared identity is no longer in evidence (2009: 97–100). Yet commercial exchange does still occur on a regular basis between the inhabitants of Tui and Valença. This is a highly localised 'Knowledge Economy' (Williams 2005: 102), in which being able to use a shared phonology associated with cross-border economic exchanges is considered symbolic capital with the potential for power and profit within the community of practice (Bourdieu 1992: 21–4). Again, our Matched Guise testing demonstrates that when speakers do not use such localised forms, our respondents do not consider them to be part of the local, in-group commercial dynamic. By not demonstrating the assumed communicative competence necessary for successful economic exchange, the status and position of these speakers in the social hierarchy are undermined. Furthermore, such commercial activities across the state border seem to reinforce the existence of localised identities; the political border, then, may become less significant than the borders that represent the localised in-group and the externalised out-group (Roudometof 2005: 128) and which are articulated through the use of the local dialect.

Of course, identification with such a community of practice and the use of certain phonological features that enhance the perception of in-group belonging does not preclude membership of other groups or the contextual use of other linguistic varieties (see, for example, Llamas and Watt 2010a, b). The renegotiation of language use and its usefulness with respect to identification practices in the borderlands is also complicated on the Galician side by its recent standardisation and its bilingual relationship with Castilian. The implication is that the localised vernacular is in direct competition for functional distribution with a standardised spoken Galician variety as well as with Castilian. However, to our respondents, communication with other *minhotes* reportedly feels more straightforward than that with compatriots who live in distant urban conurbations, as we shall see below. Indeed, in line with Williams (2005), this dichotomy does not discourage them from articulating in-group commonalities as manifestations of a locally held ideology, upheld in certain local contexts by the use of shared phonological traits. Based on our data, it seems reasonable to state that – at least for the time being – the linguistic diversity of the borderland communities in Tui has not been eroded by the availability of other linguistic options.

Palmeiro Pinheiro also postulates that the linguistic differentiation of Galician and Portuguese is a further reason for any decrease in cross-border contact and interaction (2009: 97–100). Yet recent amendments to the Galician norm have made concessions to the *reintegracionistas*' call for recognition of Galician's Portuguese derivation, and in the interviews our Galician respondents recognise that their language variety is more accentually and dialectally similar to the Portuguese spoken across the border than it is to the Galician spoken elsewhere in the region; *é un galego castelanizado*, 'it's a Castilianised form of Galician', as one puts it.[12]

From a socio-psychological perspective, representations of 'us' and 'them' are articulated by our Tui respondents about their fellow Galicians. Through 'the social positioning of self and other' (Bucholtz and Hall 2010: 8), they claim and indeed use localised speech forms to distance and differentiate themselves from other Galicians, assigning to them an out-group epithet of exclusion despite their sharing a regional and a national identity: *non comparto moito coma outros galegos; son alleos a min*, 'I don't share much with other Galicians; they are alien to me'. These findings are upheld by theories of centrality and peripherality regarding the dilution of national identity features at the borders of political states (see, for example, Llamas 2010: 227), a trend which is often to the benefit of more localised, shared identities, since neighbouring towns and villages on opposite sides of a border may have more in common with each other than they do with their own state capitals.

Socio-psychological borders are also in evidence in the Galician respondents' references to a history and ethnicity shared with the Portuguese across the national border: *somos da misma tradición*, 'we share the same tradition'. Such acknowledgement of a cross-border common ancestral heritage based on mutual origins demonstrates how individuals articulate their positive self-image (Tajfel 1978), and it also reinforces a sense of positive distinctiveness (Reizábel et al. 2004: 4, 13), embedded to a large extent in how they identify themselves as culturally, socially – and at times, even linguistically – distinct from the rest of the regional population of Galicia. In this way, individuals perceive a symbolic, non-physical boundary that assigns a sense of 'them' – the other Galicians, the non-members, the out-group – and 'us', the borderland communities, the members, the in-group (Tajfel and Turner 1979; Cohen 1985, 1986). Yet the Galician respondents appear to recognise the relevance of primordial group traits such as heritage, language and so on, but as part of a situational – and hence constructed and thus performed (Joseph 2010: 14) – response to changing contexts and to the perceived need or desire for a boundary marker between the in-group and the out-group.

Partially as a function of the region's peripheral location at the state border, an approach to identity which highlights the existence of implicitly conceptualised boundaries rather than of existing state ones may lead to a heightened political consciousness (see Martínez 1994: 8–14). Our Galician respondents are all aware of the long-standing debates regarding Galician autonomy from Spain, regional issues and the calls for integration with Portugal made by *reintegracionistas*, since such debates are often aired in the Galician media. Such ideologies stress the perceived advantages in terms of status and identity of the incorporation of Galician into the Luso linguistic family, revealing a political and perhaps even nationalistic objective. Indeed, despite the local government's standardisation and normalisation efforts over the last three decades, deep-seated perceptions of Galician's inferior status in this diglossic environment have not been eradicated, and recent threats to the official legal standing of Galician in favour of Castilian from Spanish centralist and nationalist discourse also serve to highlight the precarious position of Galician as a regional vernacular and identification marker. However, all our respondents – without exception and irrespective of their first languages – dismiss the idea of integration with a larger Luso in-group as unfeasible, some contesting that any shared identification strategies such as the use of localised linguistic forms are reserved solely for use in local spaces, within local in-groups and for very specific purposes, rather than as a precursor to any aspired-for unification under a national banner on either side of the political border.

Our study also investigated how the use of Castilian is articulated within the ideologies of Galician speakers. Consider one Galician respondent's elucidative remarks, translated for convenience:

> Listen, you need to understand, this is nothing to do with being Spanish. Here on the Minho, we are the same people, we speak the same way, but we are also Galician [. . .] and that gives us the right to speak however we want. We only use Castilian if we have to [. . .] normally with tourists [. . .] Let's face it, they cannot speak Galician or understand it so we have no choice [. . .] To be honest, I don't really feel Spanish, I feel local, different, and I am comfortable with this. Castilian is not my first language and I don't really like using it. But I certainly do not feel Portuguese; we are neighbours, we do not live in each other's houses like a family would! [RR]

In point of fact, many of the Galician respondents make the claim that Castilian is rarely used except where necessary, and this appears to be at the very least corroborated by our observational data. Although Castilian is the national language of all Spaniards, in this particular setting it does not appear to function as a core value of either a regional or a national in-group; rather, it is only employed strategically for pragmatic contextual language uses. Moreover, very often the variety offered as Castilian in the borderlands is overlaid by a strongly dialectal Galician accent, and there is also evidence of lexical interference on many occasions (the use, for example, of Gal. *auga* for Cast. *agua*, 'water', and of Gal. *graciñas* for Cast. *gracias*, 'thank you'). For these respondents, then, it would appear that language use and language choice are strategically pertinent to their configuration of other identities. Whereas in multilingual Galicia, regional identity (Galician) and national identity (Spanish) are often mutually exclusive, Portugal is ostensibly monolingual and its perceived level of linguistic uniformity would tend to negate any strong regional identification, despite the fact that, as we have seen, the northern dialects display certain marked phonological similarities to the southern Galician varieties. Indeed, regional identities are generally subsumed under the epithet of a uniform, national identity (Palmeiro Pinheiro 2009: 87); even our Valença respondents maintain a strong loyalty to the epithet of 'being Portuguese'. However, the autonomous status of Galicia from the rest of Spain affords its political reputation the label of 'minority nationalism', and offers its population an alternative regional/national identity that has little to do with a Spanish national identity.

6. Conclusion

Joseph's description of borderland communities and the role of language in local identity configuration encapsulates many of the findings discussed in this chapter:

> Groups of people who occupy contiguous territory and see themselves as having common interests tend to develop, over long stretches of time, ways of speaking that are distinctive to them, marking them out from groups who either are not geographically adjacent to them or else are perceived as having different, probably rival interests. In other words, language does tend to mark out the social features on which national belonging will come to be based – but it is only a tendency, because it also happens very frequently that the same way of speaking is shared by people with very different interests [. . .] and that markedly different ways of speaking exist among a group of people who nonetheless see themselves as part of the same nation. (Joseph 2010: 15)

Each of the points made here can equally apply across the political boundary dividing the towns of Tui and Valença. From a historical perspective, Galicians and Portuguese share certain common ascendancy, interests and linguistic roots, and irrespective of general differences in morphology, syntax and lexis, a high degree of mutual intelligibility between the dialectal varieties has been maintained over the centuries, facilitating continued and sustained cross-border communication. It is clear, however, that the perception that code-switched conversations occur is largely correct, but that in the contexts we investigated, they are always overlaid by a number of emblematic phonological traits, and this occurs because whether unconsciously or consciously, our respondents manifest a desire to accommodate to their interlocutors. It is this phonological levelling that marks the existence of a localised linguistic variety: the distinctive nature of this variety is based largely on a shared accent. By accepting that they employ this variety, the majority of respondents mark their local in-group belonging, albeit for very specific commercial reasons, and they also mark those who do not use the variety as external to the group, even when the out-group members are part of the same national entity. In other words, their localised variety would appear to have the capacity to unify when individuals from each town engage in mutually beneficial transactions across the border.

In this chapter we also considered the role of other identities, in particular those available to the Galician respondents. In belonging to different politically defined nations, the Portuguese and Galicians also have different interests external to that encapsulated by the 'local'. Interestingly, the Galician respondents tend to articulate a Galician regional national identity rather than a Spanish national identity, whereas the Portuguese fully embrace their Portuguese national identity. Thus, we can conclude that further sociopsychological borders of identity inclusion and exclusion are engendered by our inhabitants of Tui: the almost total use of Galician categorises these individuals as members of an in-group that has little to do with allegiance to their Portuguese neighbours, and more to do with a desire not to be seen as part of a Spanish national grouping, even if the latter is what is indicated on their identification papers.

Notes

1. See Beswick (2005) and Beswick (2007: 119–25).
2. For a historical account of Galician-Portuguese borderlands, see Palmeiro Pinheiro (2009).
3. Two of the seven roads assigned international status across the Spanish–Portuguese border run between Galicia and Portugal (Sidaway 2005: 190).
4. The Eje Atlántico del Noroeste Peninsular/Eixo Atlántico do Noroeste Peninsular, comprising communities of the Baixo Minho, serves as a regional lobby in relations with national governments and the EU (Palmeiro Pinheiro and Pazos Otón 2008). See also <http://www.eixoatlantico.com>.
5. See http://www.viator.com/Santiago-de-Compostela-attractions/Valenca-do-Min ho/d565-a2581 (accessed 4 March 2013).
6. Indeed, Llamas' research in the Scottish/English borderlands (2010) finds that political borders do not always mark national identity boundaries, which may be manipulated, adopted or rejected for particular ends.
7. Alternatively, an individual's use of speech forms may reflect a desire for differentiation from other speakers; this is known as *divergence* (Giles 1973: 90).
8. See the Constitución Española (1978) at http://www.constitucion.es/constitucion/index.html (accessed 4 March 2013).
9. This group has been involved with the creation of the standard since the establishment of the Comunidad Autónoma. See Beswick (2007: 84–90) for a discussion of the ideologies surrounding standardisation in Galicia.
10. Regional variation is also apparent in the Alto-Alentejo and the Algarve in the central-southern zone (Beswick 2007: 118).
11. The same pattern exists for the third-person singular subject pronoun *ele* > [ile] in Galician, [ili] in Portuguese.
12. Levelling of the open and close vowel oppositions of /o/ and /e/, lowering of atonic <o> [u] > [o] and monophthongisation of /ej/ > /e/, for example, may be accelerated by the employment of non-Galician L1 speakers in broadcasting, education, etc.

8

Perceptual Ideology across the Scottish/English Border

Chris Montgomery

1. Introduction

This chapter discusses the results of a perceptual dialectology (PD) investigation conducted in five locations along the Scottish/English border during fieldwork in 2009. PD aims to investigate non-linguists' beliefs about factors of the following sort:

> How different from, or similar to, their own speech do respondents find the speech of other areas?
> What (i.e. where) do respondents believe the dialect areas of a region to be?
> What do respondents believe about the characteristics of regional speech?
> (adapted from Preston 1988: 475–6)

In order to provide answers to these questions, perceptual dialectologists use 'draw-a-map' tasks (Preston 1982) to gather data about respondents' 'mental maps' (Gould and White 1986). PD researchers ask respondents to draw lines on blank or minimally detailed maps to indicate where the respondents believe dialect areas to exist. Respondents are usually also asked to undertake supplementary activities in which they add labels to dialect areas, and provide other comments about the areas they have drawn. Although individual maps are interesting, a major aim of the draw-a-map task is to aggregate line data relating to dialect areas (see Preston and Howe 1987).

Recent PD research in the United Kingdom (Montgomery 2007) has demonstrated the importance of three key factors that come into play when non-linguists are asked to identify dialect areas on maps. These factors – *proximity*, *cultural prominence* and *claiming/denial* – are discussed further below, and will be used to help understand the data presented in this chapter. These data include aggregate maps, numerical data relating to the recognition levels of different dialect areas, qualitative interview data and census data relating to commuting patterns.

2. Constraints on perception

I have argued elsewhere (Montgomery and Beal 2011; Montgomery 2012) for the paramount importance of the *proximity*, *cultural prominence* and *claiming/denial* factors that affect the perception of dialect areas. The last of these, *claiming/denial*, relates to the interface between social attractiveness and voice-sample placement, and is therefore least relevant to the present chapter. I therefore restrict my discussion in this section to *proximity* and *cultural prominence*. From the outset, it must be noted that the ways in which respondents perceive dialect areas are highly complex, and by dealing with the different 'factors' separately it is not my intention to argue that each operates in isolation. Instead, although the effects of each factor can be isolated in certain cases, it is assumed that many factors (including the three noted above, along with other, as yet unidentified, factors) work together for each respondent who produces a hand-drawn map.

2.1 Proximity

Proximity effects can be assigned to one of two categories: *bare proximity* and *attenuated proximity* (Montgomery 2012). Bare proximity effects are discussed by Preston (1999: xxxiv), who found that respondents complete draw-a-map tasks by drawing stigmatised areas first, and then local areas. Upon this observation, Preston formulates a theory of bare proximity which states that home or 'near-to' areas receive higher recognition levels than others, echoing the research of perceptual geographers (e.g. Gould and White 1986). In many cases, such a model of the effects of proximity provides an adequate explanation of the way in which some respondents complete their maps.

However, the theory of bare proximity does not account for the many and varied ways in which respondents might draw dialect areas. As Britain (2010a: 70–1, and this volume) has observed, there are many factors other than physical distance that might influence the way in which people use and perceive space. Thus, despite a theory of bare proximity which assumes a 'homogeneous cultural information space' (Gould and White 1986: 153),[1] such space is rarely homogeneous, as demonstrated at length by Britain (2002, 2010a). The heterogeneity of information space is one of the key reasons for variation in respondents' abilities to recognise home or near-to areas, and can explain why Preston's (1999: xxxiv) respondents would first draw stigmatised areas, and then local areas.

Although I have elsewhere demonstrated (Montgomery 2007; Montgomery and Beal 2011) that bare proximity is important in the perception of certain dialect areas, in more recent research (Montgomery 2012) other factors which lead to an attenuated proximity effect have been shown to have a good deal of importance. Attenuated proximity differs from bare proximity as it takes into account additional factors which might disrupt the flow of information which could otherwise lead to a bare effect of proximity. Such factors include obvious physical barriers such as rivers and mountain ranges, along with national boundaries such as the Scottish/English border, and other political/governmental boundaries.

2.2 Cultural prominence

The cultural prominence factor is related to increased metalinguistic knowledge gained via the media or by other mechanisms, and is something I have previously termed 'cultural salience' (Montgomery and Beal 2011: 138). Stuart-Smith has claimed that 'it is inevitable that the broadcast media will have an impact on metalinguistic awareness of linguistic varieties and variation, standard and non-standard, and the ideologies surrounding them' (2011: 3). In addition to this, it is demonstrated elsewhere (Montgomery 2012, in which I make use of the example of the perception of a nascent 'Manc', i.e. Manchester-based, dialect area) that the amount of exposure given to social and geographical varieties in the print media can also be attributed to the perceptual prominence of specific areas.

The phenomenon of cultural prominence can be thought of as one that is intertwined with ideas of proximity. Viewed through this prism, cultural prominence functions by increasing a bare proximity effect through virtual means, and bringing 'far-away' areas 'closer' to respondents through increased exposure of these areas in various forms of media and public discourse.

3. The significance of the Scottish/English border

The Scottish/English border, which has been described as 'a strong linguistic barrier' (Ihalainen 1994: 248), is extremely important in a dialectological context. In addition to its linguistic importance, the Scottish/English border also has psychological, physical and political significance to residents in the border area and beyond.

Although Watt et al. (2010: 273) note the Scottish/English border's lack of fixity over the past millennium, Llamas (2010: 229) states that the border has remained peaceful and stable in recent centuries. The stability and peace that have accompanied the relatively unusual non-federal solution to the constitution of the United Kingdom has meant that the border is highly porous. There is thus a good amount of travel between Scotland and England, as evidenced by commuting and migration data from the 2001 Census (Office for National Statistics 2007a, 2007b). I will return to Census data below, although it should be noted here that there are differing rates of trans-border commuting from England and Scotland. Ratti et al. (2010), who investigated another form of behaviour by looking for clustering patterns in landline telephone usage data, demonstrated the exceptional prominence of the Scottish/English border with respect to who calls whom in Britain (see further Watt et al. and Britain, this volume).

The stark boundary between England and Scotland shown in Ratti et al.'s (2010) research does not appear to tally with the relatively extensive face-to-face communication suggested by Census data. However, the Scottish/English border is increasingly important politically, as a result of devolution in Scotland. Devolution has meant that, despite modern border stability, England and Scotland have become increasingly distinct. Although at present the British government in London enacts a good deal of legislation which pertains directly to the whole of the United Kingdom (which, at the time of writing, still includes Scotland), there is a large quantity of Scottish-only legislation enacted by the Scottish government in Edinburgh. The independence referendum in 2014, which could result in Scotland again becoming an independent country (or if not, one governed at 'arm's length' from the British government) means that the Scottish/ English border represents a divide of increasing significance, not only politically and financially, but also ideologically.

4. Dialect variation in Great Britain

As one of the aims of PD is to compare perceptual data to those gathered via other dialec- tological methods, this section contains a very brief description of the major dialect areas in Scotland and England. It is generally agreed that there are three major dialect bounda- ries in Scotland: 'the Highland Line, the mid/north line, [and] the Scottish/English linguistic border' (Johnston 1997: 433). The Highland Line demarcates the area in which Gaelic is spoken, which is known as the *Gàidhealtachd* in that language (McColl Millar 2010). Further detail is added to this tripartite division by Stuart-Smith (2008: 48), who lists Scots varieties as 'Mid or Central Scots, Southern or Border Scots, Northern Scots (also called Doric), and Insular Scots', with Urban Scots 'spoken in the cities of Glasgow and Edinburgh and across the Central Belt'.

The border between Scotland and England has been claimed to correspond to the 'most numerous bundle of dialect isoglosses in the English-speaking world' (Aitken 1992: 895) and, predictably, it has been the site of much linguistic study (e.g. Glauser 1974, 2000; Pichler 2009; Llamas 2010; Watt et al. 2011). Although there have been other attempts (Ellis 1889; Glauser 1991) English dialects have been most recently classified by Trudgill (1999: 65), based on phonological data from the *Survey of English Dialects* (Orton and Dieth 1962–71). Trudgill outlines sixteen 'modern' dialect areas, which are subdivisions of three superordinate 'major' dialect areas: Northern, Central and South. Each of the latter is partitioned into dialect zones based on multiple linguistic criteria; the Central and South areas have prominent east–west divisions, for example. Scottish, Welsh and Northern Irish varieties are described in separate dialect surveys, reflecting the sense in which the United Kingdom's dialect map is perceived to be dis- continuous along political lines by linguists as well as by laypeople (see further Watt et al., this volume).

5. Methods and sample

For the study reported here, respondents in five locations (Brampton, Galashiels, Hexham, Langholm and Moffat) completed a draw-a-map task which asked for their large-scale perceptions of dialect regions in Great Britain. The respondents were high- school students in their mid-teens. The locations were chosen in order to investigate the impact of the Scottish/English border on the perception of dialect variation in English. Figure 8.1 shows each of the survey locations, along with the locations of the cities of Newcastle upon Tyne, Edinburgh and Glasgow.

Respondents from each of the survey locations were given a minimally detailed map which contained information relating to country borders, along with city location dots.[2] They were asked to add data to the map with a pen or pencil by responding to the follow- ing questions:

1. Label the nine well-known cities marked with a dot on the map.

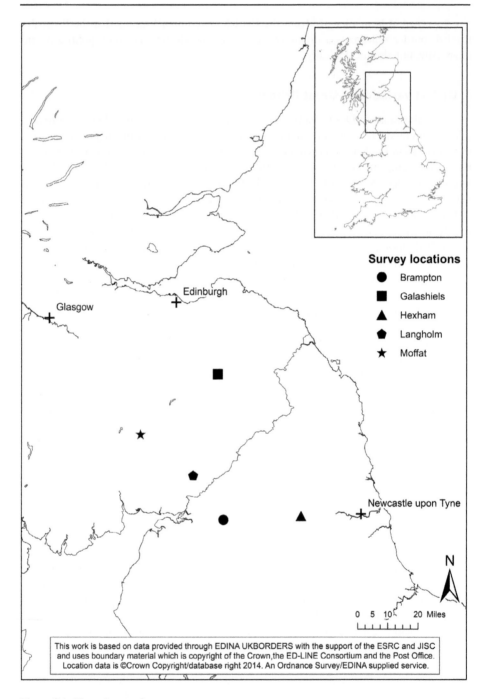

Figure 8.1 Map of research area.

2. Do you think that there is a north–south language divide in the country? If so, draw a line where you think this is.
3. Draw lines on the map where you think there are regional speech (dialect) areas.
4. Label the different areas that you have drawn on the map.
5. What do you think of the areas you've just drawn? How might you recognise people from these areas? Write some of these thoughts on the map if you have time.

The task lasted for ten minutes and, in order to assist respondents, a location map which contained a number of cities and towns in England, Scotland and Wales was projected on a screen visible to the respondents for the first five minutes of the task. In total, 151 respondents completed hand-drawn maps. Seventy-six respondents were from the three locations on the Scottish side of the border, and seventy-five from the two on the English side. The mean age of respondents was 16 years 6 months.

After the draw-a-map task had been completed, the data were processed according to the method outlined below. As part of the design of the fieldwork, processed data were used as part of another visit to some of the fieldwork sites, and aggregate maps (see below) were displayed to all participants who had taken part in the draw-a-map task. Following the presentation, a small number of respondents were invited to be interviewed about language, place and the aggregate map data they had been shown.

5.1 Data processing

PD studies which rely on draw-a-map tasks can gather different types of data, including line data relating to dialect area boundaries, dialect area name data and qualitative data relating to language attitudes. It is the line data that has mainly occupied perceptual dialectologists. Counting the lines drawn in respect of each dialect area gives a record of the relative perceptual prominence of each dialect area in the 'mental maps' of respondents. However, aggregating the line data has always been the primary aim of perceptual dialectologists (cf. Preston and Howe 1987: 363). The method employed here uses Geographical Information Systems (GIS) to produce maps which can be combined and compared with various other datasets.

GIS is a system which integrates the three basic elements of hardware, software and data 'for capturing, managing, analysing, and displaying all forms of geographically referenced information' (ESRI 2011). GIS technology functions by combining different types of data through the process of linking them to the earth's surface. This technique is termed 'georeferencing' and uses coordinate systems to tie data to a set geographical position somewhere in the world. After georeferencing, GIS permits advanced data processing (termed 'geoprocessing'). An advantage of the georeferenced and geoprocessed data that GIS uses is that they are spatially meaningful. Thus, they are a way in which language researchers can refine their analytical techniques in response to Britain's (2009: 144) critique of many of the maps used in dialectology to date, in which he points up their lack of spatial sensitivity.

Hand-drawn map data were processed according to a method discussed in detail in Montgomery and Stoeckle (2013). The respondents' maps were scanned and georeferenced and the line data extracted in order to produce final aggregate maps. Such an approach results in maps which show the placement and extent of each dialect area. Additional information revealing the percentage agreement among respondents about the placement and extent of each dialect area can be displayed. Figure 8.2 shows an aggregate map showing the 'Geordie' (Newcastle upon Tyne) area, which was constructed by aggregating lines drawn by respondents from Brampton and Hexham, the two English survey locations in this study.

6. Numerical data

In total, respondents drew 970 lines delimiting 79 separate areas, giving a mean of 6.4 areas drawn per map. This level of recognition compares well with similar research undertaken in England (Montgomery 2007: 194), in which respondents recognised an average of 4.5 areas. Overall numerical data are presented in Table 8.1. It is the differential level of recognition of dialect areas by respondents on either side of the Scottish/ English border that is of most interest here. Table 8.1 shows the twenty most recognised dialect areas for Scottish and English respondents. The data are rank-ordered. The level of recognition for each area is given in the 'Recognition' column, expressed both as a bare number referring to the number of lines drawn to indicate the area, as well as a bracketed figure relating to the percentage of respondents from either Scotland or England that drew the area. Non-Scottish dialect areas are shaded, in order to aid interpretation.

Table 8.1 shows the similarities and differences between Scottish and English respondents' recognition levels for dialect areas in Great Britain. It is clear that there is a difference in the perception of non-Scottish dialect areas across the two groups of respondents. There is a proximity effect, as expected, with Scottish respondents drawing 118 lines in recognition of Scottish dialect areas (i.e. 29 per cent of all lines drawn for 'top 20' dialect areas). By contrast, respondents from the English survey locations drew only 59 lines (14 per cent of all 'top 20' lines) in recognition of Scottish areas. Although both sets of respondents clearly favoured drawing lines in recognition of English dialects areas (along with a significant number of lines indicating 'Welsh' speakers), this disparity between recognition of Scottish and English dialect areas invites further analysis.

English respondents' 'top 10' dialect areas are predominantly English, with only the ninth and tenth slots occupied by Scottish dialect areas. The recognition rates for these areas are very similar to those found in other English locations in previous research (Montgomery and Beal 2011), and they reflect the impact of both proximity and cultural prominence. Scottish respondents' 'top 10' dialect areas contain four Scottish and six English areas. The English areas recognised by Scottish respondents are similar to those recognised by English respondents. This appears to suggest that similar proximity and cultural prominence effects can be observed acting upon respondents from both Scotland and England, at least in respect of English dialect areas.

Further consideration of the frequently recognised dialect areas by country appears to reveal the different impact of the border according to the country in which respondents live. Scottish respondents' most-recognised dialect areas were 'Geordie' and 'Weeji' (/ˈwiːdʒi/, short for 'Glaswegian', i.e. the variety spoken in Glasgow), which were both identified by 69.9 per cent of respondents. Given that 'Weeji' was the most frequently recognised city-based area among the English respondents, it might have been expected that it would have a similar recognition level to that of the 'Geordie' area. This is not the

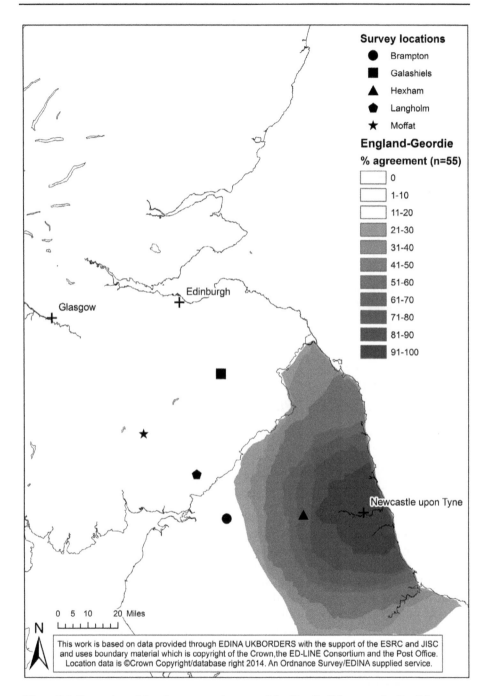

Figure 8.2 Perception of the placement and extent of the *Geordie* dialect area, by English respondents.

Table 8.1 Recognition of 'top 20' dialect areas by respondents' country; non–Scottish dialect areas have been shaded

Scottish respondents (N = 76)			English respondents (N = 75)		
Rank	Dialect area	Recognition (%)	Rank	Dialect area	Recognition (%)
1	Geordie	53 (69.9)	1	Geordie	55 (73.3)
2	Weeji	53 (69.9)	2	Scouse	53 (70.7)
3	Scouse	52 (68.4)	3	Brummie	41 (54.7)
4	Welsh	46 (60.5)	4	Cockney	40 (53.3)
5	Brummie	38 (50.0)	5	Manc	40 (53.3)
6	Cockney	27 (35.5)	6	Welsh	36 (48.0)
7	Manc	27 (35.5)	7	Cumbrian/Carlisle	31 (41.3)
8	Aberdeen	13 (17.1)	8	Yorkshire	23 (30.7)
9	Borders	12 (15.8)	9	Scottish	17 (22.7)
10	Strong/Broad Scottish	11 (14.5)	10	Weeji	15 (20.0)
11	West Country	11 (14.5)	11	Strong/Broad Scottish	11 (14.7)
12	Highlands	11 (14.5)	12	London	11 (14.7)
13	Gaelic	11 (14.5)	13	Aberdeen	10 (13.3)
14	London	10 (13.2)	14	West Country	9 (12.0)
15	Cumbrian/Carlisle	9 (11.8)	15	Bristol	8 (10.7)
16	Yorkshire	7 (9.2)	16	Cornwall	7 (9.3)
17	Scottish	7 (9.2)	17	Southern	7 (9.3)
18	Bristol	6 (7.9)	18	Highlands	6 (8.0)
19	Cardiff	6 (7.9)	19	West Cumbria	6 (8.0)
20	Lancashire	3 (3.9)	20	Midlands	5 (6.7)

case, however: the recognition rate was only 20 per cent. This suggests an attenuation of the proximity effect, with the border resulting in an interruption of the information flow, but only for English respondents. Instead of drawing smaller city-based areas, the majority of English respondents drew lines indicating either the whole of Scotland (e.g. 'Scottish') or the north of the country ('Broad Scottish').

These numerical data suggest that the border is an important factor in the perception of dialect variation in Britain, but that its impact is different for those living on opposite sides of it. This is given further consideration in the discussion of map-based and interview data in the next section.

7. Map-based data

Composite map data relating to the perception of dialect variation in Scotland are shown in Figure 8.3, with similar data shown for England in Figure 8.4. In both figures, maps are shown relating to Scottish and English perceptions. Some of the differences between

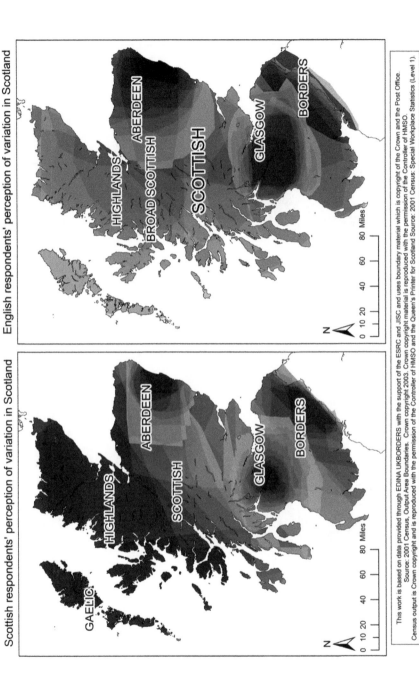

Figure 8.3 Scottish (left) and English (right) respondents' perceptions of dialect variation in Scotland.

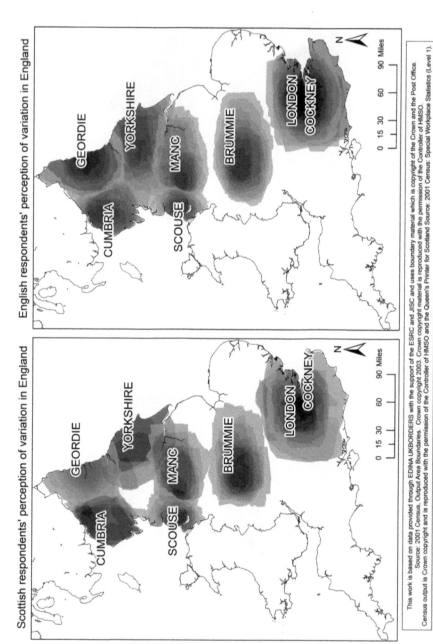

Figure 8.4 Scottish (left) and English (right) respondents' perceptions of dialect variation in England.

This work is based on data provided through EDINA UKBORDERS with the support of the ESRC and JISC and uses boundary material which is copyright of the Crown and the Post Office.
Source: 2001 Census, Output Area Boundaries. Crown copyright 2003. Crown copyright material is reproduced with the permission of the Controller of HMSO.
Census output is Crown copyright and is reproduced with the permission of the Controller of HMSO and the Queen's Printer for Scotland Source: 2001 Census: Special Workplace Statistics (Level 1).

the perceptions of dialect variation in Scotland among Scottish and English respondents can be seen in Figure 8.3, with greater acknowledgement of variation in Scotland among Scottish respondents, and less awareness on the part of English respondents.

The composite maps in Figure 8.3 display a clearly focused 'Weeji' dialect area for Scottish respondents, as well as acknowledgement of other areas. The Scottish respondents' map shows an Aberdeen dialect area, along with a Borders area, a Gaelic area and a Highlands area occupying a similar space to the 'Scottish' area. For Scottish respondents the 'Strong/Broad Scottish' area is not included, as it did not appear to relate to one specific geographical area. Instead, for this group of respondents the label was used by respondents in an idiosyncratic fashion to indicate specific parts of the country, perhaps demonstrating greater local knowledge.

The composite map of English respondents' perceptions shows fewer areas, which are in turn less focused than those drawn by their Scottish counterparts. The 'Weeji' area is included on the map, as is Aberdeen, Broad Scottish and Highlands. However, as discussed above, the most frequently drawn area was the 'Scottish' area. Respondents choosing to add this area simply drew a circle around Scotland and generally did not indicate any further subdivisions. The large 'Scottish' label on the map seems to indicate this general area, which serves as a backdrop for the other composite areas show in the figure.

The composite maps shown in Figure 8.3 clearly demonstrate that respondents' mental maps of the 'Scottish' dialect area differ considerably for respondents from Scotland and England. Scottish respondents' 'Scottish' area corresponds relatively well to the *Gàidhealtachd* area (McColl Millar 2010: 251). It therefore appears to be the case that for at least some of these respondents 'Scottish' is analogous to 'Gaelic', which occupies a similar area, although the 'Gaelic' area for Scottish respondents centres on the islands of the Outer Hebrides, as well as the north-west of mainland Scotland. By contrast, English respondents draw a general 'Scottish' area which corresponds to the area in which one might find Standard Scottish English.

The maps in Figure 8.3 show that English respondents have a generalised perception of variation in Scotland, and that Scottish respondents have more detailed mental maps of the variation in the country. This is, of course, unsurprising. That respondents would have more knowledge of their own country, not to mention an increased motivation for detailing it, is uncontroversial. It should therefore be the case that in respect of variation in England, a similar picture should emerge. However, the data in Table 8.1 have already demonstrated that this is not the case, and the maps in Figure 8.4 show that the areas drawn by English and Scottish respondents are remarkably similar to one another.

In both composite maps, a greater amount of variation is perceived in the north of England than in the south. This is most probably as a result of proximity, as discussed above. Here, five distinct areas are recognised: *Geordie, Cumbrian, Yorkshire, Scouse* (from Liverpool) and *Manc* (from Manchester), and there is very little difference between their placement and extent. The same is true of the remaining areas on the maps, which have very similar positions and distributions.

It can therefore be concluded from both the numerical and map-based data that the border affects the two sets of respondents in different ways. While the border seems to cause English respondents to focus on their own country at the expense of Scotland, Scottish respondents have a perception of dialect variation in England that is very similar to that of their counterparts in England. The Scottish respondents bolster this knowledge with a much more detailed mental map of variation in Scotland. So, despite the respondents on either side of the border having similar proximity to it (a mean straight-line distance of 30 km [19 miles] for English locations, versus 29 km [18 miles] for Scottish locations), the effect of the border is to more significantly constrain respondents from England.

The Scottish/English border appears to be operating as a 'classic' type of barrier for English respondents, by decreasing the information flow across it. However, similar disruption does not appear to be experienced by Scottish respondents, who exhibit a similar view of language variation in England to that found among the English respondents. In this way, the barrier effect of the Scottish/English border is unidirectional and is perceived differently by those living on either side of it (cf. Cohen 1985: 12).

8. Qualitative data

The qualitative data discussed below emerged from the interviews conducted with respondents from the two English survey locations (interviews could not be conducted with those in Scotland). Respondents were asked about language variation and local identity, following the types of questions suggested in Llamas (1999: 105), as well as questions about composite mental maps and ones designed to examine levels of 'folk-linguistic awareness' (Preston 1996). Of most interest for this chapter are responses that deal with the Scottish/English border, and perceptions of variation in the two countries.

Extract 8.1,[3] for instance, shows a discussion between two female respondents in Hexham. It provides clear justification for the patterns shown in the aggregate map data discussed above. These respondents claim that they can either only identify Glasgow or Edinburgh, or simply 'generalise all of Scotland'. This is in line with the data described above, which showed such patterns for respondents in both English survey locations. In general, the Hexham respondents talked much less about the Scottish/English border than about variation that was more local to them. Respondents from Brampton, which is closer to the border than is Hexham, dealt more with this topic. The Hexham respondents were less concerned with their inability (or unwillingness) to identify variation with Scotland, but their discussion suggests a good deal more about the social motivation for a less heightened awareness of the country's linguistic landscape.

Extract 8.2 shows some of the discussion between Brampton-based respondents, in which they discuss their answers to a question about whether or not they would be

1	F1	I think you can, but I can only define between Glaswegian and like an Edinburgh accent, I
2		wouldn't have picked out like an Aberdeen or like or
3		[ ]
4	M1	yeah
5	F2	yeah, I just generalise all of Scotland
6	F1	anything like that it
7		would have been just those two that I could have picked out=
8	CM	=Hmm, yeah=
9	F2	=It seems kind of flatter, like there not as like well its sort of accentuating but they're more
10		relaxed kind of way of speaking, I don't know, erm (0.5) it's hard to explain.

Extract 8.1 Extract from interview with respondents from Hexham

18	F1	=I don't mind with Geordie, but for some reason I don't like it when people say I'm Scottish
19		cos its like we're not in Scotland
20		[
21	F2	That's like a different country=
22	M1	=I think Geordies quite nice, I quite like, err I don't mind if, I mean I know I'm not but I don't
23		mind yeah I think I think I'm the same as you=
24		[ ]
25	F2	mmm
26	M1	but if someone said you've got a Scottish accent, I think I'd be offended=
27	F2	=yeah=
28	CM	=And why is that?=
29	M1	=Well, some Scottish accents, I quite like Scottish accents on old men
30	All	((laughter))
31	M1	I think it's quite nice, but I just think Scottish accents on young people are hideous=
32	CM	=So you don't want to be associated with that?
33	M1	No
34	F2	I don't like the Scottish accent
35		[ ]
36	F1	I don't mind it I think it's quite nice=
37	CM	=You don't mind it?
38	F1	Too strong is just you can't understand it, if its subtle
39		[ ]
40	M1	yeah
41	F2	I don't mind it just past the border, you know like
42		where we live kind of thing but I don't like it really far into Scotland, it's too strong and the
43		have that like ((imitates uvular fricative)) ((laughter)) it's like horrible=
44	CM	=But you don't mind it but you don't want to be associated with it?=
45	F1	=well yeah, but yes its sort of, I don't know there's something about it=
46	M1	=well you kind of want the distinction that you're from England don't you?=
47	F1	=yeah exactly=
48	M1	=I mean you don't want to be associated with Scotland, you want to be associated with
49		England=

Extract 8.2 Extract from interview with respondents from Brampton

offended if somebody misidentified them as 'Geordies'. This section of the interview makes clear that, although the Geordie dialect is perceived by these respondents to be dissimilar to the respondents' variety, it is not a major problem as far as they are concerned if the label is misattributed to them by others from outside of the area. By contrast, misidentification as Scottish is viewed as 'offensive', which is no surprise, given their description of Scottish accents as 'hideous' and 'horrible'. The national border appears to play a large role in this perception, as does the fact that Scotland is a separate country.

As the discussion proceeds, it is clear that these respondents have some knowledge of the linguistic landscape in Scotland. They touch on sociolinguistic variation (old men versus young women), and participant F2 discusses the difference between Scottish Borders varieties and those from elsewhere in the Scotland. Participant F2 also imitates a uvular fricative in her discussion of variation in the north of Scotland (the uvular [ʁ] can occasionally be heard in the north-east of Scotland, but it is localised and sporadic at best, and so cannot be viewed as a regular feature of northern or any other Scottish varieties; see Hughes et al. 2012: 132). However, they must be balanced by other comments made about 'a Scottish accent' (line 26) and general discussion about 'Scottish accents' (line 29). Such generalised comments reveal perceptions in line with those shown in the aggregate map for English respondents discussed earlier.

The interview data shown in Extracts 8.1 and 8.2 are clear examples of the fact that respondents in the English locations did not have a detailed mental map of the linguistic geography of Scotland. Participants were able to reproduce a stereotypical feature and to express personal preferences for certain speakers. However, the overriding impression from the interviews is of a perception that respondents in the English locations feel that they have very little in common with Scottish speakers, either because of the Scottish/ English border, or because of a dislike of 'the language' spoken there, or a combination of both of these factors.

9. Interaction data and dialect area recognition

Although attitudinal factors such as those discussed above undoubtedly play a role in the recognition (or otherwise) of dialect areas on either side of the Scottish/English border, other factors such as contact are bound to be important. The extent of meaningful contact between speakers of different varieties is difficult to measure in a study such as this. However, the opportunities for such contact are measurable via UK Census data. The Census questionnaires for all four countries of the UK asked questions relating to commuting, as well as a question about migration, by asking where respondents had lived one year earlier (Office for National Statistics 2004: 22–3).

Because of this focus only on one-year migration, the Census migration data have limited utility, as noted by Buchstaller and Alvanides (2010). As a result, commuting data were extracted from the Census results and are used here to model the potential for contact between speakers of other varieties. Using such Census data avoids the 'gross overgeneralisation' (Britain 2010a: 82) associated with traditional gravity models, although it should be noted that such data also relate only to adults of working age and so do not include children, teenagers or retired people. In spite of this, the routine nature of commuting and the normalisation of contact with speakers of other varieties that results from it mean that commuting represents an attractive variable to consider.

Commuting data for 2001 were extracted using the interface provided by the Centre for Interaction Data Estimation and Research (CIDER; see cids.census.ac.uk). CIDER provides origin-destination data extracted from the 1981, 1991 and 2001 UK Census results. The geography used was the 'Interaction Data Districts' (IDDs), which are derived from county and unitary authority data. There are 426 IDDs in the UK, and for present purposes data were extracted from the twenty-nine IDDs that lie within 80 km (50 miles) of the Scottish/English border. Commuting data were mapped using *ArcGIS* (www. arcgis.com). Figure 8.5 displays commuting flows from IDDs in southern Scotland, and equivalent data from northern England. The IDDs which run along the Scottish/ English border are Dumfries and Galloway and Scottish Borders on the Scottish side, and Carlisle, Tynedale, Alnwick and Berwick-upon-Tweed on the English side. The survey locations used in this study are sited in Dumfries and Galloway (Langholm and Moffat), Scottish Borders (Galashiels), Carlisle (Brampton) and Tynedale (Hexham), and the maps in Figure 8.5 are shaded so that the IDDs in which the survey locations are found are darker than the others.

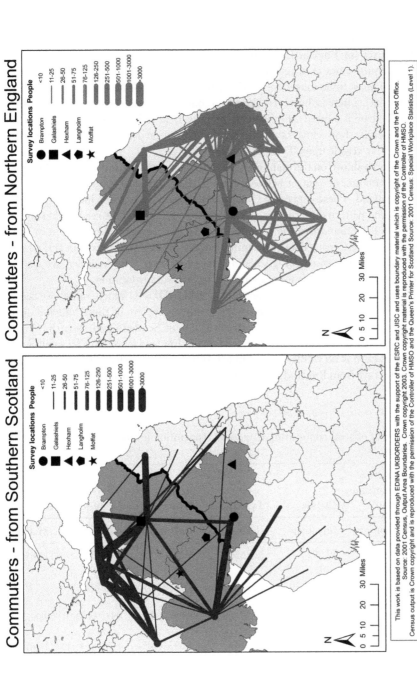

Figure 8.5 Commuting flows from Interaction Data Districts in southern Scotland (left) and northern England (right).

The maps in Figure 8.5 show that there is more commuting across the Scottish/ English border from the Scottish side than from the English side. There is a good amount of reciprocal commuting on the west side of the map, with commuting to and from the Carlisle district (in England) and the Dumfries and Galloway district (in Scotland). There is a similar amount of reciprocity on the east side of the map, though none of the survey locations is to be found on the English side of the border (in the Berwick-upon-Tweed district). There is, however, almost no commuting between Tynedale (the district in which Hexham is located) and Scottish districts. In addition to the cross-border flows, the maps clearly show clusters of interaction centred on Edinburgh in Scotland, and Carlisle and Newcastle upon Tyne in England.

The patterns shown on the maps are relatively clear, and they indicate that there might be a greater amount of contact between English dialect speakers and local people in the south of Scotland. These data can be further interrogated in order to look more closely at the commuting patterns and the possible link between these and the recognition of dialect areas. Table 8.2 summarises the commuting data and divides commuters from outside specific IDDs (the Census data also capture figures for commuting within IDDs) on the basis of their country of origin (Scotland versus England). Also included are the mean percentage recognition levels for respondents in each survey location.

Table 8.2 shows that commuting from outside IDDs is much more prevalent in England than Scotland. Examination of the country of origin of these 'outside district' commuters reveals a stark contrast between IDDs in Scotland and those in England. Whereas the ratio of commuters from Scotland and England is roughly 2:1 in all Scottish IDDs, the pattern is very different in English IDDs. In the Carlisle district 75.3 per cent of commuters are from England, while 99.5 per cent of people from outside the Tynedale

Table 8.2 'Out of area' commuting data, with recognition levels for Scottish and English dialect areas

Census Interaction area (2001) containing survey location	Carlisle	Tynedale	Scottish Borders	Dumfries & Galloway	
Survey location	Brampton	Hexham	Galashiels	Langholm	Moffat
Total workers in interaction area	52,392	22,163	100,460	144,908	144,908
'Outside District' commuters (%)	10,485 (20.7)	4,582 (20.7)	2,547 (2.5)	2,791 (1.9)	2,791 (1.9)
Of these, total from England (%)	7,897 (75.3)	4,557 (99.5)	854 (33.5)	988 (35.9)	988 (35.9)
Of these, total from Scotland (%)	2,582 (24.6)	25 (0.5)	1,693 (66.5)	1,761 (64.1)	1,761 (64.1)
% recognition of English areas	31.6	26.0	27.4	22.0	18.8
% recognition of Scottish areas	13.9	10.8	27.8	22.5	21.5

district commute from other English districts. The opportunities for contact with speakers of the English varieties are similar in the three Scottish survey locations, but in the English locations, the opportunity for contact with Scottish dialects is relatively high in the Carlisle district (in terms of bare numbers), but much diminished in Tynedale (which has only twenty-five people commuting to it from Scotland). These disparities appear to directly influence the perception of dialect variation. As a result, the Scottish survey locations have a similar mean percentage recognition level for English and Scottish dialect areas. By contrast, the decreased opportunities for contact in the Tynedale district could be one of the reasons for its having the lowest level of recognition of Scottish dialect areas of all the locations.

10. Summary and conclusions

By showing data from locations either side of the Scottish/English border, this chapter has demonstrated the importance of the border in constraining perception. The data show that the perceptual constraints of proximity and cultural prominence discussed in earlier sections are clearly important to respondents. However, the effect of the border in attenuating the impact of proximity is key to understanding the patterns shown in the respondents' hand-drawn maps. The data discussed in this chapter have shown that areas closer to respondents' home locations will generally yield a higher level of recognition than those further away. However, this proximity effect does not explain all of the patterns shown in the chapter. Instead, the role of the border in disrupting proximity effects is significant.

I have demonstrated in this chapter that the impact of the Scottish/English border means that there is a unidirectional proximity effect, whereby Scottish respondents have a 'normal' perception of the dialect landscape in Great Britain and areas further away from respondents' home locations produce lower levels of recognition, notwithstanding the impact of cultural prominence, which promotes certain areas up the 'perceptual ladder'. As a result, Scottish respondents' perceptions of dialect variation in England are very similar to those of English respondents. By contrast, English respondents have comparatively little knowledge of variation in Scotland, which I have argued is due to the effect of the border.

The effect of the border clearly has a psychological component, as evidenced by some of the interview comments from English respondents about 'a Scottish' dialect. However, it also has a physical component, as commuting patterns across the border vary according to the origin and destination locations. The finding that English respondents are more likely to commute to Scotland than vice versa is significant, as there are therefore likely to be fewer opportunities for contact between Scottish commuters and the inhabitants of the English communities as a result of this pattern.

The finding relating to the unidirectional nature of perceptual constraints for respondents on either side of the Scottish/English border is key to understanding the way in which the dialect landscape is perceived in this part of the world. It could also have important implications in other border areas, for all that this particular border could be argued to be unique (rather a truism, as all borders are unique in some sense). Unidirectionality must therefore be considered in studies of other border zones, and similar patterns might be expected in such locations.

Notes

1. 'Information space' refers to the space in which we all live (be it geographical or otherwise).
2. The decision to include these city location dots was made to ensure that respondents' geographical knowledge was consistent and that the spatial data they provided could be treated as accurate (cf. Preston 1993: 335). Further details relating to this methodological decision can be found in Montgomery (2007).
3. Transcription conventions are adapted from those used in Niedzielski and Preston (2003).

9

Wales and Welsh: Boundedness and Peripherality[1]

Nikolas Coupland

1. Introduction

Centre/periphery dynamics have played an important part in sociolinguistic accounts of minority languages. As a cohesive, indigenous minority language (as defined by Baker and Jones 1998: 99–104), Welsh is one of the north-west European 'Celtic fringe' languages, a phrase that most obviously refers to geographical peripherality. But the history of Welsh is also a history of marginalisation, in political and cultural dimensions. Correspondingly, initiatives to resist hegemonic peripheralisation and to revitalise the Welsh language can be seen as efforts to construct or regain forms of 'centredness', and the increased level of national autonomy that has followed from political devolution (since 1999) makes this sort of centring more feasible in contemporary Wales than it ever has been. However, there have also been significant issues of centre and periphery within Wales. While Cardiff, the capital city, and the surrounding urban south-east act as a socio-economic and political centre in Wales, there has been the recurring sentiment that the 'heart' or 'heartland' of Wales, ethnolinguistically speaking, is located in *Y Fro Gymraeg*, literally translated as 'the Welsh area', and associated mainly with the rural north-west and south-west of the country.

Questions of borders, boundaries and boundedness are clearly implied in contests around centre and periphery. Today Wales has a settled political border with England,[2] but centuries of anglicisation have seen linguistic and cultural influences flood across it. The Welsh Assembly government takes responsibility for Wales as a territorially bounded nation, and some believe that a nation-state is in prospect. Government-led language policy and planning (LPP) builds on the assumption that mainstreaming the Welsh language and bilingualism will decisively distinguish Wales from England, based on the presumed 'centrality of the association of Welsh identity with the language' (Aitchison and Carter 2004: 144). Yet the impact of LPP in Wales is complex and potentially divisive (Selleck 2013), and language-related boundaries of different sorts persist, both within and around Wales, despite the generally positive subjective orientations to Welsh that most people in Wales hold, as evidenced in attitudinal survey data (Coupland et al. 2006).

Overlaid on these historically shifting issues – of what is central and peripheral in Wales, and of where Wales 'starts and ends' in different respects – is the matter of how Welsh relates to English, and of boundedness in this further sense. In this chapter I explore relationships between linguistic, political and cultural boundaries in and around Wales, hoping to expose the rather uncritical assumptions that tend to be made about these links. Sociolinguistic research on borders has been extensive (though not in the Welsh case), particularly in documenting the distributional, descriptive and attitudinal characteristics of geographical/political/national boundaries (e.g. Hinskens et al. 2000; Llamas et al. 2009; Trudgill 1986). Most studies have been objectivist, in that they orient to known and presumedly fixed boundaries whose social reality is not challenged, even if research ends up establishing that language differences or linguistically mediated differences in social identity are not isomorphic with those known boundaries. In contrast, the interpretive sociolinguistic stance has developed that linguistic varieties, like sociopolitical borders, should not be treated (or not only treated) as objective entities (cf. Barth 1969; Auer and Schmidt 2010; Pietikäinen and Kelly-Holmes 2013). While Welsh and English in their idealised forms can clearly be differentiated as codes along many obvious descriptive dimensions, Welsh and English, as used and as represented in social contexts, show syncretism and selectivity of various sorts.

Urciuoli (1991, 1995) provides an overview of this constructionist perspective on language and borders, tracing origins to Hymes' (1974) argument that language codes are elements of (rather than independent of) social contexts, and to Haugen's (1966a, b) ecological view that the degree of stability that a language code has depends on particular processes of standardisation (Kristiansen and Coupland 2011). Urciuoli (1995: 533) asks 'where do borders come from?' and how do languages take on 'sharp edges'? In line with contemporary emphases in cultural and human geography, Johnstone (2010: 391) similarly argues that 'localities are products of experience and discourse' and that physical spaces are transformed into meaningful places as humans interact with them. She echoes Urciuoli's view that linguistic varieties are themselves constituted as distinctive through particular discursive actions. This is also Gal and Irvine's (1995) argument (summarised by Johnstone 2010: 392) that '"languages" and "dialects" are cultural constructs, produced by a group of people using, orienting to, and/or talking about a specific set of linguistic features, in a process that also constructs the group itself'.

In this vein, I develop a constructionist account of Wales to explore some of the diverse ways in which, and the extents to which, the Welsh language is and has been positioned as a culturally defining code. I pay attention to centre–periphery relations, arguing that particular values are attached to Welsh and to Welshness by virtue of their presumed or claimed peripherality/centredness in different cultural frames of reference. I start by reviewing two historical frames – two competing foundational 'truths' about Welsh distinctiveness – that have been widely commented on. I then examine ways in which Wales and Welshness are constructed in more local and less essentialising ways. As data I consider an eclectic mix of texts: the national anthem, extracts from LPP documents, some public notices and a bilingual menu. The texts share the quality of metacultural reflexivity; that is, they are texts that more explicitly or more implicitly project particular values onto Wales and the Welsh language.

A constructionist sociolinguistic approach to borders – in general and in relation to Wales – is compatible with (and arguably necessitated by) the conditions of late modernity. Johnstone (2010: 393) makes the case that economic and cultural globalisation is generating two contradictory sociolinguistic trends. On the one hand, increased demographic mobility and cultural homogenisation promote linguistic accommodation, levelling and the erasure of linguistic distinctiveness. On the other hand, reflexive awareness of linguistic difference is increasing, and new values for localised language are emerging. In terms of globalisation theory, this is the classical dialectic of *glocalisation* (Hannerz 1992; Robertson 1995; Appadurai 1996; Bauman 1998; Coupland 2010). Wales is being de-traditionalised, and although long-held conceptions of language and nation persist, they run headlong into late-modern value systems that commodify and exploit language and identity in new ways (Heller 2002; Duchêne and Heller 2007; Blommaert 2010). An objectivist approach to language and borders would leave no room for critical analysis of the complex and changing ideological frames that characterise bilingual Wales, and indeed of the senses in which Wales should be deemed to be bilingual. The fact that most academic and political debates about the Welsh language continue to be framed in objectivist terms provides another motivation. In my view, public debates about language and bilingualism in Wales are limited by an objectivist overdetermination of 'what Welsh is' and by under-nuanced understandings of 'what bilingualism does'.

2. Wales and Welsh in romantic nationalist discourse

We can start with a heavily idealised instance. The mythic conception of Wales as a bounded and linguistically distinctive nation is strongly visible in the Welsh national anthem. Csepeli and Örkeny (1998: 38) see the origins of European national anthems as 'paraphernalia of state which aspired not merely to command the obedience of its subjects but to rally their loyalty as citizens'. Wales has never been an independent polity, but its anthem aspires to bounded distinctiveness, and it does this by drawing from a familiar repertoire of images, claims and exhortations. Anthems are anachronistic, extolling putative national origins and heritage (the 'land of my fathers', in the Welsh case). The Welsh anthem in fact dates from 1856,[3] but it imputes a timelessness to Wales, its land and its language. Extract 9.1 is the portion of the anthem that is most commonly sung (in Welsh only) at international sporting events and on other ceremonial occasions in Wales, followed by a broad English translation.

Delineating a nationally bounded space is a primary requirement in national anthems (Csepeli and Örkeny 1998: 40). The concept of *gwlad* (including its morpho-phonemically mutated form *wlad* and its incorporation into the compound *gwladgarwyr* – 'patriots') figures repeatedly in the anthem, where it refers to 'land' in both geological and ethno-symbolic senses. The Welshness of *gwlad* is implied in the fact that the anthem is sung in Welsh (although the argument is occasionally made that Wales should have a bilingual anthem), and also in the cohesive link between *gwlad* and *[y]r hen iaith* ('the land' and 'the old language') in the second verse. Herderian associations between land, blood and heroic battles are also referenced – the battles mentioned are unspecified and they are hard to locate historically – heroic defence of one's land again being a typical theme of the genre. Perhaps the most striking boundary claim comes in *Tra mor yn fur / I'r bur hoff bau*, 'While the sea is a wall / To the pure, most loved land', imagining Wales to be a sea-bound nation, an island, notwithstanding the fact that (as I noted earlier) Wales has a long and in many senses rather permeable eastern boundary with England.

Mae hen wlad fy nhadau yn annwyl i mi,
Gwlad beirdd a chantorion, enwogion o fri;
Ei gwrol ryfelwyr, gwladgarwyr tra mâd,
Tros ryddid collasant eu gwaed.

Gwlad, gwlad, pleidiol wyf i'm gwlad;
Tra mor yn fur
I'r bur hoff bau,
O bydded i'r hen iaith barhau.

'The old land of my fathers is dear unto me,
Land of bards and singers, great men of renown;
Her warriors brave, and patriots great,
For freedom they lost their blood.

(My) country, (my) country, I'm devoted to my country;
While the sea is a wall
To the pure, most loved land,
May the old language live evermore.'

Extract 9.1 The Welsh national anthem

It would be easy to dismiss national anthems for (in Csepeli and Örkeny's terms) their collective narcissism and ethnocentrism. They are sung ceremonially; relatively few people in Wales, perhaps one-fifth, understand let alone endorse the national anthem's particular sentiments. Yet the anthem connects semantically and ideologically with popular discourses of language and national identity in Wales. It is often observed, for example, that the English word 'Wales' derives from *Wealas*, an Old English form meaning 'foreigners', as opposed to the Welsh word *Cymru*, whose first syllable/morpheme means 'with' or 'together', allowing *Y Cymru* (usually translated as 'the Welsh') to also mean 'the Comrades'. The *Wealas/Cymru* contrast supports an inter-group ('them and us') relationship between Wales and England, iconised in the lexical resources of the two languages. Referring to 'the Welsh' can be said to be othering and peripheralising from an English perspective; referring to Wales and Welsh people as *Cymru* (which is gaining popularity as a form of national reference in English discourse – 'the Cymru') centres and unifies the national in-group. This inter-group perspective again naturalises the idea of Wales being linguistically, politically and culturally bounded, including to the east, along the boundary which, according to nationalist ideology, needs to be most imperme-able. While history tells us that Offa, an Anglo-Saxon king, constructed a dyke in about AD 790 as a physical barrier between Welsh and English territory along this boundary, in order to annex the *Wealas*, it was 'his' boundary, not 'ours' – romantic, centripetal, nationalist discourse can construe Wales to be a timeless ethnolinguistic capsule, imper-meably boundaried off from England and even, in the contemporary era, from globalised modernity.

3. 'Two truths' in the history of language and culture in Wales

Influential historical and cultural analyses of Wales have argued that versions of this nationalist ideology have existed in tension with a quite different account of what defines Wales. Raymond Williams's introduction to this dualism is as follows:

> Two truths are told, as alternative prologues to the action of modern Wales. The first draws on the continuity of Welsh language and literature: from the sixth century, it is said, and thus perhaps the oldest surviving poetic tradition in Europe. The second draws on the turbulent experience of industrial South Wales, over the two last centuries, and its powerful political and communal formations. (Williams 2003: 27)

The 'first truth' is a culturally conservative conception of Wales, along the lines of the national anthem. It presumes but also lobbies for national continuity, symbolised by the Welsh language, particularly in its ceremonial realisations (e.g. in *eisteddfodau*). It expounds a politics of linguistic and cultural protectionism, particularly resistance to cultural hegemony from England, which is viewed as threatening to dilute if not displace Welsh cultural norms (see discussion of the language activist group *Cymuned*'s campaigning rhetoric in Coupland 2012, or Coupland and Bishop 2006). As in the anthem text, place, land and indeed natural landscapes are further iconic national resources (cf. Saunders Lewis's bitter poem about the physically and culturally polluting consequences of industrialisation in Merthyr Tydfil, 'Here once was Wales . . .'). Williams (2003: 27) characterises the general ideological stances of the first truth as being based in 'archaic or residual types of nationalism'.

The 'second truth' is based in socialist communitarianism as it came to be realised in industrial South Wales, which then arguably came to iconise all of Wales. Williams (2003) refers to how, in the history of industrialisation in the South Wales valleys, Wales was 'penetrated' by English capital and management, and to that extent the second truth repeats some of the inter-group (Wales vs. England) antagonism of the first truth. But the second truth is not ethnocentric, and its socialist politics are internationalist. At the height of the industrial period, coal and steel production in Wales placed it at the centre of a new global enterprise. The Welsh language is not salient in the second truth, reflecting the transregional and to some extent transnational mobility through which the communities of the Valleys were forged. The second truth finds distinctive Welsh values not in conserving the past but in building strong working communities under adverse circumstances, and, Williams suggests, in personal qualities of wit, passion, resilience and a certain arrogance.

Marxist historian G. A. Williams (known as 'Gwyn Alf') identifies the same dualism in his descriptions of *gwerin* versus proletarian Wales, although his account is more polemical. *Gwerin* translates as 'folk', but it refers more specifically to a rural, nonconformist, Welsh-speaking and (in party-political terms) Liberal ideology. Gwyn Alf argues (1985: 180) that industrialisation threw *gwerin* Wales into 'permanent crisis from 1841 onwards' and led to 'an endless drain on its people' to the extent that *gwerin* Wales developed an 'objective dependency on industrial Wales'. In his view, industrial South Wales, which fully deserved its upper-case <S> in 'South' because it was a culturally defining name, first pluralised Wales into 'two nations', then radically displaced the *gwerin* as the dominant cultural formation in Wales.[4]

Gwyn Alf is quick to de-authenticate and subvert the icons of *gwerin* Wales. He explains that Edward Williams, a London-based stonemason (1747–1826) who assumed the more ethno-symbolically Welsh celebrity name *Iolo Morganwg* ('Iolo of Glamorgan'), invented the bardic tradition that is mentioned in the Welsh national anthem (*Gwlad beirdd*, 'Land of bards') and recycled annually through the Welsh national *eisteddfod*. Gwyn Alf (1985: 162) challenges the assumption of culturally continuous, Welsh-language-mediated Welshness, writing that 'This new [bardic] Welsh nation was manufactured in London'. He describes Wales as being fundamentally disunified, a Wales of 'two western peninsulas' in the north and the south. He wrote that 'the north persists, the south innovates'. In his view it was industrialisation that, at least for a specific period, imposed a coherent value structure and sense of national purpose on Wales. The territory known as 'the Valleys' (the mining valleys of the South Wales coalfield, stretching across almost the whole of South Wales, from Llanelli to Blaenavon) sustained 'an extraordinarily rich, wide-open, very Welsh, very British . . . and increasingly American popular culture which had invented its own language [South Walian English]' (1985: 224). The Valleys provided a cultural centre for the project of Wales, until the disastrous years of harsh and abrupt de-industrialisation during the period between 1930 and 1980.

4. Language planning and national inclusiveness in contemporary Wales

It is clear, then, that the concepts 'national language' and 'national identity', and the association between language and identity, have been historically contested in Wales, and this continues to be the case. But it is also clear that neither of the two historical 'truths' is sustainable as the basis of a sociolinguistic account of contemporary Wales.

Objectively speaking, Welsh has not been spoken by a majority of the population of Wales since the late decades of the nineteenth century. Census data from 2001 showed a recovery from around 18 per cent of self-declaring Welsh speakers in 1991 to around 21 per cent. Headline statistical data on self-declaring language ability in Wales from the 2011 Census were announced on 11 December 2012[5] and showed an unexpected decrease to 19 per cent in the number and proportion of people in Wales aged three years and over who were able to speak Welsh. The data for 2001 (the latest data for which detailed analysis is available) showed significant shifts in age and areal distributions of speakers from previous decades, reflecting the statistical impact of young speakers compulsorily learning Welsh in school. They also showed that the greatest densities of young people, and correspondingly of Welsh speakers, were in urban (notably south-eastern) localities (Aitchison and Carter 2004; see also Coupland and Aldridge 2009), and these factors challenged the traditional assumption that Welsh is mainly a language of the 'heartland' rural peripheries. *Gwerin* sensibilities persist in Wales, but a rurally based, culturally conservative and linguistically protectionist ideology seems grossly out of tune with the political and cultural aspirations of a re-launched national project of the sort envisaged by the Welsh Assembly government. Equally, the Valleys communities of post-industrial South Wales have been decimated by the closure of heavy industry since 1980, leaving Gwyn Alf's 'proletariat' and all of Wales at the mercy of rampant neoliberal forces. Rural Wales and Valleys Wales have, by different routes, come to share a high level of socio-economic hardship.

Through political devolution, Wales has found itself with the opportunity, and the need, to move on from old dualisms and to remake itself as a more autonomous polity. Building national coherence has been one of its key ambitions, and this is visible in the different phases of LPP that have been developed over the last decade. Language planning in Wales has been ambitious and well funded. Following a published review of the future of the Welsh language (Welsh Assembly 2002), the policy document *Iaith Pawb*, 'Everyone's Language' (Welsh Assembly 2003), set ambitious targets for the growth of Welsh, as Extract 9.2 shows. These particular targets, as noted above, were not met, and it is not yet clear how the devolved government will react to the 2011 Census results. A current policy document, *Iaith Fyw, Iaith Byw*, 'A Living Language, A Language for Living' (Welsh Assembly 2010), consolidated earlier objectives and anticipated a 'Welsh Language Measure' (governmental Act) that would, for example, impose more specific duties on Welsh organisations to provide services in Welsh. The Measure came into force in 2011 and set out a raft of particular schemes and initiatives for encouraging the use of Welsh in families and in the community. It also introduced a scheme by which penalties could be imposed on public sector organisations, and invested a Language Commissioner with 'the primary responsibility for enforcing compliance with standards' (p. 44).

We are no longer concerned with merely stabilising the number and percentage of Welsh speakers. We want to see a sustained increase in both the number and percentage of people able to speak Welsh . . . We believe that the long-term well-being of the language is dependent on enabling as many pre-school children and young people as possible to acquire the language and as early as possible . . . But we want to look beyond mere numbers of people who can speak Welsh. We want Wales to be a truly bilingual nation, by which we mean a country where people can choose to live their lives through the medium of either Welsh or English and where the presence of the two languages is a visible and audible source of pride and strength to us all . . .

The measures set out in this Action Plan are aimed at achieving the following key targets: By 2011:

- the percentage of people in Wales able to speak Welsh has increased by 5 percentage points from the figure which emerges from the census of 2001;
- the decline in the number of communities where Welsh is spoken by over 70% of the population is arrested . . .

We shall also aim to bring about an increase in the use and visibility of the Welsh language in all aspects of everyday life, including work, leisure and social activities . . .

Extract 9.2 Extracts from *Iaith Pawb* (paragraphs 2.12–2.17)

The aim of creating a 'truly bilingual' Wales and the criterion of code 'choice' that underlies it (see Extract 9.2) has attracted critical comment (e.g. C. H. Williams 2005; Selleck 2013). The concept is interesting in that it represents Wales as a bounded national territory within which Welsh and English will function as equivalent codes, pervasively available to be 'chosen' by citizens as alternative lifestyle options: individuals will 'choose to live their lives through the medium of either Welsh or English'. Several significant obstacles are overlooked here, not least of which is the well-known unevenness in the demographic distribution of Welsh speakers within Wales. 'Choice' will be experienced quite differently in different parts of Wales – for example Gwynedd (in the north-west), where Census 2001 recorded that almost 70 per cent of the population were declared to speak Welsh, as opposed to Gwent (in the urbanised south-east), where the equivalent figure was under 10 per cent (Aitchison and Carter 2004: 90; E. Williams 2009). There is also the problem of incompatibility between the vision of speaker 'choice' and *Iaith Fyw*'s warranting of 'enforcing compliance'.

'True bilingualism' premised on code equivalence is not a coherent sociolinguistic concept, although it is easy to appreciate the Assembly government's need to develop policies that will be considered inclusive and relevant to the whole of Wales (that is, to avoid centre/periphery distinctions within Wales) and its desire to promote a view of Welsh as a code with levels of legitimacy and availability equivalent to those of English. *Iaith Pawb* and *Iaith Fyw* are, after all, not only official records of governmental policy, but textual embodiments of the ideology of language revitalisation; they are textual realisations of status planning. Yet these documents and the planning regime in general are based in a highly restrictive conception of language, and particularly of language codes in bilingualism.

5. Linguistic syncretism versus parallelism

The view of bilingualism as two equivalent language codes existing in parallel, able to be chosen at the discretion of speakers across Wales, results from a desire to redress a long history of evaluative non-equivalence between Welsh and English. The two languages (and it is a feature of language politics in Wales not only to reify Welsh and English as codes but also to erase consideration of any other languages than these two) for centuries existed in a diglossic relationship, with English functioning as a 'high', public code and Welsh (at least outside specific religious and literary genres) restricted to 'low' contexts of use. The ideological climate in which these conceptions arose has clearly changed, no doubt partly as a consequence of LPP initiatives, with Welsh having gained official status in many public domains,[6] even though there is a large perceived gap between levels of potential and actual use of Welsh in the public sphere – the gap that *Iaith Fyw* set out to close. But the whole apparatus of LPP in Wales, including its assumptions about the measurement and manipulation of the ethnolinguistic vitality of Welsh and its standing in relation to English, is built on a questionable view of languages as both bounded linguistic systems and bounded cultural commodities. In Urciuoli's terms (see the first section, above), it requires us to accept that Welsh and English are 'monolithic structures with sharp edges'. In consequence, there is little if any space to recognise bilingualism as a creative practice exploiting the malleable and often syncretic resources of language.

Figure 9.1 Two examples of 'parallel texting' in public signage in Wales.

In an earlier paper (Coupland 2012) I commented on a pervasive pattern of bilingual language display in contemporary Wales that I referred to as 'parallel text bilingualism' and that demonstrates an ideology of anti-syncretism. There is a strong trend towards public notices, institutional titles and many place names (e.g. on road signs) being presented 'in two languages'. Figure 9.1 shows two unexceptional examples. While both of these signs use multimodal semiotic resources, the linguistic elements show lexical and pragmatic redundancy. The direction sign (at the main exit from Cardiff railway station) could be said to do its directing 'twice-over' (functional parallelism) by repeating its content (formal parallelism) in Welsh and English in the two separate panels. The demarcation of Welsh from English is partly orthographic-only ('tacsi' and 'taxi' are pronounced the same way), partly orthographic-plus-phonological (e.g. 'stadium' has short /a/ in Welsh and variably long [e:] or a diphthong [ei] in varieties of Welsh English), partly lexical (e.g. 'canol' and 'centre' are standard Welsh and English words), and partly syntactic (Welsh, unlike English, puts qualifiers after head nouns in noun phrases, e.g. in *Stadiwm y Mileniwm*). The institutional sign in the second image (which in full-frame carries the main English title 'CARMARTHEN BUSINESSMENS CLUB') then shows a different sort of parallel texting across the display on the three window panes. The middle panel has an image of the Welsh dragon (the motif of the national flag) and the word 'BIZZ', a short-form for 'business' that is used in English and as an informal English loan in Welsh. But the head noun in the phrases 'clwb bizz' and 'bizz club' (which again follow different noun-phrase sequencing rules) is rendered in paralleled orthographic forms, notwithstanding that the three-part sequence turns out to be a syncretic blend of Welsh and English grammars.

Parallel texting reflects a restrictive view of bilingualism as 'double monolingualism' (Heller 2002). In the 2012 paper I argued that 'code equivalence' actually entails four specific design principles in the context of parallel-text public signage. The first is referential sameness – texts should make the same references using the resources of each language in sequence. But they should also symbolise linguistic equality, by giving equal prominence to Welsh and English text, for example in the use of fonts and text placement. They should also symbolise choice – 'read this code or that one', in the way that *Iaith Pawb* prescribes. Finally, they should respect code integrity: each code should appear in its 'proper' form. In at least these four respects, parallel texting both results from and actively promotes an ideology that favours 'language codes with sharp edges'.

Filling Welsh public spaces with paralleled bilingual text is a planned development that goes some way to meeting *Iaith Pawb*'s aspiration for Welsh and 'true bilingualism' to become 'more visible' (see Extract 9.2). Except for occasional sniping comments about the 'pedantic' nature of the practice and the expense of changing public signage, the strategy appears to meet with public approval. Since the 1960s, language activists have campaigned for more bilingual signage in Wales, which they have seen as a more equitable language policy (Merriman and Jones 2009). 'Sharpening the edges' of Welsh has been an explicit concern of LPP in Wales in other ways too. For example, government-sponsored advice has been circulated about how best to design bilingual literature, in which the need to 'keep the languages separate' is an explicit theme.[7] Terminology planning in Welsh and the publication of a continually updated terminology database is undertaken by the Assembly's Translation Service,[8] as another classical function of corpus planning. Public understandings of language and bilingualism have presumed the need for 'sharp edges' to such an extent that the institutionalising of this ideology in language planning is viewed as entirely uncontroversial.

The contrary view is that (to use Haugen's metaphor) the ecologies of language use and of language change, particularly in circumstances of contact, tend to erode boundaries around language, that codes are never uniform or complete, and that they inevitably experience syncretism: processes of 'growing together' and 'growing into' one another. This being the general case, initiatives to truncate or 'repair' syncretic action involve destabilising linguistic ecologies, and they are liable to have unintended consequences. Hill and Hill (1986) explain how the ideology of linguistic purism relegates the linguistic/textual products of syncretic linguistic processes, whether between varieties of a language or between majority and minority languages, to being considered 'degenerate'. But a minority language (although the term can easily be misleading, not least in Wales) whose boundaries with another language have become less distinct is a prime locus for anti-syncretic initiatives, driven by a fear of degeneration. That fear is compounded by a series of 'misconceptions', as described by Duranti and Ochs (1997). These include the erroneous views that language code is a precise indicator of cultural orientation (the view that one can only *be* Welsh if one *speaks* Welsh) and that culture is in itself a bounded, homogeneous entity (that Welshness is a singular identity). Syncretism has also been argued to have positive consequences. It can also be seen as a model of language development that maintains linguistic functionality and indexical value for groups in contact situations. Based on her research on East Sutherland Gaelic, Dorian (1994) makes the case that conservative, purist stances by language planners and by some speakers of older, more standard varieties of minority languages can hamper attempts at minority language revitalisation, while syncretism can leave a language more viable and versatile. These issues, of course, are key parts of the field of contestation between professional sociolinguistics and normative public opinion.

Welsh/English syncretism is multi-dimensional and extensive in ways that are too far-reaching to document here. It includes substantial lexical borrowing from English into Welsh (of the sort that is partly being 'repaired' by terminology planning) and of some morpho-syntactic features (such as plural /s/) into colloquial Welsh, but also phonological influences from English (including from long-anglicised urban south-east Wales on the pronunciation of 'new' speakers of Welsh – see Robert 2009). English usage in Wales correspondingly shows different types of influence from Welsh, particularly in pronunciation (but less so in the urban south-east, where vernacular English speech is 'very un-Welsh'). Many place names that are considered to be 'English' are better described as anglicised Welsh names. The indexical Welshness of English speech in Wales is well-attested in studies that also show the malleability of those resources in styling national identities (see examples in Coupland 2007). Under these circumstances, centripetal and standardising initiatives in relation to Welsh, based on the assumption that Welsh identity can only persist if a preferred and 'full' variety of Welsh is mainstreamed into widespread usage, would clearly challenge a complex, evolving sociolinguistic ecology.

6. Sociolinguistic niches and ethno-symbolic Welsh

In a context where competence in Welsh is very unevenly distributed (even within so-called heartland areas), but where Welsh is perceived to be revitalising and is generally well regarded, public uses and displays of Welsh are subject to contradictory pressures. Welsh has shaken off its associations of low status (as a diglossic 'low' code) and is beginning to have new associations with privilege and middle class-ness. Aitchison and Carter (2004: 91) argue that de-industrialisation and the rise of service sector employment in Wales has created a climate in which 'the ability to speak Welsh has become associated with higher status positions'. Strong LPP investment in Welsh-medium education has made it socially desirable on educational as well as ethno-national grounds. Devolution has created a more cogent political structure for which the Welsh language can potentially stand as a national index. On the other hand, in simple demographic terms, Welsh remains a minority code: Census 2001 suggests that around four-fifths of the Welsh population do not speak Welsh. More importantly, the implausibility of 'true bilingualism' in the Welsh LPP sense of that expression is transparently obvious to many. Key social domains and functions – local as well as global – continue to be dominated by English in Wales, and (as I mentioned just above) English has its own resources for performing Welshness. Moves to service the same communicative functions by both Welsh and English in parallel, of the kind that we see when Welsh TV programming duplicates English-language TV genres and formats, arguably under-uses the distinctive resources of Welsh and of more syncretic modes of bilingualism.

One consequence is that Welsh in public and particularly commercial life is becoming a niched phenomenon. There is a tendency to use Welsh language resources selectively and symbolically, reconciling the fact that most people have limited functional competence in Welsh with the fact that Welsh has positive indexicalities of place and nation, and therefore value in globalised markets as a marker of localism. This is the basis on which monolingual people in Wales may come to give their children, their houses, their pets, their boats and so on, Welsh names. They may use formulaic Welsh salutations in emails, and make some effort to sing the national anthem. These are ethno-symbolic acts of language display (Eastman and Stein 1993; Smith 2009; Coupland 2012). In the commercial sector, Welsh is able to 'add value' to products and services, particularly when names, slogans or brands can use Welsh expressions that capture particular values and meanings of Welshness that resonate in globalised markets.

One instance is commercial uptake of the concept *cwtch* which circulates widely, at least in South Wales. *Cwtch* (occasionally spelled *cwtsh*) conveys a generalised semantics of 'Welsh cosiness'. As a Welsh word it is reputedly untranslatable, as if it can be understood only by Welsh speakers (cf. the concepts *hwyl*, a nationally and sometimes religiously-oriented 'spirit' or 'enthusiasm', and *hiraeth*, a nationally oriented 'longing'). These perceived qualities allow *cwtch* to function as a rich point of culture, in turn making it ethno-symbolically exploitable. As a verb *cwtch* (transitively) means 'cuddle', or (intransitively) 'settle down' or 'get cosy'. As a noun it can again refer to a 'cuddle' or a 'hug', but also 'a small and quiet place', for example in *cwtch dan star*, 'small cupboard under the stairs'. Many commercial organisations brand themselves using the *cwtch* concept,[9] but we can briefly consider just one of them here, Cwtch Restaurant in Tyddewi/St Davids in south-west Wales.[10]

The village of St Davids is positioned very near the coast in north-west Pembrokeshire, on what is said to be a linguistic and cultural boundary-line called the Landsker Line (in Welsh *Y Ffin*, 'the Boundary'). The Landsker Line runs from St Davids south-east to Amroth on the south Pembrokeshire coast. Place names tend to be more evidently English to the south and west of the Landsker Line (south Pembrokeshire is referred to as 'Little England beyond Wales') and more evidently Welsh to its north and east.[11] But the apparently liminal position of St Davids, poised between reputedly Welsh and English language zones, is complicated by its history. Its Welsh name *Tyddewi* means 'the seat of Dewi', referring to Dewi (or David), the patron saint of Wales. The village, furthermore, is the site of a grand cathedral complex, St David's Cathedral, leading it to be known as 'the smallest city in Wales' (since having a cathedral is a conventional criterion for enjoying city status in the UK). For some, St Davids is therefore a highly 'centred' and 'centring' place in terms of Welsh ethnic identity – St David's Day (1 March) is Wales's national day, there is a St David's flag, and so on – even though it is not located inside the zone held to be *Y Fro Gymraeg* and is generally considered to be a 'rather English' cultural space.

St Davids' geographical peripherality is itself complex. Its coastal position makes it geographically 'remote', although today this remoteness is not a major obstacle to travel and in fact has positive appeal to (mainly monolingual English-speaking) tourists. Visitors are attracted to St Davids as a centre for walking, nature-watching and adventure pursuits such as coasteering, but also for its religious (and in some interpretations mystical, Celtic and New Age) associations. Historically, its cathedral was established as a religious centre strategically located on saints' and pilgrims' trails around the coast of Wales, but also supporting mobility between Wales, Cornwall and Ireland. In these various senses – geographical, cultural, linguistic – we can say that St Davids is at the same time highly peripheral and highly centred. It has a metacultural status as 'very Welsh', but has few Welsh speakers. Its Welshness has historical depth, but its appeal is also quite contemporary and touristic. St Davids is linked to nationalist (indeed *gwerin*) and Celtic mythologies, although its economic survival depends on (relatively up-market) tourism that is generally an anglicising influence.

In this context we can begin to appreciate how the semantics of *cwtch* and the branding and marketing of Cwtch Restaurant in St Davids come together. The restaurant promotes itself as a Welsh, homely, but elite establishment. Its website uses the slogan 'big on simplicity', implying that its 'award-winning' provision is based in the principled use of simple but high-quality food ingredients, simply prepared and served in comfortable ('your home from home') surroundings. The franchise incorporates rental cottages in St Davids, which it describes as 'charming, stylish and fabulously comfortable – your holiday home from home'. The restaurant and rooms' style might be described as 'boutique'. As I suggested earlier, the association between Welsh-speaking and middle class-ness is relatively new, and Cwtch Restaurant's marketing maps very well on to this development. The 'Welsh cosiness' connotation of *cwtch* adds another semantic dimension, which we can interpret in terms of centre/periphery dynamics. Cwtch Restaurant is not only 'small' in its physical size and in its homely ethos, it celebrates 'smallness' in the sense that its commercial and gastronomic principles are attuned to its position in 'peripheral' rural Wales. The Welsh language has particular salience in this construction. The restaurant's marketing takes every opportunity to style itself as an intensely local establishment, and local in an ethno-linguistically Welsh sense.

One text that amply displays this linguistically-mediated localness is the restaurant's advertised menu for St David's Day 2012. The event is already rich in metacultural significance – the patron saint's day being celebrated in the village/city that is named after him. The menu is, predictably enough, promoted as being 'all Welsh', but it is so in specific ways that extol the importance of local, Welsh-name places and products (see Figure 9.2). The text could be called an English menu, in the sense that its matrix

Cwtch* All Welsh Menu

Thursday March 1st 2012

St Davids Day Lunch and Dinner

We are celebrating the best of Welsh produce this St.David's Day with a menu that includes all things welsh – even down to the Salt we use and the Flour for our bread.

Come and celebrate the traditional day for everyone Welsh, and enjoy a complimentary Welsh Drink from Cwtch*.
Choose from:
A Glass of Monnow Valley Welsh Wine OR
Pen Lon Cardi Bay Ale OR
Gwynt Y Ddraig Cider OR
Elderwicks Elderflower Presse

To Nibble on…

Homemade bread made with Y Felin Mill Flour, Sprinkled with Halen Mon Sea Salt

To Start

Cwtch Cawl with Caerfai Caerfilly Cheese
Cawl Cenin (Wonderful Leek Soup) with Caerfai Caerfilly Cheese (v)
Abercastle Potted Crab with Lemon Mayonnaise and Bloody Mary Brekon Vodka Shot
Cold Rare Roast Welsh Black Beef with Wild Garlic Salsa Verde
Pantysgwan Goats Cheese, Roasted Pear, Baby Spinach and Walnut Salad (v) OR
Welsh Rarebit topped Portobello Mushroom (v)

Mains

Welsh Black Beef Casserole with Double Dragon Mustard Mash
12 hr Slow Roasted Pembrokeshire Pork Belly with Trealy Farm Black Pudding and Onion Gravy
Gower Mussels with Gwynt Y Ddraig Cider and Leek Cream
Fresh Fish of the Day (Solva) with Laverbread and Penclawdd Cockle Cake, Sauce Vierge
Pen Pant and Spring Meadow Minted Vegetable Cassoulet, Garlic Sauteed Potatoes (v)

Puddings

Local Rhubarb and Apple Crumble with Caerfai Cream
Dark Chocolate and Merlyn Liqueur Mousse Pots with Rachel's Vanilla Crème Fraiche
Women's Institute Homemade Bara Brith and Butter Pudding with Sticky Toffee Sauce
Gianni's Welsh Cake Ice Cream with Penderwyn Whiskey Sauce
Pembrokeshire Cheeseboard with Oatcakes and Cwtch Onion Marmalade

2 courses £15 per person
3 courses £19 per person
Lunch 12 – 2.30pm
Dinner 6pm

To make a booking please call us on 01437 720491
or email info@cwtchrestaurant.co.uk

Figure 9.2 Cwtch Restaurant's St David's Day menu, 2012.

language is English throughout: its headings, introductory blurb, pricing details, etc., are in English. The head nouns of noun-phrases describing menu options and ingredients are either in English (*wine, ale, cider, cheese*, etc.) or in languages that have donated culinary lexis (*presse, salsa*). *Cawl* is the only Welsh head noun, in *Cawl cenin*, 'leek soup'. The proprietors claim that their menu 'includes all things welsh [*sic*]'.[12] Its Welshness lies in how menu items and food ingredients are repeatedly associated (in grammatical classifiers within noun phrases) with local place names, many of them Welsh. For example, *Pen Lon Cardi Bay Ale* is a hand-made, 'artisan' beer produced on Penlon farm in Llanarth (near New Quay on the north coast of Ceredigion), and *Cardi* is a short-form for 'from Cardigan' used in both Welsh and English. *Caerfai Caerfilli Cheese* is doubly local, in that it identifies a type of cheese first made in Wales (in the town of Caerffili [the usual Welsh spelling]), but in this instance with cheese of this type made at Caerfai Farm, very close to St Davids. *Abercastle Potted Crab* presumably refers to crabs caught at Abercastle Bay, which is again only a few miles from St Davids, and so on.

Producing, supplying and consuming intensely local food is a contemporary elite food regime (Lindholm 2008: ch. 6), and very much part of the localisation response to globalisation, based in environmental politics. Prioritising 'food from somewhere' and 'slow food' (Campbell 2009) tends to be a middle-class ideological concern, and this intensifies the paradoxes on which it is based: food that is authenticated by localism minimises the cost of food miles, yet it attracts a market premium among middle-class consumers; restaurateurs can construct elite menus on the basis of the most humble of ingredients (cider, flour, salt, cheese, laverbread [seaweed], cockles, etc., in Figure 9.2), provided that they are accredited to be local; food localism is a global movement. Cwtch Restaurant's practices and promotion clearly align with the ideological regime of food localism. They promote their food as being from a set of known and particularly local 'somewheres' in 'peripheral' south-west Wales. Yet the restaurant is closely networked with many other high-end food producers and suppliers, such as the Assembly government-sponsored *Cymru Y Gwir Flas*, 'Wales the True Taste' network,[13] most of whose members use Welsh as a localising and branding resource in the way that Cwtch Restaurant does.

7. Conclusion

In this chapter I have tried to go beyond the assumption that Wales is a bounded national territory rendered coherent and 'centred' by its revitalising ancient language. There have been centuries-long contests over what defines Wales, and in particular over the status of the Welsh language in this regard, and those contests continue today. Welsh is undoubtedly a precious national resource, and has proved to be remarkably durable under the pressures of colonialism and globalisation. But these terms already over-consolidate 'the language', over-simplify relationships between language and nation, and understate the power of social change to reconfigure them. The Assembly government's model of 'true bilingualism' perpetuates these 'misconceptions' (Duranti and Ochs 1997), presuming that any upward trend in what Census reports refer to as 'the number and percentage of people able to speak Welsh' is the sole significant measure of LPP success, and that 'more Welsh' equals 'more bilingualism', 'more choice' and 'more pride and strength' in Wales (see Extract 9.2). This view of language in Wales may not bear much relevance to lived realities of bilingualism, now or in the future.

Welsh and English have never been 'equivalent' codes, and it is difficult to see how they could or should be. To plan for greater equivalence is also (in Urciuoli's terms) to plan for more 'sharpening of the edges' of these languages, with outcomes that are not obviously desirable. Sociolinguistic literatures on language standardisation and language planning have not often overlapped, yet the undesirable consequences of standardisation are precisely the consequences of corpus planning. Moves to inculcate the use of Welsh through education and in community projects do indeed appear to be boosting the demographic profile of Welsh, but the value of Welsh and of bilingualism in their many different manifestations will always need to be discovered and activated in particular local contexts and symbolic markets. The Cwtch Restaurant case is one in which a syncretic model of Welsh/English relationships – particularly Welsh place names being invoked as a linguistic index of food localism within an English matrix – is clearly functional in its own local context, as opposed to a striving for 'true bilingualism' which, as I argued earlier, is likely to undermine the potential value of creative bilingual practice.

Peripherality has featured in different ways in conventional understandings of minority languages (Pietikäinen and Kelly-Holmes 2013) and of Welsh (Coupland 2013). Welsh has been viewed as a marginal code associated with remote spaces and non-core (that is, socio-economically inferior) social functions. The politics of revitalisation is very much a project designed to re-centre Welsh, to allow it to 'compete' with English as a 'full' alternative. This is an understandable sociopolitical stance, but it is surely misjudged on many levels. On the one hand, there are markets that will continue to valorise English in Wales, not for its 'Englishness' but, in different circumstances, both for its internationality and for its potential to index Welshness. When markets value localness, and linguistic localness as one of its dimensions, they will not prioritise 'true bilingualism'. Markets tend to fetishise small languages (Kelly-Holmes 2005) and exploit their ethno-symbolic potential in specific sociolinguistic niches, as we saw with the cultural semantics of *cwtch*.

The most general conclusion to this discussion is that we need to look beyond both boundedness and peripherality in characterising Wales and Welsh, because both concepts are out of kilter with late-modern social and sociolinguistic life. Centre/periphery dynamics are not stable, because globalisation challenges the structured certainties of modernity and is liable to invert older relationships, finding new values in linguistic and other sorts of 'difference'. These processes underlie the (patchy) gentrification of south-west Wales, where some small-scale commercial initiatives are finding it valuable to market themselves using selective and syncretic bilingual repertoires. Establishing boundaries around language codes was an imperative in the foundation of nation-states (see e.g. Bert and Costa, this volume), and we see these same priorities being asserted in nationalistically-inspired LPP efforts in Wales. But the irony – bitter for some – is that globalising late modernity has already radically reduced the potential of nations to convincingly assert their own bounded priorities. 'Language and nation' rhetoric in Wales already sounds tropic and anachronistic, and at odds with contemporary social realities characterised by mobility and complexity. We should also take heed of Pennycook's argument that it is 'language practices . . . [that] create the space in which they happen' (2010: 128). Whatever Wales and the Welsh language are, they will be constructed in the local and evolving and often syncretic practices of speakers.

Notes

1. This chapter was prepared in the context of a Finnish Academy grant, with Sari Pietikäinen as Principal Investigator, for a project on 'Peripheral Multilingualism', based on comparative research on Corsican, Irish, Sámi and Welsh. I am grateful to Sari and to Misty Jaffe and Helen Kelly-Holmes, co-researchers on this project, for sharing their ideas on this theme. Charlotte Selleck and Angharad Hodgson made important contributions to some of the empirical research discussed in this chapter. I am also grateful to Wini Davies and Charlotte Selleck for helpful comments on an earlier version of this chapter, whose shortcomings remain my own.

2. East Wales has been recognised to be a borderland (meaning a zone of transition rather than a line of demarcation). Central and southern parts of the border with England are referred to as 'the Welsh Marches'. The ancient county of Monmouthshire (between the rivers Wye and Rhymney) was for several centuries an appendage to Wales, and reference was commonly made to 'Wales and Monmouthshire', harking back to the allocation of lands to Marcher Lords in the sixteenth century. The Welshness of Monmouthshire was not finally resolved until 1972. Cultural critic Raymond Williams took inspiration from his own status as a borderlander who grew up in the Marches, most obviously in his autobiographical novel *Border Country* (1964).

3. It was written by Evan James and James James from Pontypridd, and first sung in public at the National Eisteddfod (a competitive cultural festival of music and poetry) in 1874.

4. The following paragraphs fill out the detail of G. A. Williams's spiky representations of *gwerin* and proletarian Welsh 'nations', respectively:

> 'The gwerin in the form it assumed from the late nineteenth century was not and is not a class, certainly not a proletariat, to which it is often opposed . . . The gwerin was a cultivated, educated, often self-educated, responsible, self-disciplined, respectable but on the whole genially poor or perhaps small-propertied people, straddling groups perceived as classes in other, less fortunate societies. Welsh-speaking, Nonconformist, imbued with the more social virtues of Dissent, bred on the Bible and good practice, it was open to the more spiritual forms of a wider culture and was dedicated to spiritual self-improvement. It cherished many of the "traditional" habits of Welsh culture, derived ultimately from the poets' guild, nurtured country poets, skilled in verse and wordplay; it was learned in a somewhat antiquarian manner, interested in letters, and cultivated a deep pacifist patriotism, controlled by religion' (Williams 1985: 237).
>
> 'Into that industrial Wales poured anything from two-thirds to three-quarters of the actually existing Welsh population. They shifted massively into the south-east . . . These people were drawn into a society which was repeatedly modernizing and revolutionalizing itself, planting communities and uprooting them, building itself into an export metropolis of the world economy and merging inexorably into the overarching culture of the world language of English. This threatened to create two, and more, "nations" out of a Welsh people' (Williams 1985: 180–1).

5. See http://wales.gov.uk/topics/statistics/headlines/population2012/121211/?lang =en (all online sources listed in the chapter were last consulted 5 November 2013).

6. The web pages of the Assembly's Welsh Language Commissioner provide details of legislation relating to Welsh and provide full details of the Commissioner's role in relation to legal requirements. See <http://www.comisiynyddygymraeg.org/>.

7. The guide, sponsored by Barclays Bank, is available at <http://www.industry.visit-wales.co.uk/upload/pdf/a_guide_to_bilingual_design.pdf>.

8. See <http://wales.gov.uk/about/civilservice/directorates/ppcs/translationservice/terminology/>.

9. Examples include <http://www.cwtchclothing.co.uk/index.html>, <http://www.craftsfromthecwtch.co.uk/>, <http://www.cwtchcakes.co.uk/>, <http://www.jolyons.co.uk/bar-cwtch/>, <http://www.cwtchcabaret.co.uk/>, and <http://www.cwtchcamping.co.uk/> (which hires out camping chalets called 'cwtches'). In 2007 *cwtch* was voted 'the nation's favourite word' – see <http://news.bbc.co.uk/1/hi/wales/6521971.stm>.

10. See <http://cwtchrestaurant.co.uk/>. See also <http://www.cwtchcottages.co.uk/>. I am very grateful to the proprietors for giving their permission for me to represent their establishment and aspects of its promotional materials here, and to Angharad Hodgson for conducting ethnographic research at the restaurant during 2012.

11. Charlotte Selleck's village-by-village re-analysis of data for reported use of Welsh across Pembrokeshire and Ceredigion in the 2001 Census again gives some credence to the Landsker Line having contemporary relevance. The line rather neatly distinguishes villages with reported percentages above and below 20 per cent able to speak Welsh.

12. Not unlike the lower-case <w> in 'welsh' here, the menu shows many orthographic infelicities, particularly in Welsh spelling, e.g. the second spelling of *Gwynt Y Ddraig Cider* ('Dragon's wind cider') and *Halen Mon Sea Salt* ('Anglesey salt', where the Welsh name Môn should have the vowel-lengthening diacritic).

13. http://www.walesthetruetaste.co.uk/

10

The Political Border and Linguistic Identities in Ireland: What Can the Linguistic Landscape Tell Us?[1]

Jeffrey L. Kallen

1. Introducing the border

A rough north–south division in Ireland is engrained on the landscape, and pre-dates human settlement. The political border which now separates the six counties of Northern Ireland – in the United Kingdom – from the twenty-six counties of the Republic of Ireland, however, dates only from the 1920s. The paradoxically old and new nature of this border means that geographic, political, social and linguistic perspectives may each lead us to different understandings of the border, whether we are concerned with its physical placement or its role in shaping society. Our main concern here is with the modern political border and the ways in which a study of the linguistic landscape – the visual expression of language in public places – can shed light on aspects of language and identity in border areas.

The border can be seen as the culmination of a long and complex legal process, but in modern times it has been shaped especially by the Government of Ireland Act 1920 and the Anglo-Irish Treaty agreed between representatives of the British government and the self-proclaimed Irish government in 1921, and ratified by both governments in 1922. The former Act provided for the creation of two parliaments in Ireland, one in the six counties of Ulster designated as 'Northern Ireland', the other in the remaining counties, designated as 'Southern Ireland' (Government of Ireland Act 1920). The latter treaty paved the way for the adoption in 1922 of the Constitution of the Irish Free State (*Saorstát Éireann*, in Irish) and the 1937 Constitution which was its successor. Following principles established in the 1937 Constitution, the Republic of Ireland Act (1948) succinctly declared that 'the description of the State shall be the Republic of Ireland' and brought the Republic out of its association with the British Commonwealth. The United Kingdom Parliament subsequently passed the Ireland Act (1949), which declared, among other things, that 'in no event will Northern Ireland . . . cease to be part of His Majesty's dominions and of the United Kingdom without the consent of the Parliament of Northern Ireland'. The complexities of the legal and political forces which have shaped the formal status of jurisdictions in Ireland lie outside the scope of this chapter, yet what is significant for our purpose is that the political border has remained stable since the time of the Government of Ireland Act 1920: the six Ulster counties of Antrim, Armagh, Derry (or Londonderry – see discussion below), Down, Fermanagh and Tyrone constitute Northern Ireland, while three Ulster counties (Cavan, Donegal and Monaghan) and the remaining twenty-three counties (in the traditional provinces of Connacht, Leinster and Munster) form the Republic. As is shown in Figure 10.1, different perspectives on the border can lead to different graphic representations of the border area, even in the factual orientation of the cartographic map.

This legislative thread shows two opposing views of the border. The 1937 Constitution (Bunreacht na hÉireann 1942) took the stance of speaking on behalf of 'the Irish nation' (Article 1) and declared in Article 2 that 'the national territory consists of the whole island of Ireland, its islands and the territorial seas'. Article 3 was both aspirational in equating the Constitutional state with an all-Ireland concept of nation, and practical in recognising the division of Ireland as laid out in the Government of Ireland Act 1920 and provided for in subsequent documents. This article thus declared that 'pending the re-integration of the national territory, and without prejudice to the right of the Parliament and Government established by this constitution to exercise jurisdiction over the whole of that territory, the laws enacted by that Parliament shall have the like area and extent of application as the laws of Saorstát Éireann'. In contrast to the Nationalist position, the Ireland Act 1949 could be seen to offer Unionists what Murphy (1975: 128) calls 'a permanent guarantee of their ascendancy', given the Act's assurance that even the legally superordinate British Parliament could not on its own effect the unification of Ireland.

More recently, the agreement commonly known as the Good Friday Agreement or Belfast Agreement (Agreement 1998) has attempted to reconcile conflicting views of the national question. This document, which was ratified by popular vote on both sides of the border, declares (p. 33) that

> while a substantial section of the people in Northern Ireland share the legitimate wish of a majority of the people of the island of Ireland for a united Ireland, the present wish of a majority of the people of Northern Ireland . . . is to maintain the Union and, accordingly, that Northern Ireland's status as part of the United Kingdom reflects and relies upon that wish; and that it would be wrong to make any change in the status of Northern Ireland save with the consent of a majority of its people.

Accordingly, the Constitution in the Republic was amended in 1998 to delete the former Articles 2 and 3, and to substitute language which does not make a presumption of unity. Article 2 now provides that 'it is the entitlement and birthright of every person born in the island of Ireland . . . to be part of the Irish Nation', while Article 3 declares that 'it is the firm will of the Irish Nation, in harmony and friendship, to unite all the people who share the territory of the island of Ireland, in all the diversity of their identities and traditions, recognising that a united Ireland shall be brought about only by peaceful means with the consent of a majority of the people, democratically expressed, in both jurisdictions in the island' (Bunreacht na hÉireann 2004).

The border also raises questions of language and identity which are both old and new. The traditional dialects of Irish show a north–south division of considerable antiquity, in part associated with the close proximity of Ulster to Scotland: see for example O'Rahilly (1932), Wagner (1958–69) and Adams (1958). A crucial division in Ulster history which has had major linguistic consequences lies in the population displacement and movement commonly referred to as the 'Plantation of Ulster'. Although various attempts to settle populations considered loyal to the English crown date back to the time of Queen Mary I in the mid-sixteenth century, Ulster plantation initiatives which came after 1609 had particularly strong effects in bringing settlers from Scotland and England into selected areas of Ulster and in restructuring patterns of land ownership, population distribution and lines of communication. In linguistic terms, plantation and the lines of population movement which it helped to establish brought Protestant speakers of English, and to a lesser degree speakers of the Scots language, into an Ulster which had been predominantly Irish-speaking and Roman Catholic. The ways in which the balance of language distribution in Ireland shifted towards English over four centuries, and the ways in which the restoration of Irish, especially in the nineteenth century, became associated with the political nationalism that eventually led to the establishment of the Irish Free State and became incorporated into the legal fabric of the Republic, are too complex to discuss here, but see, for example, Crowley (2005) for a political overview, Ó Snodaigh (1995), Mac Póilin (1997) and O'Reilly (1999) for historical and sociological treatments of Irish in Northern Ireland, and Ní Bhaoill (2010) for an account of dialect material from Ulster Irish which includes Irish-speaking areas of County Louth. Braidwood (1964) provides a classic account of the settlement and features of Ulster English; see also Corrigan (2010) for a review of English in Northern Ireland. Maps which look at the border in traditional dialects of English and Irish are found in Kallen (2000).

Developments on both sides of the border over the last ninety years have led to different perspectives on the language question. In the Republic, Article 8 of the 1937 Constitution designates Irish as the 'first official language' (Bunreacht na hÉireann 2004: 8) though it recognises English as 'a second official language'. Irish is widely taught in primary and secondary schools, occupies a significant role in civil administration and benefits from support given to *Gaeltacht* (Irish-speaking) areas where Irish continues to be spoken as a community language. In Northern Ireland, which does not have the same general public commitment to Irish, broader historical traditions which did not necessarily associate the use of Irish with political nationalism have shifted towards a commonly held view that assumes an association between active engagement with the Irish language and broadly Nationalist politics as well as Catholic religious adherence, in contrast to a cluster of values which groups together a Protestant denominational background with Unionist political orientation and the non-use of Irish. In some parts of Northern Ireland, the use of Ulster Scots is also associated with the latter set of identity factors.

Although this set of assumptions is highly generalised and may be wrong in individual cases, it would be naive to overlook such perceptions as they are reflected in, for example, the clauses on language in the 1998 Agreement. The section on 'Economic, Social and Cultural Issues' in this document includes commitments on the Irish language from the British government to 'take resolute action to promote the language', to 'facilitate and encourage the use of the language' and to 'encourage and facilitate Irish medium education'. These commitments are hedged by the qualification that language promotion will be undertaken 'where appropriate and where people so desire', and by a general provision that 'all participants recognise the importance of respect, understanding, and tolerance' in relation not only to Irish but to 'Ulster-Scots and the languages of the various ethnic communities' (see Agreement 1998: 22–3). McCoy's (2001: 212) behind-the-scenes account of the Agreement argues that it was Nationalist negotiators from the Sinn Féin party who 'placed an emphasis on Irish language issues' during the negotiation of the Agreement and that, conversely, 'Unionist negotiators succeeded in their efforts to include the promotion of Ulster-Scots' in the provisions for cross-border language support bodies. Thus, while a full picture of language loyalty and use in Ireland would require much more detail than can be presented here, we can suggest that the use of Irish in the Republic will reflect the state's commitment to the language as well as private support for it, while usage in Northern Ireland will be more dependent on local, community-based support and, to a lesser degree (as suggested by McCoy 2001: 213–17), the broader cultural inclusiveness encouraged by the 1998 Agreement. We will also bear in mind that English, as a common language of both jurisdictions, may not be apparent as a marker of language loyalty: the use of English for some represents a definite decision not to use another language, while for others it may merely represent a choice of convenience in an increasingly Anglophone world.

2. The linguistic landscape

The study of identity and expression in Northern Ireland has often extended beyond language to include visual imagery and public performance. Rolston (1991, 2003), for example, has examined the use of murals; Bryson and McCartney (1994) examine 'flags, anthems and other national symbols'; and Santino (2001) has analysed 'public display' that includes not only posters and murals, but Lambeg drums, holy wells and spontaneous roadside memorials to those killed in the Troubles (a period of civil unrest and violence in Northern Ireland which dates from ca. 1968 onwards, and which the Agreement was designed to end). Morris (2005) further examines official symbolism in banknotes, coins, postage stamps and other forms of display on both sides of the border. The approach I take here is designed to bridge a gap between linguistic concerns and those of visual semiotics, demonstrating that the visual display of language can also add to our understanding of language and identity as expressive culture.

This approach fits within the field that has recently gained prominence under the heading of the 'linguistic landscape', or what Jaworski and Thurlow (2010) refer to as 'semiotic landscapes'. Shohamy and Waksman (2009: 314) define the identifying feature of the linguistic landscape as 'text presented and displayed in the public space'. Early work by Rosenbaum et al. (1977) pointed out the ways in which the textual display of language in public places can correlate with face-to-face language use, while Landry and Bourhis (1997: 25, 27) further argue that the linguistic landscape has both 'an informational function' which 'serves as a distinctive marker of the geographical territory inhabited by a given language community' and a 'symbolic function' which 'can contribute most directly to the positive social identity of ethnolinguistic groups'. Rather than viewing the linguistic landscape as a simple reflection of linguistic behaviour, Cenoz and Gorter (2006: 67–8) stress the dialogic nature of the linguistic landscape, arguing that it both 'reflects the relative power and status of the different languages in a specific sociolinguistic context' and 'contributes to the construction of the sociolinguistic context'. These and other approaches to the linguistic landscape suggest that if the political border in Ireland is important as a formative influence on social identities and language use, then the linguistic landscapes on each side of the political border will differ in significant ways.

3. A case study: cities and towns of the eastern border

The remainder of this chapter is devoted to a case study of the eastern part of the border between Northern Ireland and the Republic of Ireland. In provincial terms, this area covers the boundary between Ulster and Leinster and includes County Louth, which has at times been seen as part of Ulster, but is now included in Leinster. The complex and shifting nature of this border area has made it a special point of interest for historians and geographers; see Gillespie and O'Sullivan (1989) for detail. Six data points have been chosen for this study: Warrenpoint, Newry and Armagh in Northern Ireland, and Dundalk, Carrickmacross and Monaghan in the Republic (see Figure 10.1). Table 10.1 gives an overview of Census figures, including information on language and religion, for each district. These figures should not be taken as exhaustive, since the self-reporting of linguistic ability may be influenced by language attitudes as well as by day-by-day experience, and because the figures for religion aggregate subdivided data and are incomplete for small communities in the Republic. In both censuses, language data reflect the proportions for the population over the age of three years: in Northern Ireland, the percentage reflects 'some knowledge' of Irish or Ulster Scots, while in the Republic it shows persons classified as 'Irish speakers'. Local populations and figures for religion and the Irish language are based on the 2006 Census in the Republic (Census 2007) and the 2001 Census in Northern Ireland (Northern Ireland Census 2005). In order to put the border areas into perspective, Table 10.1 also gives aggregate figures for Northern Ireland (NI) and the Republic (ROI) as a whole: the general population and language figures are taken from the 2011 Census in the Republic (Census 2012) and in Northern Ireland (NISRA). All figures for Ulster Scots are from the 2011 Census. Since percentages for towns are not yet available, the percentage represents the entire district of either Armagh or Newry and Mourne. The Census in the Republic does not provide figures for Ulster Scots.

Table 10.1 Census data: population, language and religion in selected areas

Town	Languages (%)		Religion (%)			
	Population	Irish	Ulster Scots	Roman Catholic	Protestant	Other reply
Warrenpoint	7,000	21.72	3.7	85.27	5.39	9.34
Newry	26,190	19.27	3.7	83.57	6.85	9.59
Armagh	13,918	20.65	5.83	63.26	23.46	13.28
NI aggregate	1,735,711	10.65	8.08	45.14	48.36	6.51
Dundalk	33,527	36.9	—	87.43	2.37	10.20
Carrickmacross	4,181	38.0	—	—	—	—
Monaghan	6,458	35.0	—	86.81	4.70	8.49
ROI aggregate	4,370,631	41.4	—	86.83	3.80	9.37

From these figures, we note a consistency in the rate of Irish-speaking in the three data points from the Republic, running somewhat below the national average (which includes *Gaeltacht* areas), and a lower return for ability in Irish in the Northern Ireland locations, albeit one which is well above the average for the jurisdiction as a whole. Cross-border differences in the consistency of educational exposure to Irish must be considered a major factor here. The Census figures also confirm that our subject area shows relatively little use of Ulster Scots. In religious terms, five of the six data points show very similar proportions for the Catholic population, with Armagh being the odd one out: even here, though, the Protestant proportion of the population is considerably smaller than in Northern Ireland as a whole.

Figures of this kind suggest that the linguistic landscape may provide some significant cross-border similarities as well as jurisdictionally based differences. In the rest of this chapter, we will therefore concentrate on three aspects of the linguistic landscape which pertain to the border: 1) the marking of the geographical border; 2) the extent to which cross-border differences reflect different political orders with mutually exclusive signage practices; and 3) the extent to which signage across the border reflects commonality of interest, merger of features and the mutability of cross-border differences.

4. Understating the border

To illustrate the semiotic potential of maps in representing the border, we start with Figure 10.1, which contrasts an older American map (Central Intelligence Agency 1987) that is widely available on the internet with a tourist map from the *Siar Ó Thuaidh/North West Passage* public display in Monaghan that was photographed as part of this survey.[2] These maps are on the left and right of Figure 10.1, respectively. The older map displays the border prominently, designating the thick unbroken line as an 'international boundary' and using colour to distinguish between 'Northern Ireland' (beige in the original image) and 'Ireland' (a pale khaki). Each small triangle on this map designates a 'frontier post'. Although these military posts have now been dismantled as a consequence of the Northern Ireland Peace Process and the greater harmonisation of frontiers within the European Union as a whole, the choice to display these points and the terminology used to describe them underscore the notion of the political border as a concrete geographical

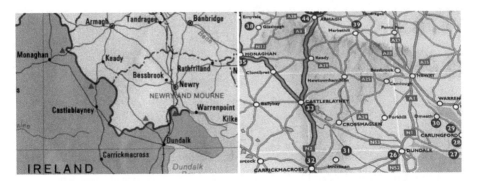

Figure 10.1 Contrasting maps of the eastern Republic of Ireland/Northern Ireland border area.

entity. The tourist map, on the other hand, does not mention a border at all. The towns in the region are presented in a seamless web of interconnected areas. Only the sharp-eyed observer will note a difference in the road numbering system such that, for example, the road designated as the N1 in the Republic (north of Dundalk) is known as the A1 in Northern Ireland.

The tendency to understate the border is a feature of border crossings throughout the sample area. Passengers on the Dublin–Belfast railway line, for example, receive no indication that they are crossing the border, and the crossing itself is only indicated by a small post whose function is not labelled. The understated border on the main Dublin–Belfast road is seen in Figure 10.2, which looks from the Republic towards Northern Ireland. The top picture shows a non-verbal 'no U-turn' sign on the left: beyond this sign is an English-language notice informing road users of speed limits in miles per hour, given in close-up at the bottom of Figure 10.2. The latter type of sign is common in border areas, and draws no attention to the political jurisdiction of Northern Ireland. Bilingual signage in Irish and English, pointing out the speed limit in kilometres per hour, is found on the

Figure 10.2 Crossing the border, Dublin–Belfast motorway (upper portion of image, long-distance view; lower portion, close-up of NI signage).

Republic of Ireland side of this crossing. It too makes no reference to the reader's entry into a different political jurisdiction.

The minimalist approach to marking the border can be seen as a matter of conse-quence when we consider the controversy that has arisen in connection with attempts to introduce 'Welcome to Northern Ireland' signage in border areas of Fermanagh and Tyrone. McAdam (2012) reports that nine such signs have recently been put up, but that several of them have subsequently been reported as missing. McAdam's report cites an Ulster Unionist party representative from Fermanagh who claimed that vandalism of the signs had originated among 'those who do not want to accept that they are living within Northern Ireland, which is part of the United Kingdom', while a Sinn Féin party repre-sentative is conversely cited as calling the erection of such signs 'pretty petty behaviour' on the part of the Ulster Unionist Minister for Regional Development. The controversy which such signage can engender suggests that while the choice to mark the border only with utilitarian road safety notices may appear unremarkable, it may actually reflect a deeper consideration of ongoing problems in the definition of national identities.

5. Contrasts in the bilingual landscape

Given the different legal positions of Irish in the two jurisdictions, it is not surprising to find a distribution which contrasts bilingual signage in the Republic with monolingual signage in Northern Ireland. Figure 10.3 illustrates such a contrast for main road signage in Monaghan (left) and Armagh (right). In Monaghan, we note not only routine bilingual-ism, but the place name choice of *Derry*, rather than the alternative *Londonderry*. The Irish word *doire*, 'oak grove', is a common element in Irish place names, and the area in question, according to Room (1994: 85–6), was denoted as *Doire Calgaich*, 'Calgach's oak wood', in the seventh century; the Londonderry form developed after 1609, at which time James I granted a charter for settlement by London merchants.

Local street signs offer greater opportunity to show variety in the association between language and typeface. The basic pattern for street signs in Northern Ireland favours monolingual signage in English, while that throughout the Republic favours bilingual Irish–English signage. As Spolsky and Cooper (1991) noted in Jerusalem, street signs very often preserve historical layers from older political regimes, or earlier decisions on writing systems, colour and other aspects of the visual presentation of language. Thus, while Figure 10.4 shows a typical monolingual street sign from Newry at the bottom of the image, the photograph from Dundalk at the top includes both an older sign with a prominent street name in Irish using a traditional Irish font underneath the English name in a smaller font, as well as an example of newer, widespread bilingual signage which, while also using an Irish font, displays it much less prominently on a single sign.

Even the smallest public notice calls for language choices which may be influenced by language policy. The contrasting approaches seen thus far are continued in Figure 10.5, which shows a monolingual notice from Warrenpoint and a bilingual sign of similar size and layout from Carrickmacross. These signs contrast not only in the choice of language, but in their pragmatic style: in terms of politeness theory, as developed by Brown and Levinson (1987), the Carrickmacross sign contains a bald, on-the-record directive in each language, while the Warrenpoint sign generates an indirect directive using an impersonal construction that relies on negative politeness.

Figure 10.3 Main road signs, Monaghan (ROI, left) and Armagh (NI, right).

Figure 10.4 Street signs in Dundalk (ROI, upper portion of image) and Newry (NI, lower portion of image).

Figure 10.5 Dog notices, Carrickmacross (ROI, left) and Warrenpoint (NI, right).

6. Blurring the boundaries

Despite the presence of such contrasting images, it would be incomplete to suggest that Northern Ireland and the Republic display mutually exclusive approaches to the linguistic landscape. Private signage, for example, is seen in Figure 10.6, which shows permanent signage for a pub in Monaghan (left) and a poster from Armagh (right). The Monaghan pub complex invokes a number of cultural references: *poc* (Anglicised as *puck*) in this context refers to the stroke of a *hurley* (the stick used in the sport of hurling), and the main pub, *An Poc Fada*, 'the long puck', is conjoined with a smaller off-licence (liquor store) signposted as *An Poc Beag*, 'the little puck'. Use of the 'Celtic' font emphasises the notion of cultural authenticity. The Armagh poster, photographed in the window of a taxi company, uses no such typographical devices, but does link language and culture by advertising an *oiche cheoil*, 'evening of music', in a bilingual poster. This poster is similar in language and function to others found throughout Ireland: for a Galway example, see Kallen (2009: Figure 17.9). Localisation is found in the poster's reference to Armagh-based singing group Macha. We can read this band name as pointing both to the County Armagh place name *Emain Macha*, known in English as Navan Fort, which, according to Room (1994: 53), also incorporates the name of the Celtic goddess Macha. Links between language and culture, then, provide opportunities for parallels on both sides of the border.

The effect of decentralised language policies in Northern Ireland can be seen in the variety of usage patterns for street names and historical reference. Our sample in Armagh showed no local street-name signage in Irish, while the Newry sample showed very little (though it is my understanding that bilingual signage in Newry is increasing). In Warrenpoint, however, bilingual street-name signage is abundant, coexisting with centrally determined monolingual signage for major roads similar to that in Figure 10.3.

Figure 10.6 Irish language with cultural reference in Monaghan (ROI, left) and Armagh (NI, right).

The Warrenpoint example shown in the upper section of Figure 10.7 gives not only a bilingual street name, with Irish in a modern Roman font in the same size and style as the English version, but the name of the local townland (administrative district) in its Irish form *Rinn Mhic Giolla Ruaid* as well as the Anglicisation *Ringmackilroy*. Linguistic connections of a different kind, however, are illustrated in the lower portion of Figure 10.7, which shows the sign for the central square known as *The Diamond* in Monaghan. Use of the name 'diamond' to denote a central area is a characteristic Ulster place name feature. The *Concise Ulster Dictionary* (Macafee 1996) defines diamond as 'the open space between roads intersecting at a crossroads, sometimes in the country, but usually forming the market square of a town'. Montgomery (2006: 49–50) gives the definition 'a type of town square dating from the period of the Plantation of Ulster', and supplies numerous citations which refer to diamonds in this sense in different parts of Ulster. Retention of the placename The Diamond in Monaghan is thus indexical of the Ulster Plantation, and links a distinctive landmark in the Republic with counterparts in Northern Ireland. The Diamond in Monaghan, however, falls in line with bilingual signage practices in the Republic, and the street sign includes a translation in Irish. This place name has been the subject of public debate elsewhere: Call for Irish (2009) reports a prominent solicitor in Ballycastle, County Antrim, calling for the Diamond there to be signposted in English, Irish and Ulster Scots so that 'all major cultures are represented'. To the best of my knowledge, while there is some signposting in this region in English and Irish as well as in English and Ulster Scots, this particular proposal has not been adopted.

As an illustration of the historical layering effect in the linguistic landscape, we may also note that the Newry sample shows modern Irish–English bilingualism in public

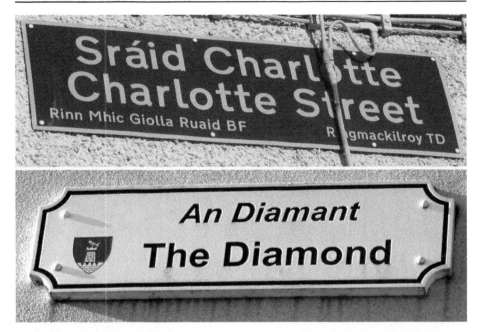

Figure 10.7 Bilingual street signage, Warrenpoint (NI, upper portion of image) and Monaghan (ROI, lower portion).

notices and in commemorations of historical features alongside an older layer of Irish usage which pre-dates the establishment of the political border. Figure 10.8 illustrates this material. The picture on the left is a detail from a piece which commemorates the accomplishment of Newry-born Terence 'Banjo' Bannon in climbing Mount Everest in 2003. The name of the local authority and substantive commentary are presented bilingually. The photograph on the right, however, comes from the Newry Town Hall (constructed in 1893), and shows the crest of the Newry Town Commissioners, dating to 1891 (see www.newryandmourne.gov.uk). This crest includes a version of the full name for Newry in Irish, in modern spelling *Iúr Cinn Trá*, 'yew tree of the head of the strand' (St Patrick is reputed to have established a monastery and planted a yew tree in the vicinity).

It is a well-known feature of dialect boundaries that zones of contact can produce intermediate forms (what Chambers and Trudgill [1998: 110–18] term 'fudged' forms) that incorporate elements from both sides of a dialect division. The range of semiotic resources found in the linguistic landscape also allows for intermediate forms: in the Irish context, a sign in English which uses a 'Celtic' font and green lettering or decoration readily incorporates elements of two potentially opposing systems of linguistic representation. In Figure 10.9, however, we see a more subtly developed picture which appears to be specific to the border area. The sign on the left is of a type commonly found in Northern Ireland and in Britain; this example comes from Warrenpoint. A similar example from Bangor, County Down, is shown in Kallen (2009: Figure 17.6). Signs of this kind are not common in the Republic, and the stylised dimpled beer glass is of a kind which is also rare in the Republic. Nevertheless, a version of this sign shows up in the Carrickmacross sample, with an identical picture, but with the fine of £500 changed to

Figure 10.8 Irish-language reference, commemoration and historical layering, Newry (NI).

Figure 10.9 Alcohol-free zone notices, Warrenpoint (NI, leftmost image) and Monaghan (ROI, centre and rightmost image).

€635. (Due to space limitations, no photograph is included here.) In Monaghan, parallel signage exemplifies two extremes. The middle photograph in Figure 10.9 shows a completely unlocalised sign: the fine is given in pounds sterling and the graphics are as in Northern Ireland. The sign on the right, however, includes both a localisation of the fine (as in Carrickmacross), as well as a change of graphics to a smooth glass which is more similar in its proportions to the type most commonly used in the Republic. The handle on this glass is somewhat anomalous, since such handles would be rare in the Republic, but perhaps reflects the continuing inspiration of the glass type found in the signs to the left. The main text of the sign on the right is local, but the small print at the bottom of the sign retains the same wording as in the Northern Ireland examples. Unlike most public signage in the Republic, bilingualism is not a feature of this sign. The overall impression, then, is strongly reminiscent of a sign type found predominantly in Northern Ireland, though it contains distinct elements of localisation.

Finally, we should note that a discussion of language and identity in the Irish linguistic landscape cannot refer only to Irish, English or Ulster Scots. As I have noted elsewhere (see Kallen 2010), the linguistic landscape in parts of Ireland has, in recent decades,

Figure 10.10 Polish shop (Armagh, NI) and branch of Lituanica chain (Carrickmacross, ROI).

incorporated a variety of languages which reflect immigration, tourism and other aspects of population movement and globalisation. Figure 10.10 gives a cross-border glimpse of so-called 'new' immigrant groups establishing shops and businesses in which other languages form part of the linguistic landscape. The photograph on the left shows a Polish shop in Armagh, while the one on the right, showing a *Lituanica* shopfront that in reality is painted in various shades of green, is from Carrickmacross. Although the main banner in the Armagh shopfront is in English, the window includes a notice for a Dublin-based baker, *Dublin Duona* (from Lithuanian *duona*, 'bread'), while the upper panel of the shop door contains a Polish-language advertisement for a money-transfer service focused on the Polish market. The Lituanica chain has shops in various parts of the Republic of Ireland and, to a lesser extent, in Britain. Although the Lituanica slogan 'The Best from Home', which is repeated under the Lituanica logo along the bottom of the shop signage, is given in English, there is no doubt from the goods on sale that 'home' refers to Lithuania or other central and eastern European countries whose foods feature prominently in the shop. Products from Dublin Duona, though not advertised in the window, are frequently sold in Lituanica shops and form a link between the two photographs.

7. Conclusion

The material we have considered here suggests that the study of the linguistic landscape offers a unique insight into questions of language and identity, particularly when identities are complex and fragmented at border areas. As we have seen, some elements of the linguistic landscape clearly mark political distinctions that inevitably become part of a person's identity through the day-to-day mechanism of life in society. The tendency in Ireland not to make overt reference to the political border, however, tells us something further about language and identity, since it is directly compatible with a desire to achieve cross-border accommodation in a situation where the border is a point of contention, though at a more remote level it also fits with the tendency towards European integration more generally.

When we turn to the community-based influences on the linguistic landscape, we see that not all expressions of linguistic identity follow from a dominant political framework. Local initiatives in some of the Northern Ireland border areas have instituted Irish–English bilingual signage that arises not as a matter of communicative necessity (as with multilingual signs at airports), but as an expression of connection to a language that, while spoken by a minority of the population, has resonances of cultural identity for the majority (see also Coupland, this volume). Local developments on the Northern Ireland side of the border thus partly parallel the position in the Republic, though the extent to which Irish is learned and given other support in the latter jurisdiction is greater than what can be found locally in the former. Regional identity finds other expression in the semiotic landscape, when we consider the retention and translation of historical features such as the 'Diamond' place name in the Republic, or the contemporary design elements shown in Figure 10.9. Such elements of the linguistic landscape suggest areal effects that retain an identity for Ulster, regardless of the political border.

Beyond these overt markers, though, the linguistic landscape can be as revealing for what it does *not* say as for what it does. We note, for example, the marked lack of public recognition for languages other than English, Irish and (in some areas) Ulster Scots. The provisions of the 1998 Agreement notwithstanding, the lack of association between the state (on either side of the border) and these other languages makes a statement about the degree to which these languages have been incorporated into the linguistic order of society. Although language policy in each jurisdiction tolerates the display of such minority languages, leaving expressions of language vitality as a matter of private initiative limits the opportunity for them to appear in public and creates a social context in which these languages may be seen as marginal. The expression of linguistic identity for those who do not feel affinities with Irish or different minority languages is also problematic. English is so widely used in Ireland that the choice of English signage in the private domain cannot communicate a distinctive identity. In the context of the Agreement of 1998, Ulster Scots could be used in contrast to Irish, but, as the Northern Ireland Census shows, the distribution of Ulster Scots is localised and applies only to a minority. The use of local dialect forms in the English of private signage can sometimes be used as a strategy, part of what Coupland (2012: 17) calls 'laconic metacultural celebration', to draw a closer association between the community and a global language such as English, but this strategy was only marginal (on a shopfront on the Dublin Road in Monaghan, referencing Dublin English) in our observation area. Questions over what can and cannot be expressed, of who has control of the linguistic landscape, and as to how elements of the linguistic landscape are both expressive and dialogic will thus continue to be worked out by participants and analysed by those with an interest in language and identity.

Note

1. I am grateful to Margaret Mannion, Dónal Mac Dónaill, Esther Ní Dhonnacha, Michael Quigley, and Micheál Ó Siochrú for advice and discussion on matters raised in this chapter. Naturally, I alone am responsible for any remaining shortcomings.
2. The photographs in this chapter are my own work: the Newry photographs date from July 2005, while all others were taken in November and December 2012. Signage changes which have taken place since this time are not discussed here due to space limitations.

11

Multilingual Luxembourg: Language and Identity at the Romance/Germanic Language Border

Daniel Redinger and Carmen Llamas

1. Introduction

Luxembourg has been described as a 'linguistic melting pot' (Hoffmann 1996: 97). This small, landlocked country, located among a cluster of international borders in north-western Europe, is situated on the linguistic border between the Romance and the Germanic language areas. In addition to having a geographical location that promotes multilingualism, Luxembourg ranks highest, by some considerable distance, of the thirty-eight countries for which the OECD gives statistics on foreign-born population (42.4 per cent in 2010; OECD Factbook 2013). Multilingualism is therefore prevalent at both the societal and the individual levels.

This chapter focuses on multilingualism in the Luxembourg educational context, and investigates the challenges faced by both policymakers and speakers living in a political and linguistic borderland. The Romance/Germanic linguistic border is mirrored in the education system, in which different languages of instruction are used to demarcate different academic subjects as well as different educational levels. Luxembourg's shared political borders with Germany, France and the French-speaking part of Belgium can be seen as shaping language-in-education policies, as German and French, the languages of Luxembourg's larger neighbouring countries, are regarded as the only legitimate media of instruction. The linguistic and spatial borders associated with Luxembourg, therefore, lead to 'imagined' educational borders.

This chapter presents data from a large-scale, comprehensive survey of secondary-school students' and teachers' language use, preferences and attitudes. The findings demonstrate that Luxembourgish, the country's national language, has emerged as a language of identity. French and German, on the other hand, while carrying clear overt prestige, are largely associated with 'otherness'.

2. Contextual background

The origins of Luxembourg date back to AD 963, when Count Sigfried (or Siegfried), a noble of Upper Lotharingia, acquired the castle *Lucilinburhuc* from the Abbot of

St Maximin and founded the independent feudal state of Luxembourg. Count Sigfried's Luxembourg was located in an area of the old Carolingian empire which was divided by a language border into two separate parts, 'Germania' and 'Romania' (Hoffmann 1980). Consequently, both Germanic and Romance varieties were spoken right from the beginnings of Luxembourg's history. In fact, the tensions between a Germanic east and Romance west go back as far as the first centuries AD, when the Celtic Treveri, the Romans and increasing numbers of Germanic-speaking Rhine Franks were living side-by-side in the area which later became Luxembourg (Hoffmann 1980).

As Luxembourg's territory increased, French gradually became the language of the nobility and the official language of the state. The linguistic prestige of French continued to grow and, by the end of the fifteenth century, French had replaced Latin in the writings of the clergy and had strengthened its position as the language of the upper classes and the emerging middle classes of merchants who extensively used French alongside German as a trading language. The peasants and serfs, however, who represented nine-tenths of the population, spoke the local Germanic dialect exclusively, as they had no use for either French or German (Davis 1994: 27). Over the following four centuries, Luxembourg changed hands several times, by turns belonging to Austria, Spain, France and the Netherlands. These various periods of foreign rule had an influence on the size and shape of Luxembourg, as parts of the original territory came under Belgian, German and French possession. In 1839 the Treaty of London finally established Luxembourg's present-day borders and Luxembourg became an independent state.

Political independence was accompanied by a newly gained self-confidence among the Luxembourg people, who started to associate their local dialect with a Luxembourg identity and used their native tongue as a characteristic differentiating them from inhabitants of the larger neighbouring countries (Gilles and Moulin 2003: 304). In 1984 West-Moselle Franconian, the Germanic dialect spoken by the majority of the population, was officially recognised as Luxembourgish, the national language of Luxembourg. French was awarded the status of legislative language, while administrative matters were to be carried out in French, German or Luxembourgish (Davis 1994: 11). However, to this day Luxembourg's administration remains almost exclusively governed by French (Fehlen 2002: 83).

As mentioned earlier, in addition to the influences of both the historical context and Luxembourg's geographical position, societal multilingualism in Luxembourg is shaped by the unusual size of its immigrant population and the presence of the various immigrant languages this entails. Successive waves of immigration throughout the twentieth century, primarily from Italy and Portugal, and the increasing use of English as a language of communication among Luxembourg's growing international workforce have contributed to the extensive multilingualism present in the country.

Luxembourg's language contact situation has undoubtedly influenced its education system, which is governed by strict language policies which have remained largely unchanged since the Education Act of 1912. The study of languages occupies a central position in Luxembourg's school curriculum, and all pupils are taught French, German and English. Moreover, French and German are employed as official languages of instruction at different stages of school-based education. Whereas German dominates as the official medium of instruction at primary school level, pupils are taught largely in French in their latter years of secondary school. Luxembourgish, on the other hand, continues to be officially excluded from almost all areas of education.

The educational focus of the study described in this chapter gives us insights into the prestige associated with the languages both in terms of the exposure they are afforded in the educational context by policymakers and their evaluations by students and teachers. Discrepancies between these points of interest do not simply demonstrate the importance of taking speakers' attitudes towards languages into consideration in language planning, they also have immediate applied value for future policymakers in the Luxembourg context.

3. Methods

3.1 The sample

The Luxembourg education system is principally split between *Lycée classique* (classical secondary school) and *Lycée technique* (technical secondary school). Classical secondary education aims to prepare students for further studies at university level. Technical secondary schools, on the other hand, mainly serve as an initiation into various professions, but do not prevent students from enrolling in higher education (Berg and Weis 2005). The classical schools are characterised by a very abrupt change of the language of instruction from German to French after the first three years of secondary education. This transition phase represents an ideal point at which to investigate attitudes towards the various languages employed in Luxembourg's schools and multilingual behaviour among students and teachers. Consequently, the classical school sample consists of students who were enrolled in their last year of German-medium education and students in their first year of French-medium education at the time of data collection. The technical schools also employ changes in the medium-of-instruction policies after the first three years, although because of the more vocational nature of these schools, students are split into numerous different educational sections. In order to keep the sample at a manageable size, only students in their last year of German-medium education were included. The sample was also stratified according to the geographical locations of the participating schools. Informants were recruited from classical and technical schools located in the north, centre and south of Luxembourg. While the northern schools sampled for this study are in close proximity to the German border, the southern schools are located on the French border. The central schools are all in Luxembourg City.

Access to two classes of students (20–25 students per class, on average) of three types (classical pre-medium-of-instruction change, classical post-medium-of-instruction change, technical pre-medium-of-instruction change) was arranged. Table 11.1 presents the distribution of students sampled. Ethnicity is based on students' self-classifications for nationality, elicited through self-completion written questionnaires (see section 3.2 for methodological details). In reality, students' perceptions of their own ethnic backgrounds may be more fluid and, therefore, may not map on to a rigid *a priori* classification of ethnic groups. Although we recognise that it is something of an oversimplification, for ease of representation only three major ethnic groups – Luxembourgish, Luxembourgish dual (one Luxembourgish parent and one parent from another ethnic background) and Portuguese – are represented separately in the table. Students originating from other ethnic backgrounds have been included in the category labelled 'Other' (further ethnic

Table 11.1 Distribution of students sampled. *Lux.* = Luxembourgish, *Lux. Dual* = Luxembourgish dual nationality, *Other* = miscellaneous nationalities (N = 367)

Region	School type	Lux.	Lux. Dual	Portuguese	Other
North	Classical	64	13	9	6
	Technical	17	2	12	6
Centre	Classical	61	15	1	17
	Technical	11	3	20	8
South	Classical	41	8	8	7
	Technical	13	4	16	5

groups are represented by Italians [14], students from former Yugoslavia [8], Germans [4] and students from France and French-speaking Belgium [8]). In total, questionnaires were administered during school hours to 367 students from six secondary schools.

3.2 Data elicitation and analysis

As mentioned above, the data elicitation technique used was a self-completed written questionnaire. These questionnaires were administered to groups of 20–30 students at a time with the first author present, to help clarify any procedural uncertainty on the part of the informants. Questionnaires were presented in Luxembourgish, French and German, as participants' choice of language constituted one of the results of the survey.

Informants initially provided details of their personal language use in terms of the languages they speak and the contexts in which they use them. They also stated their preferred language(s) of instruction. The second and third sections focused on the informants' experiences of learning the various languages used and learned in Luxembourg (Luxembourgish, French, German, English and any other language(s) spoken by the informant). They were asked to provide a rating of their competence in these languages.

The majority of the questionnaire consisted of attitude statements with which informants were required to show their level of agreement. Authentic language attitude statements drawn from qualitative interviews recorded with 70 informants from Luxembourgish, Italian and Portuguese backgrounds were presented. These statements were focused on personal language use, languages in education, the status of Luxembourgish, French and German in Luxembourg, and the role of language in the integration of immigrants. A subsample of secondary-school students was created in order to investigate attitudes towards the change of the language of instruction from German to French after the first three years of classical secondary education. The Luxembourg Minister of Education, Mady Delvaux-Stehres, was interviewed in 2007 in order to gain a better understanding of the policymakers' perspective on language use in the education system. Further statements were drawn from the language policy document *Réajustement de l'enseignement des langues plan d'action* ('Readjustment of the Teaching of Languages Plan of Action') 2007–09, published by the Luxembourg Ministry of Education. The document outlines the current position of the authorities in relation to the roles of the various languages in the education system.

The students were required to indicate their level of agreement with the attitude statements using a Visual Analogue Scale (VAS) anchored by 'Agree' at one extreme and

Figure 11.1 Visual Analogue Scale used in attitude questionnaire.

'Disagree' at the other (see Figure 11.1). Informants were instructed to position themselves on the VAS by drawing a vertical line through the horizontal agreement continuum (see further Redinger and Llamas 2009). The use of a continuous measurement scale, as opposed to a Likert scale, which usually indicates five or seven levels of agreement (for example, 'strongly disagree', 'disagree', 'neither agree nor disagree', 'agree', 'strongly agree'), allows for fine-grained measures of levels of agreement. As well as enabling very detailed measurement of students' ratings of individual attitude statements, the use of a VAS in this context makes it possible to analyse attitudinal data through hypothesis testing with mixed-effects models. Mixed-effects models allow the analysis of grouped attitude statements, while retaining detail relating to the individual statements included in the group.

Paper copies of all questionnaires were scanned and converted into digital images, enabling the measurement of informants' self-positioning on the VAS via the use of the digital image-processing software *ImageJ* (rsbweb.nih.gov/ij/). Each questionnaire contains fifty-five VAS. In total, 22,275 VAS were measured. The measurements were then analysed through hypothesis testing with linear mixed-effects models. To overcome the possibility of probability values (p-values) being anti-conservative (see Pinheiro and Bates 2000: 88 for further details), in cases where p-values were more than 0.01, the Markov Chain Monte Carlo (MCMC) sampling method was undertaken. The vast majority of significant p-values that emerge from the analysis of the data for this study are, however, smaller than 0.0001.

In recognition of the shortcomings associated with using single statements or questions as data for the study of attitudes, individual attitude statements were grouped before statistical analysis, as noted earlier. The transparency of mixed-effects models allows the researcher to group any statements, as no overall score for a given group of statements is calculated and the responses to individual questions remain visible throughout the analysis. Seven groups of statements were formed out of the twenty-three attitude statements included in the questionnaire. In addition to examining reported language use and questionnaire choice, in this chapter we focus on four of these groups:

1. affective attitudes towards Luxembourgish as a language of identity;
2. instrumental attitudes towards Luxembourgish;
3. attitudes towards Luxembourgish as a language of integration;
4. attitudes towards the usefulness of French.

4. Results

4.1 Language use and questionnaire preference

The students sampled for the study are highly multilingual. Only 6 per cent of the sample claimed to speak three or fewer languages, while 41 per cent reported being able to speak

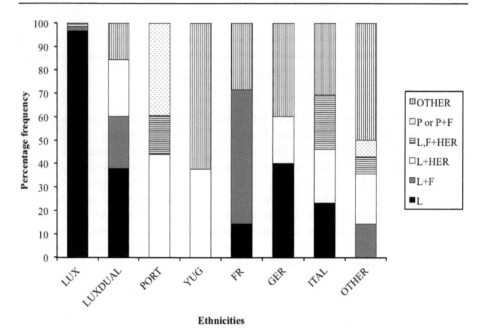

Ethnicities

Figure 11.2 Languages spoken at home by students originating from different ethnic backgrounds. Black = Luxembourgish; grey = Luxembourgish + French; white = Luxembourgish + heritage language; horizontal stripes = Luxembourgish, French + heritage language; dotted = Portuguese or Portuguese + French; vertical stripes = other.

five languages or more. The following languages were listed, in descending order of frequency: Luxembourgish, French, German, Portuguese, English, Latin, Italian, Serbian, Macedonian, Croatian, Russian, Spanish, Chinese, Dutch, Danish, Finnish and Arabic.

For ethnically Luxembourgish students, this high degree of multilingualism is not entirely reflected in their language use at home. In fact, 97 per cent of ethnically Luxembourgish students reported that they exclusively employ Luxembourgish in the home (Figure 11.2). The inherent multilingualism of Luxembourg that is implied by the official recognition of Luxembourgish, French and German is therefore rarely manifested in the homes of Luxembourgish nationals. Students other than ethnically Luxembourgish students do engage in multilingual language practices. However, students from all ethnic backgrounds employ Luxembourgish to some extent as a language of communication at home, and the use of Luxembourgish solely or in a combination with another language constitutes the most frequent medium of communication at home for the majority of students from most ethnic backgrounds.

When comparing these results to the reported use of languages with peers and friends, responses reveal that Luxembourgish constitutes the most widely-used medium of communication among members of friendship groups (Figure 11.3). For the majority of students from all ethnic groups (except Portuguese students), Luxembourgish functions as the sole medium of communication when interacting with friends or peers. This increased use of Luxembourgish as the medium of communication among students,

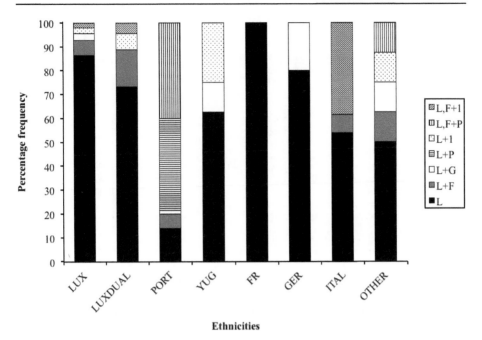

Figure 11.3 Languages spoken with friends by students from different ethnic backgrounds. Black = Luxembourgish; grey = Luxembourgish + French; white = Luxembourgish + German; horizontal stripes = Luxembourgish + Portuguese; dotted = Luxembourgish with one other language; horizontal stripes = Luxembourgish, French + Portuguese; diagonal stripes = Luxembourgish, French + one other language.

particularly given the official languages of instruction that students are faced with in the school environment, suggests that the language carries a level of covert prestige, and also perhaps indicates in-group status.

Although students of all ethnicities use Luxembourgish among themselves, the choice of language for the completion of the questionnaire is clearly related to ethnicity. This relationship is particularly visible when comparing Luxembourgish students with their Portuguese peers, where we see the Romance/Germanic distinction play out. Whereas Luxembourgish students largely opted for a Luxembourgish questionnaire, Portuguese students showed a clear preference for the French version. Italian and French students also preferred French questionnaires. Students from Germany and former Yugoslavia, on the other hand, largely took the German option. Both Luxembourgish and German questionnaires were frequently chosen by students with Luxembourgish dual nationality. However, there was also an increase in the number of French questionnaires chosen by Luxembourgish dual students when compared to their Luxembourgish peers. The collinear relationship between ethnicity and choice of language for the completion of the questionnaire is statistically highly significant ($p < 0.01$, χ^2 test). Details of the relationships between the various levels of the two variables are visualised in Figure 11.4. Even though these results may appear out of line with what was revealed regarding the degree of Luxembourgish use among peers, the high number of Luxembourgish questionnaires chosen is, in fact, surprising considering that students completed the questionnaire in

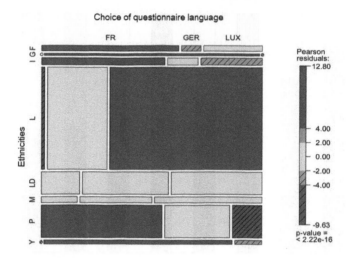

Figure 11.4 Relationship between students' ethnic background and choice of questionnaire language. For choice of questionnaire language, FR = French; GER = German; LUX = Luxembourgish. For ethnicities, F = French-speaking; G = German; I = Italian; L = Luxembourgish; LD = Luxembourgish dual; M = miscellaneous; P = Portuguese; Y = from former Yugoslavia. The sizes of the mosaic tiles are proportional to the number of informants in each category. Greyscale differences signal statistical significance, with paler shades denoting significance at the 5% level ($p < 0.05$) and darker shades indicating significance at the 1% level ($p < 0.01$).

the classroom, an environment where the use of Luxembourgish is actively discouraged. Moreover, Luxembourgish is rarely used in writing in Luxembourg's schools, and in the third section of the questionnaire students tended to report difficulties with the learning and use of Luxembourgish orthography. This insight into students' language preferences manifested through their behaviour rather than through self-reports reveals Luxembourgish to be the preferred option overall (51 per cent of students opted for a Luxembourgish questionnaire, compared with the 31 per cent and 18 per cent of students who completed German and French questionnaires, respectively), again demonstrating the covert prestige carried by the language.

We look next at language-of-instruction preferences. Once more, for ease of representation only the three largest ethnic groups included in the sample (i.e. Luxembourgish, Luxembourgish dual nationality and Portuguese) are presented in detail in Table 11.2. It is noteworthy that only a very small number of students (1 per cent Luxembourgish, 1.6 per cent Portuguese and no Luxembourgish dual students) regard the joint use of French and German – as per the current medium-of-education policy – as an ideal option. Ethnically Luxembourgish students display clear preferences for a Germanic medium of education (i.e. Luxembourgish, German or a combination thereof). The majority of Luxembourg dual nationality informants (53.4 per cent) also expressed a wish to be taught in a Germanic language (Luxembourgish, German or a combination thereof). The majority of Portuguese students (54.7 per cent) include Romance languages (French or Portuguese) in their list of preferred media of instruction. However, 28.1 per cent

Table 11.2 Self-reported medium-of-instruction preferences (%) of the three largest ethnic groups included in the sample (Luxembourgish, Luxembourgish dual nationality, Portuguese)

	Student group		
Language preference	Luxembourgish	Luxembourgish Dual	Portuguese
Luxembourgish	50.2	37.8	28.1
Lux. + French	1.4	13.3	17.2
Lux. + German	21.2	8.9	4.7
Lux. + heritage lang.	0.5	0	6.2
French	3.4	6.7	14.1
French + heritage lang.	0	0	3.1
German	6.3	6.7	0
German + French	1	0	1.6
Heritage language	N/A	0	12.5
Multiple, excl. Lux.	0.5	2.2	1.6
Multiple, incl. Lux.	10.1	15.5	3.1
Other	4.4	6.7	4.7
Any	1	2.2	3.1
Total	100	100	100

of Portuguese students nominated the sole use of Luxembourgish as their preferred medium of instruction, and 31.2 per cent of Portuguese students expressed a desire to be taught in a combination of languages including Luxembourgish.

In reported language use and preferences, then, we see evidence of divisions along ethnic lines, which largely correspond to the Germanic or Romance background of the student. However, we also note considerable agreement across ethnicities in the perceived functions of Luxembourgish, as revealed through reported use and reported language-of-instruction preference. We turn now to see whether we can observe similar divisions and commonalities in responses to attitude statements.

4.2 Affective attitudes towards Luxembourgish as a language of identity

The affective component of attitudes towards Luxembourgish and the connection between Luxembourgish and a Luxembourgish identity is examined through levels of agreement with the following three statements:

> Statement N: 'It would be sad if Luxembourgish disappeared in the future.'
> Statement P: 'Luxembourg will lose its identity if we lose the Luxembourgish language.'
> Statement W: 'Luxembourgish is the most important language in Luxembourg because it is the language of the country.'

For this group of attitude statements, all four independent variables or model parameters (i.e. ethnicity, choice of language, location of school, type of school) had a significant effect when compared with a null model through a likelihood-ratio χ^2 test. However, tests

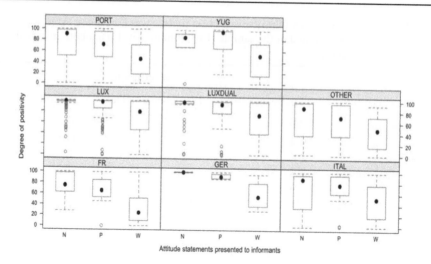

Figure 11.5 Affective attitudes towards Luxembourgish among students from different ethnic groups. PORT = Portuguese; YUG = from former Yugoslavia; LUX = Luxembourgish; LUXDUAL = Luxembourgish dual nationality; FR = French-speaking; GER = German; ITAL = Italian; OTHER = other nationalities. Likelihood-ratio χ^2 testing reveals a significant difference between the various ethnic groups ($p < 0.001$).

of collinearity revealed ethnicity to be the model parameter that in its own right has a significant effect on the informants' responses ($p < 0.001$, likelihood-ratio χ^2 test).

Despite the statistically significant differences in the attitudinal responses of the various ethnic groups, the majority of students reported positive affective attitudes towards Luxembourgish. Luxembourgish students as well as students with Luxembourgish dual nationality display the most positive affective attitudes towards Luxembourgish (Figure 11.5). The attitudes among all other ethnicities are slightly less positive. Portuguese and French-speaking students reported the most negative affective attitudes towards Luxembourgish.

Figure 11.5 reveals a general decline in degree of positivity from Statement N to P to W in all ethnic groups. The affective attitudes towards Luxembourgish are most positive among students who opted for a Luxembourgish questionnaire (Figure 11.6). The attitudes of the students who took the German option differ only slightly from those who chose Luxembourgish. Attitudes are least positive among students who completed the French questionnaire. All three groups show a similar response pattern to individual statements. Attitudes towards Luxembourgish as the most important language in Luxembourg, assessed specifically by Statement W, are the least positive among students in all three categories.

4.3 Instrumental attitudes towards Luxembourgish

The following two statements were grouped for the investigation of instrumental attitudes towards Luxembourgish:

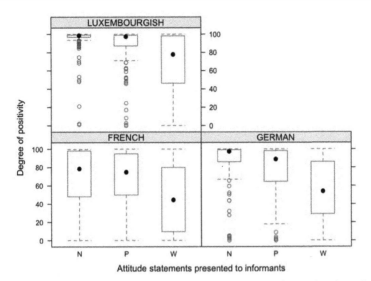

Figure 11.6 Affective attitudes towards Luxembourgish among students who chose different questionnaire languages. Likelihood–ratio testing reveals a significant difference between the different groups ($p < 0.001$).

> Statement J: Speaking Luxembourgish is not enough to get by in Luxembourg.
> Statement O: People can easily get by in Luxembourg without knowing any Luxembourgish.

Agreement with both Statements J and O indicates a negative instrumental attitude towards Luxembourgish. The responses to the VAS were therefore reverse-scored so that a high agreement score symbolises a positive instrumental attitude towards Luxembourgish. A mixed-effects model which included the choice of questionnaire language as a fixed effect yielded a significant p-value when compared with a null model (likelihood–ratio χ^2 test, $p < 0.0001$). No significant difference was found between the responses of the various ethnic groups or between students from different school types or regions. Nonetheless, Figure 11.7 reveals that students' attitudes towards the usefulness of Luxembourgish are relatively negative by comparison with their affective attitudes. Students taking the Luxembourgish questionnaire expressed the most positive instrumental attitudes towards Luxembourgish (Figure 11.8). The highest degree of positivity was found in relation to Statement O, particularly among students who chose a Luxembourgish questionnaire.

4.4 Attitudes towards Luxembourgish as a language of integration

The discrepancy between affective and instrumental attitudes towards Luxembourgish draws attention to the complex nature of the sociolinguistic situation in Luxembourg. In view of Luxembourg's high immigration rate, attitudes towards Luxembourgish as a language of integration were also investigated. The following three statements were grouped in order to assess integrative attitudes towards Luxembourgish:

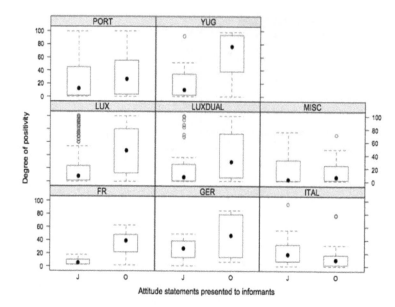

Figure 11.7 Attitudes towards the usefulness of Luxembourgish among students from different ethnic backgrounds. Likelihood-ratio χ^2 testing found no significant difference between ethnic groups. PORT = Portuguese; YUG = from former Yugoslavia; LUX = Luxembourgish; LUXDUAL = Luxembourgish dual nationality; FR = French-speaking; GER = German; ITAL = Italian; MISC = miscellaneous.

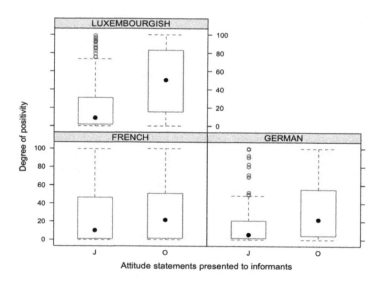

Figure 11.8 Attitudes towards the usefulness of Luxembourgish among students who chose different questionnaire languages. Likelihood-ratio χ^2 testing reveals a significant difference between the different groups ($p < 0.0001$).

Statement L: 'Immigrants can integrate better if they can speak Luxembourgish.'
Statement T: 'More efforts need to be made by the government to make immigrants learn Luxembourgish so that they can integrate better.'
Statement U: 'Immigrants need to make more efforts to learn Luxembourgish so that they can integrate better.'

Hypothesis testing with a model of ethnicity in which the effects of choice were removed yielded a significant p-value (likelihood-ratio χ^2 test, $p < 0.0001$). When undertaking the same test with a model of language choice in which the effects of ethnicity were removed, a significant p-value was also found (likelihood-ratio χ^2 test, $p < 0.05$). However, the model of ethnicity yielded a much lower p-value than the model of language choice. The students' ethnic background, therefore, has a stronger effect on their attitudes towards Luxembourgish as a language of integration than does their choice of questionnaire language.

The majority of students reported positive attitudes towards Luxembourgish as a language of integration. The most positive integrative attitudes towards Luxembourgish were found among students who chose a Luxembourgish questionnaire (Figure 11.9). Response patterns are almost identical for students who preferred the German and French versions. Among the students who chose a Luxembourgish questionnaire, the idea that immigrants themselves need to make a greater effort to learn Luxembourgish (Statement U) elicits the highest degree of agreement. This pattern is not as clear-cut among students taking the French and German options. Students in these groups show very similar responses to statements T and U, indicating a belief that both immigrants themselves and the government need to make greater efforts to make immigrants learn Luxembourgish. Students who chose a Luxembourgish questionnaire, on the other hand, place more responsibility for learning Luxembourgish on the immigrants themselves than they do on the government.

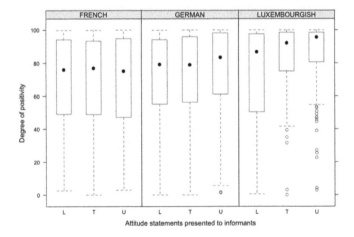

Figure 11.9 Attitudes towards Luxembourgish as a language of integration among students who chose different questionnaire languages (French, German or Luxembourgish). Likelihood-ratio χ^2 testing reveals a significant difference between the different groups ($p < 0.05$).

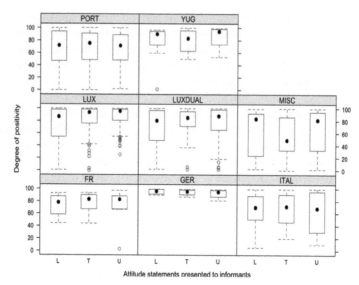

Figure 11.10 Attitudes towards Luxembourgish as a language of integration among students from different ethnic backgrounds. Likelihood-ratio χ^2 testing reveals a significant difference between the different groups ($p < 0.0001$). PORT = Portuguese; YUG = from former Yugoslavia; LUX = Luxembourgish; LUXDUAL = Luxembourgish dual nationality; FR = French-speaking; GER = German; ITAL = Italian; MISC = miscellaneous.

Students from Luxembourgish, Luxembourgish dual and German ethnic backgrounds reported the most positive attitudes towards Luxembourgish as a language of integration (Figure 11.10). On the other hand, those from Romance language backgrounds – the Portuguese, French and Italian students – show the least positive integrative attitudes towards Luxembourgish. The response pattern in relation to Statement U for students who chose the Luxembourgish questionnaire (described above) re-occurred among students from a Luxembourgish ethnic background. Overall, integrative attitudes towards Luxembourgish are more positive than instrumental attitudes towards Luxembourgish.

4.5 Attitudes towards the usefulness of French

The largely negative attitudes towards the usefulness of Luxembourgish indicate that informants have a different language at their disposal which fulfils a more utilitarian function than Luxembourgish. Responses to the following three attitude statements were grouped and analysed in order to reveal attitudes towards the usefulness of French:

> Statement K: 'In Luxembourg you must speak at least French.'
> Statement M: 'French is an important language in Luxembourg because it builds a bridge between Luxembourgish people and immigrants.'
> Statement Q: 'It is easier to find a job if you speak French rather than any other language.'

The statistical analysis revealed no significant differences between any of the independent variables. Students from all ethnic backgrounds, and from classical and technical

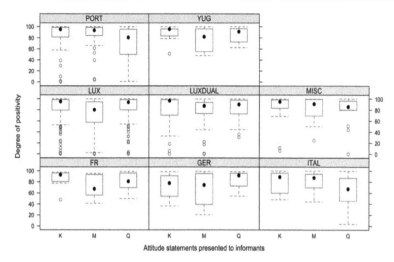

Figure 11.11 Attitudes towards the usefulness of French among students from different ethnic backgrounds. Likelihood-ratio χ^2 testing revealed no significant difference between the different groups ($p < 0.05$). PORT = Portuguese; YUG = from former Yugoslavia; LUX = Luxembourgish; LUXDUAL = Luxembourgish dual nationality; FR = French-speaking; GER = German; ITAL = Italian; MISC = miscellaneous.

schools located throughout the country reported similar attitudes towards the usefulness of French. Similarly, students' attitudes towards French were not influenced by their choice of questionnaire language. Instrumental attitudes towards French are very positive among the vast majority of all students sampled for this study (see Figure 11.11).

5. Summary and discussion

The findings presented above reveal differences along ethnic lines – and more specifically along Romance/Germanic language background lines – in both language use and language attitudes. At the same time, students are largely in agreement in terms of showing a positive attitude towards Luxembourgish as a language of identity, and a positive attitude towards French as a language necessary for advancement in society.

Differences between ethnic backgrounds are in evidence, however. On average, students from Romance language backgrounds (i.e. French, Italian, Portuguese) display less positive affective, instrumental and integrative attitudes towards Luxembourgish than do ethnically Luxembourgish, Luxembourgish dual nationality and German students. Similarly, students from Romance-language backgrounds also express the least positive attitudes towards the importance of learning Luxembourgish. All students exhibit positive instrumental attitudes towards French, however, as previously noted.

With respect to multilingual language practices, the great majority of students who categorised themselves as Luxembourgish nationals exclusively employ Luxembourgish as a medium of communication at home and with friends and peers. Students from various immigrant communities, on the other hand, engage more extensively in multilingual language practices outside the classroom through the use of their respective heritage languages. However, they also extensively communicate through the medium of Luxembourgish with family members, and particularly with friends and peers. The quantification of students' self-reported language behaviour establishes Luxembourgish as the most widely-spoken language outside the educational context for the majority of students originating from several ethnic backgrounds, not just those who categorise themselves as Luxembourgish.

We can also observe differences in the language-of-instruction preferences of students from different ethnic backgrounds. While ethnically Luxembourgish students generally appear to prefer Germanic languages of instruction, immigrant students from Romance linguistic backgrounds express a slight preference for the sole or combined use of French as a medium of instruction. However, commonalities between ethnically Luxembourgish and immigrant students can also be identified. In fact, a large proportion of students from virtually all ethnic backgrounds express a desire for the recognition of Luxembourgish (either on its own or in combination with other languages) as a medium of instruction. This increasing support for Luxembourgish can also be observed in the patterns of language choice for the completion of the questionnaire and the extensive self-reported use of Luxembourgish in classroom interactions.

On average, however, students express rather negative instrumental attitudes towards Luxembourgish. These findings draw attention to the fact that tensions in terms of linguistic prestige continue to exist between Luxembourg's national language (Luxembourgish) and the two major European languages, French and German. While the existence of students' positive attitudes towards French and German may weaken some of the evidence brought forward in support of the recognition of Luxembourgish in the educational system, the widespread preference for the use of Luxembourgish as a medium of instruction potentially reflects students' desire to increase the instrumental value of Luxembourgish in the future. Education has long been shown to function as a domain in which the status of a language can be considerably improved (Skutnabb-Kangas 2000: 500; Ferguson 2006: 33). Should Luxembourgish ever be introduced as a language of instruction in the Luxembourg classroom, the attitudinal evidence presented here suggests that it would be positively received.

6. Conclusions

The linguistic situation in Luxembourg is an under-researched area (Fehlen 2002: 81). Given the complexity of its position in respect of political and linguistic borders and its ethnically and linguistically diverse population, Luxembourg presents an ideal context for the investigation of the connections between language use, language attitudes and language planning.

Thanks to Luxembourg's borderland location its indigenous language, Luxembourgish, originated from contact between Germanic and Romance varieties: in other words, from contact between the ends of two dialect continua. Contact dialects of this kind exist all over the world at the interfaces of different dialect continua. The case of Luxembourgish is, in many ways, unusual, as the Luxembourg government officially recognised the West-Moselle Franconian dialect spoken by the vast majority of the indigenous population as Luxembourgish, the country's national language, by passing its first language law in 1984.

The findings of this study suggest that Luxembourgish is evaluated by inhabitants of Luxembourg as a language of identity.

Positive affective attitudes towards Luxembourgish increase the tensions between Luxembourgish, French and German. Moreover, these positive affective attitudes stand in contrast to the continuing exclusion of Luxembourgish from the educational sphere. A widespread desire among students for the official introduction of Luxembourgish as a medium of instruction indicates that Luxembourgish is slowly infiltrating domains which were in the past exclusively reserved for German and French. However, students simultaneously express positive instrumental attitudes towards French. These attitudinal findings draw attention to the complexity of linguistic identities among Luxembourg's students and the challenges faced by the country's policymakers whose task it is to provide an education system that satisfies the needs and desires of its multilingual population.

The emergence of Luxembourgish as a language of identity challenges the current language-in-education policies which favour politically powerful languages such as German and French. While French retains its linguistic prestige, Luxembourgish appears to be redefining its status as a language of identity and is slowly entering education, a domain that has traditionally been the preserve of French and German. Owing to the fact that Luxembourg borders on France and the French-speaking region of Belgium, Luxembourgish can be seen as a marker of differentiation from these larger neighbouring countries. In times of globalisation and the growing importance of supranational institutions such as the European Union, regional and national minorities can experience a heightened sense of their own distinctive identities (Ferguson 2006). The loosening of political borders between EU member states and the weakening of the nation-state has intensified symbolic language borders in Luxembourg, as the emergence of Luxembourgish as a language of identity has increased tensions between French, German and Luxembourgish. The success of language policies therefore depends on policymakers' understanding of the language attitudes and language behaviour of the target population, which are as complex and fluid as the contexts in which they take shape.

12

What Counts as a Linguistic Border, for Whom and with What Implications? Exploring Occitan and Francoprovençal in Rhône-Alpes, France

Michel Bert and James Costa

1. Introduction

Debates concerning the limits of the numerous Romance varieties spoken in what was once the western part of the Roman Empire have been rife for over a century (e.g. Bergounioux 1989). More recently, the creation of new administrative regions within the context of the European Union has also sparked a lively discussion about the names and circumscription of languages as those institutions seek to legitimise their own existence by drawing upon historical and linguistic forms of supporting evidence.

The current debates concerning the boundaries between language varieties in what is essentially a continuum of related forms of speech recapitulate arguments of considerable antiquity. Establishing the nature of those limits was especially important in the nineteenth century as nation-states sought to found and legitimise their existence through claims of cultural and linguistic homogeneity. The bipartite linguistic division of France between French, the language of the north, and Occitan, spoken in the south, was clearly problematic for philologists (especially in northern France) and politicians alike. Whether through natural or deliberate attrition, the original French/Occitan partition was to be erased gradually, as Occitan ever further receded as the language of everyday interactions in the south. The 'shameful' existence of Occitan, and the ideological problems it generated for the construction of a homogeneous French nation, led the linguist Bernard Cerquiglini (2007) to describe Occitan as an 'iron mask', evoking the idea of Occitan as French's hidden twin.

Situated at a distance from the major centres of debate over French and Occitan, and removed from the controversies relating to regional languages in France since the 1960s (in the Basque Country, Brittany, Catalonia, Provence, etc.), the Rhône-Alpes region is a recent administrative construct focused on Lyon, one of the major centres for the diffusion of French from the seventeenth century onwards. The region is nevertheless traversed by several linguistic boundaries, the main one being the border between Occitan and Francoprovençal.

While issues generated by questions of dialect and language boundaries in this part of France have hitherto remained within the relatively closed domain of linguistics, the emergence of an interest in language policy on the part of the regional government is currently having a modifying influence on the earlier equilibrium. This recent intervention by a new social force in local language debates calls for a reassessment of the role of regional boundaries. Indeed, the geographical limits of the extent of linguistic areas often tend to be reified as boundaries through the implementation of language policy measures, bringing tangible effects in terms of language education planning, for instance.

In Rhône-Alpes, linguistic borders are now gaining importance because they are seen as one potential tool for the legitimation of the existence of the *région*. However, while the regional government is promoting both Occitan and Francoprovençal on an equal footing, it is concomitantly downplaying the importance of this region-internal linguistic boundary so as to promote a feeling of linguistic closeness that would help to justify Rhône-Alpes' own existence as a coherent cultural area.

In this particular context, the link between identity and language is inevitably of a rather complex nature. Given the range of relevant social factors involved, and the difficulties in conceptualising identity that this diversity entails, we have chosen to follow Avanza and Laferté's (2005) sociological approach to identity. This allows us to break up the notion into three more specific categories. For Avanza and Laferté, identity is best conceived of in terms of *identification, social image* and *belonging*. Identification refers to the process through which individuals are ascribed to particular categories (for example, ethnicity or religion) by 'legitimate' institutions such as government bodies responsible for the collection and management of demographic data. Social image refers to the production of discourses, images and symbols designed to represent a particular group or territory. Again, social images can be produced by institutions, but also by various types of associations and groups (e.g. NGOs), or by, say, published travel guides. The outcome of the process is the creation, through discourse, of an authoritative representation of a social group or geographical area. In cases of the latter sort, the focus is typically an area where the production of what counts as accepted and shared reality is created, reproduced or contested. The final category, belonging, refers to the kinds of higher-order units (geographical regions, for instance) to which groups or individuals tend to affiliate themselves. Such groups can include ethnolinguistic groups, when appropriate categories are available. Belonging is constantly subject to reproduction, renegotiation and contestation, be it group-internally or group-externally.

Based on several years' worth of ethnographic sociolinguistic and dialectological research in the Rhône-Alpes and Provence regions in south-eastern France (see for instance Bert 2001; Costa 2010), this chapter focuses on how what we call 'social actors' impose limits on languages, and why. We are therefore asking the following questions: to whom are these limits important? Who can turn limits into boundaries – that is, legitimised limits that have concrete effects on groups and individuals in terms of the creation of social differences? How are those limits constructed in discourse and spatial representations? And, most importantly for the social actors themselves, what do the processes entail in terms of identity for the various groups involved? The types of actors we focus upon in this chapter are linguists, speakers, language advocates and institutions (the state and the regional government – *Conseil régional* – based in the regional capital, Lyon).

This chapter first presents the Rhône-Alpes region as one in which linguistic limits are particularly salient and meaningful for an array of different social actors. We then analyse how traditional social actors (linguists, speakers, language advocates) construct limits through language – or refrain from doing so – emphasising convergences and divergences between those limits. We finally explore the role of the regional government, as well as that of the state, in naturalising or contesting limits, and in legitimising certain boundaries through language policy, at the expense of others.

2. Language(s) in the Rhône-Alpes region

The current French administrative *régions*, of which there were twenty-two in 2014, were created, or one could say invented, between 1942 and 1960. They were subsequently given more power by the central government between 1972, when the *régions* were transformed from economic to administrative entities, and 1982, when the newly elected socialist government passed a series of major decentralisation laws.

All republican governments in France have consistently striven to avoid reviving the provinces that collectively formed the Kingdom of France until the Revolution at the end of the eighteenth century. Thus, two centuries later, the new *régions* are composed of several *départements*,[1] but they have been purposefully created so as not to replicate the borders of the former provinces. The Rhône-Alpes region, for example, comprises parts of the former provinces of Lyonnais, Languedoc, Dauphiné, Burgundy and Savoy (see Figure 12.1).[2] It should be noted that Savoy is itself a recent addition to France; it was annexed in 1860 together with the County of Nice at the time that the Italian state was formed. During the process that saw the establishment of *régions*, even long-established entities such as Brittany were partly dismantled, and the Nantes region (the Loire-Atlantique *département*) was joined to four others to form the Pays de la Loire *région*. Conversely, Provence was incorporated into a wider *région* called Provence-Alpes-Côte d'Azur with the former County of Nice and parts of the Dauphiné (and, until 1970, with Corsica). Finally, regions such as the Région Centre or Rhône-Alpes are new names invented in the 1960s, based upon geographical features. Rhône-Alpes itself consists of eight *départements* (see Figure 12.2),[3] thus constituting a very large area (43,698 km^2, or nearly 17,000 sq. miles).

In a context in which any distinctive particularity can be seen as a potential threat to French unity, it comes as no surprise that no cultural or linguistic elements were taken into account when the *régions* were designed. All the current *régions* of France, with the possible exceptions of Corsica and Alsace, embrace highly diverse cultural and linguistic areas around a regional capital. Former or traditional limits were broken down and torn apart in order to create new, apparently more rational, entities that could not be seen as competing with the citizen's main locus of identification, that is, the French nation.

As a region constructed by administrators, Rhône-Alpes is particularly emblematic of those new administrative units that took no account of limits that were meaningful to their populations. It therefore encompasses a multitude of historical, cultural and linguistic limits that still have effects in the everyday lives of people. In terms of the linguistic situation, two Romance languages are traditionally spoken within the regional territory: Francoprovençal and Occitan.[4] While the *départements* of Ain, Isère, Loire, Rhône, Savoie and Haute-Savoie are usually described as Francoprovençal-speaking areas, most

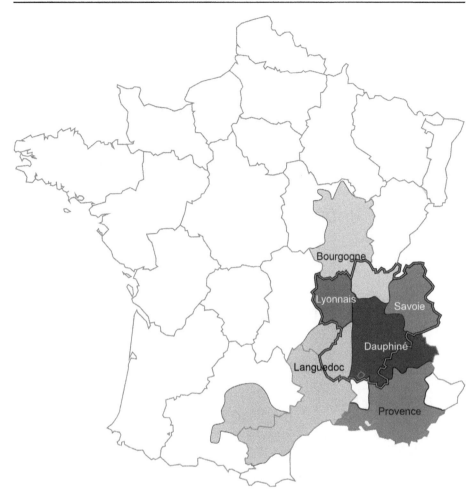

Figure 12.1 The Rhône-Alpes region in France, and the main provinces that existed in south-eastern France before the Revolution.

of the Ardèche and Drôme are habitually depicted as Occitan-speaking (see Figure 12.2 detailing the *départements* of Rhône-Alpes, and Figure 12.3, which shows the boundary between Occitan and Francoprovençal that is generally accepted by linguists and dialectologists). In reality, however, both partionings are more complex, and several important dialect boundaries run through the Rhône-Alpes region, especially in the Occitan-speaking domain (see section 3.1. below). Also, one must carefully differentiate between the two languages: with regard to Francoprovençal, linguists tend to take the view that there are no marked dialect areas (Martin 1990). Occitan in Rhône-Alpes, on the other hand, is usually divided between Provençal, in the south of Drôme and parts of southern Ardèche, Languedocian in south-western Ardèche, and Vivaro-Alpin in the remaining parts of Drôme and Ardèche (see Sumien 2009 for a summary of the classification of Occitan dialects).

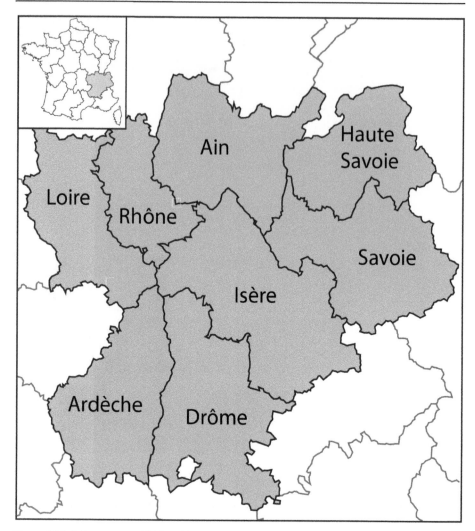

Figure 12.2 *Départements* of Rhône-Alpes.

Francoprovençal and Occitan are Romance languages descended from the Latin brought by Roman colonisers during the conquest of Gaul approximately two thousand years ago. This particular brand of Latin evolved from a mostly Celtic (Gaulish) substratum, being subsequently modified by the Germanic invasions that took place at the end of the Roman period and at the beginning of the Middle Ages. The relative importance of the Germanic superstratum is still a matter for debate, but most linguists consider Francoprovençal to have been less affected by this latter influence than was the language of the Langue d'Oïl domain, and Occitan even less so. Overall, however, both languages are part of the same Romance continuum, and in our own experience they are largely mutually comprehensible by competent speakers.

Rhône-Alpes thus plays host to a complex bundle of social, historical, cultural and linguistic boundaries. Some cultural boundaries are indexed through metalinguistic

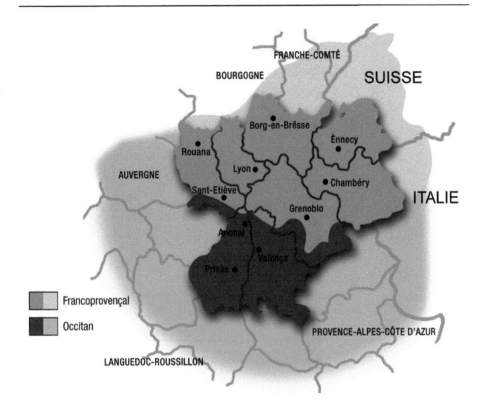

Figure 12.3 The traditional dialectological boundary between Francoprovençal and Occitan in Rhône-Alpes (map courtesy of the Rhône-Alpes region; this map is used by the regional government when promoting its languages).

discourse, and (predictably) the same limits are not meaningful in the same way to all social actors. The first social actors we consider are linguists, whose historical role has consisted in the delimitation and naming of 'languages' in the modern sense of the term as discrete and bounded entities that are resolved out of the Romance linguistic continuum.

3. The languages of linguists: Occitan and Francoprovençal

Linguists are central actors in the narrative we wish to recount here, most particularly in the case of Francoprovençal. They are especially influential when it comes to processes of identification, as their work defines what limits are acceptable in the delineation of a language. This latter process in turn has consequences on how people appropriate, or reject, the language(s) that linguists ascribe to them.

   This section examines what boundaries are relevant to this category, and how linguists effectively generated borders that established Francoprovençal and Occitan as separate and geographically circumscribed entities mapping on to to well-defined territories.

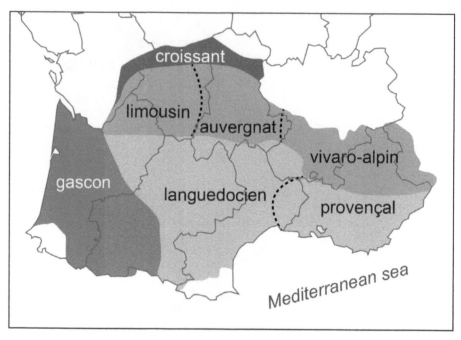

Figure 12.4 Occitan dialects in France, Italy (eleven valleys in Piedmont) and Spain (the Val
d'Aran in Catalonia).

3.1 Occitan doubts and certainties

Occitan in its current form emerged mostly beyond the boundaries of what is now
Rhône-Alpes. In spite of its having been the administrative language of several areas in
the Middle Ages, Occitan suffered a loss of status in the early modern period but then
underwent a revival of interest from as early as the beginning of the nineteenth century
(see Martel 2010a). What counted as Occitan was defined in the mid-nineteenth century
by dialectologists (Merle 2010), amateur philologists such as Simon Honnorat (Martel
2010b; Merle 1986) and the renowned Provençal writer and lexicologist Frédéric Mistral
(Mistral 1979 [1878]).[5] The northernmost boundaries of Occitan, which run through the
northern parts of the Ardèche and the Drôme *départements* (see Figure 12.4), were established long ago, but refined more recently (see Tuaillon 1964; Martin 1979; Bert 2001;
Bouvier 2003).

Identifying internal dialectal boundaries within Occitan is more problematic. The
main divide for linguists is that defined by the *ca/cha* (i.e. /k/ ~ /ʃ/) heterogloss, which
runs through the whole Occitan domain, and indeed throughout the whole of the old
Western Romania, from Italy to the Atlantic Ocean (Figure 12.5). South of that line, one
encounters such forms as /k/*antar* ('to sing') or va/k/a ('cow'), which are realised as
/ʃ/*antar*, va/ʃ/a to the north of it. This particular limit serves to mark the distinction
between northern Occitan dialects (Auvergnat, Limousin and Vivaro-Alpin) and southern ones (Gascon, Languedocian and Provençal).[6] As far as Rhône-Alpes is concerned,
linguists do not recognise any east/west divide as particularly relevant to the linguistic

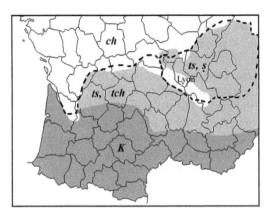

Figure 12.5 The *ca/cha* heterogloss separating northern and southern Occitan dialects. K = /k/; *tch* = /tʃ/; *ch* = /ʃ/; ş = [θ].

situation in the region, and attribute no specific role to the River Rhône in separating specific dialect groupings.

The work of linguists, while originally not meant for this particular purpose, in effect provides elements for different groups to identify with – hence the struggle that accompanied the establishment of Occitan as a distinct language. The existence of a sharp divide between French in the north of France and, in the south, a single Occitan language – called *Langue d'oc* prior to the twentieth century – is now a cornerstone of French dialectology, but its existence was the subject of fierce philological disputes at the end of the nineteenth century (Bergounioux 1989). The portrayal of Occitan as a language distinct from French could indeed be understood as questioning the unity of France and of the French people. Philologists such as Paul Meyer and Gaston Paris thus strove to prove that there was indeed no real linguistic boundary, and that all the dialects of France formed a linguistic tapestry, gradually merging into one another to form a linguistic reality organised around *Francien*, in their view the former dialect of the Paris area.

It should also be noted that nowadays a few sociolinguists consider Occitan to be a recent invention, and that what actually exists is a mosaic of several 'oc' languages (i.e. *Langues d'oc*, plural; Lafitte and Pépin 2009). In effect, this would create boundaries within the Occitan domain of Rhône-Alpes, but it does not question the limit dividing Occitan from other languages north of the domain.

3.2 Francoprovençal, an elusive linguistic reality

What lies beyond Occitan to the north is, however, less clear. Some speakers of what is now considered as Francoprovençal became members of the *Felibrige*, the literary association established in 1854 in Provence by Frédéric Mistral to promote Occitan.[7] Yet authors from the Francoprovençal domain never sought to promote their own local varieties in their writings, and instead wrote in the standard Provençal that Mistral had codified. These writers apparently had no feeling of belonging to a common entity, and never referred to the dialects of their own areas as one language with its own particular name.

Nowadays, however, linguists agree that present-day Romance-speaking France can be divided into three traditional linguistic domains: Langue d'oïl in the North, Langue d'oc in the south and Francoprovençal. This latter domain was identified as a coherent linguistic area only in 1873 by the Italian dialectologist Graziadio Ascoli (1878 [1873]) within the context of the debate, outlined above, between northern and southern dialectologists regarding the existence of dialects in France.

Originally, Francoprovençal was defined as a separate code not just because it displayed some unique and distinctive features, but also because it shared other features with either Occitan or Oïl varieties – hence its name, originally spelled *franco-provenzale*. Other names have since been proposed by linguists to circumvent confusion (Rhodanien, Moyen-rhodanien, Southeastern French and Burgondian, because of an ostensibly important Burgundian superstratum), but none of these has ever taken hold.

Beyond the question of its name, however, the limits of Francoprovençal soon became an important issue, as their circumscription encroached to a greater or lesser degree upon other languages, in particular Occitan. Eventually, two sets of phonetic features were identified as critically important: linguists distinguished Francoprovençal from Occitan according to the particular treatment of Latin *a* where the vowel is preceded by a palatal consonant (e.g. Occitan *filha* versus Francoprovençal *filli*, 'daughter'), whereas the placement of word stress on the penultimate syllable – i.e. the incidence of paroxytones – was used to differentiate Francoprovençal from Oïl varieties in the north of the domain.

The existence of the linguistic domain was further legitimised by the broad conjunction of its shape with that of a territory demarcated by Roman roads leading from Lyon to Aoste (It. *Aosta*) in present-day Italy and Geneva in present-day Switzerland, as can be seen in Figure 12.6. Within this particular framework, *Lugdunum* (Lyon), the religious capital of Gaul, could then suitably be represented as an ancient urban centre with a status that lent necessary political impetus to the development of Francoprovençal as a discrete language.

It should be noted that, as far as linguists are concerned, there are no obvious internal dialect boundaries in Francoprovençal, despite several attempts to establish some

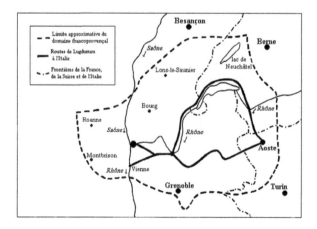

Figure 12.6 Roman roads from Lyon to Aoste and Geneva, and the Francoprovençal domain.

(Hasselrot 1934; Martin 1990). Thus, linguists do not make an issue of arguing the case for such discontinuities, contrary to what takes place among activists (see below).

The process that saw the birth of Francoprovençal as a language may be deemed thoroughly arbitrary (see also Tuaillon 1972); other choices of criterial features could potentially have resulted in a different definition of the Francoprovençal linguistic domain. Figure 12.7 shows the heteroglosses that run from east to west through the Drôme *département*, some of which could indeed also have been chosen to represent the boundary between Occitan and Francoprovençal. The linguistic choices outlined above have consequences for the people now living in those areas, consequences that at the end of the nineteenth century were largely unforeseen. Occitan has in effect been taught in schools since 1951, yet Francoprovençal cannot be taught officially. The level of vitality and organisation of Occitan activism in Rhône-Alpes, owing to the existence of strong activist networks in the Montpellier and Toulouse areas, is considerably higher than that of Francoprovençal.

At present, however, there is a consensus among linguists regarding both the existence of Francoprovençal as a language in its own right, and the border between it and Occitan in Rhône-Alpes. No obvious area of transition between the two codes is ever discernible on linguistic maps, and linguists working in the region are readily able to assign speech samples to either one or the other language. In doing so, linguists act as an organised body of scientists prescribing a particular type of identification with one language or another: a particular village or speaker is connected either to Occitan or to Francoprovençal.

It should finally be noted that one amateur linguist, Pierre Bonnaud, a former professor of geography at the Université de Clermont-Ferrand in Auvergne, has argued in favour of the existence of one Medio-Romance language that would encompass what is currently known as Francoprovençal as well as the Occitan dialects of the Alps, Auvergne and Limousin. Such a proposal, had it been widely adopted, would have led to a considerably different linguistic panorama in Rhône-Alpes: in Bonnaud's model, Occitan would only be spoken in the far south, while almost all of the remainder of the region would find itself within the domain of 'Medioromance'.[8]

4. The voice of speakers and their perception of sociocultural limits

This section considers another sort of actor involved in the definition of linguistic limits. It presents the various ways in which ordinary speakers of both Francoprovençal and Occitan conceptualise the limits of the local language they speak, and identify with such varieties to construct their identities as speakers of 'minorised' regional languages. They are grouped together as there is no significant difference between the speakers of both languages (established as such according to linguists' criteria, rather than those used by other interest groups).

4.1 Language as a local reality

To most ordinary speakers, that is, speakers who do not consider themselves as language advocates or activists, the local language or *patois* as they still generally refer to it (Bert et al. 2009) is bounded either by their village, their travels or their social network. The name usually attributed to the patois – generally 'patois of X', where X represents any

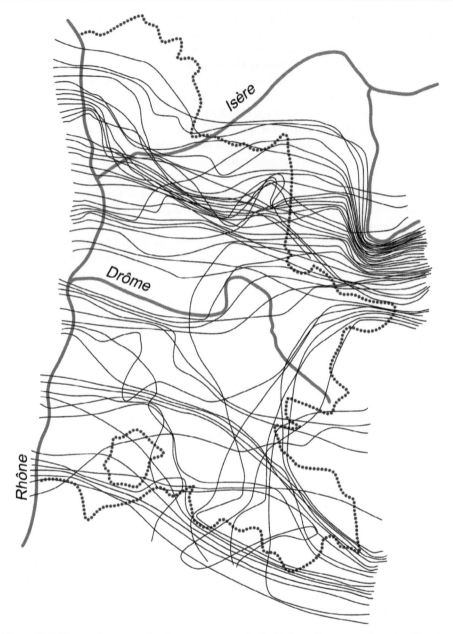

Figure 12.7 Heteroglosses running from east to west in the Drôme *département* (based on Bouvier 1976).

given village – confirms this. The patois therefore fits a lived and close-by reality, and its boundaries fit those of personal experience. With respect to linguistic identity, individual belonging is therefore primarily connected with the village, or possibly a grouping of a few villages, and, most importantly, one speaker's conception of the boundedness of the local patois may therefore not correspond to that of another speaker. Boundaries are thus traditionally not fixed, and can evolve according to interaction contexts or events such as the arrival of a newcomer.

As an illustration, during the fieldwork we conducted in 2007–08 for the Francoprovençal and Occitan in Rhône-Alpes (FORA) study (Bert et al. 2009), one 87-year-old woman in southern Drôme could name the villages where, according to her, people spoke the same patois as she did. These included several towns and villages in the vicinity, but also the city of Montpellier some 200 km (130 miles) to the south, where her son-in-law's father came from. Other nearby villages were, however, excluded from her list.

What is consistently confirmed by such examples is a clear emphasis on the maximisation of difference from nearby localities (see also Dorian 1982, who comments on the obsession of speakers of endangered languages with variation and distinctiveness), and a certain minimisation of 'foreignness' relative to more distant locations. In other words, ordinary speakers – unsurprisingly – identify linguistically with locality rather than with larger linguistic entities. What is more remarkable, however, is the lack of correspondence between the limits drawn by linguists and those identified by speakers in their everyday discourse and practice, as will be shown in the next section.

4.2 Divergence between linguists and ordinary speakers

We have noted a distinct lack of coincidence between the limits drawn by linguists and those that are meaningful to speakers. This is manifested both when speakers invoke limits that are irrelevant to linguists, and through the fact that ordinary speakers usually completely disregard the linguistic borders defined in linguistics.

4.2.1 Alleged cultural limits expressed in linguistic terms

To illustrate the first type of divergence, we take one particularly significant example in the Occitan domain, that of the Rhône. The Rhône is a major river that runs from north to south between Lyon and the Camargue area further south in Provence, eventually flowing into the Mediterranean. It marks the border between the *départements* of Drôme and Ardèche in Rhône-Alpes, and further south between the Vaucluse in Provence and the Gard in Languedoc.

The Rhône corresponds to no particular heterogloss, as all major heteroglosses in this part of France run from east to west. The border between the Provençal and Languedocian dialects of Occitan lies further west, on the River Vidourle. However, members of Occitan speech communities on both sides of the Rhône consistently invoke the river as a major linguistic border. People dwelling on one side of the river are said by those on the other to speak very differently, even in a bizarre fashion, as is the case between areas in northern Drôme and Ardèche. In some cases the speech of people on the opposite bank remains unknown, due to a lack of contact.

Although the Rhône does not in fact form a dialect boundary (see Figure 12.7), it has nevertheless acted as a political boundary since the early Middle Ages, and possibly before that. It marked the border between the Kingdom of France and the Holy Roman Empire, between Provence and Languedoc. It now forms the boundary between the Provence-Alpes-Côte d'Azur and Languedoc-Roussillon regions. In this particular case, it is therefore a strong sociohistorical sense of belonging that generates a border that later comes to be connected with linguistic issues. Here, linguistic discontinuities are posited on the basis of former political boundaries, whereas in the modern period linguistic limits are often naturalised into idealised ethnic boundaries that are subsequently used to delineate political units.

4.2.2 Limits established by linguists that go unnoticed in ordinary discourse and practice

By contrast with the situation described in 4.2.1. above, we have observed that ordinary speakers often consider some of the key boundaries established by linguists to be meaningless. We take three examples from different areas in Rhône-Alpes: a) the northern border of Francoprovençal, b) the border between Occitan and Francoprovençal and c) an important dialectal border within Occitan, in the south of the region.

Our first example concerns the northern border of Francoprovençal. In the northwest of the Francoprovençal domain, the placement of stress on the penultimate syllable, the distinctive feature that distinguishes Francoprovençal from Langue d'Oïl, has recently disappeared. As this is a recent development, however, and as linguistic traces of Francoprovençal remain in other respects, linguists consider that the language people speak in this area is still Francoprovençal.

However, in the context of a local association of language enthusiasts where speakers from the north-western area and from areas further south meet up on a regular basis, we find that participants have consistently failed to show awareness of the realisation of that particular stress placement pattern, or a lack thereof. In fact, when speakers resort to the written medium, some mark the unstressed final vowel and others do not. Yet this feature apparently goes unnoticed in the ordinary speech of other fellow association members. That is to say, this particular feature is not just unnoticed, it is not 'semiotised': it is not discursively objectified as a distinctive feature that allows the construction of difference between speakers.

Our second example shows that such important linguistic limits as language borders can be meaningless to ordinary speakers. This example is drawn from fieldwork conducted by the first author on the Occitan/Francoprovençal border (Bert 2001), and more specifically in more than twenty villages at the boundary between the north of Ardèche and the south-east of the Loire. As explained above, this linguistic frontier is grounded on the difference of the treatment of Latin *a* where it is preceded by a palatal consonant. While it does not preclude mutual comprehension, this difference leads to important structural consequences for Francoprovençal, in particular in terms of verbal, nominal and adjectival morphology (such as different conjugational paradigms between verbs in -*a* and verbs in -*i* or -*é*; feminine nouns and adjectives with final -*a* or -*i*, versus Occitan -*a*). In spite of these far-reaching effects, this feature went unnoticed by all speakers surveyed, except in one village, Tarantaise, where the speech is Occitan, and where some had noticed that in Le Bessat (a Francoprovençal-speaking village only a few kilometres away) some words ended in -*i* instead of -*a*.

This example is therefore particularly interesting, as it emphasises how different ideologies can lead to multiple strategies for constructing vernacular varieties of speech as languages, and how differences that we as linguists now deem essential can easily be dismissed within other ideological frameworks. Traditionally, speakers on both sides of what is now considered a linguistic border called their language *patois*, and difference was emphasised or downplayed for reasons of local politics rather than being foregrounded in relation to the establishment of wider entities we now call languages.

Finally, we mentioned above (see Figure 12.5) the existence of an essential demarcation in Romance linguistics, that involving the evolution of Latin *ca* and *ga*. This line runs through the north of Italy and most of the Occitan domain, and allows us to distinguish not only between northern and southern Occitan, but also between essential features of major European languages such as French, Spanish and Italian. Compare, for instance, French *chanter*, Francoprovençal, Rumantsch Grischun (a language of southeast Switzerland) and northern Occitan *chantar*, all with initial /ʃ/, against southern Occitan, Catalan, Spanish *cantar* and Italian *cantare*, with /k/. It is therefore a feature of primary importance, and in some areas in Provence it gives rise to the labelling of northerners as *Gavòts*, a mostly derogatory term.

Essential as this border may seem to linguists or lay speakers from other regions, speakers in the southern Drôme area who live on the heterogloss itself apparently do not see it as relevant, and in informal conversations that we had with them during fieldwork they seemed only to realise its existence when we happened to mention it. Even then, it was not seen as a feature upon which a difference between individuals and groups could with any relevance be based.

In the Suze-la-Rousse area in southern Drôme, however, a much more important distinction obtains in the local, and frequently mentioned and laughed-about, opposition between the pronunciation of the *-ion/-ien* suffix, for instance in the word *informacion/ informacien* ('information'). This particular feature, which is more common in the Lower Provence area but relatively marginal in northern Provence, has come to serve locally as a meaningful way to distinguish people as members of different sociolinguistic groups.

Importantly, these examples emphasise the absence of predictability in relation to what may or may not count as important linguistically in the construction of social difference. In terms of identity construction, however, this means that identification (in this case by academics) and folk feelings of belonging are potentially in conflict. As a consequence, 'speaking the same language' can indeed signify very different things to different people, in accordance with their ideological motivations.

5. Language advocates: languages as bounded, discrete entities

This section reviews the diverse positions adopted by language advocates and activists in Rhône-Alpes. Their position is very complex, as they must seek legitimacy from both the scientific establishment (mostly in order to gain access to symbolic and material resources allocated by the relevant institutions) and the people (so as to be efficient in promoting the use of the language). In this respect, the histories of language advocacy diverge considerably on both sides of the Occitan/Francoprovençal border, mainly for reasons that originate outside Rhône-Alpes, in Provence and Languedoc.

However diverse those movements may be, they are clearly part of a wider, pan-European approach to language that tends to combine language, territory and identity in an essentialised fashion. Those social movements draw on linguistics in their production of idealised linguistic territories circumscribed by well-defined language boundaries.

5.1 Francoprovençal activism: from scattered local movements to the promotion of 'Arpitan'

The existence of Francoprovençal activism is recent, little organised (outside Savoy, at least) and is less inclined to voice radical language policy claims than is the Occitan movement. Francoprovençal was, until the 1960s, mostly the preserve of dialectologists. In the 1960s, however, a brand of activism emerged in Savoy at the same time as the process that saw the establishment of the Rhône-Alpes region was taking place. Language was seen as a tool that supported the demands of Savoyard autonomists for the creation of a Savoy region within France (Bénédicte Pivot, personal communication). It comes as no surprise that Savoyard language advocates were keen on promoting the existence of what they continue to perceive and promote as a well-defined and well-delimited Savoyard dialect, although this is based on little linguistic evidence.

More recently, some younger Francoprovençal language advocates have sought to organise the movement around the concept of 'Arpitan', with certain activists seeking to establish a common orthographic system and to endorse the possibility of a standard version of the language. The term 'Arpitan' erases any indication that the language is a mixture of French and Provençal, and further naturalises it as a coherent, discrete and bounded linguistic domain with sharp external boundaries. Through the efforts of these activists, Francoprovençal would, it was hoped, no longer be the construction of a handful of linguists; it would be a language that was simply waiting to be discovered.

The aim of this latter movement is clearly part of a modernist project that apparently seeks to fuse identification with belonging, and eventually with the production of social image through music, art and other cultural and political manifestations.

5.2 The Occitan movement, 150 years later

The Occitan movement is, on the other hand, far older (in its modern form, it goes back to 1854), and far more complex (see for instance Martel 1987, 1989, 1997; Abrate 2001; Costa 2010) than the Francoprovençal pressure group described in the preceding section. The Occitan movement has since its inception been rife with ideological debates that served to express various statements of power. Disputes about orthographic issues preceded the development of the *Felibrige*, and have continued unabated to the present day.

Other debates were to follow regarding the naming of the language (Langue d'oc or Occitan), and more recently there have been attempts to redefine the various dialects of Occitan as autonomous languages, which would thus turn internal dialect boundaries into language boundaries. This means that, depending upon which revival movement they affiliate themselves with, activists do not construct linguistic borders, and accordingly their sense of belonging in relation to the borders, in the same way. Consider the maps in Figures 12.8 and 12.9, which represent meaningful borders in line with whether one subscribes to an Occitanist view of the world (Figure 12.8) or to its Provençalist counterpart (Figure 12.9). The first point of view follows, and tends to reify, that of most linguists since the nineteenth century, while the second adopts, and often essentialises, the point of view of some ordinary speakers from the Rhône area.[9]

In this case, language movements combine issues of identification and belonging, as such movements struggle to impose their own perceptions of regional linguistic

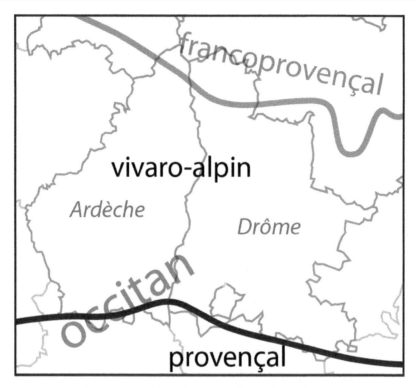

Figure 12.8 The southern part of Rhône-Alpes, according to the Occitan movement.

identification. Each particular view in turn indexes different conceptions of culture and politics (Costa 2011),[10] and seeks to modify feelings of belonging among a large number of language advocates and ordinary speakers alike. A considerable target is also the institutional level, which is key to the legitimation of identification processes and to the production of the social image aspect of identity. Ultimately, however, what is at stake in the definition of geographical limits as language boundaries is access to symbolic and material advantages, such as prestige and funding.

6. Institutional voices: national and regional

As we stated in our introduction, what makes Rhône-Alpes particularly interesting and relevant to the study of language and borders is the recent emergence of a new and inherently legitimate social actor in the process of language naming and delimiting, the regional government. This body thus has the potential to generate social image, to promote identification with its own vision of what it means to be *rhônalpin* (including linguistically) and to influence the sense of belonging among the inhabitants of the territory. In practice, it competes with an array of other types of actors, not least the state and the *départements* of which the region is composed.

The regional government has, however, adopted two main attitudes as far as regional linguistic boundaries are concerned: on the one hand, it has sought to legitimise and

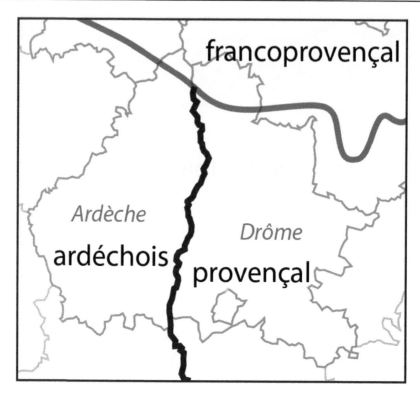

Figure 12.9 The same zone as that shown in Figure 12.8, according to promoters of Provençal as a distinct language.

officialise the linguistic division of its territory externally, following the divisions identified (or chosen) by linguists, for example through its opposition to the national government in terms of language education planning. It has therefore advocated a stance in favour of a wider national recognition for Francoprovençal in its current form. Simultaneously, it has attempted partially to erase the Francoprovençal/Occitan border internally, in order to justify the emergence of a Rhônalpine identity and to legitimise its existence as a recent administrative entity.

6.1 Region and nation

The state is a particularly influential institution, as it controls the education system. As far as Occitan is concerned, the state has followed the boundaries established in the nineteenth century, despite attempts by some Provençal language advocates to institute Provençal as a distinct entity.

It has been legal to teach some of the regional languages of France since 1951, but Francoprovençal is not among these. Following language advocates' demands over the past twenty years that the language be taught in schools, various government decisions have assigned Francoprovençal to either the Oïl domain (whereby, as a dialect of French, it does not require particular teaching provisions), or as a dialect of Occitan, which can therefore be taught (see Grinevald and Bert, forthcoming). The latter option is considered a nonsense by local language advocates, however. Legitimising the boundaries of Francoprovençal that have been established by linguists therefore places a strong obligation on the Rhône-Alpes regional government to establish a regional language policy that treats both regional languages on an equal footing. At an official level, only the borders that have been defined by linguists carry enough weight to justify political action.

6.2 Promoting a regional identity

The interest of the Rhône-Alpes government in the languages that are spoken within the territory of the region began in 2007, when it commissioned a sociolinguistic survey on the use of Francoprovençal and Occitan (Bert et al. 2009). Since then a number of language policy measures have been passed with respect to both languages. Given the lack of either historical substance or cultural unity to justify and legitimise the existence of Rhône-Alpes as a region, it is precisely this diversity that has come to characterise the region and the social image the local government wishes to promote in official discourse (see Costa and Bert 2011). Consider, for example, the following extract from the regional government's website:

> *Rhône-Alpes tire son unité de ses mille et une facettes géographiques et climatiques. Mais ce sont avant tout ses habitants qui font chaque jour de Rhône-Alpes une région dynamique, attractive où il fait bon vivre. [. . .] La région Rhône-Alpes est placée au carrefour naturel de grands axes de communication nationaux et européens. Cette situation en fait une Région ou la diversité est le maître mot. Ce puzzle à la fois géographique, climatique, sociologique et culturel pourrait être un handicap. Rhône-Alpes en a fait sa force.*[11]
> Rhône-Alpes draws its unity from its multifaceted geographic and climatic character. But above all, it is its inhabitants that daily make Rhône-Alpes a dynamic, attractive region where life is agreeable. [. . .] The Rhône-Alpes region lies at a natural crossroads between major national and European communication routes. This situation makes the region one where diversity is the keyword. This geographic, climatic, sociological and cultural mosaic could be a handicap. Rhône-Alpes has made it its strength.

Of central importance is the necessity to naturalise the existence of Rhône-Alpes in spite of its recent creation, and to create a 'charter myth' that ensures that the entity is legitimate as an administrative entity. In this respect, language proves to be a useful tool of the regional government, which can focus both on linguistic diversity as part of its constitutive diversity and on the linguistic closeness of the two languages as a way of asserting the coherence of the region as more than simply an administrative construct.

Indeed, in official public documentation regarding the language, as well as in the text that was provided to members of the regional assembly when the principle of a linguistic policy was first adopted, the language border tends to be erased (Costa and Bert 2011), in particular through the use of the expression 'vernacular languages', which means that no language names need be given.[12] Conversely, the similarities between people's speech on both sides of the boundary are emphasised in order to help to legitimise the idea of

Rhône-Alpes as a coherent ensemble. Thus, despite the official discourse appearing to celebrate diversity, unity is still sought through the existence of common features such as language, in a movement that reproduces, in a much lighter version, the nineteenth-century construction of France as 'one and indivisible'.

Issues of limits and boundaries are, as we can see from the examples discussed above, clearly connected to issues of social image production, and can be used to emphasise or neutralise tensions that can arise from the presence of diversity within a given territory. That is to say, linguistic limits can be transformed though discourse into markers of difference or sameness, depending upon the political agenda being followed at the time when these discourses are produced.

In our particular case, the limits that speakers impose on their local region are ignored by regional politics, because they emphasise the ultra-local. The limits of Savoyard as put forward by activists have indeed been wholly erased for political reasons, in order to circumvent a potential conflict with the Savoyard autonomist movement, especially at a time when the region was celebrating the 150th anniversary of the union (or annexation, depending on the social actor's point of view) of Savoy to/by France. Finally, the region acknowledges and legitimises the Occitan vision of the south of the regional domain. This discourages the creation of a new internal linguistic division, and it aligns regional choices with those of other Occitan regions.

7. Conclusion: performing diverse and potentially conflicting aspects of identity

That linguistic limits are social constructs is, of course, by no means a new element in the sociolinguistics of language borders, as is made clear in other chapters in this volume. What makes the particular case of Rhône-Alpes interesting is the lack of coincidence between the boundaries constructed by linguists and those that are meaningful to ordinary speakers. Language advocates and institutional actors are subsequently compelled to take a position with respect to these diverging points of view. Significantly, the boundaries argued for by ordinary speakers are usually disregarded by those in positions of power. The meanings those limits convey wane with the gradual passing of traditional speakers. The ideologies that led to the formation of those limits are also disappearing, and new ideologies, based on the mutually legitimising alliance of linguistics and institutions which represent the state or are underwritten by it, are gradually imposing a new type of discourse on the minority languages spoken in Rhône-Alpes.

Linguists, speakers and activists therefore perform various and conflicting aspects of identity-making and -marking through the semiotisation of linguistic features. In so doing, they carry out a type of struggle over classifications that index values and ideas which are far removed from linguistic concerns.

A first conclusion to this chapter would be that in Rhône-Alpes, linguistic boundaries are important to every type of social actor involved with regional languages, at whatever level. The edges of linguistic zones can subsequently be turned into boundaries for population-management purposes, and they can be used to generate, reinforce and legitimise difference and identity.

A second conclusion, one with more long-term implications, would be that much more research is needed in order to identify the type of social meaning that is invested by social actors in various interactional situations. This chapter only paints a very broad picture of a reality that is much more complex. The brand of language policy that the Rhône-Alpes regional government wishes to implement is of course (for now) fairly inconsequential for most of the population of the region, given the relatively small numbers of people involved. Yet it may trigger new social dynamics and generate new types of behaviour that link to the linguistic borders which have been created and naturalised by language policies.

Notes

1. In the administrative division of France, the *département* is one of the three levels of government below the national level. *Départements* were created during the French Revolution to break down former provinces, and now constitute an elected intermediate administrative level between the *communes* (towns) and the *régions*.
2. All the maps, except Figure 12.3, were produced for this chapter by Olivier Bodson, whom we wish to thank here.
3. On the process of *région* and *département* naming, see Boyer and Cardy (2011).
4. The number of speakers of either language is now very low, with less than 1 per cent of the regional population speaking either Occitan or Francoprovençal. Locally, however, for example in Ardèche, Ain or Savoy, percentages can be significantly higher, especially among the older population (Bert et al. 2009). The issues here are therefore mainly symbolic.
5. Mistral, who was the instigator of the Occitan language movement as we know it today and an inspiration for many revivalists, was awarded the Nobel Prize for his literary achievements in 1904.
6. See also Section 4.2.2.
7. For example, at the turn of the nineteenth and twentieth centuries, Paul Marietton in Lyon and the Abbé Cerlogne in the Val d'Aoste.
8. For a sketch map of the 'Medioromance' area, see http://www.creuse.fr/IMG/pdf/16-Creusois-23.pdf (accessed 5 November 2013).
9. There is a general consensus in Romance linguistics to consider the Occitan domain as one single entity. Some sociolinguists, however, support the view that Provençal is a distinct language (e.g. Blanchet 1992).
10. In particular, proponents of Provençal as a separate language tend to promote more keenly such cultural activities as the wearing of the Provençal costume, and to overemphasise their ties with rural, working-class Provence. On the other hand, they view the Occitan movement as middle-class-led and -oriented. No study has yet been conducted in terms of voting practices, however.
11. Rhône-Alpes Regional Council website, http://www.rhonealpes.fr/687-accueil-territoire.htm (accessed 5 November 2013).
12. Also, note that in French, the plural (*langues*) is not heard when the expression is spoken aloud.

13

Constructing National and International Deaf Identity: Perceived Use of American Sign Language

Elizabeth S. Parks

1. Introduction

Signing deaf people have been recognised within human society since the time of Socrates in the fifth century BC (Bauman 2008). Since Socrates' early mention, people have continued to sign with each other and to interact in unique communities, with references to signing appearing in biblical times (Luke 1: 62–72), among Benedictine monks in the fourth century, in the Ottoman Empire in the sixteenth century, during the seventeenth century with Spain's deaf education efforts through the publication of a handbook of a manual alphabet by Juan Pablo Bonet, and in France and other places in the eighteenth century as deaf educational initiatives increased internationally (Miles 2000; Deaf Jam 2012).

Distinct cultural values expressed through various forms of deafhood have been transmitted through generations of deaf people since the number of established deaf schools expanded in the late eighteenth century (Ladd 2005). Cross-national sporting events and other informal activities have brought deaf people together internationally for at least a century, and the World Federation of the Deaf (an international, non-governmental organisation uniting national deaf associations around the world) has encouraged and facilitated international interaction since it was founded in 1951 (Murray 2008; World Federation of the Deaf 2012a, b, c). In the twenty-first century, deaf people around the world are meeting and communicating with each other more than ever before. International conferences related to deaf linguistic, cultural, academic and community themes, recent growth in online video communication access and myriad other activities by and for deaf communities are dramatically increasing the frequency of international deaf interaction.

A large segment of the audiologically deaf population identify themselves as (capital-D) 'Deaf' in order to focus on their cultural identity and distinguish themselves as a unique community united by more than audiological status. This 'Deaf World' encompasses deaf people around the globe who embrace an agenda unique to their cultural and linguistic minority (Lane et al. 1996). While this convention is common in English-using parts of the world, there are places where deaf people identify themselves as a cultural community without adopting the Deaf label. Because of this diversity of perspectives and conventions for referring to deaf and hard-of-hearing people groups, I will use 'culturally deaf people' or 'the deaf community' rather than Deaf when referring to deaf people who embrace a unique deaf cultural identity. I will simply use 'deaf people' to refer to both audiological and cultural groups. I do this with the intention of being inclusive of the diverse deaf and hard-of-hearing people and communities included in my research, and their unique cultural and linguistic identities.

Although forming a distinct deaf cultural community on a global level, individual deaf communities are also impacted by their immediate social environments and exhibit unique characteristics that set them apart from each other, creating cultural borders between neighbouring deaf networks. In other words, culturally deaf people typically identify both with a global deaf entity and with their geographical location, often as a distinct national entity. The perceived and real use of sign language during negotiation of this cultural positioning is integral to deaf identity formation. As Burch states, 'The real and symbolic value of sign language remains at the crux of Deaf people's identity . . . In many ways sign language frames the perceived and real differences between this group and mainstream society' (2004: 293). Sign language not only frames differences between deaf and hearing society, but is used to delineate distinct deaf communities as well.

Ethnologue (2009) reports that there are 130 distinct sign languages in the world, but language identification research consistently adds to that number each year (Lewis 2009). One database that keeps track of human languages is the ISO (International Standards Organisation) 639-3. According to its homepage, ISO 639-3 'is a code that aims to define three-letter identifiers for all known human languages' (SIL International 2012). During the 2008–11 period, ten sign languages that were not included in the 2009 edition of the Ethnologue, which bases its set of included languages on ISO 639-3, were submitted for adoption into ISO 639-3. After review by committee, these ten languages were accepted the year following their submission. These sign languages included one in Central America, two in the Caribbean, one in South America, one in the Middle East, two in eastern Europe, one in east Africa, one in south Asia and International Sign used cross-nationally (SIL International 2012; see further below). As the expansion of research on sign language and a deepened understanding of the validity of sign language as legitimate human language continue to grow, the number of known and identified sign languages will undoubtedly continue to increase in coming years.

One of the oldest and most researched sign languages in the world is American Sign Language (ASL). Emerging in the early 1800s after the founding of the American School for the Deaf by Thomas Hopkins Gallaudet and Laurent Clerc, ASL is now used throughout the United States and most of Canada, as well as in many other countries. ASL currently has a potent influence on language use in the international deaf community, particularly in the western hemisphere. However, it is also reported to be a primary sign language in at least seventeen African and Asian countries, such as Benin, Ghana and Singapore, and is acquired bilingually in many others (Lewis 2009; Hiddinga and Crasborn 2011).

In many places around the world, ASL is intentionally taught in deaf schools which are primary sites for the emergence of deaf communities, their cultural construction and sign language development. Many international deaf leaders attend Gallaudet University (in Washington DC) or other American educational institutions where they learn ASL and then, at least potentially, transmit it to their home countries. In addition, ASL often serves as a *lingua franca* in cross-national deaf interaction, and can have significant influence on the widely accepted and ever-adapting pidgin called 'International Sign' which is used at many global deaf meetings. Despite this spread, attitudes towards ASL vary widely based on the contexts in which it is used. While some embrace it as a tool to facilitate upward international social mobility, others, perceiving ASL to be a 'killer language' (Skutnabb-Kangas 2008), believe that it is threatening their indigenous sign languages and leading to language loss and endangerment.

To date, very little investigation has been made into 'the exact nature of the influence of ASL on other signed languages or the use of ASL in other countries' (Hiddinga and Crasborn 2011). My goal in this chapter is to offer an initial building block for continued discussion about how perceived and actual use of ASL are used to create symbolic borders between and within deaf communities globally. I base my initial characterisation of these borders on research conducted in eight countries in Latin America and the Caribbean between 2008 and 2011. Listed alphabetically, these are the Dominican Republic, Ecuador, Grenada, Guatemala, Jamaica, Peru, St Vincent and the Grenadines, and Trinidad and Tobago. Each of these countries has experienced significant amounts of contact with ASL and is currently negotiating the presence of ASL in constructing its national deaf community's borders.

Attitudes towards the use of ASL and towards ASL users were investigated through extensive participant observation in deaf club and association meetings, religious services, sporting events and casual scheduled and impromptu meetings. One hundred and forty face-to-face questionnaires were administered by deaf and hearing researchers in forty different cities during the three-year research span, although each country's questionnaire participants were not necessarily asked the same set of questions. Participants were selected by focusing within each deaf social network on key stakeholders and deaf community leaders who have a high probability of reflecting and influencing broader community attitudes.

2. International acquisition of American Sign Language

Many deaf people involved in this study believe that ASL competence allows a person to participate more fully in the international deaf conversation. At the same time, they may think that ASL is also a danger to the vitality of their native sign language. For example, the deaf community of Trinidad and Tobago in the southern Caribbean has an indigenous sign language of its own, known as Trinidad and Tobago Sign Language (TTSL). ASL was introduced into Trinidadian deaf schools after an educational administrator visited Gallaudet University in the 1970s and established its use in his deaf school upon returning to Trinidad (Parks and Parks 2012). One deaf female student who experienced this language shift in the classroom stated:

> After the principal went to Gallaudet, he came back and said we couldn't use TTSL any more. I was confused by all the new signs that were so different . . . Now I understand that ASL is important for travelling because so many people

use it. But TTSL is still important and I want it to grow here in Trinidad and for ASL to be used less. TTSL is our language and our culture. It belongs to us and we can communicate with each other through it completely.

Although ASL should not be considered the sole language of the international deaf community, this perception of the importance of ASL for international deaf connection appears to be justified, at least on the academic level, as ASL does 'seem to be slowly acquiring a dominant position in international academic gatherings' (Hiddinga and Crasborn 2011: 497). With respect to language choice, the academic setting plays a more important role for most deaf people than it would for their hearing counterparts, because many deaf people acquire their first language at school instead of at home from hearing parents.

It is quite common for hearing parents of deaf children not to learn how to sign and so not to provide early language acquisition opportunities for their deaf children. Of eighty-five questionnaire responses from deaf participants in the eight countries investigated for this research, less than 5 per cent indicated that hearing parents learned to sign with their deaf children, less than 25 per cent indicated that it depended on the parents, and over 70 per cent responded that hearing parents did not learn to sign with their deaf children. If most parents do not learn to communicate with their children through sign language, how are local sign languages being transmitted between deaf generations?

The results of this study point to schools being a site of sign language acquisition for deaf people more than twice as often as any other location. Of ninety-nine questionnaire participants in the Dominican Republic, Ecuador, Guatemala, Jamaica, Peru, and Trinidad and Tobago, more than half indicated that they had first learned to sign at school. In the questionnaire, participants could select multiple acquisition sites if they felt they had learned sign language from various places simultaneously, so some indicated that they learned both at school and at a deaf association, or at school and from friends. Considered as a whole, 58 per cent of participants indicated that schools were of primary importance in their acquisition of sign language, while 28 per cent learned from friends, 13 per cent through a family member, 12 per cent through a deaf association and 4 per cent through a religious organisation. Because so many deaf people learn to sign in academic environments, then, international academic gatherings may have more significance for the Deaf World as a whole than more casual international interactions.

Deaf participants indicated that their desire to learn ASL was largely motivated by the desire to access resources available in the international deaf community that were not available locally. Countries where deaf people struggled to find employment or where social prejudice and discrimination were perceived to be especially widespread were those where deaf people most reported wanting to learn ASL. As deaf people see the acquisition of ASL as a tool towards upward mobility and opportunity, a desire among these individuals to leave the local community so as to access available resources for themselves, and to use them in the improvement of their community upon their return, appears to be increasing.

Simultaneously, however, this desire to engage in the international conversation and to access international resources is measured against the desire to fully express the indigenous deaf community's cultural identity. As deaf people engage more with the international deaf community, they also learn more about the value that the Deaf World places on the retention of unique cultural traits by individual deaf communities. For example, as national deaf associations connect with the World Federation of the Deaf, they will hear a strong message about their deaf human rights and local deaf heritage:

> Sign languages in each country are natural languages of Deaf people . . . Each natural sign language that is being used by Deaf community [*sic*] is part of the country's cultural, social, historical and religious heritage. In order to preserve the full heritage of each country, it is necessary to respect sign languages. Recognition of sign language(s) is also a way to enhance and give respect to the overall linguistic and cultural heritage of each country and of humankind. (World Federation of the Deaf 2012c, http://wfdeaf.org/human-rights)

International deaf meetings – other than academic ones – are frequently organised by the World Federation of the Deaf and its affiliates. Through the use of rhetoric like that seen in the above quote, the World Federation of the Deaf can have a compelling influence on its international network of deaf association members which, at the time of writing, included 155 member organisations located on five continents. In order to actively engage with this diverse group, deaf people must grow in flexibility so that they may communicate with deaf people who use diverse sign languages, as well as widely used second languages such as ASL and British Sign Language (BSL), and the pidgin International Sign. Because the World Federation of the Deaf uses International Sign in its meetings and online communication, and International Sign usually shares at least some aspects of its structure with ASL, ASL acquisition still aids in international engagement, especially for deaf people in countries whose sign language(s) share few similarities with ASL or whose sign vocabulary is not yet as developed as that of older sign languages such as ASL and BSL.

Thus, many deaf people find themselves negotiating the desire to engage with the Deaf World internationally through the use of ASL in academic settings, as well as with the dozens of countries that use ASL as a primary or secondary language, while simultaneously maximising the international deaf community's respect for local deaf diversity and their own desire to retain their national deaf heritage. Because national deaf leaders who access the international deaf community often increase their ASL proficiency during that engagement, they also have the potential to play a major part in determining how ASL impacts on their local community and how this ASL-use commodity is made available to others. It is important to note here that less formal international interactions between deaf people through online videoconferencing technology such as ooVoo and Skype may show few signs of ASL use if the people involved use sign language(s) that are unrelated to ASL. In addition, YouTube, the internet video file-sharing site, has provided a place where deaf people with technological access can post videos of their indigenous sign language, and is supporting the creation of a global deaf environment where diverse sign languages can be learned and celebrated.

As agency among deaf people has increased and they realise their right to determine their community's future, they are more frequently making decisions about how sign language should be used to define their own deafhood. Historically, however, deaf people have not always had the freedom or access to information that would permit them to make these choices for themselves. Deaf people in many parts of the world still find themselves in oppressive environments where correct cultural expression is defined for them, instead of by them. As shown in the aforementioned Trinidadian response, the interviewee's adoption of ASL was enforced by her educational environment. It was brought to her classroom, she was told to use it and she did use it. The introduction of ASL by educational centres, religious groups, international aid organisations, and via developing international relationships, has happened over the last century on almost every continent, and has led to a variety of responses when national deaf communities move to define themselves and subsequently draw boundaries and symbolic borders within and between themselves and others.

3. Clarifying borders between and within deaf nations

Initial research points to perceived use of ASL as being crucial in creating two types of symbolic borders. The first is a border created between a global deaf community and distinct deaf national identities. The second symbolic border is created within a national deaf community as community members clarify their identities and compete for maximum influence on its defining characteristics, while negotiating social status.

3.1 Between deaf nations

There are three primary responses to the presence of ASL in a country when the task of self-defining the symbolic border between one national deaf community and another is undertaken:

1. adoption and acceptance
2. adoption and distinction
3. mixing and rejection

I deal with each of these responses in turn below.

3.1.1 Adoption and acceptance

The first response is the adoption and acceptance of ASL within a deaf community. This is typically seen in countries where no established deaf community or deaf culture was prevalent before the arrival of ASL, which usually occurred through the founding of a deaf school or missionary endeavour in which ASL was used. Within this study sample, the southern Caribbean countries of Grenada and St Vincent and the Grenadines reflect this first type of response. Both countries have relatively small deaf communities, with an estimated population of roughly 200 deaf people each, and neither had an established sign language in use before the arrival of ASL (Parks and Parks 2012). According to deaf leaders in Grenada and St Vincent:

> There is really no Grenadian Sign Language because ASL was brought before there was ever any sign language used on the island. [deaf female, Grenada]

> Although there are some local differences in signs and facial expressions, we use ASL and St Vincent does not have its own sign language. [deaf male, St Vincent]

Although these quotes reflect recognition of the use of ASL in both countries, it should not be inferred from them that all deaf people in both communities are content with the situation of ASL having been adopted and accepted as the national deaf community's language. Grenada and St Vincent are both in the initial stages of uniting as separate national deaf communities, and it appears that the leaders of these movements are the most outspoken in their support for the development of a unique national sign language to replace ASL, even as other members of the community appear to be satisfied with continuing to use ASL and to access all the resources available through it.

At the time of the research, the St Vincent community seemed quite willing to indicate that they used a sign variety called 'ASL', but they rejected the notion that they used a sign variety called 'American Sign Language', a language that they associated with the United States. In addition, the Grenadian deaf community hoped to create a sign language dictionary that included signs unique to the Grenadian ASL variety – one that included local signs for unique food, plants and locations on the island – and that demonstrated their uniqueness as a national deaf community as compared to other ASL-using deaf communities in other countries.

It seems, then, that deaf communities that have a national identity that has adopted and accepted the use of ASL still move towards forming a symbolic border between other countries that use ASL and their own national deaf communities. This may be accomplished through distinguishing what the name 'ASL' means, by adding sign language dictionaries with local lexicons to established ASL dictionaries from other countries, or even by lobbying for the development of a completely different sign language.

3.1.2 Adoption and distinction

In contrast to countries that adopt and accept ASL as their national language, some deaf communities adopt ASL in certain domains but make efforts to distinguish it from the local sign language used in other domains. In Trinidad, deaf Trinidadians generally accept the current situation of deaf schools using ASL, although many hope for the increased use of TTSL (Trinidad and Tobago Sign Language) in the classroom. While they want to retain fluency in ASL for international travel and communication, many want to see deaf Trinidadians become fluent in the use of TTSL at home. Some deaf leaders express concern that the younger generation may lose touch with their unique deaf history by not being able to communicate with the older generation in TTSL. This concern is driven by many younger deaf people only learning and using ASL in school without significant exposure to the TTSL-using adult community that is more active in some deaf associations, deaf clubs or other organisations. Unless deaf youth become involved with these TTSL-using adults, the sign language use of the former group will be limited by their exposure to ASL alone.

Jamaican Sign Language (JSL) and ASL are used throughout Jamaica by an estimated 7,500 deaf community members, although some estimates of the deaf population are substantially higher than this (Epley et al. 2011). The Jamaican deaf community seems predominantly to identify JSL as their language, with a rapidly dwindling population using a local sign variety called Country Sign, which originated in the St Elizabeth parish. On the other hand, ASL appears to be the *lingua franca* used by deaf Jamaicans when interacting with hearing Jamaicans, with the large influx of ASL users from the United States and in many of the educational centres. Despite culturally aligning with JSL, Jamaican deaf people do not appear to have strong attitudes against the use of ASL, which may partly be a consequence of many of them having acquired ASL as their first language.

Countries such as Trinidad and Jamaica, which have adopted ASL use but kept it distinct from their indigenous language, appear to be willing to continue in a bilingual state, capitalising on the use of ASL for international and other engagements while retaining the local sign language as a unique representation of their local cultural community and values. In both of these countries, current development initiatives are working towards creating resources to ensure that the local sign language is preserved and used by future deaf generations while having generally friendly feelings towards the presence of ASL, as long as it does not hinder their local language's continued use.

3.1.3 Mixing and rejection

A third response to ASL's presence in a country other than the United States is a general rejection of its importance in current deaf identity construction, even though ASL was formerly integrated into the pre-existing local sign language. This seems to happen most often when clear domains within a community were not distinguished with respect to the use of the local sign variety and ASL. Usually, the two (or more) sign languages have been mixed to such a point that there are references to 'old signs' and 'new signs' – the old signs being used by a generation that was not exposed to ASL at a young age, and the new signs being a mixture of ASL with local sign varieties.

This mixing and rejection appears to be clearly exemplified in Ecuador. The Ecuadorian deaf community is currently involved in a language purification effort, evidenced by the creation of an Ecuadorian Sign Language (LSEC) dictionary. Part of this dictionary project's goal is to remove as much ASL influence from LSEC as possible. ASL had a significant impact on LSEC when the latter was in its formative stages in the early 1990s, and current national deaf leaders are taking steps to remove ASL influence by reclaiming old Ecuadorian signs or developing new signs that are more representative of Ecuadorian culture. In early 2011, weekly dictionary meetings were being organised in nine Ecuadorian cities to bring deaf people together with a view to identifying preferred signs and removing unwanted ASL signs from their language use. National deaf community leaders hope that the completion of the LSEC dictionary materials and the dictionary's distribution will provide resources for deaf schools and interpreters so as to enable them to work towards a standardised national sign language within the country (Eberle et al. 2012).

Deaf Dominicans in the Dominican Republic recognise that their sign language shares similarities with ASL, but many want to find a way to remove ASL influence so that there is a national sign language that uniquely represents their cultural identity. As one deaf male from Santo Domingo stated, 'We really want a Dominican Republic sign language that is separate from ASL. We don't like that the Dominican Republic community has copied other countries.' Many deaf Dominicans state that the name of their sign language is ASL, but some hasten to add that it is not the same language as used in the United States, which is American Sign Language. They indicate that local people call it ASL, but that if they meet deaf people from the United States they often have a hard time understanding them at first. Other deaf people assert that the language of the Dominican deaf community is LSD (Dominican Sign Language), a sign language distinct from ASL.

While all agree that the sign variety in the Dominican Republic is different from what is used in the United States – the two perhaps only share 70 per cent perceived similarity – they disagree about how it should be labelled (Williams and Parks 2010).

3.1.4 Summary

All three of these responses to the presence of ASL in a country's sign language use show a desire to clarify the boundaries of a national deaf community through the negotiation of the use and perceived use of ASL. While some countries willingly adopted ASL but still talk about themselves as unique deaf communities, others appear to embrace an ideology that dictates that they must first eradicate ASL's impact, or at least clearly define in which domains it is acceptable to use ASL, in order to clarify their cultural borders and exhibit a 'purified' identity. For this latter group, national deaf identity construction depends on the perception of how ASL is used (or is not used) within their community, and ASL becomes a point of constant negotiation and discussion in self-determining the group's deafhood. This leads to the discussion of the second symbolic border created by the perceived use of ASL: borders created within a deaf national community, rather than between deaf nations.

3.2 Within deaf nations

Deaf communities are often discussed as if they offer a single unified front and explanation of who they are as a deaf people group. This, however, may not accurately reflect the diversity of perspectives represented by the hundreds or thousands of individuals that make up a deaf community. As the number of people within a community grows, so too does the number of perspectives on what it means to be deaf, both as an individual and as a community. ASL often serves as a 'negotiation piece' for individuals defining deaf nations from within, just as it does in the construction of symbolic borders between deaf nations.

Based on the eight countries included in this study, it appears that deaf people often use the discussion of perceived and actual ASL use by individuals or regional communities to clarify core national deaf community membership. Boundaries were drawn between in-group and out-group members as people negotiated group and individual identity formation in the following areas:

1. regional claim to national status
2. deaf and hearing sign varieties
3. deaf social standing

3.2.1 Regional claim to national status

Unique deaf communities within a single country can form almost independently from each other, in part because deaf schools are often sites where new sign varieties emerge, and also because they may be established in locations that are geographically distant from one another. Deaf students who attend these schools are typically from the surrounding region, so as the deaf nation develops and relationships form between these deaf schools, regional deaf identities may come to exhibit unique characteristics. As a national deafhood develops, each of these regions may vie for a prominent, if not the central, role in forming and representing their nation's image. Because sign language is so crucial to a deaf community's cultural identity, aligning with or diverging from perceived and actual ASL use can critically affect a region's claim to uniqueness. As deaf regions self-identify and demarcate themselves from 'the other', ASL becomes a tool for building symbolic borders between deaf regions and staking a claim to the national deaf voice.

Some regional deaf communities are, within their country's borders, negotiating the right to act as the centre or core of the national deaf community. One example of this can clearly be seen in the Guatemalan deaf community, a locus of significant contact with ASL. Guatemalan deaf people have travelled to the United States, hearing educators and missionaries from the United States have visited many Guatemalan cities, and ASL dictionaries have made their way into Guatemala. Some deaf people are learning and using ASL as a second language, but few, if any, have learned it as their first. Deaf people in Guatemala see ASL as a language very different from their own, and in no way identify themselves culturally or linguistically with it (Parks and Parks 2008).

Deaf people indicate that there are two Guatemalan sign varieties. One of these is located in the region near the city of Quetzaltenango (often referred to locally as 'Xela') and the other is based in the capital, Guatemala City. People in these two major cities assert the distinctiveness of their local sign variety relative to that of the other city, and each makes a claim for it to be a more authentic sign variety of the indigenous Guatemalan deaf community. One of the main ways of communicating this stance is to label the other sign language variety as having been subject to more ASL influence, and thereby being less representative and respectful of local Guatemalan signs. As one deaf female from Guatemala City stated, 'Xela signs differently from Guatemala City because they have a mix of ASL, Mexican, and Guatemalan signs. They don't want to respect the Guatemala sign.'

Deaf Guatemalans associate strongly with their national community and, because ASL is seen as distinct linguistically and culturally from the sign varieties used in both Guatemala City and Quetzaltenango, they can use divergence from ASL as a claim to their own amplified national deaf identity. Both assert that the other has incorporated greater amounts of ASL into its sign variety, while their own variety is more truly respectful of deaf Guatemalan culture.

3.2.2 Deaf and hearing sign varieties

Another use of ASL in negotiating borders within a deaf nation is for distinguishing signing that is uniquely 'deaf' from the signing used by hearing people. In Jamaica, for example, although both Jamaican Sign Language (JSL) and ASL are used throughout the country, the Jamaican deaf community seems predominantly to identify JSL as their community's language. On the other hand, ASL appears to be the *lingua franca* used by deaf Jamaicans with hearing Jamaicans, with the large influx of ASL users from the United States, and in many of the educational centres. Some deaf Jamaicans did not seem to want or need hearing people to learn JSL, and indicated that it could be to their benefit simply to use ASL with the hearing community while retaining JSL as the language of the deaf community. In this framework, a person's signing and ability to code-switch could be used as a relatively easy way to distinguish between hearing and deaf members of the Jamaican deaf community. One deaf female from Montego Bay stated that, 'Deaf people use JSL, and with hearing people we use ASL because they do not understand JSL . . .

but deaf people can improve by learning ASL and teaching it to the hearing so they can support deaf people.'

Not all deaf Jamaicans indicated a desire to distinguish deaf from hearing signing via the use of JSL and ASL. The Jamaican Association of the Deaf and other sources are currently working towards the development of JSL materials to be used in deaf schools, in sign language classes for both deaf and hearing people and in various domains within the deaf community. As the use of these materials increases in schools – the primary site for deaf Jamaicans to acquire their first sign language – it is likely that the use of ASL as a *lingua franca* may decrease. Still, Jamaican deaf people do not appear to have strong negative attitudes towards the use of ASL, and may continue to use it bilingually within their community, perhaps partly due to many having acquired ASL as their first language (Epley et al. 2011).

In situations such as these, deaf people may decide that the use of ASL can serve a purpose in drawing boundaries between core deaf members of a community and peripheral hearing ones. Like many borders, the identification of in-group and out-group membership is not guaranteed purely on the basis of ASL competence, but in combination with a number of other factors, as determined by the community.

3.2.3 Deaf social standing

Social status and community membership marked by ASL use is not limited to that of hearing or deaf status. In Peru, for example, attitudes towards ASL often correspond with perspectives towards particular deaf Peruvians. Some deaf people choose to avoid using ASL (whether real or perceived) because they dislike the groups of people who willingly use it, while others shun particular individuals because of their more ASL-influenced sign variety. Of the thirty-two questionnaire participants from Peru included in this study, over half indicated that Peruvian Sign Language (LSP) was very similar to ASL, while 30 per cent indicated that LSP is unlike any other sign language used by deaf people in other parts of the world. Thus, the Peruvian community is not unified in terms of its perception of the amount of ASL influence on LSP, and, in fact, because of the great diversity present in Peruvian sign varieties at the levels of the region and other social networks, some LSP varieties may indeed be more like ASL, while others are more distinct. However, in Peru, the perceived use of ASL is just as important as its real use in terms of how borders are drawn between accepted members of the community and those who are considered outsiders. Some lexical items may be inaccurately labelled as ASL, especially when they are used by a marginalised social group, even when the forms in question are regional variations of LSP.

Some deaf Peruvians indicated that they were glad to have learned ASL because it served as the gateway to learn their own Peruvian signs later in life. Others said that it is not important what sign language is used, as long as people sign. For example, one deaf female from Arequipa, Peru, stated:

> [They] brought ASL and I did not like it. But when I went back to Chiclayo I changed my signs to match them because I respected their ability to sign. Different signs are fine, some people want to change and others do not . . . In Lima, they definitely hate ASL, but here we just want to sign.

Since deaf people in so many countries around the world have had ASL introduced into their schools and environments, the responses to its presence can vary greatly. Within a single country, such as Peru, it is not surprising that these responses can be just as diverse. As deaf people within each country negotiate what it means to be deaf within their own local, regional, national and international contexts, it is not surprising that attitudes associated with a particular language correlate with the individuals who choose to use it. Nor should we be surprised that those attitudes may be projected on to individuals when social status and related influence within each community is being negotiated.

4. Conclusion

Although all our study participants identified with a global deaf cultural world that embraces sign language and is separate from the hearing community, they also indicated that they specifically identify with deaf members of their own country as distinct from other countries. As deaf people increasingly unite and pursue national deaf identities, their motivation to embrace a deaf culture and sign language that they believe distinctively expresses who they are also increases. Concurrently, as globalisation increases among deaf nations, deaf identity on an international level is being constructed and consolidated more than ever before.

Contrary to what many researchers focus on while investigating the uniqueness of deaf cultures, deaf identity is not solely built on differences between deaf and hearing worlds. Unique deaf micro-cultures within the deaf world are also constructed in contrast with each other, and ASL is an important sociolinguistic factor that is used to establish and negotiate real and symbolic borders between international and national deaf communities. Future research investigating the formation and negotiation of deaf identities should take ASL's influence into account.

Pursuit of national deaf identity must often directly address the presence and use of ASL, a 'foreign language', in deaf social environments. Even if ASL is acquired as a first sign language, deaf nationalism appears to encourage deaf people to pursue the development of a unique sign language distinct from ASL for their country, as demonstrated in Grenada and St Vincent at the time of our research. Future study correlating the emergence of a distinct national deaf identity and the growth of a community's shared value of distancing itself from an imported language will be an important element in understanding deaf cultural development on a national level. In addition, as deaf leaders within a country pursue a united deaf nationalism, certain regional communities or specific deaf social networks may allege that another group or individual is using ASL to stake a claim as the more legitimate centre of the community. The various ways that deaf communities define membership in the core of a country's deaf social network have received very little investigation to date, although they have important implications for the negotiation of deaf regional centres as representatives of the deaf national voice. Finally, because of ASL's spread and impact on every continent in the world, it is important to continue investigation into just how widespread ASL use is on a global level, and to apply this knowledge to our understanding of the many ways that deaf people are defining their deafhood and establishing symbolic borders between self and other on every level, from individual expression to global systems.

14

Borders, Variation and Identity: Language Analysis for the Determination of Origin (LADO)[1]

Kim Wilson and Paul Foulkes

1. Introduction

In addition to conveying propositional information, spoken language conveys a complex array of indexical information. This includes short-term information relating to, for example, the speaker's health and emotional state, and their stance *vis-à-vis* the topic and interlocutor. It also includes information about longer-term properties of the speaker's regional and social background: his or her ethnicity, affiliation to a particular social class, community or group and whether or not the speaker's knowledge of a language is native(-like). The range of indexical information conveyed by speech is the preoccupying subject matter of sociolinguistics and sociophonetics (see e.g. Foulkes et al. 2010). The application of techniques and insights from these fields to forensic settings is becoming routine, most notably in speaker comparison (Foulkes and French 2012) and, to a lesser extent, speaker profiling (French and Harrison 2006). Speaker profiling is undertaken where an evidentially valuable recording (e.g. a masked robbery captured on closed-circuit television) is available, but where no suspect has as yet been apprehended. Analysis of speech may yield information about the speaker's social background or regional accent, thus reducing the potential field of suspects. A compelling example is provided by Ellis (1994), who analysed a hoax tape received by the police during the 'Yorkshire Ripper' murders in northern England in the 1970s. Ellis was able to pinpoint the speaker's origin to a narrow area of the north-eastern English city of Sunderland, and was later proved correct to within two miles. In recent years, a specialised form of speaker profiling has become established in the context of claims for asylum, whereby an individual arriving at a port of entry from another state seeks leave to remain on the grounds that to return to his or her place of origin might result in persecution. Analysis of the claimant's recorded speech may be undertaken to assess whether he or she is a genuine speaker of the language or variety. In the absence of any such claim to be an authentic speaker, the analysis may assist in identifying the asylum seeker's probable linguistic background. This application of linguistic analysis has become known as LADO – Language Analysis for the Determination of Origin. In this chapter we outline the short history of LADO, the methodologies used, key debates in the field and developments in empirical research. We conclude with a brief discussion of ongoing developments in the field.

2. Why LADO?

In the early 1990s applications for asylum rose steeply in many countries. In the UK alone, applications (excluding those for claimants' dependents) jumped from just over 4,000 in 1988 to over 44,000 in 1991 (HOSB 1992: 1). This rise had much to do with political events at the time. The collapse of the Soviet Union in 1991 prompted an increase in migration to western Europe (Kopnina 2005) and the United States (Liebert 2010). Civil wars in Somalia, the former Yugoslavia and Sri Lanka also led to an increase in asylum applications, especially to the UK (HOSB 1992: 1; 1994: 1). Applicants do not always possess the documentation that is required for asylum to be granted, and thus their true nationalities (or ethnicities or tribal membership) can be called into question. As the number of asylum applicants rose, so did the assumption that applying for political asylum was being used as a strategy by individuals who did not in fact meet the criteria for asylum as outlined in the 1951 Geneva Convention. Politicians, journalists and academics readily seized on the perceived weakness of the asylum procedure (see e.g. Daley 2002; Travis 2003; and comments in Singler 2004: 223). It was on the back of this assumption that LADO was developed as a way of offering evidence in cases where claimants cannot provide sufficient proof of their origins.

3. What exactly is LADO?

LADO is grounded on the principle, taken as axiomatic in sociolinguistics, that a person's speech conveys indexical information. Thus, in principle, aspects of an individual's background can be identified through linguistic analysis, albeit with varying levels of confidence. A crucial distinction must be drawn, however, between background – which we define as place(s) of socialisation – and nationality or citizenship. Linguistic analysis can pinpoint information pertaining to the former but not the latter (Patrick 2012). This is because, contrary to popular belief, linguistic and political borders do not always coincide, and because asylum claimants may well have complex life histories involving movement across political borders (Fraser 2012). In fact, LADO is most frequently invoked 'to distinguish between related varieties within cross border languages' (Cambier-Langeveld 2010a: 23). For this reason, some commentators have rejected outright the possibility of determining a person's nationality from his or her speech (Eades et al. 2003; Corcoran 2004), and others have questioned whether the acronym LADO is itself misleading. Reath (2004), for instance, prefers the more neutral LAAP (language analysis in the asylum procedure). Some linguists consider LADO to be feasible only in certain contexts, for example in cases relating to specific language varieties where linguistic borders are clearly defined (Maryns 2004; Singler 2004). Whether such contexts exist, however, remains unclear. Muysken (2010), for example, notes that only five countries/territories are reported to have nationals who speak only one language: North Korea, St Helena, the Falkland Islands, plus the unusual cases of the British Indian Ocean Territory (a British/American military base) and the Vatican City (Latin).

For LADO to be conducted, a recording of the claimant's speech is obtained. The analysis that is then carried out on the recording is an amalgam of techniques developed in other subdisciplines of linguistics and phonetics, especially sociolinguistics. LADO has been used in the asylum process since 1993 (FECL 1998), and is now recognised as a subfield of forensic linguistics and forensic phonetics, with a regular presence at academic conferences held by the IAFL and IAFPA.[2] It is also addressed at more general conferences such as the Sociolinguistics Symposium, and specialised workshops including those held at Wassenaar, the Netherlands (2010 – see Zwaan et al. 2010), Gothenburg, Sweden (2010)[3] and Essex, UK (2011–12).[4]

Governments in Europe, Australia, New Zealand, the USA and Canada have piloted, used or currently use LADO as a part of their asylum process (Eades and Arends 2004: 180). At present, there are five established agencies that offer LADO services, either privately or as departments of national governments. These are based in Sweden (*Verified* and *Sprakab*), the Netherlands (*De Taalstudio* and *Language Analysis Bureau of the Department of Immigration and Naturalization* (IND)) and Switzerland (*LINGUA*).

Language reports are typically requested when there is uncertainty regarding the claimed place of origin of the applicant. For example, the UK Border Agency (UKBA) (2011: 5) states that LADO is used 'to assist in establishing whether an asylum applicant is from their claimed country of nationality in cases of doubt; and to deter individuals from making fraudulent claims purely because particular countries have a perceived advantage'. This therefore means that LADO is only called for in a minority of cases. In 2008/2009 UKBA used language analysis in only 4–5 per cent of cases (but note this still accounts for as many as 487 cases in 2008 and 555 cases in 2009) (UKBA 2011: 10).

Needless to say, objectivity and accuracy in analysing an individual's linguistic attributes are imperative for the LADO analyst. An erroneous report could assist in the claimant's repatriation (potentially to an inappropriate country) which might lead to persecution, denial of basic human rights, incarceration, torture or, in extreme circumstances, even death. The costs of granting asylum to a false claimant can also be substantial, especially in countries with elaborate social services. Practitioners must therefore have an up-to-date and detailed knowledge of the relevant languages (including the local subvarieties) as well as a firm understanding of the forensic context in which they are working (Cambier-Langeveld 2010b: 89).

As yet no standard or universally agreed methods for the practice of LADO have been established. For several reasons, the field lacks transparency, as we shall see below. Moreover, there is a glaring lack of directed research to support its establishment in the asylum process or the validity of the specific methods employed. Debates have arisen among practitioners and academics regarding the qualifications of LADO experts, training and quality control procedures, as well as the set of methods adopted by each agency.

4. LADO methods and practices

When LADO was first established, agencies tended to be rather secretive about the details of their methods and employees. Needless to say, this helped to foment doubts regarding the reliability of LADO in general (FECL 1998). It is only recently that this situation has begun to change. Representatives from government and private agencies have become increasingly active in academic circles, and have started to provide insights into the workings of their agencies. The principal question that is asked of the LADO analyst is largely the same, though the exact wording may differ across agencies, jurisdictions and specific cases: in its simplest terms, is applicant X genuinely from location Y, as he or she is claiming? This can be considered a verification task. Less frequently, an analyst may instead be asked to specify a place of origin based on a speech sample (i.e. a classification task, more closely parallel to the forensic speaker profiling task outlined in the introduction to this chapter). The latter can occur when a claimant has been denied asylum and officials need evidence pointing to a destination to which the applicant should be deported. Some analysts also specialise in 'contra-expertise' and will be hired to provide a secondary language report in situations in which the first is opposed.

The agencies operating today have each developed their own working methods. These fall into two main categories – the 'native speaker/linguist method' (known to be used by the IND, Verified and Sprakab) and the 'specialised linguist method' (used by De Taalstudio and LINGUA) (Cambier-Langeveld 2010a; Baltisberger and Hubbuch 2010; Verrips 2010; Patrick 2012). The former involves a professional linguist working alongside a native-speaker consultant. The latter involves a linguist (not necessarily a native speaker) working independently.

Although the various agencies' methods conform to one or other of these types, specific procedures vary from agency to agency. For example, recorded speech for analysis might come from an interview submitted by the government requesting the analysis (FECL 1998), or from an interview conducted by the analyst in person or over the telephone (Singler 2004: 225). Alternatively, it might be conducted by a non-analyst using a set of discussion prompts provided by the agency or analyst (Baltisberger and Hubbuch 2010). There may thus be considerable differences in the quantity and quality of material available for analysis of the key indexical properties necessary for robust conclusions to be drawn. Similarly, there is no requirement for LADO reports to adhere to a particular format. There are no widespread specifications concerning the set of language features that must be analysed or the number of features that must be included as evidence of the analysts' findings. Neither are there enforced or standardised conclusion scales across practices or jurisdictions, unlike in other forensic domains such as speaker comparison in the UK (Gold and French 2011). Some conclusion scales, however, are imposed by clients (see e.g. Campbell 2013: 675). Each practice therefore has some freedom to control the methodology, format and content of its language analyses. While this flexibility can be advantageous, as the differences across languages make it near-impossible to draw up a rigid protocol for analysis, the lack of uniformity across agencies has sparked debate regarding best practice. We now turn to explore these issues in more depth.

5. Issues in linguistic analysis of asylum interviews

In order to assess the contribution that LADO can make, we must first understand what this type of analysis encompasses and the barriers it can face. A LADO report contains information about the linguistic repertoire of the claimant, based on a recording of his or her speech. This information should include reference to linguistic features at all levels which are known to correlate with social or demographic factors: segmental pronunciation, points of grammar, syntax, lexis and possibly observations about discourse strategies or pragmatics. The weight that is placed on each of these features depends in part on the language(s) in question, and in part on the preferences and experience of the analyst. For example, pronunciation of specific consonants or vowels may be vital in distinguishing between two local varieties of one language, whereas differences in vocabulary and lexis may be much more telling in another. The language report may also take into account languages that the claimant can speak other than the claimed native language, along with the claimant's proficiency in these other languages. This will be particularly applicable to parts of the world in which people are known to code-switch or to live in diglossic/ multilingual communities, both of which are common in countries that have come to be a regular point of origin of asylum seekers (see Lewis 2009; Muysken 2010). As well as discussing language features, LADO reports may also assess a claimant's cultural knowledge (Verrips 2010).

Of course, there are many general issues with language that can make LADO a very demanding task, as well as aspects of the LADO context itself that further add to its complexity. These include multilingualism, creolisation, ongoing language change, accommodation to the interlocutor, the difference between linguistic and national borders, the movement of refugees and the influences of conflict or oppression on language use. For example, multilingualism presents many barriers for language analysts, especially when the asylum seeker is in the sensitive, unique and probably stressful environment of an asylum interview. In multilingual societies, languages can have their own roles. They may be divided by formality/prestige or function: one might be used in education, while another is the language of religion and still another the language for use at home (see Muysken 2010). In an asylum interview, a claimant may feel that a specific language or variety should be used in that type of setting. It may be a formal variety, or a variety that the claimant believes the interviewer will wish to hear, regardless of whether this is actually the case. Even if using a single language, the applicant may accommodate to the perceived linguistic patterns of the interviewer (Eades and Arends 2004). Applicants may also feel inclined to exaggerate or undermine their knowledge of varieties they consider more or less valuable to the country in which they are seeking asylum as a means of increasing their desirability as potential citizens (Corcoran 2004: 206). Even the apparently straightforward matter of asking claimants to name their native language(s) may in fact be far from simple: claimants may respond with the name of their national language, when in fact their true native language may even be unrelated to it linguistically. Uncertainty of this sort is therefore potentially problematic for analysts lacking adequate knowledge of the language situation or of varieties in the relevant geographical area (de Rooij 2010; and see e.g. Rampton 1990 and Davies 2008 on problems in the definition of the native speaker). The accuracy of LADO assessment is also heavily dependent on accurate linguistic documentation, yet many of the relevant languages, varieties and regions have barely been investigated. It is also essential to bear in mind that the task of forensic speaker profiling is far from easy even with well-documented languages such as English, especially if the speaker is attempting to disguise his or her true identity.

6. The Guidelines and the Minimal Requirements for LADO

Perhaps the most prominent publication in the field of LADO is the 'Guidelines for the use of language analysis in relation to questions of national origin in refugee cases' (LNOG 2004). This document (henceforth 'the Guidelines') was laid down by a group of nineteen authors from a range of countries and disciplines. The purpose of the Guidelines was not to set out rules or regulations for the practices of LADO, but rather to assist governments (i.e. non-linguist governmental officials) 'in assessing the general validity of language analysis in the determination of national origin, nationality or citizenship' (LNOG 2004: 261). The eleven Guidelines tackle the issues of who is qualified to perform LADO and the general limitations of a linguistic analysis. They also outline several problems that arise in the LADO context, such as multilingualism and the relationship between national and linguistic borders (see further Eades 2010).

Since their publication, the Guidelines have received multiple endorsements from professional associations including IAFL, the Linguistic Society of America and the Linguistics Association of Great Britain (see Patrick 2012). However, they have also elicited strong criticism, focussing mainly on Guidelines 3 and 7, which advise against the use of native speakers where they are employed in favour of trained linguists possessing a set of recommended qualifications (Wilson 2009; Cambier-Langeveld 2010a, b; Foulkes and Wilson 2011). The debate surrounding the use of native speakers as analysts is discussed in further detail below. Arguments have also been put forward that the Guidelines are unrepresentative of the field as a whole, and that they do not provide advice to non-linguist officials who might be called upon to interpret and evaluate a LADO report (Eriksson 2008; Cambier-Langeveld 2010a, b). With respect to the latter, guiding a non-linguist through the evaluation of a language report actually lies outside the stated purpose of the Guidelines. However, guidance on what to expect in terms of the contents of reports would indeed be beneficial to non-linguists: this might, for instance, include the range of linguistic examples, adequate references to or descriptions of the language situation, or perhaps a standardised conclusion format. In future, these issues could be considered as an addition to a revised version of the Guidelines, or as the basis for a separate document. It would also encourage agencies to maintain a consistently high standard across all of their analysts and submitted reports.

The Guidelines have also been criticised for their lack of inclusivity in terms of authorship. The nineteen signatories were largely academic linguists, and few had direct or extensive experience of LADO practice. Only two agencies were represented, with the practitioners employed by these agencies being predominantly engaged in counter-expertise activities. There were no representatives of agencies using native-speaker consultants (the IND or the Swedish companies Eqvator and Sprakab, which had been founded at least three years prior to the creation of the Guidelines). At the time that the Guidelines were compiled, no agency had been willing to provide publicly available information on their methods, but there was evidence that native-speaker consultants were used by some agencies, as acknowledged by some of the signatories (Eades et al. 2003; Eades and Arends 2004: 193–4), and that this approach had been accepted by the Dutch courts (van den Boogert 2004: 2). In retrospect, the Guidelines might be interpreted as prioritising one type of approach, without any particular approach having been tested objectively.

Although originally published in 2004, and defined by co-author Patrick (2012: 535) as 'a starting point', the Guidelines have not yet been adapted or updated to accommodate what is an evolving field. In 2008 a meeting was held in Leiden, the Netherlands, between members of four LADO agencies. At this meeting, the practitioners drew up two sets of 'Minimal Requirements' pertaining to the desired qualifications of specialised linguists, and the combined native speaker and linguist team. Unlike the Guidelines, the Minimal Requirements were not published or pursued further after their initial circulation within the community. The Requirements specify the proposed minimum qualifications for LADO analysts, and include recommendations on testing, regular cross-checking of performance and ensuring an awareness of the forensic context. Emphasis is also placed on the need for an independent accreditation body to oversee LADO practices (see Fraser 2009). While it would be difficult at this time to regulate LADO without more directed research to first establish best practices, it is certainly an appealing proposition to call for an international, independent body to assist in quality control of procedures.

One of the benefits of the Minimal Requirements is that they were created predominantly by practitioners of LADO who have experience with differing methods and personnel. The Requirements, however, suffer from one of the same problems as the Guidelines: they are not based on an explicit empirical grounding. They do, however, take into account the importance of directed training, which the Guidelines do not. They also serve to assist practitioners of LADO, rather than non-linguist officials.

The combination of the Guidelines and the Minimal Requirements can be considered as a rational starting point for recommendations on how to encourage best practice in LADO by ensuring a well-defined level of expertise among analysts, as well as strict quality-control policies. When considered individually, the Guidelines are biased towards particular working methods, while the Minimal Requirements lack input from peer-reviewed research. Together, the two documents have had the input of a combination of active practitioners, academics and other interested parties. The partnership of the two documents therefore holds great potential and, with the backing of empirical data, they could be adapted into a valuable set of LADO requirements to provide guidance for the entire community.

7. The native speaker debate

The Guidelines gave rise to the most prominent debate in the field, that of whether native speakers who are not trained academically as linguists should be involved in LADO. The Guidelines state that LADO should be performed by qualified linguists, who are defined as individuals who hold higher degrees in linguistics, have authored peer-reviewed publications and are members of professional associations. They should also have an up-to-date expertise in the language(s) in question (Guideline 3 – LNOG 2004: 262). Although these requirements have been described as 'stringent' (Patrick 2012: 524), further information about the types of linguistic expertise that are preferable (if any), the additional training that should be given to LADO employees (if any), and the type of cross-checking or testing they should undergo (if any) are not given. While it is recognised that LADO falls into the field of forensic analysis, the qualifications held by those performing language analysis are not necessarily directly related to this field. Taken literally, an analyst could conform to the Guidelines if he or she has expertise in any branch of linguistics. Of course, it is unlikely that a person whose specialism is, say, morphology will have the same skills and analytical approach as one whose expertise is in forensic phonetics (Wilson 2009: 6). The biggest problem with the specialised linguist argument is the inadequate definition of 'the linguist'.

The Guidelines correctly warn that the expertise of native speakers is not the same as that of linguists, as native speakers lack the ability to analyse language at a level required in LADO. Even if a native speaker is able to identify linguistically-relevant information, he or she may lack the skills to interpret it or the vocabulary to describe it, and therefore the quality of LADO reports could suffer as a result (Eades and Arends 2004; LNOG 2004; Wilson 2009). However, once again the biggest problem with the native speaker argument is defining 'the native speaker'.

Three agencies – the IND and the two Swedish agencies Verified and Sprakab – are currently known to use native-speaker consultants, although this should not be taken to imply that they take an identical approach. A native speaker in this context is defined as a person who does not have a background in linguistics, but who has received in-house training and testing in order to equip him or her for this type of work. Despite claims that the procedures involved in native-speaker training have not been made public (Patrick 2012: 544; Fraser 2011: 124), the IND has published an overview of its recruitment and training methods (Cambier-Langeveld 2010a). For the IND, a native speaker is defined as 'a speaker who has first-hand, extensive and continuous experience with the language area and with other speakers of the language and the relevant varieties, starting from an early age' (Cambier-Langeveld 2010a: 22). Training, testing and supervision are then provided before and after a candidate is hired to ensure that he or she is capable of performing the assigned work and that it is consistently at the desired standard (see Cambier-Langeveld 2010a for more detail).

All three of the agencies using native speakers in LADO conduct their analyses under the supervision of a trained linguist (Patrick 2012: 544). It is equally important that these linguists, or indeed any who work independently in LADO, also have adequate training and testing for this unique domain of work. As Fraser (2009: 114) notes, 'people with insufficient training in the appropriate branch of linguistics can simply give too much credence to confident but inexpert opinions about language and speech'. Scepticism has also been aired in the legal literature about forensic speech analysis in general, noting that qualifications alone do not indicate a particular level of ability in the relevant analytic tasks (Edmond et al. 2011: 67). LADO demands both language and linguistic expertise, but this does not necessarily mean that they must come from the same individual source, provided that the multiple sources they come from work collectively as one. There are few languages in the world that are thoroughly documented and for which documentation is regularly kept up to date. This is particularly true in respect of the cross-border languages and national languages for which LADO is most frequently undertaken (such as Somali, Mandingo or Pashto). As such it is a significant task to find linguists with adequate academic training who also possess a native competence in the relevant languages. The ideal analyst would indeed be a highly trained native-speaker linguist, but for areas where locating such an analyst is particularly problematic it is logical to find and train a native speaker to work alongside a professional linguist – again, provided that each individual has been thoroughly vetted.

The question of whether native speakers are able to interpret their findings accurately can be mirrored by asking to what extent linguists are able to interpret *their* findings accurately. For example, while a linguist may deliver a satisfactory scientific analysis using appropriate terminology and transcription systems, if that person does not possess a native-like knowledge of the relevant variety then this lack of native knowledge may mean that he or she does not place the same emphasis on observations that a native speaker may deem as vital markers of group or community membership, particularly where less well-documented languages are concerned. As Nolan (2012: 284) states, 'the performance of the physical speech mechanism is also subject to habits, styles, tendencies, indeed vagaries, which are characteristic of the relevant speaking community [. . .] Such characteristics tend to lie below the horizon for the traditional linguist.' That is, the linguistic documentation that underpins linguists' analysis is inevitably imbued with a theoretical stance. This may result, for example, in a focus on lexically-contrastive phonemes in phonology, or a prioritisation of standard varieties of the language. This may in turn mean that systematically variable features with indexical value go unreported. Consultation with a native speaker may therefore serve to highlight linguistic features missed in an analysis carried out by a non-native. In fact, although LINGUA openly states that linguistic analysis should be done by a linguist, the native speakers who are hired to perform interviews for LINGUA are permitted to share their own impressions of the interview, which the linguist can then pursue if these impressions contradict or complement the linguist's own findings (Baltisberger and Hubbuch 2010: 18).

Although Guideline 3 was 'uncontroversial among the 19 signatories [of the Guidelines]' (Eades 2010: 38), in 2007 members of the International Association for Forensic Phonetics and Acoustics (IAFPA) and a representative of De Taalstudio discussed whether there was reason to state that it should be 'compulsory to consult a native speaker of the language variety under question' (Moosmüller 2010: 44). The group did not reach a unanimous verdict but determined that the lack of an empirical basis meant that the expertise of native speakers, supervised by linguists, should not be excluded from LADO. As a result, an interim resolution was placed on the IAFPA website to accommodate this view.[5]

It appears in retrospect that the debate over the use of native-speaker consultants was misrepresented to some extent by parties on both sides, focusing on 'untrained' native speakers. Clearly, there is cause to doubt the ability of untrained people – caricatured in some circles as members of the public plucked off the street – to perform specialised tasks of any sort, not just those involving language analysis. Nonetheless, competence in a language does permit people to observe and interpret indexical properties of speech, as has been documented in many experiments (reviewed e.g. by Thomas 2002). The problem lies in assessing the reliability and consistency of observations (Fraser 2009). It is certainly true that individuals – whether or not they are trained in linguistics – vary enormously in their capacity to notice or understand correctly the indexical meanings of linguistic features. Although such concerns may have been valid prior to the production of the Guidelines, when information on the practices of LADO was scarce, it is now clear that no agency employs consultants who have had no training. Indeed, Patrick (2012: 544) refocuses the issue in the following terms: 'The real question is not *whether*, but *how*, NENS [non-expert native speaker] knowledge should be used in LADO.' It is noteworthy in this regard that the use of native-speaker consultants is routine in forensic speaker comparison (Foulkes 2011), where analysts are expected to bear in mind a point in the IAFPA Code of Practice warning them to 'exercise particular caution if carrying out forensic analysis of any kind on recordings containing speech in languages of which they are not native speakers'.[6] Further issues for consideration and clarification include how the supervisory role of the linguist can be formalised, and how the inevitably different roles of the supervisor and consultant can be combined (Foulkes 2011; Fraser 2012). Before this can be established, it seems essential that the LADO community first agree on a narrowly defined list of minimum professional qualifications, expertise and experience that is necessary for reliable analysis, along with a definition of what additional training should be required for all practitioners who have not previously conducted this type of work. It will then be possible to determine when a solo linguist is sufficient and when a combined native speaker/linguist method is preferable as a means of meeting all of the relevant criteria. At present, there is not enough empirical evidence to support or reject outright any specific approach.

8. The beginning of empirical research

LADO has certainly evolved over the years, but remarkably little of the growing literature reports on directed empirical research or independent evaluations of agency practices. Transparency remains limited, and LADO has escaped the attention of most academic linguists. The current canon of work in the field (collected on the LARG website) is dominated by polemic, critical assessments of case studies, and literature reviews which collate research from cognate fields. Such work is selected for its potential relevance to LADO situations, but does not in itself address LADO. The LADO context is unique, and it can therefore be difficult to extrapolate valid or reliable information from the results of any indirect research. Literature reviews concerning LADO often end with a call for further empirical research in the field (Eades and Arends 2004; Reath 2004; Fraser 2009; McNamara et al. 2010; Patrick 2012), yet few have chosen to take on this vital task.

The first pieces of directed empirical research offered to the field rose from the native speaker debate outlined above. Wilson (2009) conducted a study investigating performance in an online listening test consisting of seven voices speaking English, five from Ghana and two from Nigeria (for a summary see Foulkes and Wilson 2011). Four groups of listeners were recruited (forty-two in total): speakers of Ghanaian English with no linguistics training, British undergraduate linguistics students, phoneticians (academics and PhD students, all with training in or experience of forensic phonetics) and practising LADO analysts. Their task was to identify whether the speaker was genuinely from Ghana, or a foil. All linguist groups were provided with materials on the phonetics and phonology of Ghanaian English. Results showed that Ghanaians performed with the highest level of accuracy (86 per cent correct), while LADO professionals scored 50 per cent. Once 'no decision' results were excluded, there was no significant difference in accuracy between the Ghanaians and phoneticians, both giving significantly more correct responses than did the LADO professionals.

While the performance of the LADO professionals in this task appears disturbing, there are several caveats which must be taken into consideration. The LADO professionals were not working in their typical environment; they were using fixed samples; they did not consult a native speaker; and none had expertise in the language varieties in question. The academics did not consult a native speaker or have the relevant language expertise either, but they did have an extensive and well-practised knowledge of phonetics, which gave them an advantage when working with only phonetic reference materials. A positive conclusion to draw, however, is that when they were provided with only phonetic information some academics could reach the same level of accuracy as native Ghanaians. Unfortunately, such information is not always available for geographical areas in relation to which LADO is undertaken.

Further analysis of the responses showed that the Ghanaians and linguists faced occasional problems with different speakers. One voice sample yielded an error rate of 44 per cent among the Ghanaians but only 10 per cent for the academics, whereas another sample gave error rates of 11 per cent for the native speakers and 40 per cent for the academics. We interpret this as a sign that in some cases the listener groups used different cues to dialect identification. If this finding can be generalised, it suggests that a team approach might be beneficial, where difficulties encountered by linguists would be offset by the skills of native speakers, and vice versa. Though this study does not address the native speaker debate directly, it serves as a pilot, providing a starting point for further empirical investigation, specifically of the potential of a more phonetic-based analysis and the complementary insight a native speaker may have to offer in particular cases.

A second contribution to the empirical research pool stems from a unique situation in the Netherlands. In 2007 the Dutch Parliament granted amnesty to a group of asylum seekers, while also offering some the opportunity to present their real identities to the immigration services, even if these identities were different from those originally claimed at the time asylum was granted. The nationality of the claimant therefore became known after the original casework was completed, giving the practice which took on the language analyses (the IND) an opportunity to assess their conclusions as well as the conclusions of contra-expert reports. Cambier-Langeveld (2010b) took a closer look at eight cases in which one of six counter-experts also provided a report. Five of these counter-experts were linguists and non-native speakers, while one was both a linguist and a native speaker of the language in question. This pool of experts also included signatories of the Guidelines. In each of the eight cases, the original report, conducted by the IND using a combination of a linguist and native-speaker analyst, was correct. Only one of the counter-reports agreed with the original report. This was the one written by the native-speaker/linguist analyst.

Cambier-Langeveld's investigation is based upon only a small number of cases and it cannot be proven beyond doubt that the nationality that was ultimately presented by each claimant was genuine, although all provided some documentation and at this stage in the process the claimants would have had little reason to lie about their true origins beyond a mistrust of the Dutch government. Of course, if deportation could still have led to persecution or death then that would be reason enough. Criticisms of the study focus on the implication by Cambier-Langeveld (2010b) that native-speaker competence is a requirement for a reliable LADO analysis, and that such a declaration cannot be justified based on the results of such a small number of out-dated cases (Verrips 2011; Fraser 2011). However, the conclusion reached by Cambier-Langeveld does not specify a requirement for the use of native speakers. Rather, it flags up the problems that can occur when non-native linguists are the sole analysts responsible for preparing a LADO report, and it emphasises the lack of empirical evidence in support of any one particular approach. In turn, this suggests that the consultant issue should not be presented as settled in high-profile documents such as the Guidelines (Cambier-Langeveld 2010b, 2012).

9. Improving the validity and reliability of **LADO** for the future

There is no doubt that LADO will continue to evolve. However, further published and peer-reviewed research (and ideally a thorough independent evaluation of current practices) is urgently needed to establish valid and reliable methods for LADO. Directed research on every aspect of the procedure is necessary, even if this only serves to confirm the results of other non-LADO-oriented work. As Verrips (2011: 140) notes, '[t]o ensure valid results, each link of the chain must be validated, and therefore each should be open to scrutiny and research'. The agenda for research should include best practices in interview techniques, investigation of accent/dialect disguise, how the skills of native speakers differ from those of linguists and how those skills can best be harnessed.

There are also calls to bring LADO practice into line with other forensic disciplines, for example in establishing a conclusion framework based on likelihood ratio analysis (Broeders 2010), and ensuring that practitioners conform to the general expectations that are held of independent experts (Patrick 2012). In Europe, the field may be forced to adapt and standardise as asylum procedures become harmonised across EU member states (Tax 2010). It is vital that the field be made more open to public review as we try to identify the benefits or disadvantages of current practices, even if such activity could run counter to practitioners' short-term interests (Verrips 2010). It is not enough for researchers to tackle these issues if practitioners do not take an active and public role in creating, assessing and implementing future research. Until this research is available, LADO will also benefit from a fresh circulation and review of the Guidelines.

Notes

1. We record our thanks to Tina Cambier-Langeveld and Helen Fraser for helpful discussion of several issues raised in this chapter.
2. International Association of Forensic Linguists (www.iafl.org) and International Association for Forensic Phonetics and Acoustics (www.iafpa.net). All websites cited in this chapter were last accessed on 5 November 2013.
3. https://sites.google.com/site/workshoponlado/home.
4. http://www.essex.ac.uk/larg/.
5. http://www.iafpa.net/langidres.htm.
6. http://www.iafpa.net/code.htm (point 6).

References

Abrate, L. (2001), *Occitanie 1900–1968: des idées et des hommes*, Puylaurens, France: Institut d'Etudes Occitanes.

Adams, G. B. (1958), 'The emergence of Ulster as a distinct dialect area', *Ulster Folklife*, 4: 61–73.

Agreement (1998), *Agreement Reached in the Multi-Party Negotiations* (Document agreed between the Government of Ireland and the Government of the United Kingdom of Great Britain and Northern Ireland). Online resource: https://www.gov.uk/government/uploads/system/uploads/attachment_data/file/136652/agreement.pdf (accessed 12 November 2013).

Aitchison, J. and H. Carter (2004), *Spreading the Word: The Welsh Language 2001*, Talybont: Y Lolfa.

Aitken, A. J. (1992), 'Scots', in T. McArthur (ed.), *The Oxford Companion to the English Language*, Oxford: Oxford University Press, pp. 893–9.

Alba, O. (1998), *Los sonidos del Español*, Santo Domingo, Dominican Republic: Librería La Trinitaria.

Allen, H. B. (1959), 'Canadian-American speech differences along the middle border', *Journal of the Canadian Linguistic Association* 5.1: 17–24.

Allen, H. B. (1976), *The Linguistic Atlas of the Upper Midwest in Three Volumes*, Minneapolis: University of Minnesota Press.

Alvar, M. (2010), *El Español en México: Estudios, Mapas, Textos*, vol. I, Madrid: Universidad de Alcalá de Henares.

Anderson, B. (1991), *Imagined Communities: Reflections on the Origin and Spread of Nationalism*, London: Verso.

Anderson, P. (1987), *A Structural Atlas of the English Dialects*, London: Croom Helm.

Appadurai, A. (1996), *Modernity at Large: Cultural Dimensions of Globalization*, Minneapolis: University of Minnesota Press.

Ascoli, G. I. (1878) [1873], 'Schizzi franco-provenzali', *Archivio Glottologico Italiano*, 3: 61–120.

Auer, P. and J. E. Schmidt (eds) (2010), *Language and Space: An International Handbook of Linguistic Variation, Vol. 1: Theories and Methods*, Berlin: Mouton de Gruyter.

Auer, P., F. Hinskens and P. Kerswill (2005), *Dialect Change: Convergence and Divergence in European Languages*, Cambridge: Cambridge University Press.

Avanza, M. and G. Laferté (2005), 'Dépasser la «construction des identités»? Identification, image sociale, appartenance', *Genèses*, 61.4: 134–52.

Avis, W. S. (1954), 'Speech differences along the Ontario–United States border, I: Vocabulary', *Journal of the Canadian Linguistic Association* 1.1: 13–18.

Avis, W. S. (1955), 'Speech differences along the Ontario–United States border, II: Grammar and syntax', *Journal of the Canadian Linguistic Association* 1.1: 14–19.

Avis, W. S. (1956), 'Speech differences along the Ontario–United States border, III: Pronunciation', *Journal of the Canadian Linguistic Association* 2.2: 41–59.

Azevedo, M. M. (1989), 'Vernacular features in educated speech in Brazilian Portuguese', *Hispania*, 72.4: 862–72.

Baker, C. and S. Prys Jones (1998), *Encyclopedia of Bilingualism and Bilingual Education*, Clevedon: Multilingual Matters.

Baker, W. and D. Bowie (2009), 'Religious affiliation as a correlate of linguistic behavior', *University of Pennsylvania Working Papers in Linguistics*, 15.2, Article 2. Online resource: http://repository.upenn.edu/pwpl/vol15/iss2/2/ (accessed 12 November 2013).

Baker, W., D. Eddington and L. Nay (2009), 'Dialect identification: The effects of region of origin and amount of experience', *American Speech*, 84: 48–71.

Bakos, J. (2008), 'An Examination of the Adaptation to the Northern Cities Chain Shift by Lebanese Immigrants in Dearborn, Michigan', PhD dissertation, Michigan State University. Online resource: http://bit.ly/17t66Q9 (accessed 12 November 2013).

Baltisberger, E. and P. Hubbuch (2010), 'LADO with specialized linguists – the development of LINGUA's working method', in K. Zwaan, M. Verrips and P. Muysken (eds), *Language and Origin – The Role of Language in European Asylum Procedures: Linguistic and Legal Perspectives*, Nijmegen: Wolf Legal Publishers, pp. 9–19.

Barlow, M. and S. Kemmer (2000), *Usage-Based Models of Language*, Stanford: CSLI.

Barth, F. (ed.) (1969), *Ethnic Groups and Boundaries: The Social Organisation of Cultural Difference*, Oslo: Universitetsforlaget.

Barth, F. (1994), 'Enduring and emerging issues in the analysis of ethnicity', in H. Vermeulen and C. Govers (eds), *The Anthropology of Ethnicity: Beyond 'Groups and Boundaries'*, Amsterdam: Het Spinhuis, pp. 11–32.

Bauman, H.-D. L. (2008), 'On the disconstruction of (sign) language in the Western tradition: a deaf reading of Plato's Cratylus', in H.-D. L. Bauman (ed.), *Open your Eyes: Deaf Studies Talking*, Minneapolis: University of Minnesota Press, pp. 127–45.

Bauman, Z. (1998), *Globalization: The Human Consequences*, Cambridge: Polity Press.

Bechhofer, F. and D. McCrone (2008), 'Talking the talk: national identity in England and Scotland', in A. Park, J. Curtice, K. Thomson, M. Phillips, M. C. Johnson and E. Clery (eds), *British Social Attitudes: The 24th Report*, Aldershot: Sage, pp. 81–104.

Bechhofer, F. and D. McCrone (2010), 'Choosing national identity', *Sociological Research Online*, 15.3. Online resource: http://www.socresonline.org.uk/15/3/3.html (accessed 2 December 2013).

Benjamin, B. J. (1982), 'Phonological performance in gerontological speech', *Journal of Psycholinguistic Research*, 11: 159–67.

Ben-Rafael, E., E. Olshtain and I. Geijst (1998), 'Identity and language: the social insertion of Soviet Jews in Israel', in E. Leshem and J. T. Shuval (eds), *Immigration to Israel: Sociological Perspectives* (Studies of Israeli Society, Vol. 8), Piscataway, NJ: Transaction Publishers, pp. 333–56.

Benor, S. B. (2001), 'The learned /t/: phonological variation in Orthodox Jewish English', *University of Pennsylvania Working Papers in Linguistics* 7.3: 1–16.

Benor, S. B. (2010), 'Ethnolinguistic repertoire: shifting the analytic focus in language and ethnicity', *Journal of Sociolinguistics*, 14.2: 159–83.

Berg, C. and C. Weis (2005), *Sociologie de l'enseignement des langues dans un environnement multilingue*, Luxembourg: Ministère de l'Education Nationale et de la Formation Professionnelle et Centre d'Études sur la Situation des Jeunes en Europe.

Bergounioux, G. (1989), 'Le francien (1815–1914): la linguistique au service de la patrie', *Mots. Les Langages du Politique*, 19: 23–40.

Bert, M. (2001), 'Rencontre de langues et francisation: l'exemple du Pilat', PhD dissertation, Université Lumière Lyon 2. Online resource: http://bit.ly/1clb5zQ (accessed 12 November 2013).

Bert, M., J. Costa and J.-B. Martin (2009), *Étude FORA: Francoprovençal et Occitan en Rhône-Alpes*, Lyons: Institut Pierre Gardette, INRP, ICAR, DDL. Online resource: http://icar.univ-lyon2.fr/projets/ledra/documents/Etude_FORA_rapport_d%C3%A9finitif.pdf (accessed 12 November 2013).

Beswick, J. (2005), 'Linguistic homogeneity in Galician and Portuguese borderland communities', *Estudios de Sociolingüística*, 6.1: 39–64.

Beswick, J. (2007), *Regional Nationalism in Spain: Language Use and Ethnic Identity in Galicia*, Clevedon: Multilingual Matters.

Beswick, J. (2010), 'Linguistic ideologies in institutional settings: the pronunciation of Galician in radio broadcasts', in N. Lorenzo-Dus (ed.), *Spanish at Work: Discourse and Institutional Settings in the Spanish-Speaking World*, Basingstoke: Palgrave Macmillan, pp. 35–49.

Bills, G. D. (2005), 'Las comunidades lingüísticas y el mantenimiento del español en Estados Unidos', in L. A. Ortiz López and M. Lacorte (eds), *Contactos y contextos lingüísticos: el Español en los Estados Unidos y en contacto con otras lenguas*, Madrid: Iberoamericana, pp. 55–83.

Bills, G. D., E. Hernández Chávez and A. Hudson (1995), 'The geography of language shift: distance from the Mexican border and Spanish language claiming in the southwestern U.S.', *International Journal of the Sociology of Language*, 114: 9–27.

Bills, G. D. and N. A. Vigil (2008), *The Spanish Language of New Mexico and Southern Colorado: A Linguistic Atlas*, Albuquerque: University of New Mexico Press.

Blanchet, P. (1992), *Le Provençal: essai de description sociolinguistique et différentielle*, Louvain-la-Neuve, Belgium: Peeters.

Blommaert, J. (2001), 'Investigating narrative inequality: African asylum seekers' stories in Belgium', *Discourse and Society*, 12.4: 413–49.

Blommaert, J. (2010), *The Sociolinguistics of Globalization*, Cambridge: Cambridge University Press.

Blumstein, S. E., E. B. Myers and J. Rissman (2005), 'The perception of Voice Onset Time: an fMRI investigation of phonetic category structure', *Journal of Cognitive Neuroscience*, 17.9: 1353–66.

Boberg, C. (2000), 'Geolinguistic diffusion and the U.S.–Canada border', *Language Variation and Change*, 12: 1–24.

Boberg, C. (2005), 'The North American Regional Vocabulary Survey: new variables and methods in the study of North American English', *American Speech* 80.1: 22–60.

Boberg, C. (2008), 'Regional phonetic differentiation in Standard Canadian English', *Journal of English Linguistics* 36.2: 129–54.

Boberg, C. (2010), *The English Language in Canada: Status, History and Comparative Analysis*, Cambridge: Cambridge University Press.

Boberg, C. (2012), 'English in Quebec, Canada: a minority language in contact with French', *World Englishes*, 31.4: 493–502.

Boersma, P. and D. Weenink (2013), *Praat: Doing Phonetics by Computer* [computer program]. Version 5.3.55. Online resource: http://www.praat.org/ (accessed 5 December 2013).

Bonaparte, L.-L. (1875–76), 'On the Dialects of Monmouthshire, Herefordshire, Worcestershire, Gloucestershire, Berkshire, Oxfordshire, South Warwickshire, South Northamptonshire, Buckinghamshire, Hertfordshire, Middlesex, and Surrey, with a New Classification of the English Dialects', *Transactions of the Philological Society*, 16.1: 570–9.

Bourdieu, P. (1992), *Language and Symbolic Power*, Cambridge: Polity Press.

Bouvier, J.-C. (1976), *Les Parlers provençaux de la Drôme: étude de géographie phonétique*, Paris: Klincksieck.

Bouvier, J.-C. (2003), 'L'Occitan en Provence: le dialecte provençal, ses limites et ses variétés', in J.-C. Bouvier (ed.), *Espaces du langage: géolinguistique, toponymie, culture de l'oral et de l'écrit*, Aix en Provence: Université de Provence, pp. 11–25.

Bowie, D. (2003), 'Early development of the CARD-CORD merger in Utah', *American Speech* 78: 31–51.

Bowie, D. (2010), 'The ageing voice: changing identity over time', in C. Llamas and D. Watt (eds), *Language and Identities*, Edinburgh: Edinburgh University Press, pp. 55–66.

Bowie, D., W. Morkel and E. Lund (2001), 'Early trends in Utah English', paper presented at NWAV 30, Raleigh, NC, October 2001.

Boyer, H. and H. Cardy (2011), 'Localiser, identifier, valoriser', *Mots. Les Langages du politique*, 97.3: 5–13.

Braidwood, J. (1964), 'Ulster and Elizabethan English', in G. B. Adams (ed.), *Ulster Dialects: An Introductory Symposium*, Cultra Manor: Ulster Folk Museum, pp. 5–109.

Brisk, M. E. (1972), 'The Spanish Syntax of the Pre-school Spanish-American: The Case of New Mexican Five-Year Old Children', unpublished PhD dissertation, University of New Mexico.

Britain, D. (1997), 'Dialect contact and phonological reallocation: 'Canadian Raising' in the English Fens', *Language in Society*, 26: 15–46.

Britain, D. (2001), 'Welcome to East Anglia! Two major dialect "boundaries" in the Fens', in P. Trudgill and J. Fisiak (eds), *East Anglian English*, Woodbridge: Boydell and Brewer, pp. 217–42.

Britain, D. (2002), 'Space and spatial diffusion', in J. K. Chambers, P. Trudgill and N. Schilling-Estes (eds), *The Handbook of Language Variation and Change*, Oxford: Blackwell, pp. 603–37.

Britain, D. (2003), 'Exploring the importance of the outlier in sociolinguistic dialectology', in D. Britain and J. Cheshire (eds), *Social Dialectology*, Amsterdam: Benjamins, pp. 191–208.

Britain, D. (2005), 'Innovation diffusion, "Estuary English" and local dialect differentiation: the survival of Fenland Englishes', *Linguistics*, 43: 995–1022.

Britain, D. (2009), 'Language and space: the variationist approach', in P. Auer and J.-E. Schmidt (eds), *Language and Space: An International Handbook of Linguistic Variation, Vol. 1: Theories and Methods*, Berlin: Mouton de Gruyter, pp. 142–62.

Britain, D. (2010a), 'Conceptualisations of geographic space in linguistics', in A. Lameli, R. Kehrein and S. Rabanus (eds), *Language and Space: An International Handbook of Linguistic Variation, Vol. 2: Language Mapping*, Berlin: Mouton de Gruyter, pp. 69–97.

Britain, D. (2010b), 'Supralocal regional dialect levelling', in C. Llamas and D. Watt (eds), *Language and Identities*, Edinburgh: Edinburgh University Press, pp. 193–204.

Britain, D. (2010c), 'Contact and dialectology', in R. Hickey (ed.), *Handbook of Language Contact*, Oxford: Blackwell, pp. 208–29.

Britain, D. (2012), 'English in England', in R. Hickey (ed.), *Areal Features of the Anglophone World*, Berlin: Mouton de Gruyter, pp. 23–52.

Britain, D. (2013), 'Space, diffusion and mobility', in J. K. Chambers and N. Schilling (eds), *Handbook of Language Variation and Change* (2nd edn), Oxford: Wiley-Blackwell, pp. 471–500.

Broeders, A. P. A. (2010), 'Decision making in LADO – a view from the forensic arena', in K. Zwaan, M. Verrips and P. Muysken (eds), *Language and Origin – The Role of Language in European Asylum Procedures: Linguistic and Legal Perspectives*, Nijmegen: Wolf Legal Publishers, pp. 51–60.

Brown, E. L. and D. Harper (2009), 'Phonological evidence of interlingual exemplar connections', *Studies in Hispanic and Lusophone Linguistics*, 2.2: 1–18.

Brown, P. and S. C. Levinson (1987), *Politeness: Some Universals in Language Usage*, Cambridge: Cambridge University Press.

Bryson, L. and C. McCartney (1994), *Clashing Symbols? A Report on the Use of Flags, Anthems and other National Symbols in Northern Ireland*, Belfast: Institute of Irish Studies, The Queen's University of Belfast.

Bucholtz, M. and K. Hall (2010), 'Locating identity in language', in C. Llamas and D. Watt (eds), *Language and Identities*, Edinburgh: Edinburgh University Press, pp. 18–28.

Buchstaller, I. and S. Alvanides (2010), 'Applying geographical sampling methods to regional dialectology in north east England', paper presented at NWAV 39, San Antonio, TX, November 2010.

Bunreacht na hÉireann (1942), *Bunreacht na hÉireann (Constitution of Ireland)*, Dublin: Government Sale Office.

Bunreacht na hÉireann (2004), *Bunreacht na hÉireann (Constitution of Ireland)*, Dublin: Government Publications Sale Office.

Burch, S. (2004), 'Capturing a movement: sign language preservation', *Sign Language Studies* 4.3: 293–304.

Burnett, W. (2006), 'Linguistic resistance on the Maine–New Brunswick border', *Canadian Journal of Linguistics*, 51.2/3: 161–76.

Bybee, J. (2001), *Phonology and Language Use*, Cambridge: Cambridge University Press.

Call for Irish (2009), 'Call for Irish and Ulster-Scots on same signs', *Ballymoney and Moyle Times*, 25 March.

Callahan, L. (2007), 'Spanish/English codeswitching in service encounters: accommodation to the customer's language choice and perceived linguistic affiliation', *Southwest Journal of Linguistics* 26.1: 15–38.

Cambier-Langeveld, T. (2010a), 'The validity of language analysis in the Netherlands', in K. Zwaan, M. Verrips and P. Muysken (eds), *Language and Origin – The Role of Language in European Asylum Procedures: Linguistic and Legal Perspectives*, Nijmegen: Wolf Legal Publishers, pp. 21–33.

Cambier-Langeveld, T. (2010b), 'The role of linguists and native speakers in language analysis for the determination of speaker origin', *International Journal of Speech, Language and the Law*, 17.1: 67–93.

Cambier-Langeveld, T. (2012), 'Clarification of the issues in language analysis: a rejoinder to Fraser and Verrips', *International Journal of Speech, Language and the Law*, 19.1: 95–108.

Camden, W. (1637), *Britannia*, Frankfurt: Ruland.

Campbell, H. (2009), 'Breaking new ground in food regime theory: corporate environmentalism, ecological feedbacks and the "food from somewhere" regime', *Agriculture and Human Values*, 26: 309–19.

Campbell, J. (2013), 'Language analysis in the United Kingdom's refugee status determination system: seeing through policy claims about "expert knowledge"', *Ethnic and Racial Studies*, 36.4: 670–90.

Carvalho, A. M. (1998), 'The Social Distribution of Uruguayan Portuguese in a Bilingual Border Town', unpublished PhD dissertation, University of California, Berkeley.

Carvalho, A. M. (2003), 'Rumo a uma definição do português uruguaio', *Revista Internacional de Lingüística Iberoamericana*, 2: 135–59.

Carvalho, A. M. (2006a), 'Nominal number marking in a variety of Spanish in contact with Portuguese', in C. Klee and T. Face (eds), *Selected Papers of the 8th Hispanic Linguistics Symposium and 7th Conference on the Acquisition of Spanish and Portuguese as First and Second Languages*, Somerville, MA: Cascadilla Press, pp. 154–66.

Carvalho, A. M. (2006b), 'Spanish (s) aspiration as a prestige marker on the Uruguayan–Brazilian border', *Spanish in Context*, 3.1: 85–114.

Carver, C. (1987), *American Regional Dialects*, Ann Arbor: University of Michigan Press.

Cassidy, F. G. and J. H. Hall (eds) (1985–2012), *Dictionary of American Regional English* (5 vols), Cambridge, MA: Harvard University Press.

Catford, J. (1988), *A Practical Introduction to Phonetics*, Oxford: Oxford University Press.

Cenoz, J. and D. Gorter (2006), 'Linguistic landscape and minority languages', in D. Gorter (ed.), *Linguistic Landscape: A New Approach to Multilingualism*, Clevedon: Multilingual Matters, pp. 67–80.

Census 2006 (2007), *Census 2006, Volume 9: Irish Language; Volume 13: Religion*, Dublin: Stationery Office.

Census 2011 (2012), *This Is Ireland: Highlights from Census 2011, Part 1*. Dublin: Stationery Office.

Central Intelligence Agency (1987), *United Kingdom, Northern Ireland*, Washington, DC. Online resource: http://www.loc.gov/item/89693217 (accessed 8 December 2013).

Cerquiglini, B. (2007), *Une langue orpheline*, Paris: Éditions de Minuit.

Chambers, J. K. (1994), 'An introduction to dialect topography', *English World-Wide* 15.1: 35–53.

Chambers, J. K. (1995), 'The Canada–US border as a vanishing isogloss: the evidence of *chesterfield*', *Journal of English Linguistics* 23.1–2: 155–66.

Chambers, J. K. and P. Trudgill (1998) [1980], *Dialectology* (2nd edn), Cambridge: Cambridge University Press.

Chatterton, B. (2008), 'Religious Networks as a Sociolinguistic Factor: The Case of Cardston', unpublished MA thesis, Brigham Young University. Online resource: http://contentdm.lib.byu.edu/cdm/singleitem/collection/ETD/id/1481/rec/1 (accessed 13 November 2013).

Chin, N. B. and G. Wigglesworth (2007), *Bilingualism: An Advanced Resource Book*, New York: Routledge.

Clarke, S. (2010), *Newfoundland and Labrador English*, Edinburgh: Edinburgh University Press.

Clopper, C. and D. B. Pisoni (2005), 'Perception of dialect variation', in D. B. Pisoni and R. E. Remez (eds), *The Handbook of Speech Perception*, Oxford: Blackwell, pp. 313–37.

Cohen, A. (1985), *The Symbolic Construction of Community*, London: Tavistock.

Cohen, A. (1986), 'Of symbols and boundaries, or, does Ertie's greatcoat hold the key?', in A. Cohen (ed.), *Symbolising Boundaries: Identity and Diversity in British Cultures*, Manchester: Manchester University Press, pp. 1–19.

Cohen, I. (1989), *Structuration Theory: Anthony Giddens and the Constitution of Social Life*, London: Macmillan.

Cole, R. A., J. Jakimik and W. E. Cooper (1978), 'Perceptibility of phonetic features in fluent speech', *Journal of the Acoustical Society of America*, 64.1: 44–56.

Corcoran, C. (2004), 'A critical examination of the use of language analysis interviews in asylum proceedings: a case study of a West African seeking asylum in the Netherlands', *International Journal of Speech, Language and the Law*, 11.2: 200–21.

Corrigan, K. P. (2010), *Irish English, Vol. 1: Northern Ireland*, Edinburgh: Edinburgh University Press.

Costa, J. (2010), 'Revitalisation linguistique: discours, mythes et idéologies. Approche critique de mouvements de revitalisation en Provence et en Écosse,' PhD dissertation, Grenoble: Université de Grenoble. Online resource: http://tel.archives-ouvertes.fr/docs/00/62/56/91/PDF/Costa_thesis_29112010_Final_20.pdf (accessed 13 November 2013).

Costa, J. (2011), 'Du local au global: essai de clarification idéologique préalable. Discours concurrents et revitalisation linguistique en Provence', in F. Manzano (ed.), *Unité et diversité de la linguistique*, Lyons: Publications du Centre d'Études Linguistiques / Editions de l'Université Jean Moulin, Lyon 3, pp. 233–55.

Costa, J. and M. Bert (2011), 'De l'un et du divers: la région Rhône-Alpes et la mise en récit de ses langues', *Mots. Les Langages du politique*, 97: 45–57.

Coulmas, F. (2005), *Sociolinguistics: The Study of Speakers' Choices*, Cambridge: Cambridge University Press.

Coupland, N. (2007), *Style: Language Variation and Identity*, Cambridge: Cambridge University Press.

Coupland, N. (ed.) (2010), *Handbook of Language and Globalization*, Cambridge, MA: Wiley Blackwell.

Coupland, N. (2012), 'Bilingualism on display: the framing of Welsh and English in Welsh public spaces', *Language in Society* 41: 1–27.

Coupland, N. (2013), 'Welsh tea: the centring and decentring of Wales', in S. Pietikäinen and H. Kelly-Holmes (eds), *Multilingualism and the Periphery*, Oxford: Oxford University Press, pp. 133–53.

Coupland, N. and M. Aldridge (eds) (2009), 'Sociolinguistic and subjective aspects of Welsh in Wales and its diaspora', thematic issue (Vol. 195) of the *International Journal of the Sociology of Language*.

Coupland, N. and H. Bishop (2006), 'Ideologising language and community in post-devolution Wales', in J. Wilson and K. Stapleton (eds), *Devolution and Identity*, Aldershot: Ashgate, pp. 33–50.

Coupland, N. and A. Jaworski (2004), 'Sociolinguistic perspectives on metalanguage: reflexivity, evaluation, and ideology', in A. Jaworski, N. Coupland and D. Galasiński (eds), *Metalanguage: Social and Ideological Perspectives*, New York: Walter de Gruyter, pp. 15–50.

Coupland, N., H. Bishop and P. Garrett (2006), 'One Wales? Reassessing diversity in Welsh ethnolinguistic identification', *Contemporary Wales*, 18: 1–27.

Coye, D. F. (2009), 'Dialect boundaries in New Jersey', *American Speech*, 84.4: 414–52.

Craib, I. (1992), *Anthony Giddens*, London: Routledge.

Crowley, T. (2005), *Wars of Words: The Politics of Language in Ireland 1537–2004*, Oxford: Oxford University Press.

Csepeli, G. and A. Örkeny (1998), 'The imagery of national anthems in Europe', in A. Gasparini (ed.), *Nation, Ethnnicity, Minority and Border: Contributions to an International Sociology*, Gorizia, Italy: International Institute of Sociology, pp. 37–55.

Daley, P. (2002), 'How tapes sent to Sweden alter thousands of lives', *The Age*, 27 July. Online resource: http://www.theage.com.au/articles/2002/07/26/1027497412021.html (accessed 15 November 2013).

Darby, H. (1931), 'The Role of the Fenland in English History,' unpublished PhD dissertation, University of Cambridge.

Darby, H. (1932), 'The human geography of the Fenland before the drainage', *Geographical Journal*, 80: 420–35.

Darby, H. (1934), 'The Fenland frontier in Anglo-Saxon England', *Antiquity*, 30: 185–201.

Darby, H. (1938a), 'Cambridgeshire in the nineteenth century', in H. Darby (ed.), *The Cambridge Region*, Cambridge: Cambridge University Press, pp. 116–34.

Darby, H. (1938b), 'The draining of the Fens AD 1600–1850', in H. Darby (ed.), *A Scientific Study of the Cambridge District*, London: Office of the British Association, pp. 181–93.

Davies, A. (2008), 'The native speaker in applied linguistics', in A. Davies and C. Elder (eds), *The Handbook of Applied Linguistics*, Oxford: Blackwell, pp. 431–50.

Davis, K. A. (1994), *Language Planning in Multilingual Contexts: Policies, Communities, and Schools in Luxembourg*, Amsterdam: Benjamins.

de Rooij, V.A. (2010), 'Language analysis for the determination of origin (LADO): a look into problems presented by East and Central African cases', in K. Zwaan, M. Verrips and P. Muysken (eds), *Language and Origin: The Role of Language in European Asylum*

Procedures – Linguistic and Legal Perspectives, Nijmegen: Wolf Legal Publishers, pp. 133–44.

de Vriend, F., C. Giesbers, R. van Hout and L. ten Bosch (2008), 'The Dutch–German dialect border: relating linguistic, geographic and social distances', *International Journal of Humanities and Arts Computing*, 2: 119–34.

Deaf Jam (2012), *Timeline*. Online resource: http://www.deafjam.org/timeline.html (accessed 15 November 2013).

Di Paolo, M. (1993), 'Propredicate *do* in the English of the Intermountain West', *American Speech*, 68: 339–56.

Di Paolo, M. and A. Faber (1990), 'Phonation differences and the phonetic content of the tense-lax contrast in Utah English', *Language Variation and Change*, 2: 155–204.

Diener, A. C. and J. Hagen (2009), 'Theorizing borders in a "borderless world": globalization, territory and scale', *Geography Compass*, 3.3: 1196–1216.

Diener, A. C. and J. Hagen (eds) (2010), *Borderlines and Borderlands: Political Oddities at the Edge of the Nation-State*, Lanham, MD: Rowman and Littlefield.

Diener, A. C. and J. Hagen (2012), *Borders: A Very Short Introduction*, Oxford: Oxford University Press.

Docherty, G. J. (1992), *The Timing of Voicing in British English Obstruents*, Berlin: Foris Publications.

Docherty, G. J., D. Watt, C. Llamas, D. Hall and J. Nycz (2011), 'Variation in Voice Onset Time along the Scottish/English border', *Proceedings of the 17th International Congress of Phonetic Sciences*, Hong Kong, pp. 591–4.

Docherty, G. J., C. Llamas and D. Watt (2012), 'Production and perception of a salient phonetic feature: /r/ and identity in northern Britain', paper presented at the Conference of the British Association of Academic Phoneticians (BAAP), Leeds, March.

Dodsworth, R. and M. Kohn (2012), 'Urban rejection of the vernacular: the SVS undone', *Language Variation and Change*, 24: 221–45.

Donnan, H. and T. M. Wilson (1999), *Borders: Frontiers of Identity, Nation and State*, Oxford: Berg.

Donnan, H. and T. M. Wilson (eds) (2010), *Borderlands: Ethnographic Approaches to Security, Power, and Identity*, Lanham, MD: University Press of America.

Dorian, N. C. (1982), 'Defining the speech community to include its working margins', in S. Romaine (ed.), *Sociolinguistic Variation in Speech Communities*, London: Edward Arnold, pp. 25–33.

Dorian, N. C. (1994), 'Purism vs. compromise in language revitalization and language revival', *Language in Society*, 23.4: 479–94.

Dorling, D. (2010), 'Persistent north–south divides', in N. M. Coe and A. Jones (eds), *The Economic Geography of the UK*, London: Sage, pp. 12–28.

Dorling, D. (2013), 'North–South: From Divide to Chasm', public lecture, Festival of Ideas, University of York, June 2013.

Duchêne, A. and M. Heller (eds) (2007), *Discourses of Endangerment: Ideology and Interest in the Defence of Languages*, London: Continuum.

Duranti, A. and E. Ochs (1997), 'Syncretic literacy in a Samoan American family', in L. B. Resnick, C. Pontecorvo and R. Saljo (eds), *Discourse, Tools and Reasoning: Essays on Situated Cognition*, Berlin: Springer Verlag, pp. 169–203.

Eades, D. (2010), 'Guidelines from linguists for LADO', in K. Zwaan, M. Verrips and P. Muysken (eds), *Language and Origin – The Role of Language in European Asylum Procedures: Linguistic and Legal Perspectives*, Nijmegen: Wolf Legal Publishers, pp. 35–41.

Eades, D. and J. Arends (2004), 'Using language analysis in the determination of national origin of asylum seekers: an introduction', *International Journal of Speech, Language and the Law*, 11.2: 179–99.

Eades, D., H. Fraser, J. Siegel, T. McNamara and B. Baker (2003), 'Linguistic identification in the determination of nationality: a preliminary report', *Language Policy*, 2: 179–99.

Eastman, C. M. and R. F. Stein (1993), 'Language display: authenticating claims to social identity', *Journal of Multilingual and Multicultural Development*, 14.3: 187–202.

Eberle, D., E. Parks, S. Eberle and J. Parks (2012), *Sociolinguistic Survey Report of the Ecuadorian Deaf Community* (SIL Electronic Survey Report 2012-027). Online resource: http://www-01.sil.org/silesr/2012/silesr2012-027_ESR_361_Ecuador_Deaf.pdf (accessed 15 November 2013).

Eckert, P. (2000), *Linguistic Variation as Social Practice: The Linguistic Construction of Identity at Belten High*, Malden, MA: Blackwell.

Eckert, P. and E. Wenger (1993), *Seven Principles of Learning*, Palo Alto: Institute for Research on Learning.

Eddington, D. and M. Savage (2012), 'Where are the moun[ʔə]ns in Utah?', *American Speech*, 87: 336–49.

Edmond, G., M. San Roque and K. Martire (2011), 'Unsound law: issues with ("expert") voice comparison evidence', *Melbourne University Law Review*, 35: 52–112.

Elizaincín, A. (1979), *Algunas precisiones sobre los dialectos portugueses en el Uruguay*, Montevideo: Universidad de la República.

Elizaincín, A. (1992), *Dialectos en contacto: Español y Portugués en España y América*, Montevideo: Arca.

Elizaincín, A. (2008), 'Uruguay', in A. Palacios (ed.), *El Español en América: contactos lingüísticos en Hispanoamérica*, Barcelona: Ariel, pp. 301–19.

Elizaincín, A., L. Behares and G. Barrios (1987), *Nos falemo brasilero*, Montevideo: Editorial Amesur.

Ellis, A. J. (1889), *On Early English Pronunciation, Part V: The Existing Phonology of English Dialects Compared with that of West Saxon*, London: Truebner and Co. [reprinted New York: Greenwood Press, 1968].

Ellis, S. (1994), 'The Yorkshire Ripper inquiry: Part 1', *Forensic Linguistics*, 1: 197–206.

Epley, C., E. Parks and J. Parks (2011), *A Sociolinguistic Profile of the Jamaican Deaf Community* (SIL Electronic Survey Report 2011-026). Online resource: http://www-01.sil.org/SILESR/2011/silesr2011-026.pdf (accessed 15 November 2013).

Eriksson, A. (2008), 'Guidelines? What guidelines?', paper presented at the 17th Annual Conference of the International Association for Forensic Phonetics and Acoustics, Lausanne, Switzerland, July.

Eriksson, A. (2010), 'The disguised voice: imitating accents or speech styles and impersonating individuals', in C. Llamas and D. Watt (eds), *Language and Identities*, Edinburgh: Edinburgh University Press, pp. 86–96.

ESRI (Economic and Social Research Institute) (2011), *What is GIS?* Online resource: http://www.gis.com/content/what-gis (accessed 15 November 2013).

FECL (Fortress Europe Circular Letter) (1998), 'Controversial language tests for the determination of asylum seekers' country of origin', no. 53, January–February. Online resource: http://www.fecl.org/circular/5304.htm (accessed 15 November 2013).

Fehlen, F. (2002), 'Luxembourg, a multilingual society at the Romance/Germanic language border', *Journal of Multilingual and Multicultural Development* 23: 80–97.

Ferguson, G. (2006), *Language Planning and Education*, Edinburgh: Edinburgh University Press.

Ferreira, F. (2001), 'Variation in Ibero-Romance: A Study of /s/ Reduction in Brazilian Portuguese in Comparison with Caribbean Spanish', unpublished PhD dissertation, University of New Mexico.

Fishman, J. A. (1989), *Language and Ethnicity in Minority Sociolinguistic Perspective*, Clevedon: Multilingual Matters.

Flemming, E. (2005), 'Speech perception and phonological contrast', in D. B. Pisoni and R. E. Remez (eds), *The Handbook of Speech Perception*, Oxford: Blackwell, pp. 156–81.

Flynn, N. (2013), 'Levelling and Diffusion at the North/South Border: A Sociophonetic Study of Nottingham Speakers', unpublished PhD thesis, University of York.

Foulkes, P. (2011), 'A forensic phonetic perspective on LADO practice: comments on Cambier-Langeveld', paper presented at LADO Network Seminar, University of Essex, 26 November 2011. Online resource: http://bit.ly/1avkXI3 (accessed 15 November 2013).

Foulkes, P., G. J. Docherty and M. J. Jones (2010), 'Analysing stops', in M. Di Paolo and M. Yaeger-Dror (eds), *Sociophonetics: A Student's Guide*, London: Routledge, pp. 58–71.

Foulkes, P. and J. P. French (2012), 'Forensic speaker comparison: a linguistic-acoustic perspective', in P. Tiersma and L. Solan (eds), *The Oxford Handbook of Language and Law*, Oxford: Oxford University Press, pp. 557–72.

Foulkes, P. and K. Wilson (2011), 'Language analysis for the determination of origin: an empirical study', *Proceedings of the 17th International Congress of Phonetic Sciences*, Hong Kong, August, pp. 691–94.

Fox, S. (2010), 'Ethnicity, religion, and practices: adolescents in the East End of London', in C. Llamas and D. Watt (eds), *Languages and Identities*, Edinburgh: Edinburgh University Press, pp. 144–56.

Fraser, H. (2009), 'The role of "educated native speaker" in providing language analysis for the determination of the origin of asylum seekers', *International Journal of Speech, Language and the Law* 16.1: 113–38.

Fraser, H. (2011), 'The role of linguists and native speakers in language analysis for the determination of speaker origin: a response to Tina Cambier-Langeveld', *International Journal of Speech, Language and the Law* 18.1: 121–30.

Fraser, H. (2012), 'Bayes and beyond: the complex challenges of LADO and their relevance to forensic speaker comparison', in C. Donohue, S. Ishihara and W. Steed (eds), *Quantitative Approaches to Problems in Linguistics. Studies in Honour of Phil Rose*, Munich: LINCOM Europa, pp. 215–22.

Frazer, T. C. (1978), 'South Midland pronunciation in the north central states', *American Speech*, 53: 40–8.

French, J. P. and P. Harrison (2006), 'Investigative and evidential application of forensic speech science', in A. Heaton-Armstrong, E. Shepherd, G. Gudjonsson and D. Wolchover (eds), *Witness Testimony: Psychological, Investigative and Evidential Perspectives*, Oxford: Oxford University Press, pp. 247–62.

Gal, S. and J. Irvine (1995), 'The boundaries of languages and disciplines: how ideologies construct difference', *Social Research*, 62: 967–1001.

Garrett, P. (2010), *Attitudes to Language*, Cambridge: Cambridge University Press.

Gerritsen, M. (1999), 'Divergence of dialects in a linguistic laboratory near the Belgian–Dutch–German border: similar dialects under the influence of three different standard languages', *Language Variation and Change*, 11: 43–66.

Giddens, A. (1984), *The Constitution of Society: Outline of the Theory of Structuration*, Cambridge: Polity Press.

Giesbers, C. (2008), *Dialecten op de grens van twee talen: een dialectologisch en sociolinguïstisch onderzoek in het Kleverlands dialectgebied*, Groesbeek: Uitgeverij Reijngoudt.

Giles, H. (1973), 'Accent mobility: a model and some data', *Anthropological Linguistics*, 15.2: 87–105.

Giles, H. and N. Coupland (1991), *Language: Contexts and Consequences*, Bristol, PA: Open University Press.

Gilles, P. and C. Moulin (2003), 'Luxembourgish', in A. Deumert and W. Vandenbussche (eds), *Germanic Standardizations – Past to Present*, Amsterdam: Benjamins, pp. 303–29.

Gillespie, R. and H. O'Sullivan (eds) (1989), *The Borderlands: Essays on the History of the Ulster–Leinster Border*, Belfast: Institute of Irish Studies, The Queen's University of Belfast.

Glauser, B. (1974), *The Scottish/English Linguistic Border: Lexical Aspects*, Bern: Francke.

Glauser, B. (1991), 'Transitional areas versus focal areas in English dialectology', *English World-Wide*, 12: 1–24.

Glauser, B. (2000), 'The Scottish/English border in hindsight', *International Journal of the Sociology of Language*, 145: 65–78.

Gold, E. and P. French (2011), 'International practices in forensic speaker comparison', *International Journal of Speech, Language and the Law*, 18.2: 293–307.

González, N. L. (1967), *The Spanish-Americans of New Mexico: A Heritage of Pride*, Albuquerque: University of New Mexico Press.

Gould, P. and R. White (1986), *Mental Maps* (2nd edn), Boston: Allen and Unwin.

Government of Ireland Act, 1920 (1920), 10 and 11 George 5, Ch. 67. Online resource: http://cain.ulst.ac.uk/issues/politics/docs/goi231220.htm#11 (accessed 15 November 2013).

Gregory, D. (1989), 'Presences and absences: time–space relations and structuration theory', in D. Held and J. Thompson (eds), *Social Theory of Modern Societies: Anthony Giddens and his Critics*, Cambridge: Cambridge University Press, pp. 185–214.

Grinevald, C. and M. Bert (forthcoming), 'Whose ideology, where and when? Rama (Nicaragua) and Francoprovençal (France) experiences', in P. K. Austin and J. Sallabank (eds), *Endangered Languages: Ideologies and Beliefs*, Oxford: Oxford University Press.

Gubbins, P. and M. Holt (2002), 'Introduction', in P. Gubbins and M. Holt (eds), *Beyond Boundaries: Language and Identity in Contemporary Europe*, Clevedon: Multilingual Matters, pp. 1–10.

Guia Turístico da Cidade de Valença (2014). Online resource: http://www.youblisher. com/p/223855-Valenca-Guia-Turistico/ (accessed 1 May 2014).

Guy, G. (1981), 'Parallel variability in American dialects of Spanish and Portuguese', in D. Sankoff and H. J. Cedergren (eds), *Variation Omnibus* (Vol. 40), Edmonton: Linguistic Research, pp. 85–95.

Haag, K. (1898), *Die Mundarten des Oberen Neckar- und Donaulandes (Schwäbisch-Alemannisches Grenzgebiet: Baarmundart) mit Karte*, Reutlingen: Buchdruckerei E. Hutzler.

Hall, D. (2005), 'Variation explained through contact and history: the regional French of Normandy', *University of Pennsylvania Working Papers in Linguistics*, 11.2: 17–30.

Hamburger, L. (2005), 'The main motivating factors dictating language choices in three Jewish women', *Leeds Working Papers in Linguistics and Phonetics*, 10. Online resource: http://www.leeds.ac.uk/linguistics/WPL/WP2005/Hamburger.pdf (accessed 16 November 2013).

Hannerz, U. (1992), *Cultural Complexity*, New York: Columbia University Press.

Hardill, I. and C. W. Olphert (2012), 'Staying connected: exploring mobile phone use amongst older adults in the UK', *Geoforum*, 4.6: 1306–12.

Hasselrot, B. (1934), 'Le Francoprovençal se compose-t-il de deux groupes principaux, un septentrional et un méridional?', *Studia Neophilologica*, 7: 1–17.

Haugen, E. (1966a), 'Dialect, language, nation', *American Anthropologist*, 68.6: 922–35. [extracted as 'Language standardization', in N. Coupland and A. Jaworski (eds), *Sociolinguistics: A Reader and Coursebook*, Basingstoke: Macmillan, 1997, pp. 341–52].

Haugen, E. (1966b), 'The ecology of language', in A. Dil (ed.), *The Ecology of Language: Essays by Einar Haugen*, Stanford: Stanford University Press, pp. 325–29.

Heeringa, W. and J. Nerbonne (2001), 'Dialect areas and dialect continua', *Language Variation and Change*, 13: 375–400.

Heller, M. (2002), 'Globalization and commodification of bilingualism in Canada', in D. Block and D. Cameron (eds), *Globalization and Language Teaching*, London: Routledge, pp. 47–64.

Hensey, F. (1972), *The Sociolinguistics of the Brazilian–Uruguayan Border*, The Hague: Mouton.

Hidalgo, M. G. (1983), *Language Use and Language Attitudes in Cd. Juarez, Mexico*, El Paso, TX: Center for Inter-American and Border Studies at the University of Texas at El Paso.

Hidalgo, M. G. (1986), 'Language contact, language loyalty, and language prejudice on the Mexican border', *Language in Society*, 15: 193–220.

Hiddinga, A. and O. Crasborn (2011), 'Signed languages and globalization', *Language and Society*, 40: 483–505.

Hill, J. H. and K. C. Hill (1986), *Speaking Mexicano: Syncretic Language in Central Mexico*, Tucson: University of Arizona Press.

Hinskens, F., J. L. Kallen and J. Taeldeman (2000), 'Merging and drifting apart: convergence and divergence of dialects across political borders', *International Journal of the Sociology of Language*, 145: 1–28, special issue, *Convergence and Divergence of Dialects across European Borders*, ed. J. L. Kallen, F. Hinskens and J. Taeldeman.

Hoare, R. (2001), 'An integrative approach to language attitudes and identity in Breton', *Journal of Sociolinguistics*, 5.1: 73–84.

Hoffmann, F. (1980), 'Triglossia in Luxembourg', in E. Haugen, D. McClure and D. Thomson (eds), *Minority Languages Today*, Edinburgh: Edinburgh University Press, pp. 201–7.

Hoffmann, J.-P. (1996), 'Lëtzebuergesch and its competitors: language contact in Luxembourg today', in G. Newton (ed.), *Luxembourg and Lëtzebuergesch: Language and Communication at the Crossroads of Europe*, Oxford: Clarendon Press, pp. 97–108.

HOSB (Home Office Statistical Bulletin) (1992), *Asylum Statistics, United Kingdom 1990– 91*, Issue 12. Online resource: http://bit.ly/1hNSWlw (accessed 16 November 2013).

HOSB (Home Office Statistical Bulletin) (1994), *Asylum Statistics, United Kingdom 1993*, Issue 17. http://bit.ly/HYIoQM (accessed 16 November 2013).

Huffines, M. L. (1986), 'The function of aspect in Pennsylvania German and the impact of English', *Yearbook of German-American Studies*, 21: 137–54.

Hughes, A., P. Trudgill and D. Watt (2012), *English Accents and Dialects: An Introduction to Social and Regional Varieties of English in the British Isles*, 5th edn, London: Hodder Education.

Hymes, D. (1974), *Foundations in Sociolinguistics: An Ethnographic Approach*, Philadelphia: University of Pennsylvania Press.

Hyltenstam, K. and T. Janson (1998), *Letter to the Head of the Swedish Aliens Appeals Board*, 5 January 1998.

Hyrkstedt, I. and P. Kalaja (1998), 'Attitudes toward English and its functions in Finland: a discourse-analytic study', *World Englishes*, 17.3: 345–57.

Ihalainen, O. (1994), 'The dialects of England since 1776', in R. Burchfield (ed.), *The Cambridge History of the English Language, Vol. 5: English in Britain and Overseas: Origins and Development*, Cambridge: Cambridge University Press, pp. 197–274.

Instituto de Língua Galega (ILG) (1999), *Atlas Lingüístico Galego, Vol. 3: Fonética*, A Coruña / La Coruña, Spain: Fundación Barrié de la Maza.

Ireland Act (1949), 12 and 13 George 6, Ch. 41. Online resource: http://www.legislation. gov.uk/ukpga/1949/41/pdfs/ukpga_19490041_en.pdf (accessed 16 November 2013).

Isajiw, W. (1992), 'Definitions of ethnicity', *Multicultural Canada: Encyclopedia of Canada's Peoples*, http://www.multiculturalcanada.ca/Encyclopedia/A-Z/d2/2 (accessed 16 November 2013).

Iyengar, S., M. Lepper and L. Ross (1999), 'Independence from whom? Interdependence with whom? Cultural perspectives on ingroups versus outgroups', in D. A. Prentice and D. T. Miller (eds), *Cultural Divides: Understanding and Overcoming Group Conflict*, New York: Russell Sage, pp. 273–301.

Jacquemet, M. (2000), 'Translating refugees: Kosovar interpreters as linguistic detectives', *Connect*, 1.1: 61–7.

Jacquemet, M. (2003), 'Refugee: ethnolinguist identities in the age of transidiomatic practices', paper presented at the Conference of the American Association of Anthropologists, Chicago, November.

Jaworski, A. and C. Thurlow (eds) (2010), *Semiotic Landscapes: Language, Image, Space*, London: Continuum.

Jenkins, D. L. (2009), 'The cost of linguistic loyalty: socioeconomic factors in the face of shifting demographic trends among Spanish speakers in the Southwest', *Spanish in Context*, 6.1: 7–25.

Johnson-Weiner, K. M. (1998), 'Community identity and language change in North American Anabaptist communities', *Journal of Sociolinguistics*, 2: 375–94.

Johnston, P. (1980), 'A Synchronic and Historical View of Border Area Bimoraic Vowel Systems', unpublished PhD thesis, University of Edinburgh.

Johnston, P. (1997), 'Regional variation', in C. Jones (ed.), *The Edinburgh History of the Scots Language*, Edinburgh: Edinburgh University Press, pp. 433–513.

Johnstone, B. (2010), 'Indexing the local', in N. Coupland (ed.), *Handbook of Language and Globalization*, Malden, MA: Blackwell Publishing, pp. 386–405.

Jones, C. (2002), *The English Language in Scotland: An Introduction to Scots*, East Linton: Tuckwell Press.

Joseph, J. E. (2004), *Language and Identity: National, Ethnic, Religious*, New York: Macmillan.

Joseph, J. E. (2010), 'Identity', in C. Llamas and D. Watt (eds), *Language and Identities*, Edinburgh: Edinburgh University Press, pp. 9–17.

Kallen, J. L. (2000), 'Two languages, two borders, one island: some linguistic and political borders in Ireland', *International Journal of the Sociology of Language*, 145: 29–63.

Kallen, J. L. (2009), 'Tourism and representation in the Irish linguistic landscape', in E. Shohamy and D. Gorter (eds), *Linguistic Landscape: Expanding the Scenery*, London: Routledge, pp. 270–83.

Kallen, J. L. (2010), 'Changing landscapes: language, space and policy in the Dublin linguistic landscape', in A. Jaworski and C. Thurlow (eds), *Semiotic Landscapes: Language, Image, Space*, London: Continuum, pp. 41–58.

Kay, B. (2006), *Scots: The Mither Tongue* (2nd edn), Edinburgh: Mainstream Publishing.

Kelly-Holmes, H. (2005), *Advertising as Multilingual Communication*, Basingstoke: Palgrave Macmillan.

Kendall, T. and V. Fridland (2012), 'Variation in perception and production of mid front vowels in the U.S. Southern Vowel Shift', *Journal of Phonetics*, 40.2: 289–306.

Kiely, R., D. McCrone, F. Bechhofer and R. Stewart (2000), 'Debatable land: national and local identity in a border town', *Sociological Research Online*, 5.2. Online resource: http://www.socresonline.org.uk/5/2/kiely.html (accessed 6 December 2013).

Kiely, R., F. Bechhofer, R. Stewart and D. McCrone (2001), 'The markers and rules of Scottish national identity', *The Sociological Review*, 49.1: 33–55.

Kiely, R., F. Bechhofer and D. McCrone (2005), 'Birth, blood and belonging: identity claims in post-devolution Scotland', *The Sociological Review*, 53:1, 150–71.

Kingsmore, R. K. (1995), *Ulster Scots Speech: A Sociolinguistic Study*, Tuscaloosa: University of Alabama Press.

Koch, W., M. S. Klassmann and C. V. Altenhofen (2002), *Atlas lingüístico-etnográfico da Região Sul do Brasil*, Porto Alegre, Brazil: Universidade Federal do Rio Grande do Sul.

Kontic, R. (1990), *Dialects in East Anglia and the South East of England*, Basel: Econom Druck.

Kopnina, H. (2005), *East to West Migration: Russian Migrants in Western Europe*, London: Ashgate.

Kremer, L. (1979), *Grenzmundarten und Mundartgrenzen: Untersuchungen zur*

Wortgeographischen Funktion der Staatsgrenze im Ostniederländisch-Westfälischen Grenzgebiet, Cologne: Böhlau.

Kretzschmar, W. A., Jr. (1996), 'Quantitative areal analysis of dialect features', *Language Variation and Change*, 8: 13–39.

Kristiansen, T. and N. Coupland (eds) (2011), *Standard Languages and Language Standards in a Changing Europe*, Oslo: Novus Press.

Kurath, H. (1949), *A Word Geography of the Eastern United States*, Ann Arbor: University of Michigan Press.

Kurath, H. and G. Lowman (1970), *The Dialectal Structure of Southern England*, Tuscaloosa: University of Alabama Press.

Kurath, H. and R. I. McDavid (1961), *The Pronunciation of English in the Atlantic States*, Tuscaloosa: University of Alabama Press.

Labov, W. (2001), *Principles of Linguistic Change, Vol. 2: Social Factors*, Oxford: Blackwell.

Labov, W. (2007), 'Transmission and diffusion', *Language*, 83.2: 344–87.

Labov, W. and M. Baranowski (2006), '50 msec', *Language Variation and Change*, 18: 1–18.

Labov, W., S. Ash and C. Boberg (2006), *The Atlas of North American English: Phonetics, Phonology and Sound Change*, Berlin: Mouton de Gruyter.

Ladd, P. (2005), 'Deafhood: a concept stressing possibilities, not deficits', *Scandinavian Journal of Public Health*, 33.12 (Suppl. 66): 12–17.

Lafitte, J. and G. Pépin (2009), *La 'Langue d'Oc' ou leS langueS d'Oc?: idées reçues, mythes et fantasmes face à l'histoire*, Monein, France: PyréMonde / Princi Negue.

Landry, R. and R. Y. Bourhis (1997), 'Linguistic landscape and ethnolinguistic vitality: an empirical study', *Journal of Language and Social Psychology*, 16.1: 23–49.

Lane, H., R. Hoffmeister and B. Bahan (1996), *A Journey into the Deaf-World*, San Diego: DawnSign Press.

Langstrof, C. (2009), 'On the role of vowel duration in the New Zealand English front vowel shift', *Language Variation and Change*, 21: 437–53.

Latham, R. and W. Matthews (1971), *The Diary of Samuel Pepys, Vol. 4: 1663*, London: Bell.

Lawson, S. and I. Sachdev (2004), 'Identity, language use, and attitudes: some Sylheti–Bangladeshi data from London, UK', *Journal of Language and Social Psychology*, 23.1: 49–69.

Lewis, M. P. (ed.) (2009), *Ethnologue: Languages of the World* (16th edn), Dallas: SIL International. Online resource: http://www.ethnologue.com (accessed 16 November 2013).

Liebert, S. (2010), *Irregular Migration from the Former Soviet Union to the United States*, London: Routledge.

Lillie, D. D. (1998), 'The Utah Dialect Survey: English', unpublished MA thesis, Brigham Young University.

Lindholm, C. (2008), *Culture and Authenticity*, Malden, MA: Blackwell.

Lipski, J. M. (1988), 'La discontinuidad fonética como criterio dialectológico', *Thesaurus*, 43: 310–26.

Lipski, J. M. (1994), *Latin American Spanish*, New York: Longman.

Lipski, J. M. (2008), *Varieties of Spanish in the United States*, Washington, DC: Georgetown University Press.

Lisker, L. and A. S. Abramson (1964), 'A cross-language study of voicing in initial stops: Acoustical measurements', *Word*, 20.3: 527–65.

Liss, J. M., G. Weismer and J. C. Rosenbek (1990), 'Selected acoustic characteristics of speech production in very old males', *Journal of Gerontology*, 45: 35–45.

Llamas, C. (1999), 'A new methodology: data elicitation for social and regional language variation studies', *Leeds Working Papers in Linguistics and Phonetics*, 7: 95–118.

Llamas, C. (2001), 'The sociolinguistic profiling of (r) in Middlesbrough English', in H. Van de Velde and R. van Hout (eds), *'r-atics: Sociolinguistic, Phonetic and Phonological Characteristics of /r/* (Etudes et Travaux 4), Brussels: ILVP, pp. 123–40.

Llamas, C. (2010), 'Convergence and divergence across a national border', in C. Llamas and D. Watt (eds), *Language and Identities*, Edinburgh: Edinburgh University Press, pp. 227–36.

Llamas, C. and D. Watt (eds) (2010a), *Language and Identities*, Edinburgh: Edinburgh University Press.

Llamas, C. and D. Watt (2010b), 'Introduction', in C. Llamas and D. Watt (eds), *Language and Identities*, Edinburgh: Edinburgh University Press, pp. 1–5.

Llamas, C. and D. Watt (2014 forthcoming), 'Scottish, English, British? Innovations in attitude measurement', *Language and Linguistics Compass*, 8.

Llamas, C., D. Watt and D. E. Johnson (2009), 'Linguistic accommodation and the salience of national identity markers in a border town', *Journal of Language and Social Psychology*, 28: 381–407.

LNOG (Language and National Origin Group) (2004), 'Guidelines for the use of language analysis in relation to questions of national origin in refugee cases', *International Journal of Speech, Language and the Law*, 11.2: 261–6.

Lodge, K. (1966), 'The Stockport dialect', *Le Maître phonétique*, 126: 26–30.

Lope Blanch, J. M. (1990–2000), *Atlas lingüístico de México* (6 vols), Mexico City: El Colegio de México / Fondo de Cultura Económica.

Mac Póilin, A. (ed.) (1997), *The Irish Language in Northern Ireland*, Belfast: Ultach Trust.

Macafee, C. I. (ed.) (1996), *Concise Ulster Dictionary*, Oxford: Oxford University Press.

Maddieson, I. (2005), 'Bilabial and labio-dental fricatives in Ewe', *UC Berkeley Phonology Lab Annual Report*, pp. 199–215. Online resource: http://linguistics.berkeley.edu/phonlab/annual_report/documents/2005/MaddiesonEweLabReport199-215.pdf (accessed 16 November 2013).

Maguire, W. (2014 forthcoming), 'Scotland, the north above the North', in R. Hickey (ed.), *Researching Northern English*, Amsterdam: Benjamins.

Maitz, P. (2011), 'On explaining language shift: sociology or social psychology of language?', *Multilingua*, 30: 147–75.

Mallinson, C. and B. Childs (2007), 'Communities of practice in sociolinguistic description: analyzing language and identity practices among black women in Appalachia', *Gender and Language*, 1.2: 173–206.

Malmesbury, J. (1870), *A Series of Letters of the First Earl of Malmesbury, his Family and Friends from 1745 to 1820*, London: Richard Bentley.

Marckwardt, A. H. (1957), 'Principal and subsidiary dialect areas in the north-central states', *Publications of the American Dialect Society*, 27: 3–15.

Martel, P. (1987), 'Vingt-cinq ans de luttes identitaires', in G. Vermes and J. Boutet (eds), *France, pays multilingue, Vol. 1: Les Langues de France, un enjeu historique et social,* Paris: L'Harmattan, pp. 125–42.

Martel, P. (1989), 'Un peu d'histoire: bref historique de la revendication occitane, 1978–1988', *Amiras / Repères occitans (mort et résurrection de Monsieur Occitanisme),* 20: 11–23.

Martel, P. (1997), 'Le Félibrige', in P. Nora (ed.), *Les Lieux de mémoire* (3 vols), Paris: Quarto Gallimard, pp. 3515–53.

Martel, P. (2010a), *Les Félibres et leur temps: renaissance d'oc et opinion (1850–1914),* Bordeaux: Presses Universitaires de Bordeaux.

Martel, P. (2010b), 'Du parler local à la langue: le docteur Honnorat à la découverte de l'unité de la langue d'oc', *Chroniques de Haute Provence,* 365: 35–66.

Martin, J.-B. (1979), 'La Limite entre l'occitan et le francoprovençal dans le Pilat', *Études Foréziennes,* 10: 75–88.

Martin, J.-B. (1990), 'Le Francoprovençal', in H. Metzeltin and C. Schmitt (eds), *Lexikon der Romanistischen Linguistik,* Tübingen: Max Niemeyer, pp. 671–85.

Martínez, O. (1994), *Border People: Life and Society in the U.S.–Mexico Borderlands,* Tucson: University of Arizona Press.

Maryns, K. (2004), 'Identifying the asylum speaker: reflections on the pitfalls of language analysis in the determination of national origin', *International Journal of Speech, Language and the Law,* 11.2: 240–60.

Maryns, K. and J. Blommaert (2001), 'Stylistic and thematic shifting as a narrative resource: assessing asylum seekers' narratives', *Multilingua,* 20.1: 61–84.

Maryns, K. and J. Blommaert (2002), 'Pretextuality and pretextual gaps: on re/defining linguistic inequality', *Pragmatics,* 12.1: 11–30.

May, S. (2001), *Language and Minority Rights: Ethnicity, Nationalism and the Politics of Language,* London: Longman.

McAdam, N. (2012), 'No welcome for Northern Ireland border signs as they're ripped down in protest', *Belfast Telegraph,* 9 August.

McColl Millar, R. (2010), 'An historical national identity? The case of Scots', in C. Llamas and D. Watt (eds), *Language and Identities,* Edinburgh: Edinburgh University Press, pp. 247–56.

McCoy, G. (2001), 'From cause to quango? The Peace Process and the transformation of the Irish Language Movement', in J. M. Kirk and D. P. Ó Baoill (eds), *Linguistic Politics: Language Policies for Northern Ireland, the Republic of Ireland, and Scotland,* Belfast: Cló Ollscoil na Banríona, pp. 205–18.

McNamara, T., M. Verrips and C. van den Hazelkamp (2010), 'LADO, validity and language testing', in K. Zwaan, M. Verrips and P. Muysken (eds), *Language and Origin – The Role of Language in European Asylum Procedures: Linguistic and Legal Perspectives,* Nijmegen: Wolf Legal Publishers, pp. 61–71.

Meechan, M. (1998), 'I guess we have Mormon language: American English in a Canadian setting', *Cahiers linguistiques d'Ottawa,* 26: 39–54.

Mendoza-Denton, N. (2002), 'Language and identity', in J. K. Chambers, P. Trudgill and N. Schilling-Estes (eds), *The Handbook of Language Variation and Change,* Malden, MA: Blackwell, pp. 475–99.

Merle, R. (1986), 'Le Chemin d'Honnorat: histoire d'A, ou la langue telle qu'elle doit être', *Amiras / Repères occitans,* 13: 85–98.

Merle, R. (2010), *Visions de 'l'idiome natal' à travers l'enquête impériale sur les patois (1807–1812): Langue d'Oc, Catalan, Francoprovençal – France, Italie, Suisse*, Perpinyà / Perpignan, France: El Trabucaïre.

Merriman, P. and R. Jones (2009), '"Symbols of justice": The Welsh Language Society's campaign for bilingual road signs in Wales, 1967–1980', *Journal of Historical Geography*, 35.2: 350–75.

Miles, M. (2000), 'Signing in the Seraglio: mutes, dwarfs and jestures at the Ottoman Court 1500–1700', *Disability and Society*, 15.1: 115–34.

Miller, C. (1989), 'The United States–Canadian Border as a Linguistic Boundary: The English Language in Calais, Maine and St. Stephen, New Brunswick', Undergraduate honors thesis, Harvard University.

Milroy, L. (1980), *Language and Social Networks*, Oxford: Blackwell.

Milroy, J. and L. Milroy (1985), 'Linguistic change, social network and speaker innovation', *Journal of Linguistics*, 21: 339–84.

Mistral, F. (1979) [1878], *Lou Tresor dóu Felibrige, ou dictionnaire Provençal–Français*, Raphèle-les-Arles, France: Culture Provençale et Méridionale.

Montgomery, C. (2007), 'Northern English Dialects: A Perceptual Approach', PhD thesis, University of Sheffield. Online resource: http://etheses.whiterose.ac.uk/1203/ (accessed 16 November 2013).

Montgomery, C. (2012), 'The effect of proximity in perceptual dialectology', *Journal of Sociolinguistics*, 16.5: 638–68.

Montgomery, C. and J. C. Beal (2011), 'Perceptual dialectology', in W. Maguire and A. McMahon (eds), *Analysing Variation in English*, Cambridge: Cambridge University Press, pp. 121–48.

Montgomery, C. and P. Stoeckle (2013), 'Geographic information systems and perceptual dialectology: a method for processing draw-a-map data', *Journal of Linguistic Geography*, 1.1: 52–85.

Montgomery, M. (2006), *From Ulster to America: The Scotch-Irish Heritage of American English*, Belfast: Ulster Historical Foundation.

Moore, E. (2010), 'Communities of practice and peripherality', in C. Llamas and D. Watt (eds), *Language and Identities*, Edinburgh: Edinburgh University Press, pp. 123–33.

Moosmüller, S. (2010), 'IAFPA position on language analysis in asylum procedures', in K. Zwaan, M. Verrips and P. Muysken (eds), *Language and Origin – The Role of Language in European Asylum Procedures: Linguistic and Legal Perspectives*, Nijmegen: Wolf Legal Publishers, pp. 43–7.

Morgan, M. (2001), '"Nuthin' but a G thang": grammar and language ideology in hip hop identity', in S. L. Lanehart (ed.), *Sociocultural and Historical Contexts of African American English*, Amsterdam: Benjamins, pp. 187–209.

Morkel, W. M. (2003), 'Tracing a Sound Pattern: /ay/-Monophthongization in Utah English', unpublished MA thesis, Brigham Young University.

Morris, E. (2005), *Our Own Devices: National Symbols and Political Conflict in Twentieth-Century Ireland*, Dublin: Irish Academic Press.

Moulton, W. G. (1960), 'The short vowel systems of Northern Switzerland: a study in structural dialectology', *Word*, 16: 155–82.

Moulton, W. G. (1962), 'Dialect geography and the concept of phonological space', *Word*, 18: 23–32.

Murphy, J. A. (1975), *Ireland in the Twentieth Century*, Dublin: Gill and Macmillan.

Murray, J. J. (2008), 'Coequality and transnational studies: understanding deaf lives', in H.-D. L. Bauman (ed.), *Open Your Eyes: Deaf Studies Talking*, Minneapolis: University of Minnesota Press, pp. 100–10.

Muysken, P. (2010), 'Multilingualism and LADO', in K. Zwaan, M. Verrips and P. Muysken (eds), *Language and Origin – The Role of Language in European Asylum Procedures: Linguistic and Legal Perspectives*, Nijmegen: Wolf Legal Publishers, pp. 89–98.

Nerbonne, J. (2009), 'Data-driven dialectology', *Language and Linguistics Compass*, 3.1: 175–98.

Neuhauser, S. (2011), 'Foreign accent imitation and variation of VOT and voicing in plosives', *Proceedings of the 17th International Congress of Phonetic Sciences*, Hong Kong, pp. 1462–5.

Newman, D. (2006a), 'The lines that continue to separate us: borders in our "borderless" world', *Progress in Human Geography*, 30.2: 143–61.

Newman, D. (2006b), 'Borders and bordering: towards an interdisciplinary dialogue', *European Journal of Social Theory*, 9: 171–206.

Newman, M. E. J. (2006), 'Modularity and community structure in networks', *Proceedings of the National Academy of Sciences*, 103.23: 8577–82.

Ní Bhaoill, R. (2010), *Ulster Gaelic Voices: Bailiúchán Wilhelm Doegen 1931*, Belfast: Iontaobhas Ultach / Ultach Trust.

Niedzielski, N. and D. R. Preston (2003), *Folk Linguistics*, Berlin: Mouton de Gruyter.

Nieto-Phillips, J. M. (2004), *The Language of Blood: The Making of Spanish-American Identity in New Mexico, 1880s–1930s*, Albuquerque: University of New Mexico Press.

NISRA (Northern Ireland Statistics and Research Agency), Online resource: http://www.nisra.gov.uk/Census.html (accessed 16 November 2013).

Nolan, F. (2012), 'Degrees of freedom in speech production: an argument for native speakers in LADO', *International Journal of Speech, Language and the Law*, 19.2: 263–89.

Northern Ireland Census 2001 (2005), *Key Statistics for Settlements*, London: Stationery Office.

Nylvek, J. (1992), 'Is Canadian English in Saskatchewan becoming more American?', *American Speech*, 67.3: 268–78.

OECD Factbook (2013), *Economic, Environment and Social Statistics*. Online resource: http://www.oecd-ilibrary.org/economics/oecd-factbook_18147364 (accessed 16 November 2013).

Ó Snodaigh, P. (1995), *Hidden Ulster: Protestants and the Irish Language*, Belfast: Lagan Press.

O'Brien, M. G. and L. C. Smith (2010), 'Impact of first language dialect on the production of German vowels', *International Review of Applied Linguistics in Language Teaching*, 48.4: 297–330.

Office for National Statistics (2004), *Census 2001: Definitions*, London: Stationery Office.

Office for National Statistics (2007a), *2001 Census: Special Migration Statistics*, University of Leeds and University of St Andrews: ESRC/JISC Census Programme, Census Interaction Data Service.

Office for National Statistics (2007b), *2001 Census: Special Workplace Statistics*, University of Leeds and University of St Andrews: ESRC/JISC Census Programme, Census Interaction Data Service.

Office for National Statistics (2012), *2011 Census, Key Statistics for Local Authorities in England and Wales*. Online resource: http://www.ons.gov.uk/ons/rel/census/2011-census/key-statistics-for-local-authorities-in-england-and-wales/rft-table-ks101ew.xls. (accessed 6 December 2013).

O'Rahilly, T. F. (1932), *Irish Dialects: Past and Present*, Dublin: Browne and Nolan.

O'Reilly, C. C. (1999), *The Irish Language in Northern Ireland: The Politics of Culture and Identity*, Basingstoke: Macmillan.

Orton, H. and E. Dieth (1962–71), *Survey of English Dialects*, Leeds: Published for the University of Leeds by E. J. Arnold.

Orton, H., S. Sanderson and J. Widdowson (1978), *Linguistic Atlas of England*, London: Routledge.

Padilla, A. (1999), 'Psychology', in J. Fishman (ed.), *Handbook of Language and Ethnic Identity*, Oxford: Oxford University Press, pp. 109–21.

Palácio, A. (1989), 'Um caso de permuta consonântica no dialeto do Recife', in A. Teixeira Castilho (ed.), *Português culto falado no Brasil*, Campinas, Brazil: Universidade Estadual de Campinas, pp. 25–33.

Palmeiro Pinheiro, J. L. (2009), 'Transborder cooperation and identities in Galicia and Northern Portugal', *Geopolitics*, 14.1: 79–107.

Palmeiro Pinheiro, J. L. and M. Pazos Otón (2008), 'La Eurorregión Galicia-Norte de Portugal: una aproximación a la movilidad en el contexto ibérico', *Estudios Geográficos*, 69.264: 215–45.

Paris, M. (1256), *Chronica Majora*, ed. H. R. Luard, 1872–1883 [reprinted 2012], Cambridge: Cambridge University Press.

Parks, E. and J. Parks (2008), *Sociolinguistic Survey Report of the Deaf Community of Guatemala* (SIL Electronic Survey Report 2008-016). Online resource: http://ftp.sil.org/silesr/2008/silesr2008-016.pdf (accessed 16 November 2013).

Parks, E. and J. Parks (2012), *Sociolinguistic Profiles of the Deaf Communities in Trinidad, St. Vincent, and Grenada* (SIL Electronic Survey Report 2012-004). Online resource: http://www-01.sil.org/silesr/2012/silesr2012-009.pdf (accessed 16 November 2013).

Patrick, P. L. (2012), 'Language analysis for determination of origin: objective evidence for refugee status determination', in P. M. Tiersma and L. M. Solan (eds), *The Oxford Handbook of Language and Law*, Oxford: Oxford University Press, pp. 535–46.

Pederson, L., S. L. McDaniel and C. M. Adams (eds) (1986–1993), *Linguistic Atlas of the Gulf States* (7 vols), Athens: University of Georgia Press.

Penhallurick, R. (2008), 'Welsh English: phonology', in B. Kortmann and C. Upton (eds), *Varieties of English: The British Isles*, Berlin: Mouton de Gruyter, pp. 105–21.

Pennycook, A. (2010), *Language as a Local Practice*, London: Routledge.

Peters, P., S. Kloppenburg and S. Wyatt (2010), 'Co-ordinating passages: understanding the resources needed for everyday mobility', *Mobilities*, 5: 349–68.

Pharies, D. A. (2007), *A Brief History of the Spanish Language*, Chicago: University of Chicago Press.

Pica, D. and M. Kakihara (2003), 'The duality of mobility: understanding fluid organizations and stable interaction,' in C. Ciborra, R. Mercurio, M. de Marco, M. Martinez and A. Carignani (eds), *Proceedings of the 11th European Conference on Information Systems* (ECIS 2003), Naples, pp. 1555–70.

Pichler, H. (2009), 'A Quantitative-Qualitative Analysis of Negative Auxiliaries in a Northern English Dialect: I DON'T KNOW and I DON'T THINK, innit?', unpublished PhD thesis, University of Aberdeen.

Pierrehumbert, J. B. (2001), 'Exemplar dynamics: word frequency, lenition and contrast', in J. Bybee and P. Hopper (eds), *Frequency and the Emergence of Linguistic Structure*, Amsterdam: Benjamins, pp. 137–58.

Pietikäinen, S. and H. Kelly-Holmes (eds) (2013), *Multilingualism and the Periphery*, Oxford: Oxford University Press.

Piller, I. (2001), 'Naturalization language testing and its basis in ideologies of national identity and citizenship', *International Journal of Bilingualism*, 5.3: 259–77.

Pinheiro, J. C. and D. M. Bates (2000), *Mixed-Effects Models in S and S-Plus*, New York: Springer.

Poplack, S. (1978), 'Dialect acquisition among Puerto Rican bilinguals', *Language in Society*, 7: 89–103.

Poplack, S. (1980), 'Sometimes I'll start a sentence in Spanish Y TERMINO EN ESPAÑOL: toward a typology of code-switching', *Linguistics*, 18: 581–618.

Poplack, S. (1989), 'The care and handling of a mega–corpus', in R. Fasold and D. Schiffrin (eds), *Language Change and Variation*, Amsterdam: Benjamins, pp. 411–51.

Poplack, S. (2008), 'French influence on Canadian English: issues of code-switching and borrowing', *Anglistik*, 19.2: 189–200.

Preston, D. R. (1982), 'Perceptual dialectology: mental maps of United States dialects from a Hawaiian perspective', *Hawaii Working Papers in Linguistics*, 14.2: 5–49.

Preston, D. R. (1988), 'Change in the perception of language varieties', in J. Fisiak (ed.), *Historical Dialectology: Regional and Social*, Berlin: Mouton de Gruyter, pp. 475–504.

Preston, D. R. (1993), 'Folk dialectology', in D. R. Preston (ed.), *American Dialect Research*, Amsterdam: Benjamins, pp. 333–77.

Preston, D. R. (1996), 'Whaddayaknow? The modes of folk linguistic awareness', *Language Awareness*, 5.1: 40–74.

Preston, D. R. (1999), 'Introduction', in D. R. Preston (ed.), *Handbook of Perceptual Dialectology*, Amsterdam: Benjamins, pp. xxiii–xxxix.

Preston, D. R. (2010), 'Mapping the geolinguistic spaces of the brain', in A. Lameli, R. Kehrein and S. Rabanus (eds), *Language and Space, Vol. 2: Language Mapping*, Berlin: Mouton de Gruyter, pp. 121–41.

Preston, D. R. and G. M. Howe (1987), 'Computerized studies of mental dialect maps', in K. Denning, S. Inkelas, C. McNair-Knox and J. Rickford (eds), *Variation in Language: NWAV-XV at Stanford (Proceedings of the 15th Annual Conference on New Ways of Analyzing Variation)*, Stanford: Department of Linguistics, Stanford University, pp. 361–78.

Rampton, M. B. H. (1990), 'Displacing the "native speaker": expertise, affiliation, and inheritance', *ELT Journal*, 44.2: 97–101.

Ratti, C., S. Sobolevsky, F. Calabrese, C. Andris, J. Reades, M. Martino, R. Claxton and S. Strogatz (2010), 'Redrawing the map of Great Britain from a network of human interactions', *PLoS ONE* 5.12: e14248.

Reath, A. (2004), 'Language analysis in the context of the asylum process: procedures, validity and consequences', *Language Assessment Quarterly*, 1.4: 209–33.

Redinger, D. and C. Llamas (2009), 'Innovations in the measurement and analysis of language attitudes', paper presented at the Production, Perception, Attitude Workshop, Leuven, April.

Reizábal, L., J. Valencia and M. Barrett (2004), 'National identifications and attitudes to national ingroups and outgroups amongst children living in the Basque Country', *Infant and Child Development*, 13.1: 1–20.

Republic of Ireland Act (1948), No. 22 of 1948, Irish Statute Book.

Rivera Mills, S. V. (2000), *New Perspectives on Current Sociolinguistic Knowledge with Regard to Language Use, Proficiency, and Attitudes among Hispanics in the U.S.: The Case of a Rural Northern California Community*, Lewiston, NY: Edwin Mellen Press.

Robert, E. (2009), 'Accommodating "new" speakers: an attitudinal investigation of L2 speakers of Welsh in south-east Wales', *International Journal of the Sociology of Language*, 195: 93–115.

Robertson, R. (1995), 'Glocalization: time–space homogeneity–heterogeneity', in M. Featherstone, S. Lash and R. Robertson (eds), *Global Modernities*, London: Sage, pp. 27–44.

Roeder, E. C. (1926), 'Linguistic geography', *Germanic Review*, 1: 281–308.

Rolston, B. (1991), *Politics and Painting: Murals and Conflict in Northern Ireland*, London: Associated University Presses.

Rolston, B. (2003), *Drawing Support 3: Murals and Transition in the North of Ireland*, Belfast: Beyond the Pale.

Romney, T. C. (1938), *The Mormon Colonies in Mexico*, Salt Lake City: Deseret Book Co.

Rona, J. P. (1965), *El dialecto fronterizo del norte del Uruguay*, Montevideo: Universidad de la República.

Room, A. (1994), *A Dictionary of Irish Place-Names* (revised edn), Belfast: Appletree Press.

Rosenbaum, Y., E. Nadel, R. L. Cooper and J. A. Fishman (1977), 'English on Keren Kayemet Street', in J. A. Fishman, R. L. Cooper and A. W. Conrad (eds), *The Spread of English: The Sociology of English as an Additional Language*, Rowley, MA: Newbury House, pp. 179–96.

Rosie, M. and R. Bond (2003), 'Identity matters: the personal and political significance of feeling Scottish', in C. Bromley, J. Curtice, K. Hinds and A. Park (eds), *Devolution – Scottish Answers to Scottish Questions?*, Edinburgh: Edinburgh University Press, pp. 116–36.

Roudometof, V. (2005), 'Transnationalism, cosmopolitanism, and glocalization', *Current Sociology*, 53.1: 113–35.

Ryalls, J., A. Zipprer and P. Baldauff (1997), 'A preliminary investigation of the effects of gender and race on voice onset time', *Journal of Speech, Language, and Hearing Research*, 40: 642–5.

Samant, S. (2010), 'Arab Americans and sound change in southeastern Michigan', *English Today*, 103: 27–33.

Sankoff, D., S. Tagliamonte and E. Smith (2005), *Goldvarb X: A Variable Rule Application for Macintosh and Windows*, Toronto: Department of Linguistics, University of Toronto.

Sankoff, G. and H. Blondeau (2007), 'Language change across the lifespan: /r/ in Montreal French', *Language*, 83: 560–88.

Santino, J. (2001), *Signs of War and Peace: Social Conflict and the Use of Public Symbols in Northern Ireland*, Basingstoke: Palgrave.

Scherre, M. M. P. (2001), 'Phrase-level parallelism effects on Noun Phrase number agreement', *Language Variation and Change*, 13: 91–107.

Scobbie, J. M. (2006), 'Flexibility in the face of incompatible English VOT systems', in L. Goldstein, D. H. Whalen and C. T. Best (eds), *Laboratory Phonology 8: Varieties of Phonological Competence*, Berlin: Mouton de Gruyter, pp. 367–92.

Scottish Borders Council (2010), *Scottish Borders in Figures*. Online resource: http://www.scotborders.gov.uk/download/downloads/id/2834/scottish_borders_in_figures_2010 (accessed 6 December 2013).

Selleck, C. (2013), 'Inclusive policy and exclusionary practice in secondary education in Wales', *International Journal of Bilingual Education and Bilingualism*, 16.1: 20–4.

Shackleton, R. (2010), *Quantitative Assessment of English–American Speech Relationships*, Groningen: Rijksuniversiteit Groningen.

Shohamy, E. and D. Gorter (eds) (2009), *Linguistic Landscape: Expanding the Scenery*, London: Routledge.

Shohamy, E. and S. Waksman (2009), 'Linguistic landscape as an ecological arena: modalities, meanings, negotiation, education', in E. Shohamy and D. Gorter (eds), *Linguistic Landscape: Expanding the Scenery*, London: Routledge, pp. 313–31.

Shuy, R. W. (1962), *The Northern–Midland Dialect Boundary in Illinois* (Publications of the American Dialect Society 38), Tuscaloosa: University of Alabama Press.

Sidaway, J. (2005), 'The poetry of boundaries: reflections from the Portuguese–Spanish borderlands', in H. Van Houtum, O. Kramsch and W. Zierhofer (eds), *B/ordering Space*, Aldershot: Ashgate, pp. 189–206.

SIL International (2012), *ISO 639-3 Index of All Past Change Requests*. Online resource: http://www.sil.org/iso639-3/chg_requests.asp?order=CR_Numberandchg_status=past (accessed 16 November 2013).

SIL International (2012), *ISO 639-3*. Online resource: http://www.sil.org/iso639-3/ (accessed 16 November 2013).

Silva-Corvalán, C. (2001), *Sociolingüística y pragmática del Español*, Washington, DC: Georgetown University Press.

Silverstein, M. (2003), 'Indexical order and the dialectics of sociolinguistic life', *Language and Communication*, 23: 193–229.

Simmons, M. (2001), *Spanish Pathways: Readings in the History of Hispanic New Mexico*, Albuquerque: University of New Mexico Press.

Singler, J. (2004), 'The "linguistic" asylum interview and the linguist's evaluation of it, with special reference to applicants for Liberian political asylum in Switzerland', *International Journal of Speech, Language and the Law*, 11.2: 222–39.

Skutnabb-Kangas, T. (2000), *Linguistic Genocide in Education – Or Worldwide Diversity and Human Rights*, Mahwah, NJ: Lawrence Erlbaum Associates.

Skutnabb-Kangas, T. (2008), 'Language, education, and (violation of) human rights', keynote paper presented at *Linguistic Rights in the World: The Current Situation*, Geneva, April. Online resource: http://www.esperanto-geneve-regions.info/linguisticrightsreport_en.pdf (accessed 16 November 2013).

Smith, A. D. (2009), *Ethno-Symbolism and Nationalism: A Cultural Approach*, London: Routledge.

Smits, T. (2012), 'Dialectverlies en dialectnivellering in Nederlands-Duitse grensdialecten', *Taal en Tongval*, 63: 175–95.

Speitel, H. H. and J. Y. Mather (eds) (2010), *The Linguistic Atlas of Scotland: Scots Section* (3 vols), London: Routledge.

Spolsky, B. and R. L. Cooper (1991), *The Languages of Jerusalem*, Oxford: Clarendon Press.

Stafford, P. (1985), *The East Midlands in the Early Middle Ages*, Leicester: Leicester University Press.

Stuart-Smith, J. (2008), 'Scottish English: phonology', in B. Kortmann and C. Upton (eds), *Varieties of English: The British Isles*, Berlin: Mouton de Gruyter, pp. 48–70.

Stuart-Smith, J. (2011), 'The view from the couch: changing perspectives on the role of television in changing language ideologies and use', in T. Kristiansen and N. Coupland (eds), *Standard Languages and Language Standards in a Changing Europe*, Oslo: Novus, pp. 223–39.

Sumien, D. (2009), 'Classificacion dei dialèctes occitans', *Linguistica Occitana*, 7: 1–56.

Summers, D. (1976), *The Great Level: A History of Drainage and Land Reclamation in the Fens*, Newton Abbot: David and Charles.

Sunstein, C. R. (2011), *Going to Extremes: How Like Minds Unite and Divide*, Oxford: Oxford University Press.

Syrdal, A. K. and H. K. Gopal (1986), 'A perceptual model of vowel recognition based on auditory representation of American English vowels', *Journal of the Acoustical Society of America*, 79: 1086–100.

Tagliamonte, S. and A. D'Arcy (2004), '"He's like, she's like": the quotative system in Canadian youth', *Journal of Sociolinguistics*, 8.4: 493–514.

Tajfel, H. (1978), 'Social categorization, social identity and social comparison', in H. Tajfel (ed.), *Differentiation between Social Groups: Studies in the Social Psychology of Intergroup Relations*, London: Academic Press, pp. 61–76.

Tajfel, H. and J. Turner (1979), 'An integrative theory of inter-group conflict', in W. Austin and S. Worchel (eds), *The Social Psychology of Intergroup Relations*, Monterey, CA: Brookes/Cole, pp. 33–47.

Tax, B. (2010), 'The use of expert evidence in asylum procedures by EU member states – the case for harmonized procedural safeguards', in K. Zwaan, M. Verrips and P. Muysken (eds), *Language and Origin – The Role of Language in European Asylum Procedures: Linguistic and Legal Perspectives*, Nijmegen: Wolf Legal Publishers, pp. 225–32.

Teyssier, P. (1984), *Manuel de Langue Portugaise, Portugal-Brésil*, Paris: Éditions Klincksieck.

Thomas, E. R. (2002), 'Sociolinguistic applications of speech perception experiments', *American Speech*, 77: 115–47.

Thomas, E. R. (2010), 'A longitudinal analysis of the durability of the Northern–Midland dialect boundary in Ohio', *American Speech*, 85.4: 375–430.

Thomas, E. R. (2011), *Sociophonetics: An Introduction*, Basingstoke: Palgrave Macmillan.

Thun, H. and A. Elizaincín (2000), *Atlas Lingüístico Diatópico y Diastrático del Uruguay (ADDU) – Norte*, Kiel: Westensee.

Torre, P. and J. A. Barlow (2009), 'Age-related changes in acoustic characteristics of adult speech', *Journal of Communication Disorders*, 42.5: 324–33.

Trask, R. L. (1996), *Historical Linguistics*, London: Arnold.

Travis, A. (2003), 'Language tests to uncover bogus Iraqi asylum seekers', *The Guardian*, 12 March 2003. Online resource: www.guardian.co.uk/uk/2003/mar/12/immigra tion.immigrationandpublicservices (accessed 17 November 2013).

Trudgill, P. (1986), *Dialects in Contact*, Oxford: Blackwell.

Trudgill, P. (1999), *The Dialects of England* (2nd edn), Oxford: Blackwell.

Trudgill, P. (2000), *Sociolinguistics: An Introduction to Language and Society* (4th edn), London: Penguin.

Tuaillon, G. (1964), 'Limite nord du provençal à l'est du Rhône', *Revue de Linguistique Romane*, 28: 127–42.

Tuaillon, G. (1972), 'Le Franco-provençal: progrès d'une définition', *Travaux de linguistique et de littérature*, 10.1: 293–339.

UKBA (UK Border Agency) (2011), *Language Analysis Testing of Asylum Applicants: Impacts and Economic Costs and Benefits*. Online resource: http://bit.ly/HSWQck (accessed 17 November 2013).

Urciuoli, B. (1991), 'The political topography of Spanish and English: the view from a New York Puerto Rican neighbourhood', *American Ethnologist*, 18.2: 295–310.

Urciuoli, B. (1995), 'Language and borders', *Annual Review of Anthropology*, 24: 525–46.

U.S. Bureau of the Census (2013), *State and County Quick Facts: New Mexico*. Online resource: http://quickfacts.census.gov/qfd/states/35000.html (accessed 8 December 2013).

US Religious Landscape Survey (2008), *The Pew Forum on Religion and Public Life*, Washington, DC: Pew Research Center, pp. 99–100.

van den Boogert, N. (2004), 'Language analysis in the Netherlands: general information', paper presented at EURASIL workshop, Brussels, March.

Verrips, M. (2010), 'Language analysis and contra-expertise in the Dutch asylum procedure', *International Journal of Speech, Language and the Law*, 17.2: 279–94.

Verrips, M. (2011), 'LADO and the pressure to draw strong conclusions: a response to Tina Cambier-Langeveld', *International Journal of Speech, Language and the Law*, 18.1: 131–43.

Viereck, W. (1986a), 'Dialectal speech areas in England: Orton's lexical evidence', in D. Kastovsky and A. Szwedek (eds), *Linguistics across Historical and Geographical Boundaries – In Honour of Jacek Fisiak*, Berlin: Mouton de Gruyter, pp. 725–40.

Viereck, W. (1986b), 'Dialectal speech areas in England: Orton's phonetic and grammatical evidence', *Journal of English Linguistics*, 19: 240–57.

Viereck, W. (1990), *The Computer-Developed Linguistic Atlas of England*, Tübingen: Niemeyer.

Viereck, W. (1992), 'Prince Louis Lucien Bonaparte and English dialectology', *IKER*, 7: 17–30. Online resource: http://www.euskaltzaindia.net/dok/ikerbilduma/51319.pdf (accessed 17 November 2013).

Wagner, H. (1958–1969), *Linguistic Atlas and Survey of Irish Dialects* (4 vols), Dublin: Dublin Institute for Advanced Studies.

Wales, K. (2000), 'North and South: an English linguistic divide?', *English Today*, 16.1: 4–15.

Wales, K. (2006), *Northern English: A Social and Cultural History*, Cambridge: Cambridge University Press.

Waltermire, M. (2006), 'Social and Linguistic Correlates of Spanish-Portuguese Bilingualism on the Uruguayan–Brazilian Border', unpublished PhD dissertation, University of New Mexico.

Waltermire, M. (2008), 'Social stratification and the use of language-specific variants of intervocalic /d/ along the Uruguayan–Brazilian border', *Sociolinguistic Studies*, 2.1: 31–60.

Waltermire, M. (2010), 'Variants of intervocalic /d/ as markers of sociolinguistic identity among Spanish–Portuguese bilinguals', *Spanish in Context*, 7.2: 279–304.

Waltermire, M. (2011), 'Frequency effects on the morphological conditioning of syllable-final /s/ reduction in border Uruguayan Spanish', *Journal of Language Contact*, *VARIA*, 4: 26–55.

Wastl-Walter, D. (2011), *The Ashgate Research Companion to Border Studies*, Farnham: Ashgate.

Watson-Gegeo, K. A. and D. W. Gegeo (1991), 'The impact of church affiliation on language use in Kwara'ae (Solomon Islands)', *Language and Society*, 20: 533–55.

Watt, D. and C. Ingham (1999), 'Durational evidence of the Scottish Vowel Length Rule in Berwick English', *Leeds Working Papers in Linguistics*, 8: 205–28. Online resource: http://www.leeds.ac.uk/linguistics/WPL/WP2000/WattandIng.pdf (accessed 6 December 2013).

Watt, D., C. Llamas and G. J. Docherty (2011), *Accent and Identity on the Scottish/English Border (AISEB): project homepage*. Online resource: http://www.york.ac.uk/res/aiseb/ (accessed 17 November 2013).

Watt, D., C. Llamas, G. J. Docherty, A. H. Fabricius and T. Kendall (2012), 'Interaction of merging vowels and derhotacisation in Borders English', paper presented at the Conference of the British Association of Academic Phoneticians (BAAP), Leeds, March 2012.

Watt, D., C. Llamas and D. E. Johnson (2010), 'Levels of linguistic accommodation across a national border', *Journal of English Linguistics*, 38.3: 270–89.

Watt, D., C. Llamas and D. E. Johnson (2014), 'Sociolinguistic variation on the Scottish/English border', in R. Lawson (ed.), *Sociolinguistics in Scotland*, Basingstoke: Palgrave Macmillan, pp. 79–102.

Watt, D. and J. Yurkova (2007), 'Voice Onset Time and the Scottish Vowel Length Rule in Aberdeen English', *Proceedings of the 16th International Congress of Phonetic Sciences*, Saarbrücken, pp. 1521–4.

Weinreich, U. (1954), 'Is a structural dialectology possible?', *Word*, 10: 388–400.

Wells, J. C. (1982), *Accents of English* (3 vols), Cambridge: Cambridge University Press.

Welsh Assembly (2002), *Our Language, Its Future: Policy Review of the Welsh Language / Ein Hiaith, Ei Dyfodol: Adolygiad Polisi o'r Iaith Gymraeg*. Online resource: http://bit.ly/HZAwhM (accessed 17 November 2013).

Welsh Assembly (2003), *Iaith Pawb: A National Action Plan for a Bilingual Wales*. Online resource: http://wales.gov.uk/depc/publications/welshlanguage/iaithpawb/iaith-pawbe.pdf?lang=en (accessed 17 November 2013).

Welsh Assembly (2010), *Iaith Fyw, Iaith Bw / A Living Language, A Language for Living*.

Online resource: http://wales.gov.uk/docs/dcells/publications/122902wls201217cy.pdf (accessed 17 November 2013).

Williams, C. H. (2005), 'Iaith Pawb: the doctrine of plenary inclusion', *Contemporary Wales*, 17.1: 1–27.

Williams, E. (2009), 'Language attitudes and identity in a North Wales town: "Something different about Caernarfon"', *International Journal of the Sociology of Language*, 195: 63–92.

Williams, G. (2005), 'Multimedia, minority languages and the New Economy', *Noves SL. Revista de Sociolingüística*. Online resource: http://www6.gencat.cat/llengcat/noves/hm05hivern/docs/williams.pdf (accessed 17 November 2013).

Williams, G. A. (1985), *When Was Wales?*, Harmondsworth: Penguin.

Williams, H. and E. Parks (2010), *A Sociolinguistic Survey Report of the Dominican Republic Deaf Community* (SIL Electronic Survey Report 2010-005). Online resource: http://www.silinternational.org/silesr/2010/silesr2010-005.pdf (accessed 17 November 2013).

Williams, R. (1964), *Border Country*, Harmondsworth: Penguin.

Williams, R. (2003), *Who Speaks for Wales? Nation, Culture, Identity*, ed. D. Williams, Cardiff: University of Wales Press.

Willis, C. (1972), 'Perception of vowel phonemes in Fort Erie, Ontario, and Buffalo, New York: an application of synthetic vowel categorization tests to dialectology', *Journal of Speech and Hearing Research*, 15: 246–55.

Willis, E. (2005), 'An initial investigation of Southwest Spanish vowels', *Southwest Journal of Linguistics*, 24: 185–98.

Wilson, K. (2009), 'Language Analysis for the Determination of Origin: Native Speakers vs. Trained Linguists,' unpublished MSc dissertation, University of York.

Wilson, T. M. and H. Donnan (eds) (1998), *Border Identities: Nation and State at International Frontiers*, Cambridge: Cambridge University Press.

Wilson, T. M. and H. Donnan (eds) (2012), *A Companion to Border Studies*, Hoboken, NJ: Wiley and Sons.

Wolfram, W. and N. Schilling-Estes (2003), 'Dialectology and linguistic diffusion', in B. Joseph and R. Janda (eds), *The Handbook of Historical Linguistics*, Oxford: Blackwell, pp. 713–35.

World Federation of the Deaf (2012a), *Fact Sheet*. Online resource: http://www.wfdeaf.org/databank/fact-sheet (accessed 17 November 2013).

World Federation of the Deaf (2012b), *History*. Online resource: http://www.wfdeaf.org/about/history (accessed 17 November 2013).

World Federation of the Deaf (2012c), *Human Rights*. Online resource: http://www.wfdeaf.org/human-rights (accessed 17 November 2013).

Zeller, C. (1993), 'Linguistic symmetries, asymmetries, and border effects within a Canadian/American sample', in S. Clarke (ed.), *Focus on Canada*, Amsterdam: Benjamins, pp. 179–200.

Zwaan, K., M. Verrips and P. Muysken (eds) (2010), *Language and Origin: The Role of Language in European Asylum Procedures – Linguistic and Legal Perspectives*, Nijmegen: Wolf Legal Publishers.

Index